iRPP

F OUNDED IN 1972, THE INSTITUTE FOR RESEARCH ON Public Policy is an independent, national, nonprofit organization. Its mission is to improve public policy in Canada by promoting and contributing to a policy process that is more broadly based, informed and effective.

In pursuit of this mission, IRPP

- ◆ identifies significant public policy questions that will confront Canada in the longer term future, and undertakes independent research into these questions;
- ◆ promotes wide dissemination of key results from its own and other research activities;
- ◆ encourages non-partisan discussion and criticism of public policy issues by eliciting broad participation from all sectors and regions of Canadian society and linking research with processes of social learning and policy formation.

The IRPP's independence is assured by an endowment fund, to which federal and provincial governments and the private sector have contributed.

IRPP

CRÉÉ EN 1972, L'INSTITUT DE RECHERCHE EN POLITIques publiques est un organisme national et indépendant à but non lucratif.

L'IRPP a pour mission de favoriser le développement de la pensée politique au Canada par son appui et son apport à un processus élargi, plus éclairé et plus efficace d'élaboration et d'expression des politiques publiques.

Dans le cadre de cette mission, l'IRPP a pour mandat :

◆ d'identifier les questions politiques auxquelles le Canada sera confronté dans l'avenir et d'entreprendre des recherches indépendantes à leur sujet;

◆ de favoriser une large diffusion des résultats les plus importants de ses propres recherches et de celles des autres sur ces questions;

◆ de promouvoir une analyse et une discussion objectives des questions politiques de manière à faire participer activement au débat public tous les secteurs de la société canadienne et toutes les régions du pays, et à rattacher la recherche à l'évolution sociale et à l'élaboration de politiques.

L'indépendance de l'IRPP est assurée par les revenus d'un fonds de dotation auquel ont souscrit les gouvernements fédéral et provinciaux, ainsi que le secteur privé.

As I Recall

Si je me

souviens bien

Historical

Perspectives

Edited by
The Institute
for Research on
Public Policy

With
John Meisel
Guy Rocher
Arthur Silver

Copyright © The Institute for Research on Public Policy (IRPP) 1999
All rights reserved

Printed in Canada
Dépôt légal 1999

Bibliothèque nationale du Québec
National Library of Canada

CANADIAN CATALOGUING IN PUBLICATION DATA

Main entry under title:
As I recall Si je me souviens bien: Historical perspectives
Issued also in French under title: Si je me souviens bien As I recall
Includes bibliographical references.
ISBN 0-88645-173-6

1. Canada—English-French relations. 2. Canada—History. 3. Quebec (Province)—History. 4. Quebec (Province)—History—Autonomy and independence movements. 5. Canada—Politics and government—20th century. 6. Quebec (Province)—Politics and government—20th century. 7. National characteristics, Canadian. 8. National characteristics, French-Canadian. I. Meisel, John, 1923- II. Rocher, Guy, 1924- III. Silver, A.I. (Arthur Isaac), 1940 IV. Institute for Research on Public Policy.

FC144.A8 1999 971.4 C98-901339-1
F1027.A8 1999

ADMINISTRATIVE DIRECTOR, IRPP
Suzanne Ostiguy McIntyre

PROJECT COORDINATOR
Sarah Fortin

COPY EDITOR
Brian McIntyre
Jane Broderick

TRANSLATOR
Magee & Nguyen Associées

DESIGN AND PRODUCTION
Schumacher Design

COVER ILLUSTRATION
Luc Melanson

PUBLISHED BY
Institute for Research on Public Policy (IRPP)
Institut de recherche en politiques publiques
1470 Peel Street, Suite 200
Montreal, Quebec H3A 1T1

T HIS UNDERTAKING BEGAN IN DECEMBER 1995, IMMEDIATELY AFTER THE QUEBEC referendum on sovereignty-partnership. In the three years from initial concept to final product, from *He Says/She Says* to *As I Recall Si je me souviens bien*, the project went through many twists, turns and transformations. The end result reflects many contributions without which the book could not have become what it is.

Credit for launching the project must be given to Madame Monique Jérôme-Forget, President of IRPP until December 1998, who conceived of the idea. This book would never have seen the light of the day were it not for her constant support and enthusiasm. The interest and encouragement of the IRPP Board of Directors and members of its Research Committee were just as critical. Without them, this enterprise could not have come to fruition.

The research was initiated, and the first outlines prepared, under the direction of F. Leslie Seidle, Research Director for IRPP's Governance Program. When Robert Baril arrived on the scene in 1997, the project got a second wind. He refined the conceptual framework and the structure of the book, and secured the collaboration of three eminent scholars, John Meisel, Guy Rocher and Arthur Silver. In April 1998, Sarah Fortin picked up where the others had left off, with considerable drive and the zeal of someone unaware of the challenges awaiting her. She completed the manuscript, coordinated the translation and contributed to the presentation of the book by adding illustrations and helping to design the grid.

We want to express our gratitude and appreciation to John Meisel, Guy Rocher and Arthur Silver for their valuable contributions. Their commitment to this project was unflagging.

With the exception of chapter 1, which was prepared by Arthur Silver, the articles were researched and written by Patricia Bittar, Alain Desruisseaux, Sarah Fortin and Nicholas Ignatieff. However, a project aiming for balance and objectivity cannot succeed without the comments and suggestions of many outside readers. We thank those who helped in this regard: Yves Bélanger, Jean-Thomas Bernard, Sandford Borins, Stephen Brooks, André Burelle, Robert Campbell, Stephen Clarkson, Michèle Dagenais, Serge Denis, Léon Dion, René Durocher, Fred Fletcher, Alain-G. Gagnon, Jane Jenson, Eric Kierans, Guy Laforest, Simon Langlois, Daniel Latouche, Paul-André Linteau, Antonia Maioni, Kenneth McRae, Kenneth McRoberts, Claude Morin, Desmond Morton, Alain Noël, Leslie A. Pal,

Marc Raboy, Jean-Claude Robert, Gordon Robertson, François Rocher, Michel Sarra-Bournet, Donald Smith, Brian Tanguay, Ronald Watts, Brian Young, and Robert Young. Obviously any errors are solely our responsibility.

Maureen Magee did the English translation and Brian McIntyre revised the English text. Jane Broderick did the proofreading and Sylvia Mauro the indexing. We also express our gratitude to the team of Schumacher Design, Jenny Schumacher, Anne Tremblay, Isabelle Véronneau and Claudelle Girard, who developed the concept for the cover page and designed the layout of the book. Their creative input enormously facilitated the transition from first draft to end product.

Finally, it must be said that *As I Recall Si je me souviens bien* represents a genuine collective effort. It embodies the best the Institute has to offer and we thank all of IRPP's personnel: France St-Hilaire, Acting President as of December 1998, for her judicious advice; Suzanne Ostiguy McIntyre, Administrative Director, for her involvement and support throughout the production process; Paul Howe, Research Director, for his thoughtful comments and assistance in editing the English manuscript; Chantal Létourneau, for preparing the manuscript for production; and Stéphane Baillie, Librarian, for his research assistance. The help and support of all are most appreciated.

M ANY PEOPLE PROVIDED US WITH VALUABLE HELP IN ASSEMBLING THE PHOTOS, CAR- toons and art works reproduced in this book: Suzanne Morin and Brenda Klinkow of the McCord Museum of Canadian History; Carole Ritchot of the Archives Nationales du Québec (ANQ); the staff of the National Archives of Canada (NAC), in particular Jennifer Devine; Fran Berthiaume of Canada Post Corporation; Pascale Simard of Canadian Press; Roland Forget of *La Presse*; Phil Norton of *The Gazette*; Robert Chodos of *Canadian Forum*; Maryam Abou Did of the Communist Party of Canada; Lyne Ducharme of the Office of the Commissioner of Official Languages; Peter Taylor of *The Toronto Star* Syndicate; Andrew Donato; Terry Mosher and Carole Vincent. Every effort has been made to give proper credit for all illustrations; however, in certain cases we have not been able to ascertain the copyright holder.

T HE QUESTION OF QUEBEC'S STATUS WITHIN CANADA HAS BEEN AT THE FOREFRONT of our political agenda for the past four decades. In discussions and exchanges around this question, the two linguistic communities have often held divergent, sometimes radically opposed, views of their common past. All those who keep abreast of events can see for themselves that our political discourse is peppered with references to the past, and that it is common practice for our politicians to refer only to those elements that support their particular rhetoric.

French and English Canadians continue today to hold different views of their shared history. In the writings and speeches of Quebec nationalists and sovereignists, there are frequent allusions to the wrongs done in the past, and many Quebecers believe they have not been fairly treated during the two centuries of co-habitation.[1] As Fernand Dumont observes,

> Today, Francophones may promote Quebec sovereignty in the name of greater government efficiency and claim to have exorcised the demons of their grandfathers' nationalism, [but] they do not hide the fact that their wish for independence is also nourished by memories of past humiliations.[2]

For their part, Canadians in the rest of Canada commonly conclude that Quebec has greatly benefited from its status as a British colony and a Canadian province: After the Conquest Canadian settlers were no longer subject to an authoritarian French regime and gained the same freedoms and liberties as other British subjects; the French language was recognized in the new British territory; and Francophones have come to enjoy tremendous influence on the federal political scene. Thus, Canadians outside Quebec see no grounds for historical recrimination. They feel that any damages that may have been inflicted have been amply offset by significant benefits.[3]

As summed up by historian John A. Dickinson,

> Canadian historiography has never been unified, and the two linguistic traditions are as different from one another as from foreign historiographies. No consensual view has ever existed that could reconcile all Canadians.[4]

The acuity of these discordant memories and their recurrence in our ongoing constitutional debate has led us to examine this aspect of our national unity dilemma. This collection of essays addresses the question of Canadian unity and federalism from a historical perspective through the reconstruction of 34 events which have marked relations between the two linguistic communities, from the arrival of the British in 1759 through to the 1995 referendum. The originality of this work lies in its approach: events are reviewed from both the francophone and anglophone vantage point, under the headings "As I Recall" and "Si je me souviens bien." Each event attests in its own way to the fact that our misunderstandings and confrontations are neither new nor simple.

To understand the relevance of this project, it should be remembered that a common history is generally seen to contribute to the formation of a collective national identity. But in a plurinational country like Canada, the construction of one, national historical memory is more difficult. In addition to issues also present elsewhere — the place of women, of regions and the rights and roles of ethnic minorities — the existence of two historic sensibilities poses special problems in Canada.

This situation has often been deplored and criticized by historians and politicians anxious to promote Canadian unity. As early as 1970, a study prepared for the Laurendeau-Dunton Commission found that Quebecers and Canadians were being taught different histories: "If Canada is more than ever threatened with schism, we believe we must look for the cause very largely in the manner in which today's citizens have learned the history of their country."[5] More recently, J.L. Granatstein has strongly criticized the teaching of history in Canada and called for a revival of national history:

> If Canada is to be worthy of its envied standing in the world, if it is to
> offer something to its own people and to humanity, it will have to forge
> a national spirit that can unite its increasingly diverse people. We can-
> not achieve this unanimity unless we teach our national history, cele-
> brate our founders, establish new symbols, and strengthen the terms
> of our citizenship…We have a nation to save and a future to build.[6]

Similarly, John Ralston Saul has pointed out that Canadians tend to have a negative impression of their country's history sustained by myths of victimization. Although his reproaches are not exclusively related to the rift between Quebec and Canada, they apply very well to the situation:

> Various schools of historians and politicians have sought out only the
> failures in this process, or concentrated on the wrongs done or the vic-

tories for their side…How do we so easily forget that reconciliation and reform are at the heart of the country's creation and survival?[7]

Although this dual historical legacy has sometimes given rise to interpretations that nowadays seem exaggerated and even wrong, it is our firm belief that our differences cannot be casually brushed aside by the establishment of a new symbolic order or simply dismissed by memories of common successes. In the ongoing debate over Quebec's status within the Canadian federation, it is important to acknowledge that these divergent interpretations foster mutual misunderstanding and affect relations between the two communities.

That is why the IRPP has undertaken this project. As an independent, national, bilingual institution based in Montreal, the Institute was particularly well-placed to explore past relations between Quebec and the rest of Canada. The originality of this work lies in the fact that events are summarized from the viewpoint of Anglophones and Francophones and presented separately under the headings "As I Recall" and "Si je me souviens bien."

Each of the 34 events was chosen because it had a determining influence on the evolution of Quebec-Canada relations or gave rise to conflicting interpretations. The objective was not to identify culprits or victims, destroy myths or correct questionable interpretations. Instead, our approach and the choice of events were dictated by the desire to facilitate dialogue between the two communities by allowing each side to better know and understand the other. Interpretations and perceptions make up the primary research material; our main concern was to draw a fair and balanced picture of the divergent perspectives that have taken hold.

The selected episodes are, however, not all cast from the same mould. In each case the depth of division and the magnitude of the consequences vary significantly. Moreover, the fault line varies across periods and events, involving Canadian and British authorities in some instances, French and English Canadians in others, and the federal and Quebec governments in still others. It should also be pointed out that nearly twenty of the events occurred during the last thirty years. Therefore, the greater part of the collection invokes a relatively recent past whose overall impact, in certain cases, has yet to be seen.

Given the lack of historical knowledge displayed by Canadians, it could be objected that our study gives undue importance to past events. This view may seem particularly justified in the case of the more remote events like the Conquest or the rebellions of 1837-1838.[8] Others might add that history is a lesser preoccupation in the rest of Canada than in Quebec. As Canadian novelist Nancy Huston puts it: "Yes, that is definitely the problem that this country poses for me: it is cruelly, desperately, dangerously modern; it has erased its already meagre past and it lives on the surface of its present."[9]

To these objections, we would first reply that Canada's current political and constitutional malaise can be partly explained by a lack of historical perspective or by the primarily partisan use of historical events. As Dominique Moisi notes "nations can recognize their past, rewrite or hide it."[10] We would argue that the time has come to revive our heritage, by recognizing both its positive and negative elements. A deeper understanding of perceived wrongs should generate greater empathy and facilitate the co-existence of the two communities — no matter what form this co-existence might take.

Furthermore, it should be stressed that this work deals with the collective memory of Quebecers and Canadians — "the conscious and unconscious memory or memories of an experience lived and/or made into a myth by a community whose sense of the past is an integral part of its identity"[11] — rather than their individual memories or recollections. Collective memory is often expressed indirectly, through holidays celebrated, individuals honoured or events commemorated, but it is real nevertheless. We draw on this common memory to teach history to our children, seek inspiration for the future, and debate vital issues such as the renewal of the Canadian federation.

As a consequence, the events and interpretations reported here do not have to be familiar to all in order to be significant. They are important because they help shape the contours of a collective identity. Of course, identity is as much — if not more — a function of the present and the future as it is of the past. Still, the great stories of yesteryear play a significant role in the formation of collective identities. The controversy provoked in Quebec by the May 1996 report of the Taskforce on the Teaching of History (the Lacoursière report) and J.L. Granatstein's critique points to the importance of national history in this regard.[12]

Our task was delicate. In Canada, as elsewhere, history has been deeply affected by the social sciences revolution. The image of the nation reconstructed through the works of historians has evolved considerably in recent decades, focusing more on social classes, women, regions and minorities. The image of the community that is now projected differs greatly from that which prevailed before. The debate about the new history of Quebec, a school of thought which portrays Quebec as a "normal" society whose evolution is similar to that of other North American societies, in contrast with the long-held thesis of a rural, agricultural and inward-looking society is an excellent case in point. It clearly shows how a society's self-image can be transformed and highlights the importance of the work of historians in this process of renewal.[13] Similarly, the infusion of multicultural and aboriginal perspectives into Canadian historiography has transformed Canada's self-image and probably helped undermine support for the principle of cultural duality so dear to Quebecers.[14]

These developments remind us that the relationship between the present and the past is not a one-way street. The past is not an objective reality waiting to be unveiled. The questions raised about the past, and the responses generated, vary according to the needs of the present. Thus, if the current mutual incomprehension between Quebec and the rest of Canada is undoubtedly fuelled by contradictory visions of the past, it is also the case that today's conflicts influence interpretations of this past.

In sum, despite its very real impact, collective memory is an elusive concept, difficult to fully grasp. It does not readily lend itself to concise summary. Consequently, the material assembled here explores only fragments of Quebec's and Canada's collective memories and identities. The chosen approach has meant that certain influences on the formation of collective memories were excluded.

The most glaring omission is the perspective of the First Nations. Aboriginal people appear in this collection of essays only in the context of events where they have played a role in conflicts between Quebec and the rest of Canada, as in the Oka crisis, the Meech Lake Accord, and the 1992 and 1995 referendums. This absence is partly due to our conceptual approach, but it is also the result of historical records dominated by a European vision that has marginalized and silenced Aboriginal voices.[15]

Also, because we have focused on the linguistic fault lines of the past, the provincial and regional complexity of Canada has been accorded less attention. But recognizing that this is also an important dimension of the current national unity issue, we have endeavored to present some of the principal elements feeding Western alienation as well as the driving forces behind provincial activism outside of Quebec. John Meisel's introductions in particular address these perspectives.[16]

Clearly, *As I Recall Si je me souviens bien* is not meant to be a textbook of Canadian or Quebec history. It is rather a collection of stories that should help us better understand Canada's current impasse by examining past events and present-day memories underpining Quebec's perennial drive for greater autonomy and the rest of Canada's resistance to this idea.

The book is divided into six thematic and chronological chapters. Each chapter is preceded by two introductions, one written by Guy Rocher and the other by John Meisel. The introductions provide some historical background on the reported events. Rocher describes the context for Quebec, Meisel for the rest of Canada. They have also each written a conclusion, where they offer personal interpretations of the historical relations between Quebec and the rest of Canada.

Each essay begins with a brief presentation of facts which is followed by a summary of the respective interpretations favoured by the rest of Canada and Quebec, and a conclusion which explores the long-term significance and impact of the event. Each essay and introduction can be read on its own, making it possible for the reader to go through the collection in whatever order he or she may wish. Surprisingly perhaps, the conclusions that emerge from this study are not as clear-cut as one might expect from an investigation that focuses on episodes involving antagonism and controversy. We can see in these pages the contours of two "global societies," to use Simon Langlois' phrase; yet in numerous instances, responses have been diverse and nuanced. Only a few events produced sharp and uncompromising outcomes, deeply offensive to the sensibilities of one of the parties.

This return to the past does not allow to draw definitive conclusions about future relations between Quebec and the rest of Canada. Examples of both successful accommodation and recurring or irresolvable political conflict can be seen; it is thus possible to extrapolate in either direction. However, the aim of this project was not to identify paths toward reconciliation but to encourage readers to think about alternative interpretations of Canadian history. We hope they will come away with a fresh appreciation of the historical roots of Canadian diversity that will help foster a more constructive dialogue between the two communities.

chapter 1

The First Steps

Introductions by
John Meisel
Guy Rocher

Essays prepared by
Arthur Silver

The First Steps

T HE 184-YEAR PANORAMA SURVEYED IN THIS CHAPTER ENCOMPASSES MANY SEMINAL episodes in our shared past that provide important historical background to the later case studies reviewed in this book. Like the events and developments treated in subsequent chapters, it paints a portrait of interactions between Quebec and the rest of Canada (ROC)[1] by means of a pointillist style, which builds up its canvas by setting down small, seemingly unconnected observations. When viewed together, these cohere into a broad picture of Canadian society, particularly as perceived by the two official language groups. As Guy Rocher deftly shows in his introduction, these influence current perspectives, attitudes and feelings because they act as both a memory and a mirror. He also reminds us that the view we have of the past is not static; it is a constantly changing image interpreted in diverse ways by observers. None can obtain a complete picture; each is condemned to only a partial view. One's line of vision is always influenced by the intellectual and emotional baggage of the beholder and is peculiar to a specific temporal and spatial context.

These inescapable limitations have two major consequences for this chapter and the rest of the book. They encourage a partial view of reality by conveying the impression that 1) most of Canada's conflicts arise from French/English differences, and 2) interactions between Canada's French and English communities have been overwhelmingly negative. A complementary and more positive perspective is needed.

The pivotal development treated in this chapter is Confederation in 1867, which marked the allegiance of the United Canadas and two of the Maritime Provinces to the newly born political entity called Canada. Most

Canadians, particularly in ROC, celebrate this event as a triumph of cooperation and goodwill, which at one level it certainly was. They assume that from that point on everything went more or less swimmingly on the unity front until the two conscription crises and the Quebec nationalist feelings evoked by the Quiet Revolution. The situation is much more complex than this simple view suggests.

Although some leaders of the mid-19th century saw a new country as a necessary and welcome response to the challenges confronting the United Canadas and the Maritimes, there was never universal support or wild enthusiasm for this remarkable exercise in nation-building. At various times, opposition, scepticism, reluctance and disappointment were evident in all parts of the country. It is no exaggeration to say that Canada barely squeaked through the obstacles encountered by its founders and subsequent builders. (Some would say that it is still barely squeaking through — which is correct, though to do so for 132 years is no mean feat).

The bipolar focus of this book, seeking to illuminate Francophones' and Anglophones' different perceptions of the same events, while highly useful, nevertheless masks a critical fact: neither side, particularly English Canada, is homogeneous. Consequently, ROC has exhibited deeply textured and conflicting positions on the national project bequeathed to us by the Fathers of Confederation.

The step-by-step approach to Confederation (in 1867, New Brunswick, Nova Scotia, Ontario and Quebec; in 1870, Manitoba and the North West Territories; in 1871, British Columbia; in 1873, Prince Edward Island; in 1905, Alberta and Saskatchewan; and in 1949, Newfoundland) resulted not just from the need, in some western provinces and territories, to establish a viable human and political base for European settlers. It also reflected the fact that some of the adherents to Canada had serious reservations about joining — indeed, in some cases it was necessary to offer special economic incentives like the construction of a viable rail system, special grants, or the assumption, by Ottawa, of colonial debts. Even among the four original founding colonies, New Brunswick and Nova Scotia expressed considerable anxiety over the union and entered only after overcoming substantial opposition. It is instructive to note, in this context, that what we now term "asymmetrical federalism" was very much in evidence when Canada was founded — a historic fact conveniently overlooked by many current

opponents of constitutional recognition of Quebec's unique character.

Discontent with the new arrangements and their consequences was considerable in 1867 and did not vanish as time went on. Widely separated regions and different social classes criticized their position in the federation and sought redress. In the first post-Confederation federal election, secessionists won 18 out of 19 Nova Scotia seats; in the provincial elections, the anti-Confederation Liberals under Joseph Howe won 36 out of 38 seats. Howe petitioned London for the right to take his province out of Canada, but his request was refused. Only the skill of Macdonald, and his undertaking to increase subsidies to Nova Scotia for 10 years and include Howe in the cabinet, persuaded the Nova Scotians to stay. And a little over half a century later, the secessionist Maritimes Rights Movement was

Newfoundland was the last province to join Confederation, in 1949. Following a referendum, 52.3 percent of Newfoundlanders accepted this option, as opposed to 47.4 percent who opted for responsible government. Here a young opponent stands in front of the Newfoundland flag flying at half-mast. (Canapress)

important enough to persuade Mackenzie King to establish a Royal Commission to look into the causes of Maritime discontent — a Commission which led to the redress of at least some of the grievances.

The decidedly centralist policies of Sir John A. Macdonald elicited opposition from the provinces, which met to seek redress as early as 1880, particularly against the power of the federal government to disallow provincial legislation. The tariff provisions in Macdonald's National Policy, and later Laurier's imperial preference, clearly favoured the central provinces and imposed hardship on the

West and the Maritimes. The Prairies, with the exception of Saskatchewan, resented the freight rates that discouraged the development and processing of primarily Western products and the rise of manufacturing in that region. The crisis in Manitoba, covered in the essay dealing with Louis Riel, provides another illustration of federal/provincial tensions. These deep resentments left a legacy of regional discord. It is worth noting that the first stirrings of discontent originated in Ontario (Oliver Mowat, a father of Confederation, was a prime mover!), which was later joined by Quebec, New Brunswick and Manitoba. These examples amply illustrate that French/English differences were not the only source of discontent and tension during Canada's formative years.

Another important qualification to the bipolar focus of this chapter is that antagonisms, differences and strife were not the only characteristics marking the co-existence of Canadian Anglophones and Francophones. The various incidents and developments selected for discussion, starting with the Conquest and ending with the conscription crises, convey the impression that Quebecers and the other people living in the area we now call Canada have been in a perpetual state of discord and struggle. There is an element of truth in this, but the method selected for our study exaggerates this impression. As the title *As I Recall Si je me souviens bien* indicates, the cases selected for inclusion are all ones in which clearly observable differences of opinion developed between important sections of Canada's two founding peoples. And since, in most instances, extremists on each side provided the most striking arguments and made the most noise, the apparent pattern is one of unending conflict and polarization. One gets the sense that English Canada has been consistently uncomprehending, selfish, hostile and insensitive to the interests of French Canada, and that Quebecers have been truculent, parochial and equally selfish and hostile.

It does not take inordinate tolerance for an Anglophone like myself to recognize that French Canada, as a numerical minority during much of the period under review, has had to endure unfair treatment at times. The incidents examined are real enough and have left a difficult legacy of memories that are damaging to the development of harmonious relations between the two so-called "founding races." However, put together like this, in one, concentrated chapter, they leave the reader with the impression that the Canadian experience has been an unmitigated trial for both groups, particularly Francophones. If this impression were accurate, one could neither understand why Quebec did not separate long ago, with English Canada's blessing, nor why Canada is rated throughout the world as one of the finest countries in which to live.

It is well to remember that there have been other events, developments, practices and modi operandi, more positive than those described in these pages. These, too, have entered into the collective memories of both Canadian partners. One of the factors promoting positive interactions between Canadians and Quebecers has been the existence of strong political parties. Since 1867, the Canadian party system has been a principal factor in the nation-building process and in the forging of suitable arrangements and compromises among the leading players in Canada's political game. In pursuing their central goal of attracting the maximum number of votes, they sought, as almost all still do, to find policies that would rally significant numbers of voters. This has meant that positions are defined, whenever possible, in terms acceptable to both of Canada's major linguistic groups. This moderate approach usually led to the fashioning of close working relationships between the leader of one ethnic group and the principal chieftain of the other, particularly in the days before opinion polling and spin doctors. When Ontario completed the principal East-West road establishing better links between communities from Windsor to the Quebec border, and, therefore, between Toronto and Montreal, it was not by accident that it was called the Macdonald-Cartier Freeway. The collaboration begun before Confederation by Louis-Hippolyte LaFontaine and Robert Baldwin thus continued after Canada's birth, particularly within the bosom of the governing parties.

Ever since the Conservatives profoundly alienated Quebec in 1917, as the essay entitled "Imperialism and World War" shows, the Liberal Party has held office in Canada most of the time. After 1880, the party's mediating role was strengthened by the practice of alternation, which has since become a firm party principle. According to this principle, Francophones and Anglophones have alternated as leaders of the party, thereby maximizing the chance that every other prime minister will come from Quebec. While the consequences of this can be easily exaggerated, the practice nevertheless reveals something important about the Liberal perspective on French-English relations in Canada.

The Liberal Party has also been a major player in Quebec provincial politics; it therefore provides an opportunity for many Quebecers to become involved in an organization and movement concerned with both local and national issues and developments. While not all provincial Liberals have been active in the federal party, very many have, and in doing so have entered a milieu that offers a pan-Canadian vision and pan-Canadian contacts. This has given rise to loyalties, opportunities and, yes, memories of a Canadian reality comprising both Quebec and other communities.

But, while important, provincial and federal political parties, whether from Quebec or elsewhere, are not the only agencies engaging the attention and energies of Canadians. Most individuals belong to a variety of organizations that serve their interests, engage their attention and link them to others with similar inclinations. These may be religious, professional, occupational, recreational or related to some other activity of interest to their members. The nature and scope of these voluntary associations have varied, but they have always existed in one form or another and have touched the lives of a large portion of the population. Many of them operate at local, national or even

From the Sudan crisis (1884) to WWII (1939-1945), through to the Boers War (1899) and WWI (1914-1918), Canada's participation in international conflicts has created bonds between Canadians, and many believe that the feeling of belonging to a Canadian nation was forged on the battlefields, as this WWII poster indicates. The artist, Harry Mayerovitch, has completed the dog tag of the soldier with several endings to evoke numerous origins of immigrants to Canada. Whatever his origins, this soldier was a Canadian. (NAC, C115712)

international levels, thus pulling their members into a network of friendships, activities and reference points that transcend more parochial interests. Many organizations are countrywide and focus the attention and affection of their membership on the country as a whole. They attenuate the limited view and priorities of insular preoccupations and plunge their members into inter-regional or national communities.

These types of connection often elicit new loyalties that allow people to see and judge events in a wider context. Without necessarily diminishing the attachment to one's immediate group and environment, they sometimes generate links that create cross-pressures in individuals who may therefore be obliged to reconcile inconsistent or even conflicting viewpoints. This means that a primarily Quebec-oriented perspective may be modified or attenuated by a broader regional or pan-Canadian view.

The present chapter contains many examples of ethnic or national priorities that have been modified, or even replaced, by new values. The most striking, of course, is the role and influence of the ultramontane clergy in Quebec, which, for religious, ideological and other reasons, opted for policies and arrangements that were anathema to strong nationalists like the Patriotes. But there are many other examples, such as the modification of nationalist goals because of perceived economic costs or other concerns.

For these and other reasons, most individuals compelled to make judgements on the many events and issues covered in this chapter have found themselves obliged to reconcile a variety of values, some incompatible with the emotional appeal of Quebec or Canadian nationalism. This helps explain why both Francophones and Anglophones were rarely unanimous in their reactions to the issues confronting them and why deep divisions were evident in both linguistic camps during the period under review. Indeed, in virtually every case described by Professor Silver, adherents to one side could always find allies on the other. For instance, it is revealing that on the question of how the Conquest should be interpreted — "catastrophe" (Garneau) or "providential event" (Laflèche) — two distinguished English-Canadian historians, Arthur Lower and Susan Trofimenkoff, have described it respectively as "a type of slavery" and "like rape."

Still, ethnic loyalties run deep. The scientifically suspect phrase "blood is thicker than water" does explain a good deal about how our two language families have responded to events. A good example is the diametrically opposed way in which Quebec and ROC saw the treatment accorded Louis Riel — their divergent perspectives were, without doubt, prompted by ethnic identity and allegiance.

Yet at the same time, an important lesson can be learned from the hanging of the Métis leader. Time, which is (wrongly) said to heal all things, has brought about a remarkable revision of ROC opinion. Riel's reputation is being rehabilitated; in the West, a statue in his honour has been erected and a movement is underway to have him declared a Father of Confederation. These efforts to vindicate him are not confined to Francophones or Métis.

One reason why the views of Quebecers and other Canadians sometimes converge over time is that they have created numerous links among themselves which provide ongoing opportunities for interaction and exchange of views. Their respective collective memories become somewhat blurred. The co-existence and continuous interaction between the two groups creates a mutual awareness, often only dimly perceived, of the presence of the other and of the inescapable need to take it into account when making decisions which might affect the future. This shadow presence of a partner has become an important component of the Canadian mentality. Some people are much more aware of it than others; some welcome it, while some resent it, but it is there nonetheless. And it creates a sense, often nebulous, even unconscious, of mutual dependence. While I am not prepared to push the analogy too far, this situation in some ways resembles the famous "Stockholm syndrome," whereby a deep bond tends to develop between prisoners and their long-time interrogators.[2] The co-existence of Quebecers and others in Canada, at the northern rim of the hemisphere, to the south flanked by the United States and in the east looking to Britain and France (toward all of whom many Canadians tend to have somewhat ambivalent feelings), has created a unique Canadian state of mind. This state of mind includes an undeniable awareness that one is, for better or worse, only one element in a complex set of relationships. While this does not always make for a willingness to accommodate the wishes of the other group, it means that events are perceived in a different light than if either partner were there alone. In a sense, the Canadian persona includes its own ethnic identity and fragments of others — something that is not always recognized or liked but that cannot be avoided.[3]

The phenomena sketched here must be kept in mind when considering the collective memories evoked by the cases presented in this chapter. Experiences shared by English Canadians and Quebecers provide them with collective memories of their own and help shape their perceptions. They modify the impact of the incidents described by Professor Silver and help explain why Canadians on both sides of the linguistic divide have remained together and continue to seek suitable ways in which to arrange their affairs.

The First Steps

H ISTORY IS THE PRIMARY SOURCE OF INDIVIDUAL AND COLLECTIVE IDENTITY. Whether for peoples, communities or individuals, the past serves as both memory and mirror; it provides the material from which identity is constructed. At the same time, we are always rebuilding our identity. Its image evolves through a reworking of the material from which it is composed. It is by looking into this mirror of the past that human beings, groups and societies perceive, imagine, form and modify their traits.

As memory and mirror, the past is not simply present, but always active. It is one of the main determinants of human action, both individual and societal. Psychoanalysis has demonstrated the active role played by childhood memories in the formation and motivation of our personalities and the unconscious influence of those memories on our behaviours, motivations and affections. As for nations and communities, whether their history is told through myths, legends, stories or academic studies, the past serves to underpin, feed, refresh and correct the collective memory.

It is widely recognized that history has played an essential role in the expression and evolution of French-Canadian nationalism. This was inevitable. A minority obsessed by the threat of extinction had to legitimize, in its own eyes, its solitary existence in a North American, Anglo-Saxon sea. The cost of retaining their distinctiveness had to be justified. Thus, to create and maintain "pride in our origins," French-language schools long gave the French regime a special, if not preponderant, place in the teaching of Canadian history. Students learned of the difficult struggles of the French to colonize the territory; the many religious, commercial, political and military links with various Indian tribes; the exploits of French troops

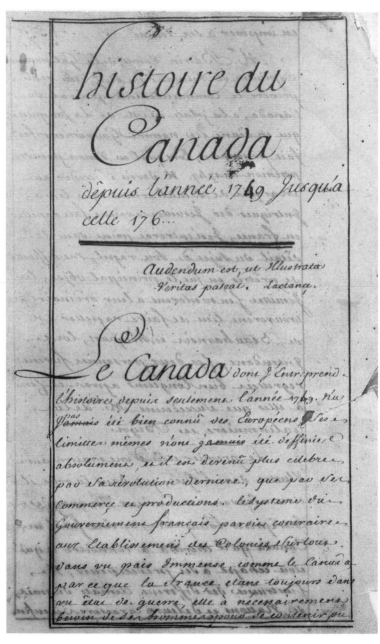

Until the turn of the 18th century, the term "Canadian" referred to the French colonists who settled in the St. Lawrence Valley. This is the cover page of what is one of the first history books telling the story of these Canadians. (Histoire du Canada, New France Collection, McCord Museum of Canadian History, C003, M1673)

against the British invaders; and the creation and establishment of religious, missionary, educational and charitable institutions. From this perspective, the Conquest was portrayed as bringing a brutal halt to this evolution. And the English regime, difficult to accept at first, was seen as a long struggle for survival.

Real or imagined, my own memory of this history is that for quite a long time many "Canadians" hoped and believed that France would re-conquer the country and thus took more time than Arthur Silver suggests, in his first essay, to recognize the "legitimacy" of the Conquest. The lingering feeling among "Canadians" that they had been "abandoned" by France was due not only to the signing of the Treaty of Paris (1763), but also to the acceptance of the fact that the French army would not be returning. The reactions to General de Gaulle's famous 1967 trip can indeed be interpreted as the "return of France": through the voice of its prestigious President, France was finally coming out of its long period of indifference toward the country it had lost and was even offering some unexpected support to the idea of Quebec independence.

The importance of the relations between different minority and majority groups in Canadian history is a line of thinking that runs through this chapter. Besides the obvious relations between the French-speaking minority and English-speaking majority, these included relations between: Quebec's anglophone minority and its francophone majority; the Catholic minority and the Protestant majority in Upper Canada, the West and the Maritime Provinces; Quebec's Protestant minority and Catholic majority; English-speaking and French-speaking Catholic minorities in the context of a French-speaking Catholic majority in Quebec and an English-speaking Protestant majority in the rest of Canada; the francophone, Catholic, Acadian minority and the anglophone, Protestant majority in New Brunswick and Nova Scotia; the aboriginal minority and the white majority; the Métis minority — particularly the francophone, Catholic Métis — and the anglophone, Protestant majority of Manitoba, antagonists in the Riel affair; and, finally, relations between new, ethnic minorities settling in the Western provinces and the British (bare) majority.

In short, relations between minorities and majorities are the threads from which the fabric of Canadian history is woven. It might even be said that this history began under the French regime when the colonists, who defined themselves as "Canadians," became a majority, in contrast with officials, traders and others passing through, who remained the "French." This history of minorities and majorities has continued right up to the present. It remains complex, both in Quebec and in Canada as a whole, and it includes the inflow of new minorities from Asia in British Columbia and the growing political activism of native peoples across Canada.

Nevertheless, the turbulent relations between the anglophone majority and francophone minority, along with the evolution of the two nationalist ideologies and of "imperialist" ideology, remain the central axis of Canadian history. Indeed, when we identify critical moments in early or contemporary Canadian history, we inevitably return to this central dynamic. It forms the backdrop for the entire fabric of Canadian history, whether political, military, social, economic or religious.

An important dimension of the history of these relations remains difficult to quantify: To what extent, and until when, did English Canadians support the imperial conception of Canada? Were they ever a majority, and, if so, when did they become a minority? We cannot turn to public opinion polls; they did not exist in the 19th century. However, based on my own recollection, I would say that early-20th century French-Canadian nationalists believed, rightly or wrongly, that English Canadians with "imperialist" convictions were in the majority. I believe this perception has played a significant role. Anti-imperialism fed the French-Canadian nationalism of the period, a nationalism which saw itself as Canadian as much as French-Canadian. French-Canadian nationalists at the time felt they were more authentically Canadian than their English-Canadian compatriots. This was true of Henri Bourassa, and even more so of Lionel Groulx, who never supported independence because he continued to cling to a certain image of Canada.

It is a cruel irony of fate that the conversion of English Canada to Canadian nationalism coincided with the transformation of French-Canadian nationalism to Quebec nationalism and the birth of various strands of the independence movement. There was a reshuffling of the two nationalist ideals but no agreement between them. It seems to me that French-Canadian nationalism was exacerbated by the rise of an English-Canadian nationalism that appeared more threatening to the Francophone minority than the imperial conception of the British Dominion of Canada. The latter's objective of assimilating — that is, anglicizing — French Canadians was so overtly expressed that fighting against it was easy, but the threat of assimilation from English-Canadian nationalism was more subtle because it was neither direct nor explicit. In the eyes of Quebec nationalists, this very "Canadian" nationalism was espousing an egalitarian and multicultural ideology which put French minorities outside Quebec on the same footing as other ethnic or cultural minorities, and could not accommodate the distinct character of Quebec.

In this regard, Arthur Silver correctly underlines the role played by the Riel affair in the evolution of relations between English and French Canadians. Through the outraged reaction of French Canadians to Riel's hanging, the "distinct" character of Quebec emerged in a particularly shocking way in the eyes of English Canada, which saw Riel as a criminal, not a hero. The solution of assimilating these troublesome French Canadians into a united, homogeneous, Anglophone Canadian family thus fed the new Canadian nationalism as much as French-Canadian nationalism.

Francophone readers will probably be surprised by the importance Silver attributes to what is called "ultramontanism." In the French tradition going back to the 17th and 18th centuries, this term has served to designate a Catholicism that is more loyal to the papacy than to royalty, and is thus more universalist than nationalist. The term was created to signify that these Catholics deferred to an authority situated "beyond the Alps" in Italy — on the other side of the mountains — as opposed to Catholic Gallicans who believed that the king should enjoy a degree of authority over the clergy and religious matters. At the same time that ultramontanism and Gallicanism were engaged in a pitched battle against each other in France under Louis XIV, they were confronting each other in the early days of the colony of New France. This conflict subsequently abated in 18th-century New France.

As I understand it, Arthur Silver uses the term "ultramontanism" in something of a derivative sense, especially in relation to events that took place after the French regime. In that case it may serve to designate an ultra-orthodox, definitively "papist" Catholicism that kept alive a cult of and devotion to the Pope and to the Vatican's authority. However, when Silver speaks of ultramontanism he is probably referring to the power of the Catholic Church and the authority of the Quebec episcopate, even in politics, and to the sustained, persistent melding of religious authority and political power. French-Canadian historians prefer to call this phenomenon "clericalism."

Clericalism is indeed a part of French-Canadian and Quebec history, and it is true that in the late 19th and early 20th centuries, just as Quebec was becoming increasingly industrialized and urbanized, clericalism appeared to win the day. A type of "ruralism," resulting from an idealized view of the French-Canadian peasant tradition, lent support to this clerical hegemony, thereby giving Quebec the reputation of being a priest-ridden province. But clerical hegemony was more fragile than it was believed to be, and it did not reign unopposed. The liberal ideology was less marginal than it appeared, especially among the French-Canadian bourgeoisie, and the struggle between these two ideologies cuts across 19th century history, particularly in the Montreal region. Moreover, if the inspiration and support for nationalism was in part drawn from clericalism, other sociological factors were also at work in the late 19th and early 20th centuries. Two of these will be discussed here: emigration from Quebec and the urbanization of Quebec.

A major demographic hemorrhage took place in Quebec in the latter half of the 19th century, as sons and whole families were forced to leave Quebec and settle in Ontario and the western provinces, particularly Manitoba, or in the United States, especially New England. Each of these groups of emigrants would have a strong impact on French-Canadian nationalism.

With regard to those who decided to move to western Canada, the settling of this francophone population outside the borders of Quebec served to create and maintain the idea of a French Canada, French-Canadians now being present in the West, not only in eastern Canada with the Acadians. This French-Canadian awareness translated into wide support for a particular cause: the defence of French-language minority rights, threatened and eroded by provincial governments in both the West and East and not sufficiently protected by the federal government. The cause of francophone minorities fuelled the nationalism of several generations of French Canadians, from the Riel affair to the Quiet Revolution. Those who went to the United States no longer belonged to French Canada. However, they became and remained "Franco-Americans" — that is, Americans who remained attached to French Canada. They created powerful and active associations to protect and promote their language and culture, which were supported by many French-language newspapers. It is a striking paradox that Franco-American leaders, journalists and intellectuals in many ways helped to inspire French-Canadian nationalism and to keep its flame burning, almost as if they had been part of French Canada.

A second sociological factor, the urbanization of Quebec from the late 19th century onwards, had the effect of fragmenting urban regions along ethnic lines. Anglophones and Francophones created their own residential areas in the cities — Montreal, Quebec, Sherbrooke and Drummondville — where both groups lived. This resulted in a highly visible difference in the standard of living between the two communities. As a consequence, French-Canadian nationalism saw the development of an important economic dimension, reflected in the creation of university institutions such as the École polytechnique, where French Canadians could be trained as engineers, and the École des hautes études commerciales, where they could be trained as accountants, businessmen and entrepreneurs. Movements such as *Achat chez-nous* (Buy at Home) and a peculiar brand of unionism that drew on both clericalism and nationalism were two other manifestations of this new economic nationalism. It played a vital role in Quebec's subsequent evolution toward the Quiet Revolution.

Finally, the role of France's nationalism should not be overlooked — from the "embarrassing" defeat of 1871 at the hands of Germany, and the loss of Alsace-Lorraine, to the start of First World War in 1914. The French nationalism of the period was in part Catholic, which gave it value for certain French-Canadian clergymen and intellectuals. Its excesses and internal battles, over the Dreyfus affair (1890s) for example, robbed it of any influence it otherwise might have had, but its romanticism provided the rhetorical energy that was sometimes lacking in French-Canadian nationalism.

French nationalism, however, could not set the tone for a minority nationalism like the one that took root in French Canada, with Quebec as its centre. In the essays contained in the following chapters, we will retrace the route taken by French-Canadian nationalism as it evolved toward Quebec nationalism.

The Conquest
(1760)

T HE CONQUEST WAS THE BASIS FOR ALL RELATIONS BETWEEN FRENCH AND ENGLISH Canadians, for it made English Canada's very existence possible. Until then, Canada was the name of the St. Lawrence Valley colony settled and administered by Frenchmen. Its conquest was part of a global conflict in which France and Britain struggled for commercial and imperial supremacy on all the seas and in all corners of the world.[1]

France surrendered Canada in 1760, but its retention by Britain was not certain until the peace of 1763. In previous wars, territories captured by one side had often been returned to the other during peace-table trade offs (Acadia, France's colony in present-day Nova Scotia, had been taken and returned several times before passing permanently to British hands by a treaty of 1713.) So, if Canada now remained British property, it was because French diplomacy gave it up for advantages elsewhere.

Between 1760 and 1763 Canada was run by the British army, which, being uncertain about the colony's ultimate fate, changed existing conditions as little as possible. Peace, however, brought a radically new approach. In a Royal Proclamation of October 1763, Britain announced that English laws and institutions, including an elected legislative assembly, would be introduced, and that anglophone immigration would be encouraged.

This policy proved unrealistic. In the two decades after the Conquest, only a few hundred Anglophones arrived. The attempt to introduce English laws thus produced confusion and instability, and it was quickly found to be unworkable. Nor was a legislative assembly feasible: under English law, Roman Catholics would have been excluded; yet, the Canadian population was essentially Roman

Catholic. "If it...be constantly remembered," wrote Governor Sir Guy Carleton in 1768, "that on the Canadian Stock we can only depend for an increase in population in [this Province], the Policy of continuing to them their Customs and Usages will be sufficiently evinced."[2]

The Royal Proclamation proved ill-conceived in other ways too. The boundaries it set for Canada (which it renamed Quebec) corresponded to the actual region of settlement (the St. Lawrence Valley between Vaudreuil and Gaspé) in which France had provided regular government and enforcement of its laws.[3] Outside that region, though France had claimed sovereignty and sought to exclude European rivals, it had treated native populations as allies rather than subjects, respecting their autonomy and territory.[4] The Royal Proclamation followed that precedent, banning white settlement outside the established colonies. But it went further: it completely detached the interior from the supervision of Quebec, thus proving insensitive to the needs of Canadian fur traders and ineffective in excluding American expansionists from the West.[5]

In the Quebec Act of 1774, the British Parliament adopted a new course. It expanded Quebec to include former dependencies: Labrador, southern Ontario and the Ohio-Michigan-Illinois region; it also confirmed the use of French civil laws, maintained seigneurialism, gave legal enforcement to the collection of tithes by the Catholic Church, made Catholics eligible for public office, and provided for government by a governor and appointed council, a system similar to that of the French regime.

Though this was intended to satisfy the Canadians, the provisions for autocratic government, seigneurialism, Catholic establishment, and the attachment of the Ohio Valley to Quebec seemed "intolerable" to the Anglo-American colonies, whose revolution it helped bring on. The success of that revolution upset Carleton's expectation that Quebec would always remain French, for it provoked an exodus of loyalist refugees from the United States, of whom some six to 10 thousand came to Quebec. Shocked and angry to find that the Quebec Act deprived them of traditional English rights of private property, political representation, and common law, the Loyalists demanded changes.

Accordingly, a new constitution was instituted in 1791. Quebec would be divided at the Ottawa River, preserving the old French province (now to be called

Lower Canada), while creating a new province (Upper Canada) to the west, where most of the Loyalists had settled. Each would have an elected legislative assembly. In Upper Canada, English laws and property would be introduced, while in Lower Canada, French law and Catholic establishment would remain in force.[6]

   Thus, three decades after the Conquest, the former French province of Canada, now called Lower Canada, remained in many ways what it had been before 1760. Its population was essentially francophone — the word "Canadian" was still used only to refer to the French-speaking population established before the Conquest — though it had acquired a small anglophone minority; its legal, seigneurial and Catholic institutions remained in place. And now, while a British governor controlled the administration at Quebec, Canadians would be represented in legislating for the province, making it possible, according to the British Prime Minister, William Pitt, for them "to be governed to their satisfaction."[7]

si je me souviens bien

Canadians had reason for anxiety at the moment of the Conquest.
Only a few years before, British authorities had uprooted (continued)

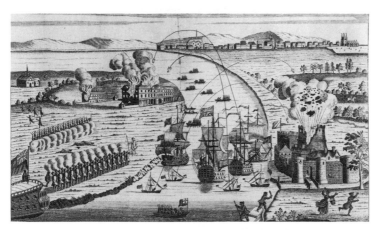

Plate illustrating the siege and capture of Quebec, printed in the *London Gazette* in 1759. (NAC, C77769)

the Acadian population from Nova Scotia, scattering it throughout
the Atlantic colonies, and many feared they might do the same in
Canada. In reality, most people were not disturbed. For ordinary habi-
tants, the Conquest ended the military conscription of the French
regime, though not corvées (compulsory labour for the state),
seigneurial dues or Church tithes. Most had little chance of meeting
an Anglophone, and, in the short term, their lives changed little.[8]

Those most affected by the Conquest were members of the
seigneurial aristocracy whose careers were in the French army or
administration. About a hundred left Canada after 1760, though
most left their families behind to maintain their estates.[9] The first
British governors, themselves members of a military aristocracy,
favoured the ambitions of Canadian seigneurs. Under the Quebec
Act, it was the members of that class who were appointed to the
governor's council, and after 1791 members of the seigneurial aristocracy continued to be favoured by governors in the distribution of
patronage.[10] Such appointments were important to seigneurs,
because they no longer enjoyed privileges they had held under the
French regime, such as exclusive rights to fur trade profits and commissions in the French Marines.

The fate of Canadian merchants after the Conquest has
been the subject of intense debate. Many difficulties faced them:
they had to find new British contacts to supply trade goods, credit
and a market for their furs; they faced suspicion and sometimes
obstruction from British post commanders in the West; those who
previously enjoyed contracts to supply military garrisons could no
longer count on them; all faced unprecedented competition, as the
removal of old restrictions opened the trade to all comers, including
new arrivals from Britain and her other colonies. Noted historians at
the Université de Montréal long argued that those disadvantages
were so great that they made it impossible for Canadian businessmen to survive. The Conquest thus led to the elimination of the
business class from French-Canadian society, leaving it without a

dynamic and progressive lay leadership and exposing it to ideological backwardness and economic exploitation.[11] Other historians have
rejected that idea, notably Fernand Ouellet, who has demonstrated
that, in the short run at least, Canadian merchants carried on.
Seven years after the surrender of Canada, 87 percent of the
traders were still French Canadians, and they comprised more than
three-quarters of the fur dealers until the American Revolution.[12]

Nevertheless, by the 1790s, British merchants had assumed
an overwhelmingly dominant position in commerce. Historians may
disagree about the explanation – whether French-Canadian businessmen were incapable of adapting to new economic conditions,
whether the Conquest cut them off, or whether post-Conquest difficulties discouraged them from entering new ventures in the late
18th century[13] – but the end result was that control of business, outside of small local enterprises, had passed to Anglophones.

For the Church, the Conquest brought uncertainty followed
by reassurance. The last French bishop of Quebec died in June of
1760; but – although the terms of surrender, the Treaty of Paris, and
the Royal Proclamation all promised religious freedom to Canadian
Catholics – it took six years for the British authorities to find a way
to permit a new bishop to take office without giving recognition to
Roman or French jurisdiction. Church leaders continued to be nervous about the security of their religion, and some historians have
argued that they had to serve British interests, preaching obedience
to British rule, in order to maintain it.[14] Yet the Church could hardly
have preached otherwise. Since the time of St. Paul, it had taught
that Christians owed loyal obedience to their legitimate sovereigns;
and according to traditional understanding, British rule after the
Treaty of 1763 was as legitimate as French rule before. "They are our
masters now," said the Vicar-General of Quebec, "and we owe them
the same duty we owed the French when they were our masters."[15]

Thus, the first generation managed to adapt to the
Conquest. Especially after the passing of the Quebec Act, which

protected their special institutions, authority and privileges, the clergy and aristocrats in particular could even rally to British authority with some enthusiasm.

In later generations, too, some people saw a positive side to the Conquest. The acting bishop of Trois-Rivières, Louis-François Laflèche, wrote in 1865 that it had been a providential event, sent by God to isolate French Canada from the anticlerical French Revolution, thus enabling her to preserve her Catholic character intact.[16] Many who made careers in politics after the coming of responsible government thanked the Conquest for the parliamentary institutions Britain had brought to Canada.[17]

At the same time, there has always been a bitter sense that the Conquest brought Canada under foreign rule. The great historian of the 1840s, François-Xavier Garneau, wrote of it as a terrible catastrophe that had torn French Canada away from the very source of its French personality and brought it under "foreign domination...the greatest evil that can befall a people."[18] This domination was not merely political. A later historian, Lionel Groulx, would write in 1921 that the Conquest had imposed the influence of "English culture" and a "Protestant and Saxon atmosphere" upon Quebec, subjecting even the "souls" of French Canadians to "the law of the conqueror."[19] And the idea of the Université de Montréal historians that the Conquest had deprived French Canada of a business class implied the establishment of a permanent economic domination as well. In short, "For those who understand the true importance of national independence, this Anglo-American conquest is a major disaster in the history of French Canada..."[20] For however much French Canada retained of its society, institutions identity and territory in the first decades after 1760, it could not escape, in the long run, the presence of a new – English – Canada to which the Conquest gave rise. Now, when the American Revolution produced its exodus of Loyalists, and when, in 1815, the end of the Napoleonic Wars produced an even greater exodus of emigrants from the

Si je me souviens bien

British Isles, there was a British Canadian territory in which they could settle. By 1840, under Britain's aegis, Anglophones had become a majority in the former New France, and French Canadians were only a minority element in a country dominated by others. ◆

as i recall

At the time of the Conquest, British ideas about Canada were confused and divided. The Royal Proclamation itself flew in the face of an important body of official opinion and owed much to the personality and ideas of a single minister, Lord Halifax.[21] The few Britons who arrived in Canada during the 1760s and 1770s were also divided. The first British governors considered the maintenance of French laws and institutions reasonable and appropriate to the needs of the population. Since they belonged to the military aristocracy, they

The victory of the English over the French in 1759 resulted in multiple interpretations. We see here one of the very first ones, a passage from the diary of Malcolm Fraser, a lieutenant in the 78th Regiment, the Fraser Highlanders: "... it is hoped ere long will be the means of subjecting the whole country to the British Dominion; and if so, this has been a greater acquisition to the British Empire than all that England has acquired by conquest since it was a nation ..." (*Journal of Wolfe's Campaign of 1759*, McCord Museum of Canadian History, C170, M277)

naturally favoured the continuance of seigneurialism in Canada
(General James Murray and other officers actually acquired
seigneuries). In this, however, they incurred the opposition of some
merchants, who had been led by the Royal Proclamation to expect
English laws and institutions to be established and felt cheated
when the French system was kept. The Quebec Act naturally disappointed such people, and it is not surprising that some of them
eagerly sympathized with the American revolutionaries.

Neither the merchants nor the soldiers of the first generation constituted an English Canada. Only in the 19th century did
Anglophones begin to call themselves Canadian, though it would
take a long time more for their Canadianism to be separated from
their sense of Britishness.

Anglophones' views of the Conquest have changed along
with their sense of their own identity. Nineteenth-century admirers
of British institutions sometimes thought French Canadians ought
to be grateful for the Conquest, which had brought those advantages to them.[22] Twentieth-century historians have shown more sen-
sitivity to the situation of a nationality given into the power of
another. "Conquest is a type of slavery," wrote A. R. M. Lower. And
Susan Trofimenkoff compared it to rape.[23] Yet few English Canadians
have seen the Conquest as an ongoing phenomenon. Most would
consider that the relationship of domination which it created was
ended, or undone, if not by the Quebec Act in 1774, then at least by
the granting of responsible government in the 1840s. When George
Brown, the Ontario Grit leader, spoke in the Canadian legislature's
Confederation debate in 1865, he began by referring to the end of
the Conquest: "Here we sit today seeking amicably to find a remedy
for constitutional evils and injustice complained of − by the van-
quished? No sir − but complained of by the conquerors!"[24]

To think that the Conquest had ended was necessary for
those who, after Confederation, dreamed of forging a united
Canadian nation. Thus, William Foster, in an 1871 pamphlet written to

promote a Canadian national spirit, suggested that French
Canadians had transferred their loyalty instantly and willingly from
France to Britain. According to Foster, that loyalty became a bond
linking French Canadians to the Loyalists, and, when war broke out
in 1812, it brought forth a "heroic devotion" in Canada's "inhabitants
of French and British origin." Thus began a shared experience which
Foster hoped would continue in "a common belief in a glorious
future" for the Canadian nation.[25] ◆

English Canadians, as they developed a sense of Canadian nationality,
increasingly saw the Conquest merely as an event that had brought French and
English together to form that nationality. For English Canadians today, writes a
British Columbia political scientist, "the Conquest made Quebec part of Canada,
and the Canadian identity was subtly shaped by the French component."[26]

That sentence sums up precisely what still makes the Conquest disturbing
to so many Francophones: that it "made Quebec part of Canada." Until the
Conquest, Quebec *was* Canada! The Conquest changed the very meaning of the
word. As Anglophones came to call themselves Canadian, the original Canadians
were obliged to qualify their own name, referring to themselves as *French-
Canadian*. Ultimately, "Canada" would apply to a vast anglophone-dominated
country. The name and identity of the francophone population had been taken
over by others.[27] That implies, of course, that Confederation itself is an extension
of the Conquest — an idea which may seem strange to English Canadians but has
a serious history in francophone Quebec. In the 1860s, even promoters of
Confederation had to admit that British imperial power limited French Canada's
ability to opt out of the scheme.[28] In 1921, Lionel Groulx wrote that the "evil of
the Conquest was aggravated after 1867 by the evil of federalism,"[29] and, in 1952,
Michel Brunet argued that modern Canadian nationhood was merely a psycho-
logical equivalent of the British Empire invented by English Canadians to compensate for the empire's decline.[30] More recently, a Laval University anthropologist
has claimed that Confederation was a creation of British imperial power that aimed
at the permanent dominance of English Canada over the French Canadians.[31]

Thus, for the Conquest to have "made Quebec part of Canada" is not so innocent as Anglophones may think. For many Francophones at least, it means that Canada is "a country built on the Conquest."[32]

The Rebellion of 1837-1838

U NDER THE 1791 CONSTITUTION, LOWER AND UPPER CANADA EACH HAD A BRITISH governor who, with a group of officials appointed by him, controlled the provincial administration; an elected assembly and a council appointed by the governor shared legislative power. The franchise was limited to property holders, but, as farmers comprised the majority of the population, property was widely distributed and most households were represented in the assemblies. This arrangement was not designed to establish the rule of the people but to balance and harmonize the influences of three distinct elements: the Crown (represented by the governor), the aristocracy (in the appointed councils), and the electorate.

The early 19th century saw a repudiation of this concept of government, as liberal and enlightened ideas spread to Canada from Britain, Europe and the United States.[1] Between 1807 and 1810, the Lower Canadian assembly fought to establish its independence from the governor's influence;[2] after 1818, it increasingly sought control over his budget and complained about the appointed legislative council, whose members often rejected bills that the assembly had passed. By the 1830s, reformers were demanding that the council be abolished or made elective.

In both Canadas, such demands were associated with social or economic grievances. Those appointed to executive positions or legislative councils belonged to economically privileged classes: seigneurs or owners of great blocks of private land, directors of large business corporations receiving government aid, and bishops of the established Catholic and Anglican Churches. While these men had political and economic power concentrated in their hands, ordinary people faced serious difficulties. By the mid-1820s in Lower Canada, good farmland in the seigneuries was scarce and seigneurs reacted by increasing dues and other exactions. In Upper Canada, settlers struggled against both the wilderness and an unfair land distribution system that kept them in poverty and their neighbourhoods underdeveloped.[3]

In 1834, Lower Canada's assembly passed a set of 92 resolutions summing up their grievances and demands. They wanted an elected legislative council, executive responsibility to the assembly and reform of the land distribution system. British attempts to compromise with leaders of the reform (or "Patriote") party broke down in 1836, and Patriote politicians declared a legislative boycott, returning to their constituencies to rally support in mass assemblies and public meetings. Meanwhile, a committee of the Upper Canadian assembly, led by William Lyon Mackenzie, had issued its own voluminous report on grievances, which contained many of the same complaints as the 92 resolutions.

The Lower Canadian boycott threatened to paralyze government, since credits could not be voted if the assembly did not meet. So the British Parliament passed resolutions of its own, refusing Patriote demands and authorizing colonial governors to spend money from the assemblies' accounts without their authorization. This only intensified the protest movement in the Canadian countryside, especially in western Lower Canada. By November 1837, the government was nervous enough to start mobilizing volunteers and arresting Patriote

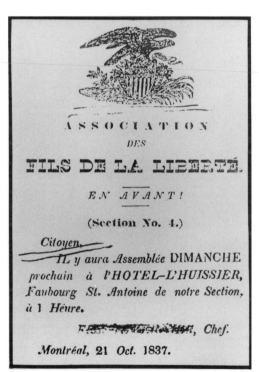

A semi-political and semi-military association inspired by the American Sons of Liberty, the "Fils de la Liberté" was created by the Patriotes as a counterweight to the English Doric Club. This poster invites Montrealers to a public meeting (ANQ, Montreal Center, Le Jour collection, P348, Patriotes file)

leaders. When protesters forcibly released two arrested men, the army launched a serious assault on Patriote strongholds in the Richelieu Valley. Though beaten back at the village of St-Denis on 23 November, it soon crushed resistance in the region and turned to the other main Patriote concentration at St-Eustache, north of Montreal. On 14 December, in a battle that cost the lives of between 70 and 100 rebels, the town was taken, looted and burned.[4]

Upper Canadian authorities responded to the Montreal district troubles by sending troops to Lower Canada, thus encouraging protesters in the western province to take action themselves. "Let me advise every friend of the people," wrote Mackenzie, "to provide himself with a rifle, or a musket or gun...keep your eyes on Lower Canada."[5] By 5 December, Mackenzie had gathered about a thousand men just north of Toronto, but their attempt to take the town ended in farcical catastrophe and they were quickly dispersed.

Canadian émigrés spent the following months in the United States trying to work up support and organize anew, but their attempts at a second rebellion in November 1838, with border crossings near Napierville in Lower Canada and Prescott in Upper Canada, were quickly dispersed. A severe repression followed. While only two leaders of the 1837 uprising had been hanged in Upper Canada, and none in Lower Canada, there were 10 hangings in Upper Canada in 1838 and 12 in the lower province; dozens of men from both Canadas were sent into penal exile. In Lower Canada, looting and burning by troops were even more serious than the year before.

si je me souviens bien ————

There was no single French-Canadian attitude toward the Patriotes or the rebellions. The population was divided along class lines, and the rebellion itself was confined to the Montreal district.

Parliamentary reformers were mostly lawyers or other professional men, often from modest family backgrounds. Together with storekeepers and other small merchants, they controlled the assembly in the 19th century. But the executive and legislative

Si je me souviens bien

As long as the aristocracy benefited, gov't was going to stay
the same -

councils contained members of the old aristocratic elites: seigneurs
and bishops of the Church. The struggle to make government
responsible to the elected assembly can thus be seen as a fight by
members of a rising middle class to take power from the old elites.

During the summer and fall of 1837, peasants also turned
against those elites. For some time, Lower Canadian farmers had
been losing ground in the wheat export market, while seigneurial
dues and privileges, tithes and other clerical taxes had been getting
more and more burdensome, especially in the Montreal district.
Thus, as farmers were drawn into the agitation begun by Patriote
politicians, they directed it more and more against aristocratic privilege and seigneurial exactions; and when violence erupted,
seigneurial manor houses were often the targets of popular action.[6]

ethnicity because mixed

The rebellion also involved ethnic conflict. French-Canadian
seigneurs might have enjoyed an advantage over ordinary lawyers and
notaries when it came to government patronage, but an even greater
advantage was enjoyed by Anglophones.[7] This seemed to indicate ethnic prejudice on the part of British governors, and it helped to make
the Patriotes conscious of an ethnic dimension in their conflict with the
governor. Patriotes also clashed with the great merchants of Montreal
and Quebec who, in the 19th century, were overwhelmingly
Anglophone. The latter looked for government support to promote
immigration and provide infrastructure that would enable them to capture the trade of Upper Canada and the American West. But their interests were not necessarily those of rural French-Canadian voters, and
when the assembly hesitated to spend money on them, the anglophone merchants turned for support to the governor and appointed
councils. Thus, an anglophone alliance in government and business
stood against the Patriotes and provoked their resentment.[8]

In fact, the question of nationality could hardly have been
avoided. In telling French Canadians in 1791 that Britain had "no
intention of imposing English laws upon them" and that "they ought
to be governed to their satisfaction," the British Prime Minister

Si je me souviens bien

seemed to be indicating that Lower Canada was to be run as a
French-Canadian province.[9] This was certainly the understanding of
the Patriotes, whose parliamentary leader, Louis-Joseph Papineau,
claimed that the whole reason for having separate provinces of
Upper and Lower Canada was that "everything was and still is different between one and the other: religion, laws, usages, customs,
and languages." It was, moreover, so that "the defence of their laws
and institutions [would] be entrusted to themselves" that French
Canadians had been granted an elected assembly in 1791.[10] At any
rate, the Patriotes wanted a local government responsible to the
local majority, "an administration that will be French-Canadian in
feeling, French-Canadian in its interests, French-Canadian even in its
prejudices."[11] English Lower Canadians were welcome to participate,
but it had to be as Lower Canadians, not as Englishmen.

The French Coln. did not want to deal with Englishmen they wanted to deal with Franco-Anglo-cda when it come to inter provincial affairs.

It was this element of the Patriote program that would be
most prized by later generations. The anticlerical tendencies of the
radical reformers and the illegality of their actions in 1837 could hardly be approved in a French Canada that was becoming more and more
influenced by its clergy in the second half of the 19th century.[12] But
their nationalism remained attractive. And for nationalists in the 20th
century, it was the implied separatism of the Patriote rebellion that
summed up its real meaning: "an uprising of the more advanced section of French Canadian nationalists against English domination."[13]

Papineau become a misunderstood leader of the 20th separatists.

Thus, radical separatists of the 1960s and 1970s looked to
the Patriotes for inspiration and considered themselves "the heirs
of Papineau and the revolutionary Patriotes of 1837-1838."[14] ◆

as i recall

The proportion of recent immigrants in the Upper Canadian population was much higher than in Lower Canada, and this helps to
explain why governors in the western province could count on more

popular support than their counterparts in Quebec. Upper Canadian reformers could not be sure of winning majorities in provincial elections, and those of 1836 returned a pro-government majority. When Mackenzie began organizing in the countryside, therefore, he did not have the same support from other legislators as his counterparts in Lower Canada. He had never been a leader among legislative reformers – unlike Louis-Joseph Papineau, who had been Speaker of the Assembly and leader of a large reform caucus. All this helps to explain why the Upper Canadian rebellion was put down so easily, even without the presence of British troops – local volunteers were enough to do the job.

Mackenzie, for his part, tried to establish contacts with Lower Canadian Patriotes, and many of his supporters saw themselves as engaged in the same struggle as Lower Canadians. This Ontario tendency to see the rebellions as waging a common fight against autocratic government would be encouraged by the cooperation of French- and English-Canadian reformers during the 1840s.

Lower Canada's Anglophones were more conscious of national conflict. Their suspicion of French-Canadian political influence had appeared by the turn of the century, as the revolutionary and Napoleonic wars raised fears that French agents were at work in Lower Canada.[15] Anglophones who occupied official positions through the governor's patronage were particularly vulnerable to such suspicions, and they were joined by anglophone merchants frustrated by the assembly's coldness to projects which they considered necessary to the prosperity of the country. In 1809, the merchant Hugh Gray wrote that it had been a mistake to grant French Canadians an assembly, since most were too ignorant of public affairs, while the lack of any representative tradition in French Canada left even the best educated unprepared for responsible conduct of a British-style legislature.[16] In 1822, anglophone merchants supported an abortive attempt to undermine French-Canadian nationalism by re-uniting Upper and Lower Canada. And after the

[handwritten margin note: Anglos felt that giving French's an assembly it was a mistake, ig they were not 'wise' enough in English parliamentary way.]

passing of the 92 Resolutions, Anglo-Montrealers formed volunteer "rifle corps" to combat "French republicanism" and "disloyalty."[17] ◆

Anglophones and Francophones alike have often looked back on the rebellions as an important step toward responsible government, holding up both Papineau and Mackenzie as heroes of democratic reform. At the same time, many have questioned the usefulness of their rebellions — especially Mackenzie's — arguing that responsible government would have come without them. Whatever their importance in the history of democratic reform, the rebellions would have a drastic effect on French-English relations because of the 1838 investigation into their causes by Lord Durham and the union of the two Canadas, which Britain would impose as a result of his report.

The Rebellions set the stage
For what was to be of
French-English relations in Lower/Upper Canada.

The Union of the Canadas (1840)

I N MAY 1838, THE EARL OF DURHAM ARRIVED AT QUEBEC TO BE BOTH GOVERNOR AND investigator, with instructions to report on the causes of the recent rebellions. Five months later, after a trip to Upper Canada and a fast visit across the border at Niagara, he returned to Britain, leaving a staff to finish the investigation. His report was completed in January 1839.

Durham attributed the Canadian uprisings to three principal causes:[1] the defective character of the 1791 constitution,[2] economic underdevelopment, and French-Canadian nationalism. The 1791 constitution had been "ill-contrived," wrote Durham, because it was foolish to think that men who participated in the making of laws would accept having no say over the administration of them. If this were not changed, Canadians would always be discontented and resentful of Britain. Governors, therefore, must submit their executive to the influence of the assembly, "by entrusting its administration to such men as could command a majority."[1] Making government responsible to the assembly would aid the economic development of the colonies. Canadian assemblies had not voted money for economic development programs, because the lack of ministerial responsibility had made them mistrustful of the executive officers who would have spent it.

Yet, it was hard to see how responsible government could be given to Lower Canada, where French-Canadian nationalists seemed likely to dominate the assembly. They had shown, by their past actions, that they did not share the view of economic development held by English-speaking North Americans. "The English population," wrote Durham,

> ...looked on the American Provinces as a vast field for settlement
> and speculation, and...regarded it as the chief business of

government to promote...the increase of population and the accumulation of property.

French-Canadian politicians, on the other hand, viewing the province "as
the patrimony of their own race," refused to spend money "required for
improvement," especially for projects that would increase the prosperity of British
immigrants or promote the growth of commerce with Great Britain.[2]
Durham did not blame French Canadians for that attitude. Britain herself
had encouraged them, in 1791, to think of Lower Canada as a province set aside
for their nationality; yet it had frustrated that expectation by allowing British emigrants to settle there. Moreover, Lower Canadian governors had unfairly excluded French Canadians from a fair share of patronage, thus provoking feelings of
national resentment.

Yet, French Canadians too had need of economic development. Isolated
from France by the Conquest, they had not been able to share in the modernization that had occurred in that country since then; isolated by language and
nationalism from other North Americans, they had not picked up modern ideas
from them either. So their agricultural economy remained old-fashioned,
seigneurial backward and unable to properly support their growing population.
Already large numbers were emigrating to the United States to seek opportunities
their own province could not provide.

Since French-Canadian nationalism blocked the prosperity of all, it had to
be eliminated. Durham therefore recommended that Upper and Lower Canada be
merged. In a single legislative assembly, French-Canadian politicians would be
forced to come to terms with an English-Canadian majority. The combined English
population of Upper and Lower Canada was already larger than the French, and
immigration would give it an even greater advance. With responsible government,
the English-dominated legislative assembly of a united Canada could proceed with
the programs of economic development the country needed. Outnumbered, out-
voted, yet attracted by the very prosperity that these reforms would bring, French
Canadians would abandon their dreams of a separate nationality, learn English, as
the French of Louisiana were doing, and join the majority population.

In 1840, the British Parliament passed an Act of Union that reflected much
of Durham's report. The two Canadas would be joined under a single government

with a single legislature. Laws and legislative records would be published in English only. French Canada would be absorbed within a larger English-Canadian province. *It sure did not happen that way.*

Yet, Britain did not grant full responsible government. What is more, to win Upper Canadian support for the Union, it agreed that Upper Canada should have the same number of representatives in the assembly as Lower Canada, though it had only two-thirds the population.

Even before the Union went into effect, Upper-Canadian reform politicians contacted Louis-Hippolyte LaFontaine, a former Patriote MLA, with a proposal for political alliance: LaFontaine's party would accept the Union and work with Upper Canadian reformers to win full responsible government; the Upper Canadians, for their part, would help to preserve French-Canadian laws, institutions and identity. If the two groups together could win a majority in the assembly, they could carry out their program, since governors were now instructed to work "in harmony" with the assembly and could not go too far against it.

The strategy worked. Hopes of merging French and English laws were quickly abandoned, and separate legal administrations were maintained for *what in essence* Upper and Lower Canada. In 1842, separate officials were appointed to supervise *1840's* publicly funded schools in the two sections. A year later, the assembly appealed *meant.* to Britain to restore French as an official language; in 1848, the British government did so. As time went by, the assembly passed more and more laws that were applicable only to one or the other of the former provinces. In effect, a sort of quasi-federalism had emerged, in which a single legislature and government ran parallel administrations for an Upper and Lower Canada, which retained separate *popular box* identities.[3] Responsible government soon followed; it was contained in the instructions of Lord Elgin, who became governor in 1847, and confirmed by his *Responsible gou't* signing of the Rebellion Losses Bill in 1849.

Responsible government allowed LaFontaine, his Upper Canadian ally, Robert Baldwin, and their successors to form popularly supported administrations — and the system of parliamentary representation ensured that French Canadians would play an important role in them. By 1851, Upper Canada's population exceeded that of Lower Canada, yet both sections still had the same number of seats in the assembly. The constitution of 1840 thus ended up

As always
French cat.
got
Their
wong

protecting French Canadians from the worst consequences of the minority position it had imposed upon them.[4]

Meanwhile, the Union did force French and English to work together in politics, with inevitable compromises and mutual influences. Though their civil laws never merged, they did influence each other during the mid-19th century. French and English politicians and businessmen found common interests in business and economic development based on a Laurentian transportation system: the Union legislature quickly authorized completion of canals along the St. Lawrence and soon backed construction of thousands of kilometres of railway; in 1854 it virtually abolished Lower Canada's seigneurial tenure, which had previously been defended as a French-Canadian national institution.[5]

Monument to the memory of Robert Baldwin and Louis-Hippolyte LaFontaine whose political alliance during the 1840s made it possible for Canadians to have responsible government. (NAC, C970)

si je me souviens bien

French Canadians were universally opposed to the imposition of the Union. Clergy and laity, conservative and liberal alike, signed petitions against the measure, which seemed intended to end their nationality; which gave no official place to their language; which, by

merging the budgets of the two provinces, would force Lower
Canadian taxpayers to help pay off Upper Canada's enormous public
debt; which skewed parliamentary representation in favour of Upper
Canada; and, above all, which deprived them of their distinctive
homeland and, for the first time in their history, made them a
minority in their own country. *Minority in your own country*

Once the Union came into effect, divisions appeared within
French-Canadian opinion. While LaFontaine adopted the strategy of
cooperation with Baldwin's reformers, other former Patriotes wanted to work for the repeal of the Union and to put the regaining of
French Canada's autonomy ahead of responsible government. To —
them, LaFontaine appeared a turncoat, abandoning the cause of his
own nationality. *Nationality Quebec is above will of ... presedence*

Since the reform alliance could succeed only if LaFontaine
brought to it a sufficient number of seats to give it a majority in the
assembly, he had to rally French-Canadian voters behind him – and
he looked for help in persuading them. As it happened, the Catholic
clergy was enjoying a growing influence over public opinion in the
1840s, and LaFontaine turned to this increasingly ultramontane cler- *The clergymen have always been of huge influence.*
gy to win the necessary support.[6] His opponents, true to their
Patriote liberalism, argued for abolition of compulsory tithes, for a
nondenominational public school system free from clerical control,
and against Church claims to lands once held by the Jesuit order but
now used by government for the support of education. LaFontaine's
party supported the clergy on all these issues; in return, the clergy
and clerical newspapers lent their influence to his party.

The end result was the success of LaFontaine's strategy; but with *The backward ways of Quebec.*
it, as the historian Jacques Monet has pointed out, came a rigid conser-
vatism that increasingly characterized majority politics in French Canada.[7] *ultramontane*

Ultramontanism gave new intensity to French-Canadian *ultramontanism*
nationalism, since it taught that the French-Canadian nation was
divinely created with a special God-given purpose, and that French
Canadians had a religious duty to maintain their nationality within

Lower Canada.[8] It also rejected the 19th century trend toward state-run nondenominational public schools, insisting that education must be a religious function and under clerical control. Thus, while Upper Canada moved toward neutral public schools, Lower Canada established parallel systems of Catholic and Protestant schools, giving the clergy more and more control over the running of the Catholic schools. Ultimately, the influence of ultramontanism, by making Catholicism the very heart of the French-Canadian identity, made it difficult to distinguish the two things, so that what was Catholic seemed *ipso facto* to be French-Canadian, and what was opposed by the Church seemed necessarily to be anti-French Canadian. Thus, Upper Canadian liberals, in advocating separation of Church and State, and more particularly in opposing public funding of religious schools, appeared to be enemies of French Canada.

The influence of ultramontanism on LaFontaine's party made it difficult to maintain the alliance with Upper Canadian reformers, and in 1854 his successor, A.-N. Morin, brought the party into a new coalition with English-Canadian Tories; it would dominate Canadian politics until the end of the century.

The opposition between LaFontaine and his more thorough-going liberal and nationalist opponents has been reflected in French-Canadian historical writing. An optimistic view is presented by Jacques Monet, who sees the 1840s as a triumph over assimilation, in which French and English worked together for their mutual advantage, while each preserved its own identity – and in which privileged elites lost hold of power, and government became responsible to public opinion. In effect, the 1840s see the undoing of the Conquest and the triumph of liberty under the British Crown.[9]

For nationalist historians, the picture is very different. French Canadians might have escaped assimilation, "but they did not escape annexation, political subordination, or provincialization."[10] No longer the majority in their own homeland, they were now a minority in a province imposed by British power; they were obliged to accept the business development schemes which English merchants had always demanded, and which, in the past, French Canadians had been able to block. It was the English middle class who had really won power, and all that French Canada had saved was a share of patronage and a limited identity. Worst of all, to keep the support of voters in the face of this defeat, French-Canadian politicians had to "go to Canossa," betraying the liberalism of the Patriotes by conceding to the clergy an inordinate influence in the social cultural and even political life of French Canada — a conservative influence which would freeze the development of Quebec society for over a century.[11] Far from ending the Conquest, the Union had only confirmed it.

Whether federalist or separatist, French Canadians could not be indifferent to the memory of Lord Durham, who had proposed the Union as a way to destroy French-Canadian nationality. His name remains a symbol of anglicization and of anglophone hostility to French-Canadian distinctiveness. ◆

Lord Durham

as i recall

While English Lower Canadians were generally glad of the Union, Upper Canadians were not so keen, and it was only by offering equal representation to the less populous province that Britain secured their consent.

Many English-Canadian supporters of the Union hoped that it might bring French and English together "to be *one people*." That did not necessarily mean the replacement of all things French by things English.

In the revision and consolidation of the laws, for instance, no one ever dreamt of rejecting every French law or custom, or adopting none but English. The great object will be to prepare a code of laws that shall embody all that suits the country...no matter for its origin.[12]

In essence what the Union did.

In this view, French Canadians were expected to abandon their language, though government would not *force* them to do so. It was assumed that if people were free to make their own decisions, they would choose what was in their own interest, and that if French Canadians were put into a common political society with other British North Americans, they would decide on their own that it was in their individual best interest to adopt the language of the majority.[13]

But the disappearance of French was not in itself a necessary goal. What was essential was that French and English should work together for prosperity and economic progress. The acceptance by French-Canadian politicians of the economic development program advocated by the great merchants and English-Canadian politicians made it easy for the latter to support the restoration of official French and the maintenance of separate laws and school systems in Lower Canada.

But the influence of ultramontanism among French Canadians contributed to an increasing anglophone discontent with the Union in the later 1850s and 1860s. Reform continued to enjoy majority support in Upper Canada, where thoroughgoing liberals, nicknamed Grits, fought for separation of Church and State, for the secularization of lands that had been reserved for the support of Protestant clergy, and for nondenominational public schools.

Upper Canadian Catholics (almost 18 percent of the population in the 1850s) were able to resist these tendencies to some extent. For the system of representation in the assembly allowed a large block of MLAs from Lower Canada, allied with a smaller number from Upper Canada, to form an overall majority and to pass laws granting Catholics in Upper Canada government-funded schools separate from the nondenominational ones. When such laws were passed in 1855 and 1863, against the votes of a majority of Upper Canadian MLAs, Grits expressed a popular frustration. They blamed the system of representation, which gave Lower Canada more MLAs in proportion to population than Upper Canada, caused more provincial money to be spent in Lower than in Upper Canada, and allowed Lower Canadians to prevent the adoption of measures wanted by Upper Canadians.

English-Canadian Tories were not as unhappy about the Union as were Grits. After 1854, it was the strength of their French-Canadian allies that enabled their Conservative coalition to hold power, and they had no reason to wish for a change. But Tory MPs found it harder and harder to face their constituents unless they accepted the need for constitutional change. In 1864, the recognition of that need would lead them to support Confederation.

Today, most Anglophones probably have little idea that there ever was a Union of the Canadas. But if Samuel LaSelva is right to say that English Canadians look on the Conquest as having "made Quebec part of Canada"[14] then the Union may seem significant to them as a demonstration that French and English Canadians could work together within that Canada, in mutual respect and for their common benefit. ◆

While the Union failed to anglicize French Canadians, it did force them into a minority position. It thus limited the scope of their national life and forced them to compromise with the majority. Ultimately, however, it was Upper Canadian frustration that brought the Union to an end and forced politicians to seek a new relationship between the two Canadas. It would be Confederation.

Frustration of equal representation when having most of the population.

Confederation (1867)

I<small>T WAS</small> G<small>EORGE</small> B<small>ROWN, THE LEADER OF THE</small> G<small>RITS, WHO LAUNCHED THE MOVE</small> toward Confederation. His idea was to transform the Canadian union into a federation, thus ending a situation of which Upper Canadians had long been complaining. If each province had a government to control its own local affairs, Lower Canadian votes would no longer be able to foist separate Catholic schools on Upper Canada or spend Upper Canadian tax dollars on Lower Canadian institutions or local projects. At the same time, French Canadians, finding themselves in "a position of comparative independence," would have no reason to fear representation in proportion to population in the federal legislature and would find it easier to cooperate with English Canadians in matters of common interest. Thus, in Brown's view, "The disruption of the existing union and the establishment of a Canadian federal system is the only remedy for existing evils."[1]

In 1864, Brown persuaded George-Étienne Cartier, leader of Lower Canada's majority party, the "Bleus," and John A. Macdonald, leader of Upper Canada's Tories, to work with him. Cartier and Macdonald agreed to a federation but proposed to enlarge it by inviting the Maritime Colonies to join. They hoped this would facilitate the development of trade between Canada and those colonies and would make it easier to build a railroad between them. Such considerations seemed particularly important at the time because the United States was getting ready to cancel the 1854 reciprocity treaty, which had provided for limited free trade between it and the British North American provinces. An interprovincial railway would also have a military function. During the winter of 1861-62, when war with the United States had seemed imminent, the lack of a rail link had made it extremely difficult for British troops to reach Canada. Disputes with the United

States were frequent in the 1860s, and there was a general feeling that British North Americans needed to see to their military defences, especially since Britain could not continue to ensure them on its own. A British North American confederation seemed useful in this situation.

Cartier, Macdonald and Brown formed a coalition in June 1864 to seek a general confederation, but with the understanding that if that failed, they would secure a federation of the two Canadas only. That September, at Charlottetown, they put their proposal to representatives of Nova Scotia, New Brunswick and Prince Edward Island, and secured an agreement in principle. In October, a new conference, in which Newfoundland delegates also participated, convened in Quebec to work out a detailed plan of confederation.

It soon became clear that there were differences of opinion about how the confederation should be structured. The Canadians, who controlled the agenda and prepared the resolutions to be discussed, were determined that representation in the federal assembly (to be called the House of Commons) must be based on population; Maritimers, however, feared that such a system would leave them with no effective voice in federal affairs.[2] Delegates also disagreed about how centralized or decentralized the confederation should be. In the end, despite the fears of the smaller provinces, the Quebec Resolutions affirmed the principle of representation by population, but they were ambiguous enough in other respects that people could see in them either centralization or decentralization, according to their own manner of interpretation.[3]

The Quebec Resolutions were repudiated outright by Newfoundland and Prince Edward Island. In New Brunswick, they were a major issue in the 1865 elections, which saw the downfall of Leonard Tilley's confederationist government and the formation of a new administration opposed to the scheme. This government, however, proved unstable, and new elections had to be held in 1866. Aided by thousands of Canadian dollars contributed to his campaign, and by a new American war scare that underlined the need for action on military defence, Tilley came back to power and received legislative authorization to attend a new conference in London to further refine the confederation scheme. This was as much as Nova Scotia's premier, Charles Tupper, could get in his province. Only in the Canadas were the Quebec Resolutions debated and approved by the legislature.

Majorities of both Upper and Lower Canadian MPs voted in favour of them, though the majority among Lower Canadians was a modest one.

During the winter of 1866-67, the London conference revised and refined the Quebec Resolutions, and, in March 1867, they were passed by the British Parliament as the British North America Act (BNA Act). Confederation went into effect on July 1st of that year.

Painting by Charles W. Simpson (1927) representing the Fathers of Confederation, created on the occasion of the 60th anniversary of Confederation. (NAC C13943)

si je me souviens bien

The French-language public debate on Confederation took place [*Acadians out of the loop.*]
almost exclusively in Lower Canada. Acadians in the Maritimes had no
representatives in their provincial governments, no newspapers to discuss public questions from an Acadian point of view, no national society or other forum for discussion. The first French-language
newspaper in New Brunswick did not appear until a week after
Confederation had come into effect. By then, it was too late to do anything but "resign ourselves to our fate and try to make the best of it."[4]

In Canada, all francophone members of the government were
from Lower Canada, and their sense of French-Canadian nationality was
overwhelmingly identified with that province. "The French Canadians
are really a nation," wrote Louis-François Laflèche in the midst of the
Confederation debate; "the St. Lawrence Valley is their homeland."[5]

Accordingly, the French-language debate on Confederation
turned on the question of how much autonomy Lower Canada was
going to acquire. The Lower Canadian "Rouges," or Liberals (the
only major party not invited to join in the coalition government),
feared that the confederation would be far too centralized, that
Ottawa would be able to dominate the provinces and that French
Canada would, therefore, be at the mercy of an Anglo-Protestant
majority. "Without finances, without power to undertake major public works, the local legislature will hardly be more than a big municipal council..."[6] In fact, to call this a *confederation* was merely to
"disguise" its reality. "This quasi-legislative union is just a step
toward a complete and absolute legislative union."[7] Now, instead of
being united with one anglophone province only, French Canada
would be overwhelmed by a number of them in a larger version of
the 1840 Union. No wonder Rouges referred to the BNA Act as an
"anglifying bill."[8]

French-Canadian pro-Confederationists had a very different
view of what the new system would be. After meeting some of them
during the fall of 1864, the governor of New Brunswick reported that
" 'federal union' in the mouth of a Lower Canadian means the inde-

pendence of his province from all English or Protestant influences..."[9]
That certainly was the idea that Bleu leaders tried to get across.
When Étienne-Pascal Taché, the chairman of the Quebec conference
and head of Canada's coalition government, spoke in the legislative
council, he stated that Confederation would be "tantamount to a separation of the provinces, and Lower Canada would thereby preserve
its autonomy together with all the institutions it held so dear."[10] In an
autonomous province of Quebec, French Canadians would cease to be
the minority they had been under the Union, and would "become forever the national and religious majority."[11] This was the key to their
national future: the control of all their distinct institutions and local
interests. By creating a separate province of Quebec with its own government, legislature and French Canadian majority, Confederation

> recognizes the French Canadians as a distinct and
> separate nationality. As such, we form a state within
> the state. We enjoy the full exercise of our rights and
> the formal recognition of our national independence.[12]

Not that Bleu leaders expected that independence to be complete. They and their English-speaking counterparts had a number of
things in common: satisfaction with their parliamentary form of government and loyalty to Britain[13]; fear of the United States and a sense of the
need for common defence[14]; and, above all, economic interests. Cartier,
whose constituency was Montreal, whose legal practice counted the
Grand Trunk Railway as one of its clients, and whose income came partly
from Montreal commercial property, shared the ambitions of Montreal's
anglophone businessmen who aimed to make their city the centre of an
interprovincial transportation system and the focus of manufacturing
and commerce for British North America. He was well aware that
Montreal's prosperity had been built on its transport connections with
Upper Canada, on its role as shipper of Upper Canadian wheat and lumber to European markets, and as a provider of manufactured goods to
Upper Canadian consumers — and he hoped to see Montreal's hinterland
further expanded.[15] An effective central government was needed to

promote those ambitions, for the development of the interprovincial economy would not only increase the profits of Quebec businessmen, it would provide much-needed jobs for ordinary French Canadians, who, by the 1860s, were emigrating to the United States in search of employment in far greater numbers than when Durham had noted the phenomenon.[16]

But as the Bleus presented Confederation to French-Canadian voters, the central government would have no more power than was strictly needed to achieve those military and commercial goals. Cartier himself told a Lower Canadian audience that in the constitutional negotiations, "I was careful to make sure that the federal government would receive only that amount of power which was strictly necessary to serve the general interests of the Confederation."[17] In the legislature, he described the central government as dealing "with the matters of defence, tariff, excise and public works," but not nationality, religious institutions or identity.[18] Bleu editors agreed:

> in Confederation the central government will have
> powers only over questions of common interest to all
> provinces...But the future of our race, the preserva-
> tion of everything that constitutes our national char-
> acter, will depend directly on the local legislature.[19]
> Nor would the federal government have any power to
> interfere with the provincial one.
> Each of these governments will have absolute power
> within its own jurisdictions, each will be equally sover-
> eign in its own sphere of activity, and those spheres will
> be entirely distinct and separate from each other...[20]

In fact, as the French-speaking sponsors of Confederation described it, the new regime was a sort of sovereignty-association for Quebec: "We've made an alliance with our neighbours to promote our common interests while keeping for ourselves exclusive control over all our own affairs."[21] And in that federal alliance, Quebec was to be the French-Canadian country, the political expression of the French-Canadian nationality. ◆

as i recall

Like French Canadians, Anglophones were divided between propo-
nents and opponents of Confederation; but they were also divided
about what kind of a confederation they wanted. Some, like
Conservative leader John A. Macdonald, favoured a highly centralized system. Indeed, Macdonald admitted to the legislature that he
would have preferred a legislative union and had accepted a federal
one only out of necessity. Even so, he described it as highly centralized, with "all the great subjects of legislation" and "all the powers
which are incident to sovereignty" going to the central authority,
while provincial powers would merely be subordinate.[22] Indeed, he
predicted in private to a fellow politician that he would see "both
local Parliaments and Governments absorbed in the General power."[23]

centraliz
rivals
vs.
federats

   Macdonald's views were thus very far from those which the
Bleus were defending; but they were not shared by all Anglophones.
The sense of local identity and the desire not to be swallowed up by
a Canadian majority were strong in the Maritimes. Both Macdonald
and Brown would comment in the Canadian assembly that a legislative union would have been unacceptable to the Maritimers as well
as to the French Canadians.[24] Indeed, for Newfoundlanders, Prince
Edward Islanders, and a great many voters in New Brunswick and
Nova Scotia, the scheme adopted at Quebec and London was not
decentralized enough or designed to give sufficient voice to the
provinces in federal affairs.[25]

   Nor did all Upper Canadians share Macdonald's views. The
push for a federal arrangement had begun, after all, with Upper
Canadian Grits, and provincial control over matters such as education, social and cultural affairs, property and municipal institutions
was a fundamental goal for them. Indeed, many Upper Canadian
reformers expressed the same view of provincial autonomy as the
Bleus: each level of government, provincial as much as federal,
would be sovereign within its own jurisdictions, each receiving sovereign authority in the same way from the imperial parliament. *The
Globe* of Toronto called for provincial legislatures "empowered by

the imperial Legislature and the Crown," with which the federal government "will not be allowed to interfere." Under Confederation, it
claimed, "The people of Ontario have got the absolute control of
their local affairs..."[26] ◆

The realities of gov't one people. Whatever their views on Confederation, no one expected that it would
turn British North Americans into one single people overnight. Even Macdonald,
who wished Confederation to make "one people and one government," recognized that French Canadians needed to be able to go on being "what they are now
— a nationality."[27] The populations of the different provinces in 1867 simply did
not have enough common values, outlook or contact to form a single national
community,[28] and few would have disagreed with Cartier's assertion that
Confederation was creating only "a political nationality with which neither the
national origin, nor the religion of any individual would interfere," and in which
the provinces would retain their distinct identities.[29]

Nevertheless, Confederation awakened dreams in some people's minds of
something more than a mere political nationality. Such, at least, was the case with
five young men (four Ontarians and one Nova Scotian) who met by chance in
Ottawa in early 1868, and discovered that the new constitution had inspired in
all of them the dream of a great nation unified by a "strong national spirit" and a
sense of dedication to a common cause. They expressed their own dedication by
forming a club to promote "the higher interests of their country," to encourage
others to put "Canada First" — ahead of private interests — and inculcate a common outlook and set of values.[30]

During the decades after Confederation, English-speaking journalists,
teachers and politicians would increasingly pick up this idea of a Canadian
nationality unified by a common "national spirit." As we shall see, the desire
to create a unified national spirit would be associated, at the end of the 19th
century, with measures to promote anglicization and to curtail the use of
French. In the middle decades of the 20th century, it would be associated with
an expansion of the federal government and attempts to make it into a more
"national" government.[31]

Attempts to forge a single Canadian identity or spirit naturally upset French Canadians, who retained a strong sense of their own national identity. And 20th century moves to centralize power in Ottawa would go against their long-held view that Quebec's autonomy was the essential guarantee that Confederation had offered them for their national future.

Ottawa vs. Quebec ; the confederation.

The Hanging of Louis Riel (1885)

DURING THE WINTER OF 1868-69, GEORGE-ÉTIENNE CARTIER WENT TO LONDON to arrange the transfer to Canada of the Hudson's Bay Company's immense territory lying to the dominion's north and west. News of this arrangement provoked great anxiety in the North-West's main settlement, the Red River colony, centred on present-day Winnipeg. Red River had a population of about 12,000, of whom 1600 or so were whites (Hudson's Bay Company personnel, missionaries, descendants of Scottish emigrants brought by Lord Selkirk in 1812, and recently arrived settlers from Ontario), and most of the rest Métis, the children of marriages between white fur traders and Indian women. Of the Métis, about 5800 were French-speaking and 4100 were Anglophones. *Hudson's Bay & Canada.*

Naturally, Ontario settlers were pleased with the transfer. But others worried about how the end of the fur-trade economy would affect their lives, whether their property would be secure, and whether their interests would be represented in the new government. French Catholics feared that Anglo-Protestant immigration would overwhelm them; and everyone resented the fact that they had not been consulted about the change.

During the fall of 1869, a group of French-Métis forcibly prevented the new Canadian governor from entering the territory, then proceeded to take possession of Fort Garry, the administrative centre of Red River, and to seize the Company's stores. Their leader was Louis Riel, a Métis recently returned from a classical education in Montreal. *Resistance to Cdn. gov't entering the Red river region.*

When news of the resistance reached Ottawa, the government stopped the transfer and sent three envoys to investigate the problem. They got to Red River around the beginning of 1870 and assured everyone that Canada wished to respect their rights. They urged the local population to draw up a list of their demands and send them to Ottawa for negotiation. Accordingly, a convention of equal numbers from French and English parishes met and drew up a "bill of rights." The convention also agreed to a "provisional government" to run the colony until an understanding with Canada could be put into effect,[1] and Riel was accepted as its head.

Manitoba was formed

Three local men took the bill of rights to Ottawa that spring. Their discussions with federal ministers were successful, and the result was the Manitoba Act, which Parliament passed in May. This created a small province, Manitoba, in the region of Red River. Like Quebec, Manitoba would have a bilingual legislature and courts. It would legally recognize Métis title to lands occupied until then and would include a reserve of 570,000 hectares of land for Métis families. News of the Act was received with satisfaction at Red River, and the transfer to Canada was completed at the end of the summer.

Meanwhile, in early December, Riel had captured a number of Canadians attempting to organize resistance against him. He kept them imprisoned for most of the winter, and, in March, one of them, a turbulent, unruly and untamable man named Thomas Scott, was "court-martialled" and "executed" by a Métis firing squad. This killing created a problem, for while the British and Canadian governments had been willing to overlook Riel's other actions, they could not ignore what was legally an act of murder. Though the Red River delegates, especially Father N.-J. Ritchot, pleaded for a complete and general amnesty, neither Ottawa nor London could bring itself to issue one.[2] In Manitoba, warrants were issued for the arrest of Scott's killers, and, though officials did not act on them, there were violent attempts at vigilante justice during the fall and winter of 1870-71, directed by recently arrived Anglophones against Métis thought to have been involved in Scott's death. Riel fled to the United States, and many others followed.

But Riel did not stay away. In the 1872 federal elections, he was nominated for the Manitoba riding of Provencher. Though he withdrew that time, he was elected in 1873 and again in 1874. In April 1874, he went to Ottawa to claim his seat. But with a murder charge still outstanding against him, he was legally a fugitive from justice, and when his presence in Ottawa was discovered the Commons voted to expel him. At the same time, it set up a committee to inquire into his allegations that he had been promised an amnesty in 1870. The evidence was inconclusive, the testimony contradictory, and the committee's report left the matter unresolved.

That fall, Ambroise Lépine, head of the court martial that had condemned Scott, was tried in Manitoba for Scott's murder. Found guilty by a half-English, half-French-Métis jury, Lépine was condemned to death. But in January 1875 the Governor General commuted the sentence, and in February, the Government proposed a complete and general amnesty for participants in the Red River uprising, on condition that it would not apply to Riel and Lépine for five more years.

Riel spent the next year with friends in Quebec and the United States, but in 1876, he began to have religious hallucinations of such intensity that his protectors had him confined in a psychiatric hospital. Upon his release in 1878, he went to the United States and eventually settled down as a teacher in Montana.

Meanwhile, the Canadian Prairies faced a rush of settlement, largely from Ontario and almost all English-speaking. By 1885, the French-origin group, including Métis and newcomers, made up only 10 percent of the Manitoba population and only 14 percent in the rest of the Prairies. Traditional ways of life came under pressure as farms, fences, towns and a railroad appeared. By 1884, francophone Métis in the Saskatchewan district felt so threatened by these developments, and so frustrated by Ottawa's slow response to their appeals for protection, that they sent for Louis Riel, hoping he could help them attract government attention.

Riel arrived at the Métis settlement of Batoche in June 1884, and, supported at first by English-Canadian settlers with grievances of their own, began to organize public meetings and prepare petitions. In early 1885, he lost patience for such measures and moved to establish a "provisional government." This lost him the support of settlers and of Catholic missionaries, but he went ahead, threatening a "war of extermination" unless the nearby mounted police detachment left the territory.[3] Finally, on 26 March, an armed clash between Riel's men and a group of Mounties and volunteers ended with a dozen dead and 11 wounded.

Reacting quickly, Ottawa raised a volunteer force, with battalions from Nova Scotia, Quebec, Ontario and Manitoba, to put down the rebellion. By mid-May, they had reached Batoche and taken it; a few days later Riel himself was arrested. He was tried for high treason in late July at Regina. Unable to deny that he had led a rebellion, his lawyers pleaded the defence of insanity. But the medical testimony was divided, and Riel's behaviour at the trial seemed lucid and rational. The jury, therefore, found him sane and guilty, and he was sentenced to death. His lawyers appealed his case to the Manitoba Court of Queen's Bench and the Judicial Committee of the Privy Council, but the verdict was upheld. Riel was hanged on November 16, 1885.

si je me souviens bien

With no telegraph, regular mail delivery or professional reporters at Red River, Canadian newspapers had to rely on indirect sources of information. The most important were articles from the St. Paul or Chicago press. But as these were expensive and time-consuming to translate, French-language papers could not carry very many of them. They relied at first on statements made in Parliament, but increasingly on letters sent to Quebec by Francophones at Red River. Such letters, usually from people close to Riel, insisted that he had the support of "almost the entire Red River population" – "French-Canadian and English alike."[4] This created the impression that Riel represented the whole community, and that his power was based on popular approval.

Consequently, when Thomas Scott was killed, Quebecers – even though they were shocked and horrified by "a crime which cannot be too much deplored" and which "we condemn as energetically as possible"[5] – nevertheless felt that it had to be accepted as the act of a popularly supported government. "To ask the people of Red River to hand over to us its leaders, its government, its jurors, to be condemned to death as felons and murderers, would be to subject that whole society to the will of another society."[6]

In reality, Red River was not united. Riel drew active support from among the French Métis and Catholic missionaries, though even they were not unanimous. English-Canadian settlers opposed him; so did many anglophone Métis, though others were torn

Si je me souviens bien

Riel was not as liked as many thought.

between loyalty to their francophone cousins and dislike of Riel's violent methods.[7] English-language newspapers drew attention to these divisions and the opposition to Riel, thus making his movement seem essentially francophone. But such a representation of the uprising disturbed French-Canadian editors. If all of Red River was united behind Riel, as their correspondents assured them, why did Ontario papers single out the French, unless it was only "a pretext to demand the expulsion of the French from the North-West?"[8] That suspicion was reinforced when English Canadians called for the punishment of Scott's murderers. Since Scott's killing had been the work of a *de facto* government supported by the whole community, demands for Riel's arrest must be motivated by prejudice against his nationality. "If Riel, the French Canadian, had been the victim instead of Scott, nobody in Ontario would have bothered about it."[9]

French-Canadian opinion, therefore, supported the demand for an amnesty, and events of the early 1870s – the assaults on Métis in Manitoba, Riel's expulsion from the Commons and the trial of Lépine – only intensified that support. In the summer of 1874, A.-A. Dorion, leader of the Quebec federal Liberal caucus, warned Prime Minister Alexander Mackenzie that "sympathy for Riel and his companions is getting stronger and stronger in Lower Canada and it will soon be a difficulty in the way of any Government."[10]

The amnesty that Mackenzie finally produced did not completely satisfy French-Canadian opinion. The five-year delay before it would apply to Riel and Lépine seemed an additional "injustice, and an insult to us."[11] Nevertheless, Quebec Liberals were able to defend it. After all, despite the delay, Riel and Lépine were being amnestied.[12] In practice, the amnesty ended assaults on Métis in Manitoba,[13] and allowed the Métis question to fade from political discussion. In 1884, when Riel arrived in Saskatchewan, French-Canadian newspapers paid him virtually no attention – until he turned to rebellion.

When the 1885 rebellion began, French Canadians showed a determination to put it down. The government must "act quickly

and strike hard," said Montreal's leading French-language paper.[14]
Two French-Canadian battalions formed part of the North-West
expedition, and enthusiastic crowds turned out to cheer for them at
Montreal and Quebec.[15]

Yet at the same time, the rebellion revived memories from the
1870s, and, with them, some mixed feelings. "The cause of the Métis is
dear to us," commented one editorialist. "We are too closely related to
be indifferent to their fate."[16] They were certainly wrong to rebel, but it
was Ottawa's neglect of their grievances that had "pushed them into it
over a long period of time."[17] As for Riel, people remembered his past
confinement and considered him "a lunatic of the first order."[18]

These views affected French-Canadian reaction to Riel's trial.
No one could deny that he had started a rebellion, but it was
expected that the Métis' grievances would be taken as mitigating
factors that dictated mercy. In any case, it was unthinkable that Riel
could be found guilty, since he was "a lunatic, entirely without
responsibility for his acts" – a man who had started the rebellion
"without realizing what he was doing."[19] When the trial ended with a
verdict of guilty and a sentence of death, French Canadians were
shocked. Thousands signed telegrams and petitions calling on the
federal cabinet to spare Riel's life; rallies, demonstrations and public
meetings were held throughout Quebec for the same purpose.

Ordinarily, people argued, an insane man would not be condemned in such a case; if an exception was made for Riel, it could
only be because of his nationality, because English Canadians wanted to hurt French Canada by hurting him. They had already seemed
to be doing that in the 1870s. "Riel is only a symbol: it's the French-
Canadian and Catholic element that they'd like to see dancing at the
end of a rope."[20] This seemed all the more plausible since Riel had
been tried by an anglophone magistrate and an all-English jury.[21]

When the execution took place, therefore, French Canadians,
convinced that Riel had been hanged only "because he was French,"[22]
took to the streets in angry demonstrations. At a giant rally in

Si je me souviens bien

Montreal, the leader of the Quebec Liberal Party, Honoré Mercier, called the execution an attack on the French-Canadian nation − "a blow struck at the heart of our race."[23] And since French Canada was under attack, it must unite its ranks to defend itself. Conservatives and

Caricature by John Wilson Bengough published in *Grip* in August 1885, a few weeks after Louis Riel was sentenced to death for high treason. ("A Riel ugly position," NAC, C22249)

Liberals must join together to form a single French-Canadian national party and fortify their nationality within their province of Quebec.

Mercier campaigned on these lines until the 1886 provincial elections, in which a number of former Bleus, angry about Riel, broke from their party and ran as "National Conservatives." With their support, Mercier formed a "National Government" of Quebec in early 1887. Over the next five years, he repeatedly affirmed the distinctive national character of Quebec — Catholic and French Canadian — and in so doing raised fears among English Canadians that the Confederation's very survival was threatened by French Canada's distinctiveness. ◆

English-Canadian newspapers, picking up dispatches from St. Paul, printed a different version of Red River news from that of their francophone counterparts. Since most of Riel's opponents were Anglophones, and since they were the ones who left for the US while he controlled the colony, interviews, letters and reports that appeared in the St. Paul and Chicago press tended to emphasise divisions in the Red River population and opposition to Riel. Anglophone newspaper readers thus formed the impression that Riel was not a true representative of the Red River people, but that he had imposed himself by force and ruled by violence. "The situation of those whites and half-breeds who oppose the rebellion is daily getting more precarious," reported a correspondent in December, "and many talk of leaving for the States."[24] In holding Canadians prisoner for weeks and months, with no charge, no trial and no legal authority, he and his friends were acting as "high-handed...Czars or Sultans."[25]

But if Riel was a self-imposed despot, then the killing of Thomas Scott was simply a cold-blooded murder; the idea that it was an execution carried out by a *de facto* government was totally implausible. Indeed, the killing of Scott only confirmed that Riel's power was based on "terrorism."[26] Consequently, there could be no question, as far as most English Canadians were concerned, of granting an amnesty – at least not "in connection with the trial of those who murdered Scott."[27]

Even the confidence shown by the Manitoba voters did not at first change Ontarians' opinion that Riel was "a reckless adventurer whose hands are red with the blood of a...deliberate act of murder."[28] Yet, by the fall of 1874, after his second election to Parliament, the amnesty committee's report, and four years of agitation, English Canadians were coming to recognize that Francophones honestly believed Riel and Lépine had acted with a sense of legitimacy in killing Scott. Many, therefore, were coming to support an amnesty – if not because they agreed with the francophone view, at least "because they do not desire to wound the mistaken sympathies and misplaced sensitiveness of their French-speaking fellow-citizens..."[29] It was time to put an end to the "disunion and discord between the people of Quebec and Ontario."[30]

So English Canadians generally accepted the 1875 amnesty, especially since the five-year delay for Riel and Lépine acknowledged that a murder had been committed, even if its authors would not be punished. Riel soon faded from people's thoughts. His appearance in Saskatchewan in 1884 attracted little attention and less concern – until he turned to rebellion.

When the rebellion broke out, there was a strong sense in English Canada that the country was seriously threatened, and a great pride in the "citizen-soldiers" who volunteered to defend it. Indeed, those who hoped for the emergence of a real Canadian nation were heartened by the sight of men from Nova Scotia, Quebec and Ontario all "fighting for a common cause and a common country"; it seemed that as a result, the "Canadian nation has been fused by a common overwhelming warmth..."[31] But the reaction to Riel's trial and execution dashed that hope.

Few English Canadians were surprised by the trial's result. "The evidence was clear and convincing."[32] The defence had not even tried to deny that Riel had started a rebellion. The Métis' sufferings could not extenuate his crime, since he had not been living in Canada to share them. Indeed, two witnesses, including a Catholic missionary, had testified that Riel had been willing to abandon the Métis and leave the country if the government would pay him $35,000. Apparently, he had wanted to exploit the Métis grievances "to make a big stake for himself."[33]

As for his madness, the medical experts were not agreed, and Riel's own speech to the jury, marked by coherence and clarity, "leads many to believe that Riel is sound in mind."[34] He might be a "crank" when it came to religious matters, "but that does not absolve him from responsibility nor lessen his guilt."[35]

Moreover, Riel was a recidivist. Amnestied for his first crime, he had repeated it on a larger scale "and will do so again if he gets off."[36] This time he had even incited Indians to violence, and innocent priests and settlers had been murdered as a result. This could not be tolerated; society could not survive unless such people were deprived of "all power to repeat their crimes." Riel's execution was thus necessary for "the safety of society."[37]

The attitude of French Canadians, therefore, seemed shocking. How could they be so unanimously opposed to the sentence in the face of such overwhelming reasons for carrying it out, unless they were motivated simply by racial prejudice? In fact, "no one can believe that if Louis Riel were an Englishman that Quebec would have taken the slightest interest in his fate."[38] When French Canadians protested after the execution, it looked as though they were angry only because one of their people had been executed for crimes for which a man of any other nationality would have been executed. They seemed to want a privileged status for themselves: "One law for the English-speaking people and a less severe one for the French."[39] Unwilling to live under the same law and be part of the same nation as everyone else, they seemed determined "not in any way to regard themselves as one with us."[40]

French always wanting special privellege.

Mercier's nationalism only intensified these impressions – raising fears among English Canadians that the Confederation's very survival was threatened by French Canada's distinctiveness. "We are drifting more and more into a state of distrust," observed the *Hamilton Spectator*, "more and more into that frame of mind which makes mutual effort for the upbuilding of our common country impossible." And the reason was French Quebecers' "conviction...that they are a race apart, having interests differing from the interests of other Canadians."[41] ◆

The idea that Riel was a victim of English-Canadian prejudice remained an important theme in French-Canadian history until the 1960s. Since then, Quebec's professional historians have lost interest in Riel, as they've concentrated on Quebec's own social and economic development. But the old idea has

Monument erected to the memory of Métis leader Louis Riel in Regina, Saskatchewan. (*La Presse*)

remained important in the media and general opinion. In 1980, as Quebecers prepared for their first referendum on separation, they were reminded of Riel, whose persecution, they were told, had worked to exclude French Canadians from the West.[42] In 1983, a Franco-Ontarian paper still described him as a victim of francophobe "English prejudice."[43] Although not many people today may actually know the facts of Riel's life and death,[44] his name remains a symbol of English-Canadian ill will and injustice toward French Canada.

Among Anglophones, attitudes have changed radically since Riel's time. In the mid-20th century, English-language historians began to adopt the French-Canadian view of Riel's execution, and by the 1970s, historian Desmond Morton could comment that French Canada's "version of the facts has triumphed" in the popular culture of English Canada.[45] At the same time, Riel came to be seen by Anglophones less as a French-Catholic figure and more as a westerner resisting the dominance of central Canada, or as a representative of Aboriginal peoples.[46]

The Riel affair had its greatest impact on English Canada during the three decades following his death. By provoking intense suspicion of French-Canadian distinctiveness, it led to an assimilationist drive that would seriously affect the position of Francophones throughout Canada.

→ What Riel means to French Anglophones.

The Minority
Rights Disputes
(1871-1916)

F RENCH-ENGLISH RELATIONS IN CANADA HAVE BEEN AFFECTED BY THE ASSOCIATION, and sometimes the confusion of two distinct types of minority rights: the right of Catholics to tax-supported religious schools and the right of the French language to be used in public institutions.

In the 19th century, most Catholics outside Quebec were not Francophones. The 1871 census showed that only 27 percent of Ontario's Catholics were of French origin, 47 percent of New Brunswick's and 32 percent of Nova Scotia's. In Prince Edward Island, which joined Confederation in 1873 and where Catholic school rights became an issue three years later, only 23 percent of Catholics were of French origin according to the census of 1881.

The Catholic schools issue arose when British North American governments, like those in other countries influenced by 19th century liberalism, moved to establish tax-funded public school systems, supervised by government officials and teaching a nondenominational program. The Catholic Church opposed such schools, arguing that religious doctrine could not be separated from other subjects without depriving Catholic children of the education their religion required them to have. Ultramontanes also argued that divine and natural law made education the responsibility of the Church and the family, and that the State had no right to interfere.[1]

In Upper Canada, under a pre-Confederation compromise, the government established a nondenominational public school system but allowed separate Catholic schools a share of public funding. This compromise was made permanent at Confederation by Section 93 of the British North America (BNA) Act, which forbade provinces to pass laws that would "prejudicially affect" denominational school rights already held by law. But, while separate Catholic schools had indeed been established by law in Upper Canada before Confederation, that was not the case in the Maritime colonies. Nova Scotia stopped funding denominational schools and set up a single, public system in 1864. In New Brunswick there were no separate Catholic schools, although the public system established in 1858 was so decentralized that public schools in Catholic districts could, in practice, be run as if they were denominational.

The weakness of Section 93 was seen in 1871, when New Brunswick passed a law that centralized its public school system and imposed a common curriculum. When Catholics asked Ottawa to disallow this measure, Sir John Macdonald, as Minister of Justice, replied that Section 93 did not apply, since separate Catholic schools had not been established by law in New Brunswick. An appeal to the courts confirmed Macdonald's opinion. Three attempts (in 1872, 1873 and 1875) by an anglophone Catholic MP, John Costigan, to have

Illustration published in the *Canadian Illustrated News* in 1875 recalling the Caraquet upheavals. (*Death of Constable Gifford*, McCord Museum of Canadian History, M984.306.1597)

Parliament overrule Macdonald failed, and, in the winter of 1874-75, Catholic resistance became more direct. In January, violence erupted in the Acadian village of Caraquet, when New Brunswick authorities tried to coerce the local school board, and two men were killed. This shocked Catholic leaders and provincial authorities into negotiating a compromise: the public system would remain, but material offensive to Catholic consciences would be removed from the program; Catholic clergy and members of religious orders would be able to teach in the schools; and Catholic religious instruction could be given after regular classes were over.

None of this had anything to do with French-language rights. British North American governments had been pragmatic and flexible in allowing local communities to use their own languages in their schools, whether public or separate. In Nova Scotia, under a law of 1841, public funding had been available to German, Gaelic and French-language schools, and in Upper Canada, the Board of Public Instruction had allowed local schools to teach in French or German where the community spoke that language.[2] In New Brunswick, French was used in the schools of Acadian communities, and that practice was not affected by the law of 1871. Instruction continued to be given in French, and the provincial government authorized new French-language texts and appointed francophone school inspectors.[3] Similarly, when Prince Edward Island established a nondenominational public school system in 1877, it announced that French could still be used in francophone districts.[4]

The early school controversies, therefore, were not about language but about religion. But if provincial governments accepted the use of French in their schools, it was not because they recognized it as an official language protected by constitutional right. Under section 133 of the BNA Act, French enjoyed official status only in the federal and Quebec parliaments and courts; no other province was constitutionally bilingual until Manitoba was established in 1870. Official equality for English and French languages was one of the demands the Red River delegates brought to Ottawa in the spring of 1870, and it was incorporated into the Manitoba Act. The principle was extended to the rest of the Prairies by an 1877 amendment to the federal Northwest Territories Act.[5]

At the same time, Catholic school rights were also extended to the North-West. When the first government of Manitoba set up a public school system in

1871, it was based on denominational lines, with separate Catholic and Protestant sections. In 1875, the federal government provided for a publicly funded Catholic school system in the territories as well.

By 1890, anglophone settlement in the Prairies had left French-speakers there hopelessly outnumbered and obliged them, in practice, to learn the majority language despite the official status of French. In 1889, Joseph Royal, the French-Canadian lieutenant-governor of the Northwest Territories, opened the session of the territorial assembly in English only, and the assembly itself expressed a desire to drop French altogether. Since that would require federal authorization, a resolution was introduced in Parliament by an Ontario MP, D'Alton McCarthy, in early 1890. Passed in amended form, it gave the territorial government the required permission. Meanwhile, Manitoba decided to drop its official use of French as well — a decision that would go effectively unchallenged until the 1970s — and passed a new school law replacing its dual structure with a single, nondenominational system.

It was the Manitoba school law that caused the real controversy at the time. Catholics believed it violated both the BNA Act and the Manitoba Act, but in 1892 the Privy Council ruled that the constitution did allow Manitoba to act as it had. Catholics now turned to another constitutional provision by which they could petition the federal government to help them. Early in 1895, the Privy Council confirmed that Ottawa did have the power to intervene, and even to pass legislation restoring Catholic schools in Manitoba — though whether or not to do so was a political question.

Embarrassed by this situation (for the country was badly divided on the desirability of federal intervention), the Conservative government stalled for a year, then finally brought a remedial bill before Parliament in 1896, so late that Parliament's five-year life came to an end before it could be passed.

In the elections that followed, Conservatives expected to win Catholic votes because they had put forward a remedial bill. But Liberals, led by a French-Canadian Catholic, Wilfrid Laurier, promised to get an even better deal for Manitoba Catholics, by compromise and negotiation, without infringing on provincial jurisdiction over education. The Liberals carried the election, with their majority based in Quebec, and soon announced a compromise agreement with Manitoba: the public school system would remain, but in Catholic districts, priests could give religious instruction in the schools after regular classes; Catholic school inspectors and teachers would be hired; and textbooks would not contain material offensive to Catholics. Though this agreement was terribly disappointing to those who had hoped for a return of Catholic schools, Laurier remained in power, carrying Quebec in the elections of 1900, 1904 and 1908.[6] Yet, in 1905, he disappointed Catholics and Francophones again, when he introduced legislation creating the provinces of Saskatchewan and Alberta out of sections of the Northwest Territory. Though he included a guarantee for Catholic schools in these provinces, it was far weaker than what they had had in 1875 — and though Quebec Conservatives called for the establishment of official bilingualism in the new provinces, Laurier refused, in the name of provincial autonomy, leaving them free to be English only.

Language also became an issue in other parts of the country. The early 20th century saw the end of Ontario's flexibility on language policy, and in 1912 the department of education issued Regulation 17 requiring the province's public and separate schools to teach in English only. In 1916, Manitoba would follow suit, ending all minority language instruction in its

Postcard showing schoolchildren on strike to protest Regulation 17 adopted by the Ontario government in 1912. (Archives of the Centre de recherche Lionel-Groulx, Laurendeau and Perrault Families Collection, P1/T4, 10.5)

schools as well. Thus, the period from the late 1880s to the middle of the First World War saw a major assault on Catholic schools and the French language in Ontario and the West.[7]

si je me souviens bien

As Catholics, French-speaking Lower Canadians had a natural sympathy for their co-religionists in other provinces. Indeed, they felt a special responsibility for Catholicism, since ultramontane writers and speakers taught that their nationality had a divine mission to promote the Catholic cause. Yet at the same time, they saw their own national safety in Quebec's autonomy, and they were wary of any minority guarantee that would mean privileges for Protestantism that might interfere with Quebec's Catholic character and autonomy. Thus, the French-Canadian Fathers of Confederation went to the Quebec conference supporting a simple proposal for absolute provincial control of education; this was amended to protect the Protestant and Catholic schools of Ontario and Quebec, thanks to the initiative of an anglophone Catholic. Accordingly, when the Archbishop of Halifax asked a French-Canadian minister, Hector Langevin, for help in securing from the London conference equally strong protection for Catholic schools in the Maritimes, Langevin was reluctant: "as Catholics," he and Cartier would "be happy to see our co-religionists of the lower Provinces obtain the advantages in question," but they would not bring it up themselves, since it was a matter of the Maritime provinces' jurisdiction.[8] Apparently it never did come up, for five years later, in a debate on the New Brunswick schools controversy, Cartier would tell the Commons: "In all our discussions on the subject of Confederation, there was never any question of the rights of Catholics in that province."[9]

Even in the Canadas, minority guarantees were not always welcome. In Lower Canada, they would mean privileges for Protestantism that might interfere with Quebec's Catholic character.

Si je me souviens bien

Thus in the summer of 1866, when two bills promising new privileges for Protestants in Quebec and Catholics in Ontario were withdrawn, French-Canadian MPs and newspaper editors of both political parties expressed approval. According to one paper, "they preferred that there should be no concession of privileges to any religious minority in the proposed constitution."[10]

In the New Brunswick schools controversy, French Canadians showed the same attitudes. As Catholics, they sympathized with their co-religionists as victims of an "unjust" law that deprived them of "religious rights, paternal rights, and the right of true freedom of conscience."[11] But when Parliament was asked to remedy their situation, either directly or by having the constitution amended to include more effective minority guarantees, most Quebec MPs held back. Cartier warned that any federal interference on behalf of New Brunswick Catholics would weaken the control that provincial autonomy gave Quebecers over their own schools. The Constitution had been conceived to give power over education to the provinces, and that was particularly important to French Canadians. "I insisted very strongly on that in the discussions on the Union proposal, for I wanted the province of Quebec to have that right."[12] However much they might wish to support Catholic minorities, Quebec MPs "must protect above all the interests of Quebec." Federal interference on behalf of a minority would be a dangerous precedent that "would be invoked against Lower Canada any day when there would be a wish to infringe upon our rights."[13]

Meanwhile, Quebec politicians had at first been no more active in securing minority rights in the West than in the Maritimes. When Riel's uprising led to the entrenchment of just such rights in Manitoba, Quebecers acknowledged that they were an unforeseen advantage. "Let's admit frankly what everyone is saying under his breath: all this madness has served us well; [without the Red River uprising], the French population of the North-West would have found itself badly off in the political organization we were intending to provide."[14]

In fact, French Quebecers had been little aware of Manitoba's francophone population until the Red River uprising drew it to their attention. Afterwards, the news of violent assaults on francophone Métis by anglophone settlers in Manitoba, the arrest and trial of Lépine, and the five-year struggle to obtain an amnesty ensured that Quebecers would remain focused on the French element in the West.

Similarly, French Canadians in Quebec had hardly been aware of an Acadian community in the Maritimes when the schools controversy began — most thought it had ended with the 18th century expulsions. The New Brunswick Catholic spokesmen were Anglophones and the issue itself was religious. But news of the 1875 violence at Caraquet changed that. Caraquet was an Acadian town; the Catholics whose rights were at stake there were not just Irish, they were "Acadians" — "French" — or even "French Canadians."[15] The fact that the Caraquet crisis coincided with the climax of the Métis amnesty controversy, underlined the French element common to the two affairs. In both cases, French groups seemed under attack, and the implications were frightening: "Trampled under foot in Manitoba, crushed in New Brunswick, we are threatened with annihilation."[16]

The New Brunswick and North-West controversies thus created a growing awareness of and concern for French-Catholic groups outside Quebec, which seemed threatened by English-Canadian persecution. The 1885 trial and hanging of Louis Riel brought that concern to a peak, and the attacks on the French language and Catholic schools in the West after 1889 appeared to be a continuation of the same fanaticism that had caused Riel's death and aimed to exclude French Canadians from participation in the life of the Confederation.

All this led French Canadians to change their conceptions of Confederation. It was no longer satisfactory to look on it as an association of provinces in which Quebec alone was French; there had to be a recognition of French in the West as well. So, by the 1890s, minority rights seemed important to French Canadians in a way that they had not in 1867. It now seemed to them that "the whole federal system depends

on this fundamental basis: respect and protection for the minorities."[17]
The 1895 Privy Council decision seemed to confirm that view, and, by the
end of the decade, it was leading to the emergence of a whole new theory of Canadian nationhood: a perfectly bicultural Canada, with "official
use of both languages in each and every province of the confederation."[18]
That was the vision that would be popularized by Henri Bourassa in the
20th century: "a Canada that would be French and English in each of its
parts as well as in its whole."[19]

　　This dualist vision of Canada was bound to be frustrated in a
period when governments were dropping French from their legislatures and schools, and the bitterness which that created among
French Canadians would help provoke the terrible confrontations over
conscription in 1917 between them and Canadian anglophones.　◆

Many Ontarians supported Confederation in order to end a situation
that had allowed Lower Canadian votes to expand separate schools
in Upper Canada. Consequently, they were not eager to entrench
new Catholic school rights in the Constitution, though they were willing to protect those already established, as *The Globe* acknowledged:

> Under our present Parliamentary system, it is never safe
> to say that the Romish Bishops in Canada cannot with a
> little labour get all they may ask. Under Confederation,
> while gladly 'crying quits' and leaving them what they
> now have and can keep in spite of us, we should be
> placed in a position to refuse them anything more.[20]

Maritimers were unwilling to compromise public schooling
even to that extent.

　　When it came to language, there was more willingness to
compromise, though not to entrench languages in the Constitution
beyond Section 133. Even those who hoped for an eventual

amalgamation of races in a single, English-speaking nation were ready to accept the use of French as a practical matter as long as French Canadians continued to speak it. Thus, the *Toronto Leader* defended the establishment of French as an official language in the federal Parliament even though it expected English to dominate simply because it was the language of the majority and MPs would find it desirable to speak English in order to be understood. "In the process of time, we may outgrow the use of two languages in the Confederate legislature..." But the process could not be forced: it "must be the result of natural causes, and be due to the wishes of the people who speak the French language."[21]

Thus, a pragmatic recognition of the needs of cultural communities on an *ad hoc* basis was a common approach in the 1860s. Canadians of that time did not have our present-day ideas of equality of rights or status across the country and had no difficulty accepting different rights in different places. The Manitoba Act reflected that approach. English Canadians had certainly not expected the establishment of French language and Catholic schools in the North-West, and when it was learned that the Red River bill of rights demanded such things, objections were raised. It was "a bad policy and a bad beginning" to western development to impose official languages before the region had been settled. After it was settled, its population should be free to use whatever language they wanted and not be saddled with official languages in advance "for the sake of conciliating Mr. Riel and his few hundred malcontents."[22] Despite such objections, Liberal and Conservative MPs alike accepted the Manitoba Act – some for the sake of peace with Red River, others because "justice" seemed to require it – and it passed in the Commons without a formal division. In 1875 and 1877, when Catholic schools and official bilingualism were put into the Northwest Territories Act, not a word of protest was raised by the Ontario press. Even those who hoped that a true Canadian nationality would emerge from Confederation did not oppose such

When the separate schools question arose in New Brunswick, the protection of minorities was placed on the political agenda. This cartoon published in the *Canadian Illustrated News* in February 1875 lists all the questions which had to be addressed by the prime minister, including minority rights. (McCord Museum of Canadian History, M993X.5.782)

measures. They were not yet convinced that a common feeling of patriotism had to express itself in a single language. As we have seen, many thought in the summer of 1885 that the way in which French and English Canadians had fought side by side in the North-West campaign had forged such patriotism.

But the reaction to Riel's trial and hanging in 1885 changed all that. The Riel protests and the Mercier regime to which they gave rise seemed to show that without a common identity and set of common values even the political nation would fail. Indeed, the trend of world events, with the recent unifications in Italy and Germany, seemed to confirm that viable countries needed to be based on single nationalities. Canada, therefore, needed to forge a common identity. "It would seem almost impossible," more and more people believed, "that a nation could be one in sympathies without first being one in language..."[23]

Such ideas can be seen in the assimilationist movement after 1889. When D'Alton McCarthy introduced his bill to authorize the end of official French in the Northwest Territories in 1890, he maintained that it was "in the interest of the national unity of the Dominion that there should be community of language among the people of Canada."[24] And the Equal Rights Association, formed to promote national unity in the same period, called for the abolition of separate schools on the grounds that children could not form a sense of common citizenship unless they shared a common classroom experience.[25]

The argument that national unity required cultural assimilation gained force after 1896, as massive immigration brought to the country an unprecedented variety of languages, cultures and identities. To English Canadians already convinced that French Canada's distinctiveness was a threat to the country's survival, this new diversity seemed a major challenge. Unless these people could be brought together in a common nationality, it seemed, the country was faced with chaos. And no means to bring them together seemed more likely to be effective than a common school system teaching a common language. This idea was an important factor in Manitoba's decision to scrap minority languages in 1916. ◆

By the early 20th century, French and English Canadians had moved to completely opposite conceptions of Confederation and of what was necessary for it to survive: French Canadians had come to see it as a partnership of two cultural nations, each with its language and schools entrenched in all parts of the country; English Canadians were increasingly convinced that only the forging of a single nationality through cultural and linguistic assimilation would enable Canada to survive as a country.

Imperialism and
World War
(1884-1917)

A T THE TIME OF CONFEDERATION, CANADA WAS NEITHER A SUBJUGATED COLONY NOR yet independent. It controlled its own domestic affairs, raised and spent its own taxes and passed its own laws, but it had no control over its foreign relations. As far as the rest of the world was concerned, Canada had no existence separate from Great Britain. Most Canadians expected this situation to evolve gradually toward independence, with Canada becoming more Britain's ally than her colony.

After the mid-1880s, however, the idea of independence had to compete with new proposals for unification of the empire that would allow Canada and the other self-governing colonies, or "dominions," to participate as equals with the United Kingdom in making common policies and pursuing common goals. In Britain, where the rising power of Germany, the United States and others was provoking feelings of insecurity, imperial unity seemed attractive as a way to reinforce Britain's world position with the help of her own colonies.

Although imperialists never managed to formulate a practical plan for imperial power-sharing, various forms of cooperation were pursued in the late 19th and early 20th centuries; the most controversial was military cooperation. Britain first asked for Canadian aid during the Sudan crisis of 1884. Sir John A. Macdonald's government refused to send troops but did allow British authorities to recruit a few hundred French-Canadian and Mohawk boatmen to transport their expedition up the Nile. By the time of the Boer War, in 1899, the imperial idea had gained strength, and it was harder to say no to such requests. As the war approached, Ottawa came under pressure from British authorities and pro-imperial lobby groups. The cabinet itself was divided, with Sir Wilfrid Laurier, the prime minister, opposed to sending troops. Yet, when the war began, Laurier gave in and authorized a 1000-man contingent. Other groups of volunteers followed, and by 1902, when the war ended, more than 7000 Canadians had signed up.

Laurier's decision to send Canadians to South Africa provoked Henri Bourassa, a young Liberal MP, to resign his parliamentary seat in protest. Bourassa would become the centre of opposition to imperialism in the following decades. After the Boer War, Germany's ambitious naval construction program caused growing anxiety in Britain, and, in 1909, the British government asked the dominions for cash contributions to help maintain British naval strength. Laurier was reluctant. He feared — and Bourassa constantly reinforced his fear — that giving in to such demands would only undermine Canada's autonomy and responsible government. Yet pro-imperial sentiment was strong, and Laurier compromised with a bill to create a small Canadian navy. This would relieve the British of some responsibility for protecting Canadian waters

Both a politician and a journalist, Henri Bourassa (1868-1952) was one of the leading spokesmen of French-Canadian nationalism in the first half of the 20th century. (Archives of the Centre de recherche Lionel-Groulx, Lionel-Groulx Collection)

and enable them to divert resources to the German threat. While imperialists thought this bill gave Britain too little, Bourassa considered it a surrender to British militarism. In the 1911 election campaign, Bourassa's Nationalist League cooperated with the Quebec wing of the Conservative party, helping to defeat Laurier's Liberals and bring Robert Borden's Conservatives to power.

Three years later, World War I began. Legally, Britain's declaration of war meant that Canada was at war. Practically, only the Canadian Parliament could decide whether to do anything about it. Public opinion was almost unanimous in supporting active participation, and large numbers of men volunteered to fight. The first Canadian contingent left for Europe in the fall of 1914, and more followed; by the beginning of 1916 the government was committed to maintaining a force of half a million men.

But French and English Canadians did not participate equally. The army was ill-prepared to accommodate French-speaking troops. Its officer training in the preceding years had been conducted in English. Consequently, fewer than four percent of graduates from the Royal Military College, and only 12 percent of those who had taken a staff course for senior officers, were French Canadians.[1] On the eve of the war, only nine percent of the officers in Canada's permanent force were French Canadians.[2] With so few officers, it was difficult to maintain effective French-speaking battalions, and many French Canadians who volunteered found themselves in mainly anglophone regiments.

Because of this, and for other reasons discussed below, recruitment levels in Quebec were lower than elsewhere. Even after the first year of the war, when figures were distorted by the high proportion of British-born men among the volunteers, the gap was significant: between October 1915 and October 1917, 60 battalions were raised in the West, 75 in Ontario, but only 13 in Quebec. Even the Maritimes, whose population was only 45 percent of Quebec's, raised two more battalions.[3] Clearly there was less enthusiasm in Quebec than elsewhere.

This would cause a serious problem in 1917, when Borden became convinced that voluntary recruitment was not meeting the army's needs, and decided to raise the necessary men by conscription. Anticipating opposition from French Canada, he asked Laurier to join him in a coalition. Laurier refused, but the bulk of his English-Canadian followers abandoned him, voting for conscription and entering a political union with Borden. The result was alienation in Quebec, expressed in angry demonstrations and the dynamiting of the summer home of a conscriptionist newspaper publisher.

In that December's federal elections, western Liberals backed Borden in a "Union Government," leaving Laurier with only a remnant of his party, largely confined to Quebec. The result was the election of a government from which all French-Canadian participation was excluded. Not a single French-Quebec or Acadian MP was returned to the government benches; the federal government was now, literally, an English-Canadian government.[4]

as i recall

The idea of imperial federation did not recommend itself to all English Canadians. The *Toronto Daily News* called it "so magnificently absurd that Canadians laugh at it, and Britishers sneer at the colonialists who are silly enough to believe that such a scheme would not involve the loss of every immunity, right and liberty of self-governing provinces..."[5]

Nevertheless, imperial unity held attractions for many. During the late 1880s, disappointment in Canada's rate of economic development led to a search for special trading relations abroad. Free trade with the US was talked of, but that raised fears of annexation.[6] Imperial union, on the other hand, offered improved trade arrangements that would be more consistent with English Canadians' strong tradition of loyalty to Britain.

Imperialists also had more idealistic arguments. Since the 18th century, Britain had been associated with ideas of political and civil liberty and had been admired for its parliamentary institutions, which seemed to embody and promote that liberty. So, in the eyes of many, the maintenance of British power and influence meant the spread of liberty, tolerance and the rule of law. In the late 19th century, those ideas came to be associated with a movement for social reform that aimed to apply Christian principles of brotherhood, charity and justice to solving the problems of urban poverty, unhealthy living conditions and social injustice, which were being created by industrialization. Much of the energy and idealism of that movement to reform domestic society was also directed toward the imperial field – and imperialists hoped that this would raise the level of Canadian politics, which otherwise seemed bogged down in patronage, corruption and petty local interests.[7]

Imperial unity also seemed necessary for military defence. Canadians had always depended on British power to guarantee their autonomy. But in the late 19th century, Britain seemed less able to provide that guarantee on her own. She and the self-governing dominions, however, might do it if they combined forces for their common defence. Indeed, accepting free help from Britain while contributing nothing in return seemed morally despicable and unworthy of a mature people.

> "It is nothing short of disgraceful," wrote a pamphleteer,
> that Canada should accept British consular aid,
> British supremacy on the seas, and British backing
> [in disputes with the US] without paying one penny
> toward the imperial defence which is behind all
> these things.[8]

Such a situation only perpetuated a colonial status which Canadian imperialists despised. "I, that write these lines," proclaimed one, "am an Imperialist because I will not be a Colonial."[9] Instead of remaining a colony, Canada had to become Britain's partner, taking her place among the nations of the world – as a nation within the empire.[10]

Most English Canadians, however, were not prepared to surrender Canada's autonomy or her potential for future independence. They might, in times of crisis, be glad to see their country come to the aid of the empire; but it had to do so as a nation.

One aspect of imperialism in English Canada was bound to create trouble. After the Riel affair, as we have seen, many English Canadians, fearing that French Canada's distinctiveness might destroy Confederation, began to support anglicization. For such people, the empire offered an extra justification for their policies. The first president of the Canadian Imperial Federation League was D'Alton McCarthy, the author of the 1890 bill to end official use of French in the Northwest Territories. French must give way, he argued, so that the two Canadian races might become fused in a "British country."[11] Apparently, he considered it impossible "that French might be an official language in a part of the British Empire."[12] Manitoba's Provincial Secretary agreed; his province was dropping French because it could not "tolerate a foreign language in a British province."[13]

The Boer War illustrates all these tendencies. Although English-Canadian opinion was by no means united, a majority did become convinced that Canada must contribute to the defence of an imperial system on which her own security depended; some hoped the war would open commercial opportunities in South Africa; most agreed that (as Wilfrid Laurier asserted) the British cause was "the cause of justice, the cause of humanity, of civil rights and religious liberty."[14] But they wanted Canada's participation to be national in character.

First president of the Canadian Imperial Federation League, D'Alton McCarthy (1836- 1898) was one of the major promoters of the imperial ideal and of British Canada. (NAC, PA25697)

When Laurier proposed to send volunteers in small units under junior officers to be absorbed into the British army, G.T. Denison, President of the British Empire League, objected. Canadian volunteers should go as a national contingent, he insisted, under Canadian command: "They should feel that they represent our country, and that the honour of all who stay at home is in their keeping."[15]

Unfortunately, the Boer war also evoked suspicion of French-Canadian distinctiveness and its potential to sabotage Canada's destiny as Anglophones saw it. Within Laurier's cabinet, the strongest opposition to participation came from Joseph-Israel Tarte, who, as party organizer in Quebec during the 1896 elections, had given the Liberal campaign a particularly French-Canadian nationalist emphasis. So, when the government hesitated to send volunteers, some English Canadians blamed French Canada for standing in the way of Canada's national duty. Canadians are British, proclaimed the *Montreal Star*,

"and they will have their government British or they will know the reason why."[16] In Toronto, *The News* complained that "there will never be
a united Canada as long as the French Canadians can prevent it," and
urged English Canadians to liberate themselves "from the dominance
of an inferior people..."[17] Responding to such calls, angry crowds
burned effigies of Tarte in demonstrations in Toronto and Kingston.[18]

In the end, pro-war opinion had its way, and, as many a Boer
War monument in Canadian towns and cities still testifies, English
Canadians generally looked on Canada's participation as a proud
achievement of an emerging, young Canadian nation.

Neither the sense of Canadian nationhood nor the desire to
play a part in the world as Britain's partner had diminished by 1914.
Sympathy for Britain, a belief in the nobility of her cause and a
sense that Canada's own security depended on the maintenance of
her power, all inspired support for an active Canadian role in the
world war. But from the beginning there was also an insistence that
Canada was participating as a nation, not a colony. The prime minister, Robert Borden, explained that this was "a struggle in which we
have taken part of our own free will and because we realize the
world-compelling considerations which its issues involve." Canada
was fighting to oppose aggression and brutal violation of international law and order. Allied with other "civilized states," she was
defending "civilization and humanity" and "the cause of freedom."[19]

This understanding of Canada's purpose in the war attracted
Protestant social reformers, idealists and activists. The cause of world
civilization appealed to the same idealism, dedication and sense of
justice as the cause of reform did at home. That led to the passage
during the war of some notable reforms: prohibition, women's suf-
frage and an income tax.[20] But it also led to exaggerated demands on
young men to fight, and to intolerance and bad feeling toward those
who were reluctant to do so. French Canadians in particular were victims of such attitudes, since they enlisted at much lower rates than
others did. In the summer of 1915, the Orange *Sentinel,* which spoke

for an association that was particularly hostile to French-Canadian distinctiveness, complained that French Canadians "enlist in retail and desert in wholesale." Two years later, even John Dafoe, the nationalist and Liberal editor of the *Manitoba Free Press,* attacked French Canadians as "the only known race of white men to quit."[21]

Such feelings only reinforced the assimilating tendency that had been growing since the Riel affair. Thus, the commander of the Canadian force overseas opposed the creation of distinctive French-Canadian battalions. "They should not be kept separate," he said, "they are Canadians the same as everybody else, and the sooner it is so regarded the better it will be for the national life of our country."[22] At the same time, desire for unity, together with wartime suspicion of strangers, provoked new hostility toward minority languages. So, in Manitoba, where many immigrants who were former subjects of enemy countries spoke German, Ukrainian, Polish, etc., English was made the only language of public schools in 1916 – and French got swept away with the immigrant languages. ◆

Si je me souviens bien

The imperial idea did not, at first, provoke particular opposition from French Canadians. They too were protected by imperial power and might profit from imperial connections. Nor were they immune to the high ideals of the imperialists. Ultramontanism, with its theory that particular nations were chosen by God to spread Christian values and Christian way of life, made it easy to sympathize with that aspect of imperialism.[23] Thus, the French-Canadian boatmen who volunteered for the Sudan expedition in 1884 were compared in the French-Canadian press to the Zouaves (French Canadians who, in the 1860s, had served in the French army at Rome to defend the papacy against Garibaldi), and their mission was portrayed as noble, lofty and Christian.

At the same time, just as English Canadians would later insist that volunteers for South Africa must go as a Canadian national corps, the French-Canadian press portrayed the *voyageurs* of 1884-85 as a French-Canadian national contingent. Praise from British officers and French reporters for the skills and courage of French Canadians were reported as signs of recognition for French Canada itself: "Bravo, Jean-Baptiste!"[24] This implied that the empire could accept French Canadians even with their distinctiveness. Indeed, the empire could be seen as a mosaic of diverse nationalities — an "immense assembly of nations come from the far corners of the earth," as A.B. Routhier later described it — with a "variety of races and colours, beliefs and languages..."[25]

Such a view of the empire became increasingly difficult to hold in the late 19th century, as English-Canadian assimilationists associated their cause with imperialism. The more men like D'Alton McCarthy appealed to the empire to justify their moves against the French language and French-Canadian identity, the less the empire looked like a mosaic and the more it appeared a hostile force. This could already be seen at the time of the Boer War.

Not that all French Canadians were opposed to that war. Some volunteered to fight: a company officered by French Canadians (though only half its enlisted men were French-Canadian) was given a proud send-off by a part of the French-Canadian public and press.[26] Yet at the same time, Montreal's *Nouveau Monde* expressed "sympathy" for the Boers, whom it compared with French Canadians, fighting to protect their distinctive identity against assimilating and bullying Anglo-Saxons.[27] That comparison only seemed more apt when Laurier's delays led to a francophobic reaction. The campaign for a Canadian contingent seemed to bring out the "anti-French element" ("mangeurs de français") among English Canadians — the kind of people who burned Tarte in effigy "because he is French, and not sufficiently imperialist to please those gentlemen of the superior race."[28]

If the bullying and assimilating character of many English-Canadian imperialists turned French Canadians away from the empire, so did the fear of losing Canada's autonomy. Henri Bourassa argued that sending troops to South Africa would set a precedent that would bind Canadians to fight for Britain in all her foreign wars, even when Canada's interests were not involved. Not that he was advocating independence: He agreed that Canada still needed British protection, and he professed a strong attachment to the British liberal tradition.[29] But he considered the recent expansionist imperialism to be a base departure from that tradition: "a regime of land-grabbing and military domination...stupid, brutal, and boastful," that sought "the world supremacy of the Anglo-Saxon race..."[30]

Despite such fears, most French Canadians supported participation in the world war when it began in August 1914. Men were ready to volunteer, and Archbishop Bruchési of Montreal declared that it was Canada's duty to aid Britain in every possible way. *L'Action Sociale,* said to represent the Archbishop of Quebec, affirmed that Britain was engaged in a just war in which Canadians "owe her our most wholehearted cooperation."[31]

Bourassa's own newspaper, *Le Devoir,* was not so sure. An editorial of August 18 worried that if Canadians acknowledged a duty to fight in the present war, they might be bound to fight "in every other conflict that Britain gets mixed up in, whether it's in Europe, Asia, or Africa, and regardless of who Britain's allies or enemies might be."[32] Bourassa himself hesitated at first, not wanting to contradict the clergy, but soon began to oppose the war effort more openly.

His opposition was not unconnected to the campaign against Regulation 17, which increasingly held French Canadians' attention during the war. In 1915, the Quebec legislature called on Ontario to respect the rights of its minority, then authorized Quebec municipalities to contribute money for the maintenance of French schools in Ontario. Neither the courts' decision that Regulation 17 was constitutional, nor a 1917 papal encyclical calling on French Canadians

A poster calling on French Canadians to follow the example of Dollard des Ormeaux, a French Canadian hero of the early 17th century. (NAC, C93228)

to stop agitating against it, could assuage the bitterness that people
felt or prevent them from relating this issue to the war. "In the
name of religion, liberty and faithfulness to the British flag," wrote
Bourassa, "French Canadians are enjoined to fight the Prussians of
Europe. Shall we let the Prussians of Ontario impose their domination like masters...?"[33] Bourassa's colleague, Armand Lavergne, went
further: Franco-Ontarians, he said, were victims of a persecution
even worse than what the Germans had imposed in Europe. "Until
they have been completely freed of this persecution, I cannot consider for an instant the idea of deserting their cause for a somewhat interesting adventure in a foreign country."[34]

But Regulation 17 was only a culmination of the bullying and
anglicizing wave that had been sweeping through English Canada
since the late 1880s, and which would lead to Manitoba's 1916 decision to run all its schools in English. Even the structures of the
Canadian army seemed to manifest the same anglicizing pressure.
No wonder French Canadians were less eager than others to enlist.

The adoption of conscription in June 1917 brought even the
bishops into line with Bourassa, for although they had supported
the war effort, they had always opposed compulsion. In Ottawa, one
or two French-Canadian ministers accepted the measure, but
Quebecers repudiated them in the December elections.

The results of those elections were so shocking that separatist resolutions were soon being discussed in the Quebec legislature and in various municipal councils and political riding
associations.[35] Worse consequences followed: An attempt to round
up conscripts at Quebec City in March 1918 led to the outbreak of
rioting, which ended only when troops opened fire, killing four and
wounding at least 35.[36] ◆

In English Canada, it is commonplace to say that Canadian nationhood
was achieved on the battlefields of Europe during the First World War.[37] Pride in

battles won and echoes of the wartime spirit of national dedication help to explain that impression. At the same time, the war moved Canada dramatically toward independence. Its military contribution won it the right to participate in the peace conference and sign the treaty in its own name. It became a full member of the League of Nations and other international bodies; and in 1931, by the Statute of Westminster, Britain recognized that Canada was legally as well as practically independent.

But the war had other, more sinister meanings. In the 1917 elections, English and French Canadians expressed opposing views not merely on conscription but on the whole meaning of Canada. A Toronto newspaper, *The Star*, noted it the following day: French Canadians considered Canada a bilingual country, while English Canadians saw it as an English country with a bilingual province.[38] Seeing Canada as "an English country," English Canadians had not only dropped the use of French in governments and schools outside Quebec; they had developed national institutions — including an army — that were English in language and character, and had pursued an external policy based on their idea of Canada as part of a community of English-speaking nations. What is more, the elections of 1917 showed that they could form a national government without the support or acquiescence of French Canada and pursue those policies despite French Canada's opposition. No wonder separatist resolutions were discussed in Quebec!

The idea of Quebec independence remained in the air after the war, encouraged by the influential historian, priest and teacher, Lionel Groulx. In scathing evaluations of Confederation, published in 1917 and 1927, Groulx blamed English Canadians for sabotaging it by violating minority rights and bullying French Canada. This could not continue forever. A 1923 Groulx-inspired publication of the nationalist league, *Action Française*, announced that Quebec's independence was at hand and called on French Canadians to prepare for it.[39]

The divisions and bitterness of World War I were not forgotten by W.L. Mackenzie King, the Liberal leader and prime minister for most of the 1920s and 1930s. His foreign policy was marked by an aversion to any commitments (especially to Britain) that might entangle Canada in another war — and even when he realized that he could not stay out of a major conflict with Germany, he tried to convince French Canadians that the war was unsought and unavoidable.[40] When it finally began, King marked Canada's independence by waiting a week before officially joining it. Then, in the October 1939 Quebec election campaign, his francophone cabinet colleagues toured the province with a promise that if Quebecers voted Liberal, conscription would not be used in this war.

However, when the expansion of hostilities at the end of 1941 created a strong pro-conscription movement in English Canada, King looked for a way out of that promise. In a plebiscite held across the country, he asked voters to release him from it. The result echoed that of 1917. While the rest of Canada gave King a massive Yes, Quebec overwhelmingly voted No. This was the critical moment, although King waited two more years before sending conscripts overseas. French

It is, therefore, neither as a province nor as an ethnical group that we have adopted this stand. If we refuse to relieve the Government of its 1939 and 1940 promises, we do so as Canadian citizens, placing Canada's interests above all. In this country, we believe, there is a majority of Canadians to whom Canada is the fatherland and for whom the motto: CANADA FIRST, has never been merely an electoral cry but the expression of a deep sentiment and a supreme conviction. We appeal to these Canadians. We ask them to place their country above race and partisan outbursts. Do they want to enact legislation to stop the plunge over the abyss and which forcefully expresses the voice of the majority from ocean to ocean? With the calmness and all the strenght of free men let them answer a resounding "NO" to Mr. King's Plebiscite.

God Save Our Country! Long Live Canada!

THE LEAGUE FOR THE DEFENCE OF CANADA,
by its Directors

(signed) Dr. J. B. PRINCE, President,
André LAURENDEAU, Secretary.

354, St. Catherine East
Room 50
Montreal   MA. 2837

L'Imprimerie Populaire, Limitée, Montréal ⬛1

The Plebiscite

P2/A, 119

MANIFESTO

issued by

**The
League for the Defence of Canada**

◆

« No province or ethnical group can refrain or be silent »

◆

With the calmness and all the strength of free men, let them answer a resounding

NO

to Mr. King's Plebiscite.

Opponents of the plebiscite created the League for the Defence of Canada. This excerpt from their manifesto invites Canadians to vote No: "We are asking them to place the fatherland above race or electoral passion." (Archives of the Centre de recherche Lionel-Groulx, Laurendeau and Perrault Families Collection, P2/A, 119)

Canadians who campaigned for a No vote understood the promise of 1939 as a bargain between the two nationalities: the minority would accept Canada's participation in the war, and the majority would refrain from doing what it had the power to do, that is impose conscription. For English Canada to release King from his promise was to unilaterally go back on its part of the bargain.[41]

In English Canada, King has generally been admired for his handling of conscription. He is said to have shown French Canadians that he didn't want to impose it and that he held it off as long as possible, thus keeping their confidence and maintaining Canadian unity.

But while King kept Quebec votes (for the Conservatives would have introduced conscription even sooner than he did), he could not avoid a fundamental fact: the dualist vision of Canada, to which French Canadians had increasingly adhered since the end of the 19th century, had been as blatantly repudiated in 1942 as in 1917. Two decades later, as the modern separatist movement organized itself in Quebec, the memory of the 1942 plebiscite, in which English Canada "imposed" conscription, forcing French Canadians "to serve our country in a unilingual English army," was brought up as evidence of the inability of Confederation to accommodate the two nationalities.[42]

chapter 2

The Making of the Welfare State

Introductions by
John Meisel
Guy Rocher

Essays prepared by
Alain Desruisseaux
and Sarah Fortin

The Making of
the Welfare State

T HE ESSAYS IN THIS CHAPTER EXPLORE THE DEVELOPMENT OF THE WELFARE STATE IN
Canada. They provide an excellent inventory of the kind of factors that
affect most of the cases discussed in this volume. These factors include demographic context, historical antecedents, the economic and sociopolitical milieu,
the personalities and organizations involved and, above all, the respective underlying values of people residing in Quebec and the rest of Canada (ROC).

Because, however, the time period covered by each chapter is usually fairly long the importance of each factor frequently changes over the span of the relevant period. This chapter finds Quebec in its rather inward-looking, pre-Quiet
Revolution phase at the outset, whereas it subsequently assumes the characteristics of a more modern, bustling, daring society. In the earlier period, attitudes
toward welfare and social security were shaped by the all-powerful and ubiqui-
tous Catholic Church. This, as well as the French language and a long history as
a somewhat isolated minority, gave the society a deep sense of cohesiveness and
community. Therefore, there was a predisposition to support wide-ranging community services undertaken by the Church, rather than the state. However, the
influence of the Church declined and Quebec took on the project of building a
modern society; public bodies took over the funding and administration of welfare programs. A strong but secularized sense of mutual aid and collective solidarity bound Quebecers together in support of the welfare state.

The story on the ROC side was quite different: Although the Social Gospel
— a Church-inspired philanthropy — was a factor, support for the welfare state
largely manifested itself through various voluntary associations and, above all,
political parties. The presence in English Canada of the Co-operative

Commonwealth Federation (CCF) and its successor, the New Democratic Party (NDP), had a major impact on social legislation. These social democratic parties never held office in Ottawa but they forced the central parties, particularly the Liberals, to espouse progressive social policies. Their occasional control of provincial governments also lent impetus to the creation of the welfare state. As the essay on health insurance suggests, it was the example of Tommy Douglas' Saskatchewan CCF government that ultimately led to the adoption of a national system of health care. The key role played by the CCF and the NDP in the evolution of the Canadian welfare state points to the importance of political parties and the party system in resolving divisive issues. Over the years, the increasing fragmentation of Canada's party system has, therefore, made it more difficult to arrive at national consensus.

However, a lack of such agreement is nothing new. The essays in this chapter show that, from the start, provincial agreement for social security policy was sometimes hard-won. There was fear that projects initiated and funded by Ottawa would distort provincial spending patterns and compel lower levels of government to adopt an agenda partly drafted in the country's capital. Significantly, Quebec was not the only province to fear this kind of intrusion; Canada's history contains many examples of provinces being allied with Quebec against the federal government and other provinces. Since many of the social projects involved redistribution of income among regions — a positive characteristic of Canadian federalism —often the poorer and smaller provinces welcomed Ottawa's ideas much more than the wealthier ones, which would have to help foot the bill.

Despite this unease, most Canadians and their provincial governments have come to accept the principle behind equalization payments — redistribution of resources from richer to poorer provinces. The ravages of the Great Depression and the legacy of the Second World War largely explain this new attitude; they have acted as powerful catalysts for a fundamental change in the way in which Canadians think about their country.

Contemporary readers, accustomed to periodic fluctuations in the economic climate, might be inclined to underestimate the pervasive and profound influence the Depression cast on the minds of Canadians for many years, particularly in its immediate aftermath. The impact of the worldwide crisis was dramatic: gross national expenditures between 1929 and 1933 were estimated to have dropped by 42 percent, and by 1933 almost one third of the labour force was unemployed; one in five Canadians became dependent on government relief. In the four western provinces, which were dependent on exports, the effects were particularly devastating. There was a growing sense that the state had to become more active in assisting individuals who, through no fault of their own, were in dire need.

The considerable regional variation in the effects of the Depression also made it evident to many Canadians that arrangements had to be made for hard-hit areas to be assisted by more fortunate ones. New forms of federal-provincial, and possibly interprovincial, cooperation were needed. This realization led to the establishment of the 1937 Royal Commission on Dominion-Provincial Relations (Rowell-Sirois Commission), whose mandate was to examine the "economic and fiscal basis of Confederation and the distribution of legislative powers in the light of the economic and social developments of the last 70 years." The recommendations of the Commission, released in 1940, were generally centralizing and many of them were unacceptable to various provincial governments. Nevertheless, several of the projects described in this chapter deal with initiatives first identified and explored by the Rowell-Sirois Commission. They show that important changes affecting members of a federation can be made without formal constitutional amendment.

The Depression was barely over when war broke out. In the 1940s, the need to cope with the economic dislocation that resulted from the shift from a wartime to a peacetime economy was another major impetus for launching the welfare state, insofar as Ottawa was concerned. Not only did veterans have to be absorbed into the labour force, but Canada's industrial war machine had to be transformed. Toward the end of hostilities and after the two armistices, large-scale unemployment was feared — an apprehension exacerbated by the spectre of the Great Depression. Furthermore, a great many Canadians (not only those of British origin) found inspiration in the contribution they and their countrymen had made, under Canadian colours, to the Allied war effort. The exhilaration of that experience nourished a new kind of Canadian nationalism — one no longer linked to Britain — and it was widely felt that those who had made sacrifices in the war were entitled to the decent standard of living that could be provided by a Canadian welfare state.

To better understand how the welfare state was put in place in Canada, it is important to realize that the professionalization of government, and the emergence of a specialized and skilled public service, occurred in Ottawa before it materialized in the provinces. In the immediate postwar years, the federal government benefited from the presence of an impressive cadre of highly competent and motivated public servants. The provinces, on the other hand, were largely mired in old-fashioned, parish-pump, patronage-driven politics. There was little room for a meritocratic civil service that would attract highly professional public servants.

The senior public service built up by the King administration was impressive. Many were former academics and virtually all subscribed to the theories of full employment advanced by John Maynard Keynes, the British economist. In essence, Keynes argued that when the economy contracts, governments should inject purchasing power into the community by embarking on schemes involving large-scale public projects and other public expenditures. Keynesian economics dictated that Ottawa institute major programs directing funds from the public coffers into private pockets and, presumably, from there into various private, job-creating ventures. Mothers' Allowances were a good example, but virtually all welfare state projects fitted nicely into the Keynesian model and thus were strongly favoured by Ottawa and, ultimately, many of the provinces.

One consequence of Ottawa's advantage was that, in the normal pattern of federal-provincial negotiations, it took the initiative with well-prepared documents, to which provincial politicians responded as best they could, often flying by the seats of their pants. In most instances, provinces were unable to bolster their position by drawing on carefully researched analysis of the kind underpinning the federal case. This pattern was dramatically broken in the course of negotiating over a new pensions scheme. On that occasion, Quebec presented a plan of its own, which, in the eyes of most participants, was far superior to the federal proposals. Allow me a personal recollection, I was told by the then Premier of Ontario, John Robarts, that it was this experience which persuaded him to establish an Advisory Committee on Confederation, served by a competent bureaucracy, to assist him in future dealings with the other provinces and Ottawa. It was thus the example of Quebec, soon followed by Ontario, which led to the emergence in the provinces of ministries focusing on interprovincial relations.

Quebec's sophisticated preparatory work on the pension plan came as a surprise, because many thought that Quebec lacked the infrastructure needed for such analysis. Universities in ROC grew much faster than their counterparts in Quebec; particularly in the sciences, engineering and the social sciences. Therefore, governments outside Quebec had greater opportunities to attract well-trained specialists. Ottawa was first to make good use of these opportunities, followed by provinces such as Saskatchewan. Quebec was a latecomer but, as so often happens, made up for its slow start dramatically. In the advent of the Lesage government, university graduates, notably from the social science faculty at Laval University, came to play a major role in the Quebec public service and the many quasi-public agencies established during the Quiet Revolution. Ultimately, the role of these "technocrats" was more important in Quebec than elsewhere in the country, a situation which often gave Quebec a decided advantage in negotiations. Eventually, most provinces developed similar capabilities for policy development.

In reviewing how Quebec and ROC approach questions of public support of the needy and of the welfare state generally, I am vividly reminded of the insightful analysis of social structure developed during the 19th century by Ferdinand Tönnies. He made a fundamental distinction between *Gemeinschaft* (communal society) and *Gesellschaft* (associational society). In the former, people feel they belong together because they are of the same kind; ties are warm, informal and self-evident. In the latter, bonds are voluntary and largely based on the rational pursuit of self-interest. While the analogy is not perfect, to my mind, francophone Quebec still exhibits many of the characteristics of *Gemeinschaft*, despite the fact that it is now a much more heterogeneous and textured society than it once was. The history of Quebec has left a vestigial sense of shared community. The rest of the country is held together less by emotional ties (although these cannot be dismissed altogether) and more by a rational pursuit of self-interest. These different wellsprings of communal sentiment have also shaped attitudes toward economic redistribution and the welfare state.

The Making of
the Welfare State

C ANADA MOVED TOWARD A WELFARE STATE MODEL DURING THE 1930S AND THE YEARS following the Second World War. It was hardly the first country to choose that path: Great Britain (in 1901) and New Zealand had already put in place the basic elements of health insurance, and Imperial Germany, under Bismarck, had led the way as early as the 1880s with a system of health insurance and old-age pensions. In fact, Canada was rather late in joining the welfare movement.

It is difficult to appreciate today how many changes this transformation required, not just in terms of structures, but in the mindset of political leaders and senior civil servants, capitalists and business leaders, the clergy and the public. What it entailed was a fundamental, sociopolitical transformation. In the 19th and early 20th centuries, Canada was in many respects the very image of an economic colony, its development largely shaped by the involvement of British and American capital and capitalists. Because of its semi-colonial status and its adherence to the socioeconomic ideology of liberalism, the Canadian state took a typically laissez-faire approach, at both the federal and provincial level, and was primarily concerned with providing the necessary infrastructure (ports, railway and road networks) for economic development.

From approximately 1890 to 1920, however, some people became alarmed by the deterioration of living conditions for a growing proportion of Canadians; in cities and mining towns, rapid urbanization and industrialization created an exploited working class made up of rural-born workers and immigrants. Similar conditions in Europe had precipitated the spread of socialist ideology, which the new immigrants brought to Canada. In response to these social changes, and to what was perceived as the socialist threat, some religious groups and members of the clergy were won over to the idea of social reformism. This movement was known in Protestant circles as the Social Gospel. The Catholic equivalent was the Social Doctrine of the Church, which was set out in Pope Pius IX's Encyclical *Rerum Novarium*.

Though the Christian social reform movement did not succeed in influencing the federal government, it may well have paved the way for the welfare state in several respects. It critiqued the ills of unbridled capitalism, fanned the fears of the socialist menace and helped bring about social legislation in some provinces, particularly in Western Canada where new political parties, such as Social Credit and the Co-operative Commonwealth Federation (CCF), the first socialist-inspired party, were very influential and where many European immigrants had introduced their left-wing ideas.

But in the end, it took an exceptionally serious economic crisis, the Great Depression of the 1930s, as well as a justification rooted more in economics than in religion, to prompt the Canadian state to legislate in social matters. The Depression forced the state to take over the work of private charities, which found themselves unable to come to the assistance of masses of newly unemployed workers. This was the beginning of what came to be known in Quebec as *secours direct* (direct assistance). But the state was not able to provide a subsidy program of this kind for very long, at least not out of its own coffers. The obvious solution was a system of public insurance.

As the essays in this chapter demonstrate, however, this process involved much hesitation, resistance and procrastination. Among the obstacles to the development of the welfare state were the interests of businessmen and financiers, who were not prepared to help finance social programs; the dominance of liberal ideology, which prized the virtues of personal initiative and saw social policies as a threat to the work ethic; the weakness of the state itself, which was ill-equipped in human and financial resources to conceptualize and adopt these policies; and, lastly, the absence of an economic theory conducive to such ideas.

A further obstacle stood in the way of the development of social policies: the nature of the Canadian Confederation. In 1867, when the division of powers had been negotiated, jurisdiction over social policies was conferred on the level of government closest to the people i.e., the provinces. Each provincial government discharged this responsibility in its own way, with varying degrees of success. In 1921, the Quebec Liberal government of Louis-Alexandre Taschereau adopted the Public Charities Act. Its purpose was to provide to those termed "indigent" (i.e., "the poor," "illegitimate children," "unwed mothers" and the "physically handicapped") a basic level of assistance plus any institutional health care they might require. In this respect, Public Assistance was one of the first social welfare programs and the precursor of a hospital insurance program, though without the principle of collective insurance.

But the Public Charities Act was not an unemployment insurance law, and it had not been conceived as an instrument capable of coping with an economic crisis of the magnitude of the Depression. The federal government had to contribute unemployment relief, but in order to legislate in this area it had to confront the problem of provincial jurisdiction. This was a formidable obstacle, one that has continually affected the development of the whole range of Canadian social policies from the beginning of the 1930s to the present. The Quebec government consistently opposed federal intervention, except for the brief periods when the federal government could count on the "understanding" of a Liberal provincial government like that of Adélard Godbout (1936, 1939-44) or, to a lesser degree, those of Jean Lesage (1960-66) and Robert Bourassa (1970-76, 1985-94). But even these governments came under pressure from the French-Canadian, and later Québécois, nationalist movement, ever the fierce adversary of federal government intrusion into provincial jurisdiction.

Several factors helped shape Quebec-Canada relations in the field of social policy. In the first place, the federal government was well ahead of the provinces in acquiring the human and intellectual resources needed to intervene in the field of social policy. In order to meet its wartime obligations, it recruited an impressive bevy of senior civil servants at the very time that a number of energetic statesmen came to power. This strong bureaucracy was to play a crucial role in the formulation and implementation of federal social policies and thus in the establishment of the welfare state. With bureaucratic backing, the federal government appointed major commissions of inquiry and provided them with the means to produce outstanding reports and background studies. Notable examples are the Royal Commission on Dominion-Provincial Relations (the Rowell-Sirois Commission, 1937-40); the Advisory Committee on Post-War Reconstruction, which commissioned the famous *Report on Social Security for Canada* (1943) by L.C. Marsh; and the Royal Commission on National Development in the Arts, Letters and Sciences (the Massey-Lévesque Commission, 1949-51).

At the same time, the Quebec government was not completely inactive. The Liberal governments of Louis-Alexandre Taschereau (1920-36) and, later, Adélard Godbout demonstrated a degree of openness toward social questions. This was reflected in the *Report of the Quebec Social Insurance Commission* (the Montpetit report, 1933), the reports of the Provincial Commission of Inquiry into Hospitals (1943), the Royal Commission of Inquiry on Constitutional Problems (the Tremblay Commission, 1956), appointed by Maurice Duplessis to counter the Rowell-Sirois and Massey-Lévesque reports, and two commissions of inquiry into health services (1951 and 1972). But Quebec's weak civil service was clearly outmatched by Ottawa. Not until 1960 would the Quebec government sharply change tack, by recruiting a new generation of university graduates who would build a Quebec bureaucracy capable of dealing with the federal civil service on an equal footing.

Union Nationale election poster depicting Maurice Duplessis as "the intrepid defender of our rights." A conservative and advocate of increased political autonomy, Duplessis was a major opponent of the implementation of social programs in Canada. (NAC, C87690)

The federal government nevertheless had a wide lead. The "war effort" had provided it with considerable resources, while postwar planning, geared to its advantage, gave it considerable room to manoeuvre, and it was able, in the end, to win a series of concessions from the provinces on a range of issues, including unemployment insurance, hospital insurance, university financing and pensions. But its crowning achievement was taking the lion's share of individual and corporate income tax revenue, which resulted in enormous spending power that would give it control over everything else. The constitutional debate that accompanied the making of the Canadian welfare state concerned not merely legal questions: it was, above all, economic and political, conducted in the context of longstanding inequality in the balance of power between the provincial and federal governments.

A second factor that was to have a critical influence on the adoption of the welfare state model was the publication, in 1936, of *The General Theory of Employment, Interest and Money*, in which the British economist John Maynard Keynes laid down the theoretical foundations of an interventionist and social-democratic welfare state. Indeed, Keynes sketched the broad outlines of a program of action to achieve full employment through government policies and investments intended to encourage consumer spending and thereby stimulate economic activity. Not only did Keynesianism provide a justification for social policy; it also served to legitimize the federal government's policy initiatives. The new economic doctrine was accepted in Ottawa well before it was in Quebec, where it was taken up in earnest only at the beginning of the 1960s with the arrival of many young economists in the civil service.

The making of the welfare state cannot be fully understood without considering a third factor: the increasingly important role played by trade unionism, in both Quebec and the rest of Canada. In Quebec, trade unionism had undergone a split: the so-called "international" unions, which, as in the rest of Canada, were actually American-based; and Catholic unionism, founded by the clergy to counter the nondenominational influence of the international unions. Unions focused on improving the working and employment conditions of their own members, but the changing ideology of Quebec trade unionism led it to support legislative initiatives in the social policy field, particularly unemployment insurance and hospital insurance.

The Catholic Church, omnipresent in Quebec society, also played an important role — though in this case as a fetter on the development of the welfare state. Because priests and nuns had assumed responsibility for establishing and running most of Quebec's health and welfare institutions, as well as its social services, government involvement was long seen as unnecessary. The Catholic social doctrine to which the clergy subscribed held that the state would play only an auxiliary role in these matters, restricting itself to supporting the activities and institutions of the Church and private charities. Elevated almost to the status of a dogma, because its source was the papacy itself, this doctrine was respected in both spirit and practice through a close alliance between the higher clergy and the political power structure. The supplementary role assigned to the state in the social doctrine of the Church dovetailed neatly with the ultra-conservative ideology of the Duplessis government, which ruled Quebec from 1944 to 1959. Any form of state intervention was seen as having been inspired by a dangerously statist and socializing ideology. It was only with the death of Duplessis in 1959, and the rapid decline and eventual eclipse of the public role of the Catholic Church after 1960, that Quebec embarked on the transformation labelled the Quiet Revolution.

The Canadian government was slow to adopt the welfare state model and Quebec was even slower. However, when Quebec finally started down that road in 1960, it did so with a burst of energy that allowed it to make up for lost time.

Unemployment Insurance (1940)

THE ESTABLISHMENT OF A NATIONAL UNEMPLOYMENT INSURANCE PROGRAM HAD BEEN included in the platform of the Liberal Party of Canada since 1911,[1] but the first unemployment insurance act was not adopted until March 12, 1935, by the Conservative government of R. B. Bennett. Returned to office in the autumn of 1935, Prime Minister King, convinced that Bennett's legislation intruded upon a field of provincial jurisdiction, decided to refer it to the courts.[2] In June 1936, the Supreme Court ruled that the law was unconstitutional, a decision upheld by the Privy Council in London on January 28, 1937. Barring an amendment to the Canadian Constitution, the federal government would not be able to legislate in the field of unemployment insurance.

In January 1938, the National Employment Commission, appointed two years earlier, submitted its report, which recommended the establishment of a national unemployment insurance program. That same year, Prime Minister King invited the provinces to relinquish their jurisdiction over unemployment insurance to the federal government, but only those provinces with Liberal governments agreed. The dissident provinces were Quebec, Alberta and New Brunswick, governed respectively by the Union Nationale, Social Credit and Conservative parties.[3]

In the 1939 provincial election, Maurice Duplessis' government was defeated, thereby eliminating one of the program's fiercest opponents and ushering in a new climate of cooperation between Quebec and Ottawa.[4] In May 1940, the Royal Commission on Dominion-Provincial Relations, the Rowell-Sirois Commission, appointed three years earlier, released its report recommending the establishment of a national program of unemployment insurance. At the same time, by the simple expedient of a letter of understanding, and without consulting the Legislative Assembly,[5] Premier Godbout of Quebec finally agreed to relinquish full jurisdiction over unemployment insurance to the federal government. As he said in his letter to Prime Minister King:

> With all this in mind, we do not think we could rightly withhold our assent to the suggested amendment to the British North America Act, and we feel that, in giving it, we are doing nothing but carrying out our duty toward our province and our country as well.[6]

The New Brunswick government quickly followed suit, as did Alberta's soon after.

as i recall

During the 1920s and 1930s, there was no consensus in English Canada on the matter of unemployment insurance. Supported by trade unionists, it was criticized in business circles. Prime Ministers Bennett and King, believing that the employment crisis

In Stratford, Ontario (1934), strikers asked for the establishment of unemployment insurance: "We fight for full and free unemployment insurance." (NAC, PA125093; Communist Party of Canada)

was a temporary phenomenon, were reluctant to commit the government to a program that promised to be the largest and costliest ever launched in Canada. Bennett and King believed, as did many others, that an unemployment insurance program would undermine the work ethic.[7] The first unemployment insurance act, adopted by the Bennett government in 1935, was, in fact, compatible with this principle, seeking primarily to contain the federal government's growing deficit and halt the transfer of relief payments to the needy, whose ranks had multiplied in the wake of the 1929 crash.[8] Similarly, the constitutional arguments put forward by King had long served as an excuse for inaction, even though many of the provinces wished to see Ottawa step into the field. As the historian James Struthers observes: "Throughout the Depression, it was Ottawa, not the provinces, that consistently invoked the constitution and the sanctity of provincial rights as justification for its limited responsibility for the jobless."[9]

Yet it is also true that some provinces refused, at different points, to give up their jurisdiction over unemployment insurance. In 1937, New Brunswick and Alberta demanded that the full range of federal-provincial disputes be reviewed before specific issues like unemployment insurance were addressed.[10]

As time passed, the proposal for a national unemployment insurance program began to win increasing support from the Canadian public and from the banking and financial community.[11] King himself even became a strong supporter.[12] The Depression of the early 1930s, the introduction of Keynesian ideas into academia and then into the federal civil service, and the desire to accumulate funds to help pay for the war effort all contributed to the acceptance of the plan.[13] ◆

si je me souviens bien

During these years, Quebec nationalism was expressed, politically, in terms of the defence of provincial autonomy. The 1935 general election saw Bennett's Conservatives virtually wiped off the map in Quebec, not least because their interventionist designs were so at odds with the principle of provincial autonomy.[14] When Duplessis responded to Ottawa's request for control over unemployment insurance with a categorical refusal, he won the approval of nationalists, who were opposed to what they saw as a centralizing measure. By ceding to Ottawa jurisdiction over unemployment insurance, nationalists realized they would be giving up enormous power. As André Laurendeau warned:

> Under no circumstances can we compromise on the question of social legislation: we must have complete control. Any other position would be suicidal for French Canada, for to give way this time would soon lead to concessions on other issues. We will be masters of our own social and economic life, masters of our own education, or else we are doomed to disappear as a people. Are we ready to sign our own death warrant?[15]

Others regarded unemployment insurance as a futile, even harmful, measure. At the time, many people still associated economic development with agriculture, and corporatism was still held up as the industrial relations model most compatible with Catholic moral values. For example, economist François-Albert Angers believed that "before we can solve the labour problem, indeed in order to resolve it, we must first find a solution to our agricultural problems, both in the West and in the East."[16]

Premier Godbout's consent to the 1940 constitutional amendment was therefore strongly opposed by nationalists. As historian Jean-Guy Genest writes, "nationalists interpreted this gesture as an act of treason against the French-Canadian ethnic group."[17]

However, the Liberal government benefited from the support of many unions,[18] and in 1933 the Social Insurance Commission, appointed by the Quebec government at the outset of the Depression and chaired by Édouard Montpetit, had recommended that the federal government create an unemployment insurance system.[19] ◆

On July 10 1940, with the agreement of all provinces, the Canadian Constitution was amended to give the federal government jurisdiction over unemployment insurance. This was followed on August 7 by the granting of Royal Assent to the act establishing unemployment insurance.

Just as André Laurendeau had expected, this first breach of provincial jurisdiction would not be the last. In the aftermath of the Second World War, Ottawa set out to create a wide social security net, justifying its activity in this field by citing its responsibilities in economic development, which included ensuring a "high and stable level of employment."[20] Although the provinces raised a number of objections, the federal plan was slowly put in place, one piece at a time. With the adoption in 1968 of the Medical Care Act, the plan for a full welfare state outlined in 1945 was virtually complete.[21]

Nor did the constitutional change that transferred responsibility for unemployment insurance to the federal government put an end to the debate, since unemployment insurance policies overlap with two other fields of provincial jurisdiction: social policy and employment policy. In the context of the 1960s Quiet Revolution, Quebec would steadily begin to occupy the field of job training, leading to duplication that would become the subject of recurring disputes with the federal government.[22]

Over the years, many voices in Quebec have demanded that Quebec be given sole responsibility for the social security system, including the Unemployment Insurance Fund; by 1990, this position was widely accepted by all concerned in the province.[23] In 1992, during the Charlottetown constitutional negotiations, job training and development was one of the fields of jurisdiction Ottawa agreed to relinquish, though the unemployment insurance fund would remain in federal hands.[24]

After the failure of the Charlottetown referendum, bilateral negotiations were undertaken to seek an administrative arrangement that would give substance to what had been negotiated at Charlottetown. On May 30, 1996, Prime Minister Chrétien announced that the federal government would recognize the provinces' exclusive responsibility for job training.[25] In December 1996, Alberta and New Brunswick became the first provinces to sign such agreements, and Quebec followed suit.

Tax   Rental
Agreements
(1947-1954)

I N ITS APRIL 1941 BUDGET SPEECH, FOLLOWING THE RECOMMENDATIONS OF THE
Rowell-Sirois Commission,[1] the federal government announced that it wished
to control all taxes on personal income and corporate profits as well as succession duties for the duration of the war plus one year. In return, the provincial
governments would receive unconditional grants and special subsidies. After
much negotiation, eight out of nine provinces, including Quebec, accepted the
federal proposal. In April 1942, Premier Adélard Godbout of Quebec tabled a
bill stipulating that his province would, in return for an annual subsidy, grant
Ottawa the exclusive right to collect personal and corporate income taxes until
the end of the war. The bill also stipulated that the federal government would,
one year after the end of the war, reduce its tax rates and authorize Quebec to
partially recover its tax fields.[2] The law was passed on May 13, 1942. One year
later, Ontario, the only holdout, gave in to pressure from its electorate and con-
sented to the federal proposal.[3]

As soon as the war was over, all the provincial governments tried to recover
their lost tax fields. At the very least, they wanted to increase their monetary compensation from Ottawa.[4] During the Reconstruction Conference in August 1945,
the federal government presented its fiscal proposals, based on its new Keynesian
economic policy.[5] Ottawa suggested reserving for itself the exclusive use of personal and corporate income taxes, as well as succession duties. In return, it would
undertake to compensate the provinces based on population.[6] The premiers were
unable to come to any agreement and the conference ended in a stalemate.

In 1947 Ottawa came to an agreement with eight provinces by separately
negotiating with each.[7] In exchange for certain compensation, the provinces

agreed to refrain from collecting personal and corporate income tax for five years, and succession duties for four years. Ontario and Quebec, particularly protective of their fields of jurisdiction, refused to subscribe to the plan. The tax agreements were renegotiated in 1952 and the Ontario government, now under the leadership of Leslie Frost, finally agreed to participate.

In January 1954, the Quebec government, facing a considerable increase in public expenditures for health and education, and concerned with defending its autonomy,[8] announced its intention to exercise its constitutional rights and collect its own personal income tax – much to Ottawa's annoyance. In its budget speech of April 1954, Ottawa announced its refusal to deduct an amount equivalent to that which Quebecers paid to the provincial treasury from the amount they paid to the federal tax department: "If the federal government automatically allowed as a credit against its tax any tax a province unilaterally chose to impose, the province would in effect be determining the effective rate of federal tax."[9] In early September, Prime Minister Louis Saint-Laurent strongly criticized the position of Premier Maurice Duplessis, arguing that Quebec did not need special treatment: "Quebec is a province like the others."[10] With neither side giving way, double taxation was about to be imposed on Quebecers.

It took several months and much effort to break the fiscal impasse. In January 1955, the governments of Canada and Quebec announced they had reached an acceptable solution: Quebec would collect personal income tax equivalent to 10 percent of federal income tax, which would, in turn, be reduced by the same amount.[11]

as i recall

The federal government's proposal that it have exclusive access to personal and corporate income taxes and succession duties enjoyed strong public support in English Canada. The principle which had guided Ottawa's approach to this issue was summed up by Douglas Abbott, the Minister of Finance, in 1953:

> Any allocation of tax sources which would be adequate to meet the needs of the wealthier provinces

would leave the less well-off provinces unable to balance their budgets or to provide services at anything
like the national average...No federal-provincial fiscal
arrangement can alter the facts of geography or
change the location of rich natural resources, but
federal-provincial arrangements should be designated to moderate, rather than aggravate, these regional inequalities of wealth and resources.[12]

After the 1945 federal proposals were made public, all
provinces complained that the level of compensation was insufficient to meet their financial obligations. Not surprisingly, however,
the "have not" provinces tended to support the thrust of the proposals.[13] Premier Douglas of Saskatchewan, for instance, strongly
supported the centralization of fiscal and monetary policy, arguing
that only Ottawa could mount new social programs.[14] Soon after the
1946 federal budget speech, the governments of Manitoba,
Saskatchewan, New Brunswick and Prince Edward Island announced
they were ready to make a deal. Premiers Hart of British Columbia
and Macdonald of Nova Scotia proved to be more resolute, calling
for concessions in other fields.

To overcome resistance from the provinces, Ottawa agreed
to adapt its calculation of compensation to the particular situation
of each province, offering three different funding formulas that
proved to be more generous than previous arrangements.[15] "We will
be better off signing than not signing," said Nova Scotia's premier,
Angus Macdonald.[16] Tax rental agreements soon became an integral
part of the English-Canadian political scene.

Only the George Drew government in Ontario truly opposed
Ottawa's plan. Although Quebec has often been seen as the only
province dissenting in tax matters, it was Ontario that in many
cases took the lead in defending provincial autonomy. In 1941,
Mitchell Hepburn, the Ontario premier, had described the Rowell-
Sirois Commission's recommendations as a "scrapping of

The Duplessis government's decision to collect its own income tax did not meet strong opposition in the rest of Canada, but, given the abuses of power committed by this government (police brutality and censorship), some people questioned the real motives underlying his autonomist stance. (*Canadian Forum*, 1953)

Confederation, that robs the provinces of their fiscal independence and of their full autonomy."[17] While acknowledging the necessity of a strong central government, Premier Drew was also deeply committed to provincial autonomy: "No matter what the intention may be, the almost inevitable result of the acceptance of such an arrangement would be the ultimate abandonment of the federal system in favour of a unitary system of government in Canada."[18] Only in 1952 did Ontario adhere to the tax agreements. "In retrospect, it seems reasonably clear that in the particular tensions of the time [Premier Frost] had made up his mind that the country's best interest required Ontario's agreement," explains R. M. Burns.[19] ◆

si je me souviens bien

Even at the time of the tabling of the Rowell-Sirois Commission's report in 1940, nationalists in Quebec repeatedly warned Premier

Godbout to guard against centralization.[20] In April 1942, when he agreed to transfer all of his fiscal powers to Ottawa, they reacted swiftly. In the Legislative Assembly, Maurice Duplessis then Leader of the Opposition, declared: "This bill is one of the worst threats to Quebec's autonomy."[21]

During the general election of August 1944, Godbout unsuccessfully denied that he had "given up part of the province's authority and prestige, abdicated a single constitutional right or sacrificed a single iota of provincial autonomy."[22] The Liberal party was defeated.

In April 1946, four months after Ontario had made its position clear, Quebec made its stand known. Reaffirming the provinces' sovereignty in their areas of jurisdiction, Quebec proposed a compromise whereby it would rent personal and corporate income tax to the federal government, with compensation, and in exchange the federal government would withdraw from all provincial tax fields. The memorandum stated:

> It is easy to see that a province having no revenue
> but subsides from the central government would
> cease to be a sovereign state. It would become a kind
> of inferior governmental organism under the supervi-
> sion of the authority from which it gets all its means
> of subsistence.[23]

Had it been accepted, this solution would have meant federal recognition of provincial ownership of tax fields.

Pressure from nationalist circles, with the support of the trade unions,[24] was a prime force behind Duplessis' opposition. The role of the Montreal Chamber of Commerce in this respect was particularly important: It strongly supported provincial autonomy and proposed that the Premier levy a tax of five percent on personal income. Duplessis rejected that solution, reasoning that he was "not interested in five percent autonomy."[25] He did, however, consent to appoint a Royal Commission of Inquiry on Constitutional Problems (the Tremblay Commission), in February 1953.

The people of Quebec showed little interest in the discussions and did not seem inclined to push the Premier into taking on this new battle. Some feared that this lack of concern would be an advantage to the federal government.[26] According to political analyst Léon Dion, it was Prime Minister Saint-Laurent's statement in the fall of 1954 – "Quebec is a province like the others" – that gave Duplessis what he needed to secure public support:

> Saint-Laurent's untimely statement had the effect of a
> bomb. Nationalist circles rose up, the media raged and
> public opinion, until then divided between Saint-
> Laurent and Duplessis the way it would later be divid-
> ed between Trudeau and Lévesque, favoured Duplessis
> to a far greater degree than he had expected.[27]

Most witnesses before the Tremblay Commission in the winter of 1954 recognized that "Quebec was right to demand a larger share of fiscal resources and to want to uphold its autonomy."[28] The Commission concluded that the Duplessis government's imposition of an income tax was "in general, supported by taxpayers, even though it established a system of double taxation for more than 300,000 citizens."[29] Several observers had criticized Duplessis for being all talk and no action. Gérard Filion remarked, "If the provinces, and particularly Quebec, had taken advantage of all their legislative and taxation rights, Ottawa would have had less of a chance to gain a foothold in their territory."[30] Duplessis' decision to collect personal income tax was thus seen as a positive sign.[31] As for the nationalists, they were elated: "[This victory] symbolized an end to Quebec's rear-guard action and a turning point in federal-provincial relations,"[32] explains Michael Behiels. ◆

By establishing a provincial income tax, the Duplessis government asserted its opposition to the centralizing aims of the federal government and, by the same token, its will to define its own fiscal policies.

Ottawa, however, did not come out of these negotiations empty-handed, since Duplessis had retreated on two major issues: the principles of total deduction and of provincial priority in the field of direct taxation. More importantly, however, the solution reached with Quebec opened up the way for a more flexible approach to fiscal relations. Under the Tax Rental Agreements, from 1947 to 1957, the provinces had abandoned their fiscal room to Ottawa. Starting in 1957, the Tax Sharing Arrangements marked the beginning of a new approach involving conventional tax-sharing between the central government and the provinces and equalization.[33]

Federal Grants to Universities (1951)

I N RESPONSE TO THE GROWING INFLUENCE OF THE UNITED STATES, THE CANADIAN government appointed the Royal Commission on National Development in the Arts, Letters and Sciences (the Massey Commission) in 1949. Two years later, the Commission made public its recommendations, among which figured federal financial assistance to universities. That same year, the federal government disbursed $7.1 million for the nation's universities.[1] At first, Quebec accepted the federal payments,[2] but subsequently required its universities to turn down further transfers. Much to the displeasure of many Quebec universities, the federal funds simply accumulated without being spent.[3]

as i recall

Federal grants to universities met with little opposition in English Canada. In general, the public approved of the central government's actions and saw nothing wrong with its funding programs in a field of provincial jurisdiction. The English-Canadian academic world, as well as its artistic and intellectual communities, gave a similarly warm welcome to the conclusions of the Massey report.[4] In fact, in a brief to the Massey Commission, the National Conference of Canadian Universities had recommended the adoption of a program of federal aid on the basis of student enrolment, arguing that the poorest provinces were not in a position to support higher education.[5]

According to constitutional expert Frank R. Scott, the central government was in no way interfering in provincial affairs: "Legally there is no invasion of any legislative field in a province if the federal Crown, legal proprietor of public funds, offers a subsidy to any institution or group engaged in educational or cultural work, since the making of gifts is not the same as enacting laws."[6] ◆

si je me souviens bien

The Duplessis government's opposition to federal grants to universities received support from both the Montreal Chamber of Commerce and many Quebec intellectuals. The historian Michel Brunet, for example, regarded federal aid to universities as "one of the elements of a far-reaching program of political unification, conceived and executed by the principal leaders of Anglo-Canadian society."[7] Ironically, Pierre Elliott Trudeau, best known at the time for his opposition to the Duplessis regime, found himself siding with the leader of the Union Nationale on this issue. In Trudeau's view, governments should exercise their prerogative to distribute funds raised through taxation only within their own jurisdictions:

It remains the duty of each government to ensure that it does not collect taxes for that part of the public interest not within its jurisdiction. If the federal government has a surplus of funds large enough to give grants to *all* the universities, and if it cannot justify its action by claiming that it is an equalization measure (since it gives grants to all universities) or an anti-cyclical measure (since we are in an inflationary period), this government is plainly guilty of infringing the principle of the proportional division of fiscal resources that underlies any federal system: it has levied for education, which is not within its competence, funds that – had the matter been left to the provinces – might or might not have been used for universities, depending on the wishes of the provincial electorates and their respective governments.[8]

Not everyone shared Trudeau's opinion. Father Georges-Henri Lévesque, the founder of the school of social sciences at Laval University and a member of the Massey Commission, defended the legitimacy of the federal grants. According to Lévesque, a distinction had to be drawn between education, which was within provincial jurisdiction, and culture, an open field in which the federal government could get involved: "The French culture is the common heritage of all Canadians, and the federal government has the right and the duty to do all that it can to encourage its development..."[9]

The underfinancing of universities and the arbitrary and haphazard allocation of funds also prompted several universities to take a stance in favour of the federal grants. Thus, the Association canadienne française pour l'avancement des sciences, which maintained fairly cordial relations with the Union Nationale government, recommended that the grants be accepted.[10] Balancing precariously on the federal-provincial fence, the administrators of Université Laval and the Université de Montréal also recommended that the federal grants be accepted, provided the provincial government was not opposed. For its part, McGill University raised its tuition fees and put the blame on the provincial government: "In refusing the federal government's offer, the province has deprived McGill of $615,000," commented Cyril James, Principal of the university.[11] ◆

According to Jean-Claude Robert, "the refusal of federal grants harmed Quebec universities to a degree that is still hard to appreciate but which significantly impeded their growth."[12] It was only after Duplessis' death that his successor, Paul Sauvé, could re-open the question of federal grants to universities and finally get the federal government to agree to a new mode of financing. This measure saw the Quebec government gain an additional tax point to finance universities, in lieu of direct transfers to the universities through the Canadian Universities Foundation.[13]

From then on, it was possible for a provincial government to opt out of a federal program without incurring a financial loss. This concession was important for subsequent federal-provincial relations, particularly during negotiations over the financing of shared-cost programs in 1964 and 1965, the Canada Pension Plan in 1965 and the Canada Assistance Plan in 1966, in the course of which Quebec would end up with a *de facto* distinct status.[14]

Canada and Quebec Pension Plans (1965)

I N THE EARLY 1960s, THE GOVERN- ments of Quebec, Ontario and Canada had a growing interest in the question of pension funds. In 1927, the King government had addressed the issue by implementing the Old Age Pensions Act. That program, however, was intended only as income support for the most destitute people[1]; workers' pension funds remained the responsibility of private enterprise. Thus it was a question of writing legislation that would allow a person's accumulated pension funds to be transferred from employer to employer so that a worker who changed jobs would not be penalized. The goal was to improve the mobility of the work force while ensuring greater income security for Canadians.

To follow through on his electoral promise, Prime Minister Pearson announced, in May 1963, his intention to create a national

The first pension cheque ever paid in the Dominion of Canada was issued to Mr. W. H. Derby, a resident of British Columbia, in 1927. (NAC, PA-203149)

universal, contributory pension plan. His White Paper, tabled in the summer of 1963, proposed the establishment of a public plan to be financed gradually – i.e., contributions would increase as contributors retired in ever greater numbers. A few days before the federal election, however, Premier Lesage of Quebec cautioned federal political parties against any attempt to unilaterally establish a pension program, as he wished to see Quebec set up its own pension plan.[2] The Constitution was on Quebec's side, since the provinces did have precedence over pension matters.

The impasse became a real political crisis during the spring 1964 Federal-Provincial Conference of First Ministers, when Quebec submitted its own pension-fund proposal based on three main principles: 1) universality, 2) the option of a funded scheme — i.e., an immediate accumulation of funds, and 3) a central deposit fund. All the delegates at the conference found the Quebec plan superior to the federal proposal.[3] This reaction embarrassed many federal civil servants, who had underestimated Quebec's determination to create its own plan.[4] The conference ended in total disagreement over the pension plan, tax allocations and joint programs.[5] Lesage and Pearson held separate press conferences, which was an unprecedented occurrence. Lesage stated, "We must say that the Quebec government is not satisfied and that we will very soon have to study much more carefully than ever before what we should state in the next budget." The implication was clear: Quebec was about to impose double taxation, for which Ottawa's intransigence would be blamed.[6]

The federal plan seemed doomed by the end of the conference. Tensions between Ottawa and Quebec were such that several observers expressed a fear that the country would fall apart. As one participant put it, "I think we suddenly realized that, by God, the country might break up."[7]

Over the next 16 days, intense secret negotiations between representatives of Ottawa and Quebec broke the impasse. On April 20, 1964, Lesage and Pearson announced that they had come to an agreement. Quebec would have its own pension plan. It would, however, be identical to Canada's in every respect.[8]

as i recall

When Prime Minister Pearson announced his intention to create a national universal, contributory pension plan in 1963, some provinces, especially Ontario, appeared to be reluctant. At that time, Premier Robarts declared that Ontario might not participate in the federal plan because Ontario had already enacted its own legislation on the question. Supported by Manitoba and anxious about the plan's related costs and impact on the private insurance industry, he urged the federal government to delay moving on its project. Ontario's legislation entrusted insurers with responsibility for providing pension plans, but required that the accumulated funds be portable. Insurance companies preferred the Ontario approach and attacked the federal proposal. Regardless, the federal authorities, bolstered by support from the public, trade unions and the Canadian left, particularly the New Democratic Party (NDP), paid little heed to pressure from the financial and insurance communities.[9]

The announcement that Ottawa and Quebec had come to an agreement was greeted with enthusiasm by most provincial governments, who "liked the broader coverage, the averting of conflict and, most of all, their gains from the pension fund and the boost in their share of income taxes."[10] The Ontario government, however, found the plan too generous and bridled at the special treatment afforded Quebec. It began to consider a program of its own to avoid *de facto* distinct status for Quebec, but ended up joining the federal plan. "I could have opted out," said John Robarts, "just the way Quebec opted out, but it seemed to me that there wouldn't be any national pension plan...So I made that very agonizing decision that we would stay with them..."[11]

In Ottawa, Tommy Douglas, Leader of the NDP, called the accord "a real victory for national unity" but to John Diefenbaker, Leader of the Opposition, "the new pension plan [was] the biggest monstrosity ever produced in this field."[12] ◆

Si je me souviens bien

In Quebec, the motivating factor in creating a public pension plan was the desire to establish a capital reserve which could be used for economic development. As Jean Lesage remarked, "Such considerable funds should be channelled into the speedy development of public and private sectors, so that Quebec's economic and social objectives can be achieved as rapidly and efficiently as possible."[13]

During the Quiet Revolution, the Quebec government had launched several large-scale projects that required vast sums of money. A pension plan would allow Quebec to free itself from the financial choker imposed by the anglophone financial syndicate.[14] Attempts by the Quebec government to obtain the necessary funds for projects like the nationalization of electricity were rejected by the Canadian financial community.[15] The Ontario model, which required the private sector to administer pension funds, was just as unsatisfactory to the Quebec government as the Ottawa proposal: it was potentially biased in favour of Ontario's economic interests because Quebec's insurance and trust companies were less developed.[16] It was the French model, with its Caisse des dépôts et consignations (Deposit and Consignment Office), set up in 1816, that Quebecers chose to emulate.

Thus the April 1964 compromise was a great victory for the Quebec Liberals. In the Quebec legislature, the Minister of Education, Paul Gérin-Lajoie, declared, "April 20, 1964, will become an outstanding date in the annals of Canada and the men who have taken part in these events will see their names in the pages of history."[17] Claude Ryan wondered in *Le Devoir:* "Are we at a turning point in the history of Confederation? It is too early to make such a big statement, but at least a ray of light has appeared. Let us rejoice!"[18] ◆

On March 29, 1965, the Act instituting the Canada Pension Plan was adopted by a large majority. On June 23, Quebec adopted both the Act respecting the Quebec Pension Plan and the Act instituting the Caisse de dépôt et placement du Québec (Quebec Deposit and Investment Fund). The Caisse would become one of Canada's major investors, by the early 1990s a powerful financial institution worth $41 billion.[19]

On the economic-development front, the Caisse would contribute to the financing of the James Bay hydro-electric project and to the success of private enterprises such as Provigo and Vidéotron. In so doing, it has played a key role in the growth of a new business class and the assertion of a French-language presence in the business world. At the same time, the Caisse's purchase of bonds from the Quebec government, while Canadian investors were rejecting them, has effectively allowed Quebec to become more independent of the Canadian financial community.[20]

The pension plan negotiations marked a turning point in the history of Canada-Quebec relations. Some believed it confirmed Quebec's distinct status[21]; others thought it strengthened Ottawa's position in the area of social policy.[22] This, however, would not be the last time that the right of opting out would be debated. It would come to haunt future intergovernmental negotiations — over medicare, for example — and constitutional debates, from Victoria to Charlottetown.

Hospital Insurance

and Health

Insurance

(1957-1968)

I N 1946, SASKATCHEWAN TOOK THE FIRST IMPORTANT STEP IN CANADIAN HEALTH POL-
icy when its Co-operative Commonwealth Federation (CCF) government, led
by Tommy Douglas, instituted a plan. Although Saskatchewan's initiative quickly
became the envy of the other provinces, the federal government remained reluctant to introduce a national program.[1] It was not until the autumn of 1955, when
Prime Minister Saint-Laurent undertook to implement hospital insurance as soon
as a "substantial majority" of the provinces gave their support, that Ottawa
became involved. On April 12, 1957, the Hospital Insurance and Diagnostic
Services Act was adopted.[2]

The Act defined the national parameters that had to be respected by
provinces wishing to establish their own hospital insurance programs. The federal government undertook to transfer to the provinces about half of the costs
involved in offering free hospital care; those provinces that did not respond to the
federal incentives would be depriving their citizens of a considerable amount of
money. When the Act came into effect on July 1, 1958, the four western provinces
and Newfoundland took part in the program. They were later joined by Ontario
and Nova Scotia (in 1959), Prince Edward Island and New Brunswick (in 1960)
and, lastly, Quebec (in 1961).[3] Thus by 1961 all of the provinces and territories
were participating in the program, and by March 31, 1963, 99 percent of
Canadians were covered by hospital insurance. This program marked the first
step toward a substantial narrowing of the scope of private insurance and the
introduction of universal access to health services.

Eleven years later, in July 1968, the second major health policy — the
medical care insurance program, or Medicare — came into effect. Once again,

Saskatchewan had taken the initiative by adopting a Medical Care Insurance Act as early as 1961. The Medicare program offered federal financial assistance to the provinces provided they respected five principles: accessibility, universality, portability, public management and comprehensive services. On July 1, 1968, when the program started, only Saskatchewan and British Columbia were providing eligible programs, but by 1971 all of the provinces had introduced a universal medical insurance plan.

as i recall

The public debate over hospital insurance was launched in the early 1940s in English Canada[4] generally and even earlier in the western provinces[5]; hospital insurance was at the heart of Canadian thinking about social policy. In 1945, not only did the platforms of all of the federal political parties include the introduction of health insurance, but public opinion polls indicated that 80 percent of the population was in favour of such a program.[6]

Doctors and insurers, however, were not that eager. In the 1950s, the Canadian Medical Association took a position against the hospital insurance plan: "Anxious doctors warned that a government plan would rob them of their independence, lower their standards, and interfere with the intimate doctor-patient relationship."[7] Private insurance companies argued that the government should only cover those who were uninsurable.[8]

In the 1960s, the same groups fought vigorously against the adoption of a universal and compulsory medical insurance program. This time, they had a number of provincial governments on their side: Alberta, Ontario and British Columbia had in fact adopted policies to assist their poorest residents, leaving the majority with the burden of purchasing private insurance if they so wished; and in 1965 a majority of Canadians preferred this option.[9] The premier of Ontario, John Robarts, criticized the federal program in the following terms:

"Medicare is a glowing example of a Machiavellian scheme that is in my humble opinion one of the greatest political frauds that has been perpetrated on the people of this country."[10]

The development of the two health-care programs was also largely shaped by beliefs that held sway within the federal government. The reluctance to adopt the hospital insurance program was due in large part to the influence of a number of cabinet ministers, including Prime Minister Saint-Laurent (as well as his predecessor, W.L.M. King), who either were reluctant to establish such a costly program or preferred a program that would cover only the poorest people. In the end, the hospital insurance program was adopted only after considerable debate, argument and delay.[11] These obstacles were surmounted by a combination of factors, including public pressure, growing support for the CCF party and the influence of Ontario Premier Leslie Frost[12] and the federal Minister of Health, Paul Martin.[13] The support of Prime Minister Pearson and many members of his cabinet for a national program of universal health insurance stands in stark contrast to the earlier experience.[14] ◆

si je me souviens bien

Despite the pressure – principally mounted by the labour movement[15] – in favour of health-policy reform, Maurice Duplessis' government opposed the introduction of the federal-provincial hospital insurance in Quebec as representing federal intrusion into an area of provincial jurisdiction. As a conservative, the Quebec premier also objected to state interventionism, preferring to leave health-care services to the Church and other private organizations. Quebec's position changed, however, when Jean Lesage's Liberals took office in 1960. The Union Nationale remained opposed, predicting that the program would create a statist system at odds with the social doctrine of the Church. A Union Nationale member of the legislature, Jean-Jacques Bertrand, declared: "We agree with Catholic sociologists that the state should only play an auxiliary role and that it should avoid entering headlong into a field where the dividing line between social doctrine and socialism is so easy to cross."[16]

The adoption of Medicare was more tumultuous. As soon as the federal proposals were publicized, the Lesage government announced that it intended to launch its own plan: "When our plan is introduced, it will be operated outside any joint federal-provincial program in line with our general policy of opting out in all areas within our competence," vowed Premier Lesage at the July 1965 federal-provincial conference.[17] To this end, a research group was formed in the autumn of 1965, followed in November 1966 by the establishment of a Commission of Inquiry on Health and Social Welfare (the Castonguay Commission) charged with reviewing the whole range of health and social services in Quebec. In the spirit of the Quiet Revolution, the resulting reform of the health-care system was far-reaching,[18] but this was not easy: As it did elsewhere in Canada, compulsory and universal Medicare sparked strong opposition from the Quebec business community, insurance industry and, especially, medical specialists.

The Castonguay Commission recommended a host of reforms that would directly affect the status, administration and mission of every institution involved in providing health or social services. It proposed an overall social-development policy based on an integrated approach to social services, health services and income security.[19] The Commission's main recommendation was that Quebec establish a full and universal insurance plan, financed through a one-percent tax on income.

Submitted in August 1967, the Commission's report touched off a wave of public and media enthusiasm. In fact, Medicare enjoyed more support in Quebec than it did elsewhere in Canada. In January 1968, no fewer than 64 percent of people polled in Quebec, compared to 55 percent nationally, agreed that

such a program should be established even if it would require a
tax increase.[20]

Bolstered by its previous success in negotiations over grants
to universities in 1959 and the pension plan and financing of
shared-cost programs in 1965,[21] the Quebec government strove to
win concessions from Ottawa over the financing of the program and
the rules governing the right to opt out. However, they were unsuc-
cessful this time around. Ottawa had been careful to specify that
Medicare was not a shared-cost program and that it intended to
subsidize the participating provinces according to a predetermined
scale. Premier Bertrand sharply attacked the federal government's
decision to increase income taxes by two percentage points. As he
said at the Federal-Provincial Conference of finance ministers in
November 1968: "We cannot tolerate that the federal government
should feel free to levy additional taxes on our citizens in order to
finance programs outside Quebec which we know to fall within
provincial jurisdiction."[22] The dilemma was clear: either Quebec
would agree to participate in the program under Ottawa's conditions, or it would see Quebec taxpayers lose out on a significant
amount of money that was rightfully theirs.

Pressured by the opposition and by public opinion, and with
an election deadline approaching, the Union Nationale government
decided to accept the federal offer. The Health Insurance Act was
tabled on March 10, 1970, and adopted in July. It became effective
only in November, after special legislation was enacted to force an
end to a 10-day strike by medical specialists. ◆

Despite its wish to preserve its autonomy, the Quebec government was
unable to resist the lure of money. In this sense, the adoption of the national
Medicare program vividly illustrates the strength of federal spending power as
well as the limits of the opting out formula as a mechanism of accommodation.
In 1959, Quebec had been able to take advantage of this formula in the case of

grants to universities, and again in 1965 with the pension plan and the hospital insurance program. However, Quebec was unable to repeat its success in the case of the Health Insurance Act.[23]

The federal government's intervention in areas of provincial jurisdiction, notably in the field of health and education, would prove to be a recurrent source of tension between Ottawa and the provinces, especially Quebec. During the 1980s and 1990s, the restriction of the federal spending power would be at the centre of constitutional discussions.

Following the introduction of the Canadian Health and Social Transfer (CHST) in 1995, which cut billions of dollars in transfers to the provinces, the allocation of jurisdiction and the financing of social programs again became a source of dispute. In December 1997 all of the provinces except Quebec agreed to enter into intergovernmental negotiations to reach a framework agreement on the "Canadian social union." This pact would define a series of principles on social policy, outline approaches to collaboration on the use of the federal spending power and specify mechanisms for dealing with intergovernmental disputes.[24] While Quebec finally agreed to take part in these negotiations in August 1998, after a provincial consensus on opting out with full compensation was announced, it was the only province to refuse to sign the deal on the social union in February 1999.

chapter 3

Defining the Canadian Identity

Introductions by
John Meisel
Guy Rocher

Essays prepared by
Alain Desruisseaux,
Sarah Fortin and
Nicholas Ignatieff

Defining the
Canadian Identity

P ROBABLY NOTHING IN CANADIAN HISTORY HAS SO SIGNIFICANTLY CHANGED THE WAY
Canadians think about their country as the events discussed in this chapter.
Starting after the Second World War, this process of change was most sharply
focused on specific policies during the era dominated by the Royal Commission
on Bilingualism and Biculturalism (the B&B Commission, 1963-67).

Regardless of formal agreements and constitutional niceties, the actual situation from the mid-18th century until well after the Second World War was that
Canada's economic and political power was mostly in the hands of the anglophone elite, who gave the country a British "feel". The English language and the
trappings of the British state dominated our institutions and political practices
and were, in the minds of most, the defining features of Canada. Ours was essentially a British country with a francophone component that occupied a unique but
somewhat secondary place. Large-scale postwar immigration from the United
Kingdom strengthened these characteristics.

Canada's anglophone political and economic leaders and the Quebec
Church elite, supported by a large network of notables, had reached an accommodation based on the understanding that each party was to enjoy freedom of
action within its own sphere. The clergy and its allies were supreme in Quebec,
while the rest of the country — its commerce and industry in particular — was
firmly controlled by Anglophones, most of whom were of British descent and
maintained emotional ties with the "mother country." Broadly, this was the situation until the mid-20th century.

Subsequent changes substantially altered that status quo, causing tension and necessitating new ways of thinking about the political context of

Canadian life. The first major transformations, which came soon after the Second World War, saw a marked attenuation of British influence. Even before the events covered in this chapter, a number of measures heralded Canada's progression from "colony to nation," to use the phrase made famous by Arthur Lower in his book of the same title. Thus, in 1947, the first Canadian Citizenship Act defined Canada's people as Canadians; in 1949, appeals to the Judicial Committee of the Privy Council in London were abolished, making the Supreme Court of Canada the final court of appeal; and, in 1952, the tradition of appointing highly placed Britons as governors-general was broken when Vincent Massey, a Canadian, was appointed to the vice-regal post, commencing a tradition of sending only Canadians to Rideau Hall.

Canadians celebrate the Centennial of Confederation on Parliament Hill on July 1, 1967. By this time, Canada had acquired most of the attributes of an independent state. (Canapress)

Canada rapidly lost its British veneer. An increasing number of Canadians saw their homeland as a unique partnership of Francophones and Anglophones, and later as a dual entity comprising Quebec and ROC. While not all Anglophones accepted the "Compact Theory of Confederation" dear to the Tremblay Commission (1953-56) and many Quebec nationalists, there was widespread acceptance of the idea that Canada was fundamentally a francophone-anglophone partnership, made stronger by mutual recognition of the other's language. The Official Languages Act of 1969, although focused on language use by the federal government, became an important symbol of Canada's dualism.

But just as this dualism acquired general acceptance, its impact was attenuated by the emergence of multiculturalism. That development first received serious recognition in the B&B Commission report, since the Commission's mandate led it examine the situation of "other ethnic groups." Before the Second World War, large-scale immigration from continental Europe, particularly to the western provinces, had created a constituency with concerns far removed from the usual preoccupations of Quebec and central Canada. After the war, substantial numbers of newcomers swelled the populations of those provinces. Accordingly, the Pearson government appointed to the Commission two articulate representatives of the "third force," thereby ensuring their voice would be heard. One of the volumes of the Commission's report addressed the question of how the country could adjust to the presence of Canadians whose origins were neither French nor English.

When the Commission put multiculturalism on the political agenda, many so-called "ethnic" Canadians welcomed this new perspective. But its recommendations in this sphere were less far-reaching than those on strengthening the French fact in Canada. This drew considerable criticism from Canadians of other ethnic groups.

Whatever the B&B Commission's impact, multiculturalism was in the wind. It became enshrined in formal policy and, briefly, in the creation of a Ministry of State for Multiculturalism. Although multiculturalism never quite took hold fully in Canada (mainly because it was overtaken by other developments), it did divert attention and energy away from the dualist vision of Canada, to Quebec's consternation.

Multiculturalism in turn had to cede to newer forces. Although this occurred after the period covered by this chapter, it is necessary to note it here because it affects the definition of Canadian identity. The impact of multicultural groups joining the "founding races" as primary constituent building blocks of Canada was blunted by profound societal change. First, multiculturalism itself underwent a major transformation as increasing numbers of new Canadians were non-European, constituting visible minorities whose culture often diverged substantially from that of the original Canadian settlers. More important, the aboriginal population, previously neglected, emerged as a primary thread in the Canadian tapestry. Finally, there was the preoccupation of many Canadians with rights-based entitlements — women, the physically challenged and individuals pursuing alternative lifestyles, to name a few groups. In 1982, the Charter of Rights and Freedoms endowed some of those groups with collective rights, giving them interests and identities sometimes at odds with the traditional definition of Canada. Both dualism and multiculturalism thus lost some of their earlier relevance.

The changing perspectives on Canada cannot obliterate a basic reality — our country comprises two well-established, distinct cultures: one French, centred in Quebec, and the other English, spread across ROC. Their life together is often marred by deep misunderstanding and distrust, although it can also be shown that they have frequently managed to arrive at consensus and mutual enrichment through joint viewpoints and action. The catalogue of differences and divergences is long. So the question arises: are there fundamental irritants bedevilling relations between Anglophones and Francophones?

One issue stands out: Quebecers find it incomprehensible that some Anglos cannot see that the preservation of their language is of primordial importance to them and justifies the adoption of seemingly draconian measures to ensure its survival in Quebec. This failure they see as indicative of a monumental lack of interest on the part of Anglos and an inability to place themselves in Quebecers' shoes. In the face of what they interpret as a flagrant rejection by ROC, Quebecers, not surprisingly, feel a sense of neglect that predisposes them to separate ways. A good example is the reaction triggered by the opposition to the presence of French-language broadcasting in the early days of the Canadian Broadcasting Corporation; Francophones felt they were unwanted in Canada and their particular situation in North America not understood. Hector Charlesworth's statement at the time: "If there is a separatist feeling in Quebec, it has been provoked in no small degree by the narrow-minded hostility of certain groups of English-speaking Canadians" — is a common observation that could be repeated many times in many contexts, but is remarkable because it was made as early as 1937.[1]

Yet, oddly enough, many Anglophones also believe their viewpoint is ignored and that they suffer neglect. ROC disenchantment usually takes two forms. First, outsiders often find Quebecers overly self-absorbed and uninterested in what goes on beyond their immediate world. This may be no more than a (possibly unconscious) resentment of Quebecers generally seeing themselves as Quebecers first and Canadians second, unlike most other Canadians, who tend to identify with Canada more than their province. The essay on the adoption of the Canadian flag illustrates this point, but Anglophones frequently invoke other examples: the meagre coverage of Canada by the Quebec print media, the assumption that Canadians outside Quebec are bereft of any nationalism or the belief that ROC is a homogeneous mass with uniform attitudes toward Quebec and other issues.

The second grievance concerns Quebec's failure to acknowledge anglophone efforts to adapt to Quebec's needs or appreciate the positive steps taken to accommodate it. Thus it is sometimes felt by non-Quebecers that the bipartisan B&B Commission produced many extremely useful reforms: equal opportunities for Francophones in Ottawa and its environs; the use of French in the federal government; and the strengthening of the French presence in Montreal, which contributed to the French language becoming dominant in the city's business establishments. Quebec's language laws certainly contributed to some of these developments, but many English Canadians nevertheless thought, and still think, that the B&B experience was a positive contribution to the well-being of Canadians, and particularly Quebecers. The Commission may have failed to address the problems created by the influx of Allophones into Quebec, but this does not diminish its accomplishments. In short, it is felt that Quebecers are quick to identify slights but slow to note the steps taken to assist them in realizing their dreams.

Defining the
Canadian Identity

T HE French-Canadian nationalism of the first half of the 20th century is a more complex phenomenon than it would appear at first glance: It was as much Canadian as French-Canadian, a paradoxical characteristic to which not enough importance is granted nowadays. This nationalism strove to protect and promote the survival and interests of the French-Canadian community, and its field of action was not limited to Quebec. It extended to all parts of Canada where there were minority, French-speaking communities — i.e., from coast to coast. In particular, the right to French primary and secondary education in provinces other than Quebec, a right that had long been denied, was the subject of endless requests and demands.

The reasoning behind these interventions was based on a certain "Canadian idea," a vision of Canada as a national entity of which the French-Canadian community was rightly a part. From the French-Canadian nationalist perspective of the first part of the century, the Canadian idea was more a "project" than a reality: The image of a bilingual Canada in which the two linguistic and cultural communities would be on equal footing and collaborate in building a country that belonged to them — a truly independent country. For this "project" to come to fruition, Canada would have to leave the British Empire and become a member of the League of Nations as quickly as possible. To this end, French-Canadian nationalists called for the abolition of colonial political structures, which they considered outdated, and the adoption of the symbols of an independent Canada. Thus, seeking legal solutions from the Privy Council in London, using Dominion to designate Canada, holding British citizenship and paying allegiance to the British monarchy were all denounced as archaic ties from which

Canada should free itself. Moreover, using as the Canadian flag the Union Jack, and later the Red Ensign, the flag of the British merchant navy, was seen as one of the most humiliating symbols of outdated colonialism.

Allow me to share a personal recollection here: At the classical college I attended, students could choose, among the extracurricular activities offered, between Académie française and Académie anglaise. There we learned the art of public speaking, in French or in English. I chose the latter. As the subject of my first speech (not only the first speech of my life, but also the first in English!), I chose Why We Need a Canadian Flag, which I delivered with youthful passion. That was in 1938. It would be another 25 years before Canada adopted its own flag.

In the eyes of a Quebecer who grew up in the French-Canadian national-ist climate of the time, Canadians to the west and east of Quebec developed their own "Canadian" identity at a breathtakingly slow and painstaking pace. English Canadians appeared to be satisfied with Canada's colonial status within the British Empire and to want to perpetuate at any cost the Dominion's dependence on and loyalty to England, a loyalty that had become ridiculously outdated. French-Canadian nationalists strongly believed they were much more Canadian than English Canadians, who, more British than Canadian, were keeping Canada from becoming independent.

It is possible to imagine a Canadian history that would have seen English Canadians progressively adopt a Canadian identity that they would have shared with their French-Canadian, nationalist partners. But the essays in this chapter demonstrate the evolution of two national identities, which diverged rather than converged. In English Canada, a truly Canadian identity gradually came to replace the prevailing British identity, and a new Canadian nationalism was grad-ually expressed through the adoption of a Canadian flag (1965), a Canadian national anthem (1964-80) and a national capital Act (1958), and decisions in various spheres, such as the 1960s decision to appoint a Canadian to the position of principal of McGill University, after a long line of mainly British principals. With the adoption of a Canadian policy of official bilingualism (1969), the French-Canadian nationalist "project" seemed to have come to fruition, or at least to be in the process of doing so.

However, the meeting of identities never took place. At the very time when Canadian identity was maturing in English Canada, the sense of belonging to French

Canada, which had prevailed among Quebecers until the mid-20th century, was giving way to the emergence of a sense of belonging to Quebec. This evolution was symbolized by the replacement of the traditional "Province of Quebec" — henceforth regarded as negating the concept of Quebec as a country — by "Quebec."

In my opinion, the critical phase of this evolution, and of contemporary Canadian history, was the early 1960s to 1971 beginning with the Pearson government and ending with the Trudeau government. Of all the prime ministers who preceded and succeeded him, Prime Minister Lester B. Pearson was the most sensitive to both the dramatic and tragic sides of Canada's political evolution. His concern prompted him to appoint the Royal Commission on Bilingualism and Biculturalism (the B&B Commission), which had as its task to sound out the Canadian national psyche. The Commission was subject to pressure from the solidly established ethnic communities in western Canada, which resisted bilingualism and biculturalism, and to the emerging Quebec separatist movement, which, though still marginal, was very militant.

That critical period ended in 1971 when the Trudeau government adopted the definition of a multicultural rather than a bicultural Canada. The latter had been envisioned by Pearson and advocated by the B&B Commission. In Quebec, the Commission's report was received with a great deal of ambivalence. The interests of francophone minorities did not appear to be sufficiently protected. The change in direction signalled by the multicultural definition of Canada was thus an even more cruel disappointment to those who had hoped for a recognition of "two founding peoples." The designation of multiculturalism reduced French-Canadian culture to the same level as all the others, turned its back on Canadian history and evoked the ahistorical idea of an equality of all cultures and all ethnic communities.

The image of a multicultural Canada never really took hold in Quebec and received a very negative press. Without directly confronting the federal government's multiculturalism, the Quebec government developed an immigration and citizenship policy that recognized the ethnic pluralism within Quebec, but in its own way by giving priority to the French language and culture.

The B&B Commission report, especially interpreted by the Trudeau government, had considerable influence on the divergent evolution of Canadian and Quebec identities. It may be seen as the turning point, when the divergence of the two identities, which had been long in the making, could no longer be avoided. From that point onward, each went its own way. The 1960s and 1970s, which had been envisioned as a period of reconciliation of points of view and identities, and which might have been so, turned out to be the breaking-up period. The longstanding latent misapprehension by Quebecers, especially nationalist Quebecers, of the Canadian image and identity taking shape in the rest of Canada exploded during that decade. In this sense, it marked a turning point in Canadian history: The crisis began then — but is not yet over.

It was during that period that the division and opposition between the federalists and sovereignists first appeared in Quebec. In 1960, Quebecers still divided their political allegiances between the Liberals and Conservatives (or, within Quebec, the Union Nationale Party, which had replaced the Conservative Party in the 1930s). After 1970, Quebecers had to position themselves vis-à-vis the indépendantiste movement.

In traditional Quebec political culture, the government of Quebec was closer to the population than the federal government. Ottawa was seen as a distant, anglophone city. The feeling of being "Canadian," which had prevailed among Quebecers for a long time, already contained a degree of Quebec identity. This undoubtedly constituted fertile ground for the rapid emergence of a new Quebec identity, which, for many, was ready to replace the Canadian one.

The Creation of the Canadian Broadcasting Corporation (1932)

I NITIATED IN 1919 WITH A LICENCE GRANTED TO THE MARCONI COMPANY (CFCF) in Montreal, commercial and private radio broadcasting, or wireless telephony as it was called at the time, developed without government intervention until the early 1930s. In the context of growing Canadian nationalism, domination of the airwaves by American programs prompted the federal government to appoint the Royal Commission of Inquiry on Broadcasting (the Aird Commission) to look into the question. Its report, tabled in September 1929, recommended that radio broadcasting be organized as a public service and that a "national company" be set up. Although the Aird Commission made no special reference to the production of French programs, it recommended that programming in each province be locally determined.[1]

In 1932, following an inquiry of the Special Committee of the House of Commons on Radio Broadcasting and rulings by the Supreme Court of Canada and the Privy Council in London giving control over broadcasting to the federal government, the Canadian Radio Broadcasting Act, providing for the creation of the Canadian Radio Broadcasting Commission (CRBC, which became the CBC in 1936), was finally adopted, with only one dissenting vote.

With a mandate to create a broadcasting system with Canadian content accessible to all Canadians, the CRBC undertook to implement a pan-Canadian network. The year following its creation it began to broadcast from coast to coast. Half of the weekly seven hours devoted to pan-Canadian programing was reserved for French-language broadcasts.

as i recall

When the idea of Canadian nationhood was beginning to emerge, Ottawa's decision to legislate radio broadcasting was generally well received in English Canada.[2] During public hearings in 1932 by the House of Commons Special Committee on Radio Broadcasting, the general view favoured some form of public ownership and control of the airwaves.[3] The main justifications for government intervention were: to strengthen national unity, to ensure high-quality Canadian programming as a means of public education, and to control the quantity and quality of advertising. The Canadian Radio League was undoubtedly the most active and eloquent organization in this debate. Graham Spry, one of the League's leaders, asked Canadians to choose between "Canada and the United States," saying, "Here is an important state enterprise that should exercise a real and significant influence in defining the Canadian nation."[4]

The federal government adopted the goal of national unity. Prime Minister Bennett announced in the House that complete control of the airwaves had to be assured, in order to make the national broadcasting service "a great agency for the communication of matters of national concern and for the diffusion of national thoughts and ideals, and [an] agency by which national consciousness may be fostered and sustained and national unity still further strengthened."[5]

During the debates leading up to the adoption of the Radio Broadcasting Act, the language question was addressed in a less explicit manner than the questions of ownership, programming or even provincial jurisdiction. Testifying before the Special Committee in 1932, the Chairman of the Aird Commission had, however, let it be known that, as a rule, the language of communication in broadcasting across the country would be English.[6] Thus, the CRBC's decision in May 1933 to broadcast programs in French on the entire network provoked a flood of protests from English-language listeners.[7] Extremist groups such as the Ku Klux Klan, Protestant Vigilance Committee, Royal Black Knights of Ireland

AN APPRECIATION

HECTOR CHARLESWORTH—"Thanks for the applause."

Caricature of George Shields published in the *Evening Post* in 1934 illustrating the discontent stirred up by the broadcasting of French programs by the new Canadian Radio Broadcasting Commission.

and Sons of England protested against what they regarded as a violation of the rights of the majority.[8]

"There was a queer mixture of prejudice, bigotry and fear – but not necessarily antagonism – to French as a language,"[9] commented historian E. Austin Weir about this episode. Recalling this period, Hector Charlesworth, CRBC Chairman at the time, wrote: "If there is a separatist feeling in Quebec it has been provoked in no small degree by the narrow-minded hostility of certain groups of English-speaking Canadians."[10]

According to Frank Peers, French programming reminded English Canadians that Canada was a bilingual country, and the reminder was not always welcome. "For many quarters in English Canada, the Commission was looked upon as an instrument of French domination, or at least as a French-dominated organization."[11] A poll commissioned in 1934 by the *Regina Star* showed that 87 percent of respondents objected to the use of French on the air.[12] Said F. W. Turnbull, a Conservative Member of Parliament for Regina:

> The French language is not an official language of
> the whole of Canada, and is confined in its applica-
> tion to the terms of the British North America Act.
> When the radio commission does anything at all
> which appears to be forcing what I may call the
> Quebec view on the rest of the country, these people
> resent it, and instead of building up unity it is build-
> ing up a wall of hostility against it."[13] ◆

Si je me souviens bien

As in the rest of the country, attitudes in Quebec toward the federal plan to legislate radio broadcasting partly depended on one's interests in the industry. The newspaper *La Presse,* which owned CKAC, the first Francophone radio station in North America, was opposed to

Si je me souviens bien

nationalization of the airwaves, arguing that the French language
would be threatened and that centralization would aggravate the
conflict between the two linguistic communities.[14] The Quebec government activly opposed the federal initiatives and led a legal dispute over the matter. Quebec nationalists were opposed to federal
interference in a field they believed to be provincial jurisdiction.[15]
Quebec had already adopted its own Radio Broadcasting Act in 1929.

Some public figures from French Canada – among them
Édouard Montpetit, a University of Montreal economist, and Georges
Pelletier, editor of *Le Devoir* – were, however, favourable to Ottawa's
intervention and had joined the Canadian Radio League.[16] Several members of the French-Canadian elite, as well as their English-Canadian
peers, were concerned about the Americanization of the airwaves[17] and
the quality of programming.[18] Thus protection of the national identity, as
conveyed through public radio, was seen a positive objective.

For these federalists, bilingualism was a question of fair play[19];
they insisted on equality in programming and advertising. Thus in
April 1937, *Le Devoir* came to the defence of Gladstone Murray,
General Manager of the new Canadian Broadcasting Corporation,
who had stated that radio broadcasting could help the two communities better understand one another's language.[20]

However, some people, faced with the reactions provoked by
French-language broadcasting in English Canada, the French network's slowness in providing service to all Francophones in Canada[21]
and persistent bilingualism on private French stations,[22] ended up
encouraging the autonomy of the French network.[23] ◆

Linguistic tensions provoked by bilingual programming gave rise to a
gradual separation of French-language and English-language programs.
Complete autonomy of both networks was finally achieved in December 1937
with the opening of a 50,000-watt station in Montreal, leaving the old 5000-
watt transmitter to fulfil the needs of the Anglo-Quebec community. The

establishment of a national radio network, initially designed to strengthen Canadian unity, would have the paradoxical effect of promoting the distinctiveness of Quebec.[24]

The same kind of linguistic concerns arose when the national television network was created in 1951.[25] In subsequent years, the CBC's role sporadically came back to haunt relations between the two communities, specifically during the conscription crisis of the early 1940s,[26] the Radio-Canada producers' strike of 1958,[27] the FLQ era and the 1970 October Crisis,[28] the election of the Parti Québécois in 1976,[29] the referendums of 1980, 1992 and 1995,[30] and, lastly, upon the establishment of the English-language news network.[31] To this day, the field of telecommunications remains a subject that causes considerable tension and rivalry between the federal and Quebec governments.[32]

The Royal
Commission on
Bilingualism and
Biculturalism
(1963-1970)

P RIME MINISTER LESTER B. PEARSON LAUNCHED THE ROYAL COMMISSION ON
Bilingualism and Biculturalism (the B&B Commission) in 1963 shortly
after his government came to power. At the time, during what is known as the
Quiet Revolution, the modernization of the Quebec state was in full swing.
The provincial government led by Jean Lesage, had as its slogan "Maîtres chez
nous" (Masters in Our Own House).

In December 1962, responding to the changes underway in Quebec,
Pearson had attracted much attention with a House of Commons speech on
Canadian unity that he later called "the speech in the House of which I am most
proud."[1] In that speech Pearson admitted that a serious problem existed as a
result of French and English Canadians' different interpretations of
Confederation, a comment that was then unprecedented for an English-Canadian
politician. His speech reflected his openness to the traditional French-Canadian
view of Confederation:

> Confederation may not have been technically a treaty or a compact
> between states, but it was an understanding or a settlement between
> the two founding races of Canada made on the basis of an accept-
> able and equal partnership...Outside Quebec, and as Canada grew
> from coast to coast, this understanding was more often honoured in
> the breach than in the observance.[2]

Furthermore, Pearson called for an inquiry into "the bicultural and bilin-
gual situation in our country," a formula which was retained for the Royal
Commission he went on to create in 1963 under the chairmanship of André
Laurendeau and Davidson Dunton.[3]

The mandate of the B&B Commission was to "recommend what steps should be taken to develop the Canadian Confederation on the basis of an equal partnership between the two founding races."[4] It held a series of public meetings across the country and published a preliminary report that shook Canadians by asserting, "Canada, without being fully conscious of the fact, is passing through the greatest crisis in its history."[5] An extensive program of research into the socioeconomic and cultural status of the country's two major language groups was undertaken. The Commission completed its work in 1970.

The Commission's recommendations included the adoption of an Official Languages Act, extension of official bilingualism to the federal government, creation of bilingual districts with official language services where language minorities made up at least 10 percent of the population, and declaration of official bilingualism in the provinces of Ontario and New Brunswick.

as i recall

In its *Preliminary Report,* the B&B Commission wrote that it had found "tragically little awareness of the feelings and aspirations of French-speaking Canadians" in English Canada:

> Few had come to grips with the questions that Quebec's resurgence poses for all Canadians...To very many, Canada appears as essentially an English-speaking country with a French-speaking minority, to which certain limited rights have been given. So far most do not seem to have understood, or to be ready to meet the implications of 'equal partnership'.[6]

Laurendeau observed that many English Canadians believed the Commission was creating a problem, rather than addressing an existing one.[7] Former federal Tory Minister Gordon Churchill was one proponent of this view: "I was opposed to [the Commission] from the start. I thought it would do nothing but create disunity...Instead of creating unity, it has created more disunity than I have known in my lifetime, except in 1917

over the conscription crisis."[8] The Commission was also widely criticized
by English-Canadian politicians for its $7.6-million research program, a
then unprecedented sum in the history of Canadian royal commissions.

Of the two topics addressed by the Commission, bilingualism
and biculturalism, it was the latter that would be the harder to sell. In
western Canada, the Commission encountered strong opposition from
Ukrainian Canadians, for whom the Commission's "two founding
nations" vision suggested second-class citizenship, and who considered themselves co-founders of western settlements.[9] Laurendeau
made the following observation about the Prairies in his diary:

> Having been built by very diverse ethnic groups, these
> provinces have had delicate problems to resolve. They
> have succeeded in finding a certain balance and fear
> that biculturalism will put this balance in danger.[10]

Although some English Canadians viewed biculturalism as a
safeguard against cultural annexation by the United States, many
"were fearful that recognition of a dual society might lead to a
splintering of the country."[11] This concern was expressed in 1969 by
sociologist John Porter, who, in response to the Commission's final
report, wrote that "they would bring us together through bilingualism, but keep us apart through culture."[12]

By contrast, bilingualism – the recognition of two principal languages – won enough support in English Canada for important federal civil service reforms to be undertaken. In 1968, reflecting the hope
for national unity that was invested in official bilingualism, New
Democrat David Lewis made the following judgement:

> For the first time in the 40-odd years I have lived
> here, there is an atmosphere and climate in English
> speaking Canada which makes possible the accep-
> tance of the fact that bilingualism is part of the
> Canadian mosaic. This is something that, until we had
> the B&B commission, would not have been possible
> to expect in many parts of this country.[13] ◆

si je me souviens bien

The Commission's *Preliminary Report* conveyed the impatience of French Canadians with the fact that "the principal institutions in the country are frustrating their desire to live their lives fully as French Canadians." French Canadians in Quebec, the report noted, are conscious of belonging to a distinct society, one which is "taking a very hard look at itself" and "showing a very clear determination to achieve 'liberation'." Noting that the crisis arose chiefly from divergences between French Quebec and English Canada, the report observed that French-language minorities outside Quebec had been "thrown off balance by the evolution of Quebec."[14]

Federalist intellectuals, including Pierre Elliott Trudeau and Marc Lalonde, published a critique of the *Preliminary Report* in *Cité Libre*, in which they ridiculed the Commission's methods as unscientific, described its vision of a crisis in relations between French and English Canadians as exaggerated and rejected the need for fundamental reform of Confederation.[15]

From the opposite end of the spectrum, the Commission met with vociferous protest from advocates of independence. Commissioner Paul Lacoste recalled:

> It was in Quebec that hearings were the most difficult, even arduous at times, for the Commissioners. The most-nationalist elements were systematically hostile to the Commission and made a lot of noise, creating the impression in some towns that there was almost general refusal of the process.[16]

René Lévesque attacked the Commission's vision of bilingualism and biculturalism in English Canada as "a fool's bargain" for Quebec, given the historical record of Francophone assimilation outside Quebec.[17] On the other hand, Quebec Premier Daniel Johnson, elected in 1966 under the slogan "Égalité ou indépendance," (Equality or Independence), found ammunition in the Commission's report for his campaign for special status for Quebec in federal-provincial negotiations.[18]

Si je me souviens bien

Cartoon showing Quebec as a recalcitrant showgirl refusing to "get into the cake"
baked by André Laurendeau and Davidson Dunton on the occasion of the Centenary
of Confederation. The two dispirited bakers have to explain themselves to Lester B.
Pearson. (Donald MacPherson, 1967, Toronto Star Syndicate)

Sociologist Guy Rocher summed up the disappointment of
many Quebec nationalists with the Commission's recommendations,
particularly the failure to address political/institutional reforms:

> To the francophone community in Quebec, anx-
> ious and suspicious and haunted by plans of sepa-
> ration, the Laurendeau-Dunton Commission
> presented the prospect of a bilingual Canada in
> which French was forever destined to remain the
> minority language – probably more and more the
> minority – while at the same time being demo-
> graphically threatened within Quebec itself...It
> opened the doors to Canada but invited Quebec,

Si je me souviens bien

in exchange, to run the enormous risk of seeing
itself progressively deprived of any effective
political power, in Quebec City as in Ottawa.[19] ◆

After Pierre Elliott Trudeau's rise to power in 1968, biculturalism and the vision of an equal partnership between two founding nations, which had guided the B&B Commission during Laurendeau's tenure, were ignored out of fear that any reference to culture would lend credence to the two-nations thesis.[20] The Commission's recommendations on bilingualism, however, were largely adopted by the federal government in the Official Languages Act of 1969. Volume IV of the Commission's final report also provided the government with recommendations concerning multiculturalism, which served as preparation for the federal policy adopted in 1971.[21]

The Commission's warnings about the need to address the broader political dimension of the partnership accelerated movement toward constitutional reform. In November 1967 (the month following publication of Volume I of the Commission's final report) Premier Robarts of Ontario hosted the Confederation of Tomorrow conference in Toronto with all the provincial premiers in attendance. A federal-provincial conference on constitutional reform followed in February of 1968.

The Canadian Flag (1965)

A S A COLONY AND LATER A DOMINION WITHIN THE BRITISH EMPIRE, CANADA had as its flag the Union Jack. In 1925, the federal government began to consider the possibility of giving Canada its own national flag. Liberal Prime Minister Mackenzie King assigned a Privy Council committee the task of examining various design possibilities and submitting a report to Parliament. The plan, however, was not warmly received in the House of Commons. Historian George F. G. Stanley recalls: "When the flag question was raised in the House of Commons, the supporters of the Union Flag charged King with 'flag-waving,' an activity engaged in only by unsophisticated Americans, and with disloyalty to the Mother Country."[1] The King government abandoned the project.

In 1945, a decree was issued authorizing the use on federal buildings of the Canadian Red Ensign, a red flag featuring the Union Jack and the arms of the Canadian provinces, until another national flag could be adopted.[2]

The following year, the King government again thought the time was right for a distinctive Canadian flag and created a parliamentary committee to this end. But almost immediately the endeavour became a bone of contention. At the request of the Duplessis government, the Quebec Legislative Assembly unanimously adopted a resolution demanding that the Canadian flag be exempted from "all foreign symbols." But in the House of Commons, the Conservatives — joined by the Liberals in Ontario, the West and the Maritimes — informed the government that the Canadian flag should feature the Union Jack.[3] Faced with this situation, the King government once again abandoned the project. Consequently, none of the 2,695 sketches that had been submitted to the committee were put to a vote in Parliament. It took another 20 years before the project was revived.

At the beginning of 1964, Prime Minister Lester B. Pearson informed the House of Commons that the government wished to adopt a national flag. The Centennial of Confederation was approaching and the prime minister had made a solemn promise during the 1963 election campaign to provide Canada with its own flag before the first two years of his mandate were completed.

In October 1964, the Joint Committee of the Senate and the House of Commons responsible for studying the various proposals retained three sketches: a Red Ensign bearing the *fleur-de-lys* and the Union Jack, a design consisting of three maple leaves between two sky-blue borders, and a red flag displaying a stylized red maple leaf on a white square.[4] The members of the Committee were unanimous in recommending the single-leaf design. Most Conservatives, however, strongly favoured the first of the three designs, featuring the Union Jack and the *fleur-de-lys*. To put an end to the Conservatives' filibustering, the Pearson gov-

Prime Minister Lester B. Pearson unveils the Canadian flag. (Duncan Cameron, NAC, PA 136153)

ernment, on December 14, 1964, resorted to the motion of closure, a controversial measure that had not been imposed since 1956.[5] The next day, the House of Commons approved the single-leaf design by a vote of 163 to 78; the new Maple Leaf flag became official on February 15, 1965.

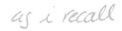

The parliamentary debates sparked by the adoption of a Canadian flag revealed the persistent attachment of many English Canadians for British symbols. With the support of groups such as the Canadian Corps Association and the Royal Canadian Legion,[6] Conservative leader John Diefenbaker favoured the Red Ensign bearing the *fleur-de-lys* and the Union Jack. The former prime minister explained his viewpoint in his memoirs:

> Pearson believed that a distinctive flag was one in which there should be no relationship with the past, nothing to indicate our heritage; the greatness of the French régime or the contribution of Great Britain. One Canada, I believed, should be symbolized by a flag containing both the Union Jack and the *fleur-de-lys*...Neither [of these] was a sign of subservience to a colonial past. There was no colonialism in honouring our history.[7]

Among the public, however, the flag debate did not provoke the protest that Diefenbaker had hoped for. New Democratic, Ralliement créditiste and Social Credit MPs, however, were in favour of adopting the new flag.

When the new Canadian flag became official, it was celebrated quietly. *The Globe and Mail* greeted it politely while deploring the fact that the parliamentary debates preceding its adoption had diverted the attention of MPs away from more pressing matters.[8] In a letter to *The Toronto Star*, an Ontario reader, reacting to the extensive debate around adoption of the Maple Leaf, wrote, "If all Canadians will fight as vigorously *under* the new flag as they have *over* it, there is still hope for us as a great nation."[9]

Historian J. M. Bumsted, who considered the Pearson initiative a great success, stated, "The Baby Boomers took to the new flag almost instantly...and Confederation Year (1967) was utilized to promote it generally, and extremely successfully."[10] ◆

si je me souviens bien

The debate over the choice of a new flag did not cause as much of a stir in Quebec. But clearly Francophones did not have the same attachment to the Red Ensign as English Canadians did. This was, in fact, a source of dissension in the Conservative ranks in Ottawa: of the 10 Tory MPs from Quebec, only three remained loyal to the party and voted against Pearson's motion of closure. Four defied Diefenbaker and supported the government, and three others were absent from the House at the time of the vote. Leading Quebec's Conservative dissidents was the MP for Trois-Rivières, Léon Balcer. He later described the split in his party:

> Among the Conservatives, the caucus debates began
> to take on the air of a pitched battle. The party's
> anglophone majority started a crusade to save that
> vestige of colonialism, the Red Ensign. At every cau-
> cus meeting, we Quebec MPs argued in favour of rec-
> ognizing the right of Francophones as well as
> Anglophones to be part of a modern Canada that
> would not be the vassal of any other country.
> Diefenbaker, being the excellent debater he was, used
> all of his talents in leading his group to turn their
> backs on the very legitimate aspirations of his
> Quebec colleagues.[11]

Si je me souviens bien

Among the Quebec public, the Maple Leaf was greeted sober-
ly. Claude Ryan, editorialist for *Le Devoir*, described the reaction:

> No one felt wildly enthusiastic about the new flag;
> everyone felt, without daring to say so publicly, that
> we were again faced with a compromise, that the flag
> expressed a unity which was deeply desired but not
> yet achieved.[12]

Premier Jean Lesage compared the adoption of the new
flag to passage from adolescence to adulthood for Canada. "Our
young country has just shed its *toga praetexta* and put on its *toga
virilis*,"[13] he declared. The Leader of the Opposition, Daniel
Johnson, however, said that Quebec had preceded Canada by 17
years when, in 1948, it adopted the *fleur-de-lys* as the "flag of the
French-Canadian nation."[14] ◆

While the Maple Leaf is widely accepted today, a survey conducted in
1994 by Canadian Heritage revealed that Quebecers did not attach the same
importance to it as Canadians from other provinces. While Canadians outside
Quebec ranked the flag as the most important symbol of Canada, Quebecers put
it in sixth place, behind the Canadian Charter of Rights and Freedoms, national
parks, historic sites, bilingualism and the national anthem.[15] Moreover, the program of distributing Canadian flags, started in 1995 by Sheila Copps, Minister of
Canadian Heritage, has had little success in Quebec. As of August 1996, when
500,000 flags had been distributed free of charge, only 8.5 percent of the requests
had come from Quebec,[16] even though Quebecers make up 24 percent of the
Canadian population.

Official
Bilingualism (1969)

I N 1968, AFTER MORE THAN FIVE YEARS' WORK, THE ROYAL COMMISSION OF INQUIRY on Bilingualism and Biculturalism recommended giving Canadians the opportunity to communicate with the federal government in either English or French for the purpose of obtaining federal government jobs and, as far as possible, to work in their preferred language. It went on to recommend strengthening French-language minorities and making linguistic duality a visible feature of the country and its primary institutions.[1]

A degree of bilingualism was evident in the public sector before the adoption of the Act. The French language had been allowed in Parliament since 1867[2] and had gradually appeared on postage stamps (1927), bank notes (1936) and government-issued cheques (1945-1962).[3] But bilingualism never really made its way into the federal bureaucracy. In 1938, an amendment to the Civil Service Act required officials to speak the language of the majority of the people they were to serve. However, it was routinely ignored by the bureaucrats, and less than five years after its adoption it was, for all intents and purposes, forgotten: "For close to thirty years after the civil service legislation of 1918, a traditionally English-speaking administration in Ottawa had remained consistent in its patterns of recruitment and promotion at the expense of 'adequate representation' for French Canadians..."[4].

The government's indifference toward the French question is also revealed in Mackenzie King's 1947 committee investigating bilingualism in the public service: it left no record, either in the form of a report or policy.[5] It was precisely this situation that the Official Languages Act was meant to change.

The Act stipulated that "the English and French languages are the official languages of Canada for all purposes of the Parliament and Government of

In 1908, for the first time a series of eight bilingual stamps was issued to commemorate the Tricentennial of Quebec City. This one recalls the arrival of Jacques Cartier at Stadacona in 1535, a native village located near the site where Quebec City would be founded by Samuel de Champlain in 1608. Not all Canadian stamps became bilingual until 1927.(Canada Post Corporation)

Canada and possess and enjoy equality of status and equal rights and privileges as to their use in all institutions of the Parliament and Government of Canada."[6]

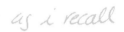

as i recall

The introduction of the French language to certain Canadian symbols and on the airwaves of the new Canadian Radio Broadcasting Commission in the 1930s met with strong opposition from English Canada.[7] The attitude of the federal government on language matters since the 1870s had ill-prepared English-speaking Canadians for this expression of the French reality in Canada, for Ottawa had provided tacit or active support for the unilingual English policies of several provinces.[8]

For English Canadians, the French-language provisions of in the Constitution (section 133) were adequate, and the attempts by French Canadians to achieve greater equality in language matters were treated with indifference and even hostility.[9] It was long presumed that the principles of efficiency and rationality worked against the wider use of French in the public service.[10]

It is not surprising, then, that many English Canadians were not overly receptive to the Official Languages Act:

> the great majority of English speakers regard Canada
> as an English-speaking country...They consider it the
> duty of ethnic minorities, not excepting the French,
> to adjust to English. French might be used as a
> regional language in Quebec to cater to its French-
> speaking majority, but elsewhere in Canada it is
> wrong to 'stuff French down our throats.'[11]

In the House of Commons, a vocal minority fiercely opposed the Bill. Some thought increased services in French a much too costly response to the demands of Francophones in Quebec.[12] Others believed the policy to be misguided: language conflict in Quebec and the increasingly loud demonstrations in favour of French unilingualism led some to think that bilingualism did not respond to the aspirations of Quebecers'.[13] The Official Languages Act was seen as a discriminatory policy that would reduce the opportunities for advancement in the public service for those who did not speak French – a situation that would undermine national unity:

> In the public service of Canada, bilingualism...is an
> unmentioned but potent condition of employment, and
> certainly of advancement. If this policy is further but-
> tressed by legislation such as that now before us, it will
> effectively debar from the public service all but a hand-
> ful of Canadians whose mother tongue is other than
> French. If such an obvious step is taken to alienate
> western Canadian citizens from their capital and central

government, it will not be surprising if the voice of
western separatism becomes louder and louder.[14]

In 1990, the belief that official bilingualism "benefits dispro-
portionately a small bilingual elite" was still widely held by opponents of the policy.[15]

According to Kenneth McRoberts, the ideal of a bilingual
Canada is at odds with the daily experience of many Canadians. A
survey conducted in 1985 revealed that only 14 percent of
Anglophones across Canada had contact with the French language
on a daily basis; 52 percent never heard French spoken, and 34
percent only occasionally.[16] Not surprisingly, opposition to the
Official Languages Act has been especially strong in the western
provinces, where Francophones make up a very small percentage
of the population.[17]

"...don't turn the box around that way, Ricky...you know your father can't stand all that
French in the morning..."

Cartoon by Sydney Barron showing the daily tensions that bilingualism aroused (Syd
Barron, 1967, Toronto Star Syndicate)

Though the provinces had unanimously endorsed the recommendation of the Laurendeau-Dunton (B&B) Commission that Francophones outside Quebec enjoy the same rights as Quebec anglophones, in February 1968[18] most provincial governments were reluctant to implement a policy on bilingualism. Only New Brunswick declared itself officially bilingual, in 1970, under a policy that was entrenched in the Constitution in 1982. In the 1970s and 1980s, the Ontario government also took initiatives to improve the status of French in the province, by offering, for the first time, full secondary education in French in publicly supported schools,[19] authorizing the use of French in the Legislative Assembly (1970), adopting a law on French-language services (1972), creating a French television network (1984) and adopting the French Language Services Act (1986).[20]

But the Official Languages Act has enjoyed considerable support from Canadian elites, especially politicians.[21] Conservative Senator Edgar Fournier of New Brunswick replied to those opposed to the "discriminatory" Official Languages Act: "What about the discrimination against us [French Canadians] for so long? Do they [the opponents] expect Canada to be a one-way street? We have had it for too long."[22] Supporters of bilingualism considered the Act an appropriate response to the aspirations of French-speaking Canadians. When the bill was tabled, Prime Minister Trudeau asserted, "this bill is of the greatest importance in promoting national unity." David Lewis, Leader of the New Democratic Party (NDP), fully agreed:

> I regard this measure as redressing a profound oversight which has haunted Canadians for the first century of our existence as a country, an oversight which has harmed harmonious development among the citizens of this nation. I consider it as a step long overdue.[23]

Others thought the policy on bilingualism would enhance
Canadian distinctiveness, as NDP MP Lorne Nystrom observed in
the House of Commons:

> [this piece of legislation] should help make Canada
> more distinct in identity and culture from the United
> States. I believe it will add to the individuality of Canada
> as a nation and promote the Canadian conscience and
> attitude on national unity throughout the world."[24]

Over time, the ideal of individual bilingualism, as personified
by Pierre Elliott Trudeau, was supported by an increasing number of
English Canadians. Although official bilingualism continues to be
opposed by some groups, such as the Confederation of Regions
Party, the Association for the Preservation of English in Canada and
the Reform Party of Canada,[25] the majority of English Canadians
believe that "having two official languages in Canada makes a more
interesting and even better country." Many of these people consider
it important that their children learn French, which has resulted in a
large increase in the number of French immersion classes across
Canada throughout the 1980s and 1990s.[26] ◆

si je me souviens bien

Until the mid-20th century, French Canadians directed their efforts
in language matters to the federal scene. Their main demands were
that the education and language rights of French-language minority
communities be respected, that the policy of bilingualism be applied
in Ottawa and that French Canadians be equally represented in the
federal public service.[27]

In light of this historical struggle to obtain pan-Canadian linguistic equity, the Official Languages Act was a welcome policy.
Renaude Lapointe, editorialist at *La Presse,* noted, "Those of us
who have been demanding the official equality of the two languages

at the federal level for such a long time see this Act as a victory of great significance."[28] According to historians François Cardin and Claude Couture, the Official Languages Act was "generally well received in Quebec"[29]

In nationalist circles, however, reaction to the Act was more critical. During the 1960s, nationalists had grown increasingly aware of the anglicization of immigrants in Quebec, and as a consequence the new federal law did not meet their expectations. When the report of the Royal Commission on Bilingualism and Biculturalism was tabled, Quebec nationalists were already arguing that its recommendations were not sufficient to appease Francophone dissatisfaction.[30] For many, the province had become the only appropriate arena for the application of a language policy, and by the time Parliament finally adopted the Official Languages Act there was a growing consensus among Quebec opinion leaders in favour of official unilingualism.[31] As Eric Waddell observes, this focus on Quebec was partly due to the failure of the pan-Canadian strategy of promoting bilingualism adopted by the French-Canadian elite in the first half of the 20th century.[32]

Nowadays, the personalist approach adopted by the federal government in managing the language question is still often seen as designed to undercut efforts to protect and promote the French language within Quebec. Nationalists prefer the territorial model and are opposed to symmetrical treatment for francophone minorities outside Quebec and the anglophone minority in Quebec.[33] Pierre Fournier sums up this view:

> For two decades, the federal government has used the francophone minorities as an instrument of blackmail to combat Québécois nationalism. To a large extent, pan-Canadian bilingualism and reinforcement of minority rights are elegant pretexts for reducing Quebec's latitude in defending its francophone majority and, more important, for challenging its wish to repatriate the powers necessary to be effective.[34] ◆

Despite objections from opponents and divided public opinion, the House of Commons adopted the Official Languages Act on July 9, 1969, with the support of all the parties; only 17 MPs, including former prime minister John Diefenbaker, voted against it. Since its inception, and in spite of the controversies it continues to fuel, the Act has taken on ever greater importance and has become a key element of "Canadianness" for a great number of citizens.

In 1982, the basic principles of the Official Languages Act were entrenched in the Canadian Charter of Rights and Freedoms; several years later, on September 15, 1988, a new version of the Act was promulgated. It elucidated the rights and obligations of each citizen in terms of official languages and expressed the government's commitment to "'enhancing the vitality of the English and French linguistic minority communities' and fostering the full recognition and use of English and French in Canadian society."[35]

In 1995, after 25 years of implementation, the Commissioner of Official Languages made a positive assessment of the Official Languages Act, especially concerning the presence of Francophones in the civil service,[36] the availability of services to language minorities[37] and schooling in minority languages.[38] Compared to the situation that prevailed before its adoption, progress has been made: "Many Canadians have forgotten that 30 years ago it was not at all certain that a French-speaking Canadian could telephone or write a government office in Ottawa and receive a reply in his or her language. Sometimes, service was not available in French…even in Quebec."[39]

However, when measured against the expectations of the Act — the linguistic health of official minorities, individual bilingualism and national unity, for instance — the assessment is less positive. The rate of assimilation of Francophones outside Quebec is high,[40] individual bilingualism is prevalent only among minorities and Francophones,[41] and there has been no substantial change in the sense of belonging of Quebecers, who still overwhelmingly identify themselves as Quebecers first.[42]

Federal Multiculturalism Policy (1971)

T HE MULTICULTURALISM POLICY ANNOUNCED BY PRIME MINISTER TRUDEAU IN 1971 WAS based on Book IV of the Report of the Royal Commission on Bilingualism and Biculturalism, entitled *The Cultural Contribution of the Other Ethnic Groups*. This study responded to concerns voiced by some ethnic groups that the bilingualism/biculturalism mandate downgraded their contribution to Canadian society and made them second-class citizens. Canada being a country of considerable immigration — 26.7 percent of Canadian citizens, as of 1971, were of neither French nor British descent — the widening of the Commission's mandate and the adoption of a multiculturalism policy were largely the consequence of pressure from cultural minorities.

Four main thrusts were included in the 1971 policy: 1) federal assistance to cultural groups, 2) an effort to overcome cultural barriers to full participation in Canadian society, 3) the promotion of dialogue between cultural groups, and 4) language instruction for immigrants. As Raymond Breton has noted, the federal government was already involved in these areas, but the new policy represented "a significant shift in the magnitude of the programs, the range of pursuits and the emphasis given to the four areas."[1]

Most important, however, was Trudeau's symbolic affirmation that "although there are two official languages, there is no official culture, nor does any ethnic group take precedence over any other."[2] In Trudeau's words, multiculturalism within a bilingual framework would enhance the "cultural freedom" of Canadians and thereby advance Canadian unity by breaking down "discriminatory attitudes and cultural jealousies."

The Trudeau government underscored the symbolic importance of the multiculturalism policy by incorporating it in the Canadian Charter of Rights

and Freedoms. Section 27 states: "This Charter shall be interpreted in a manner consistent with the preservation and enhancement of the multicultural
heritage of Canadians." The importance accorded to multicultural programming, however, never matched the symbolic importance of the policy. The
Parliamentary Standing Committee on Multiculturalism reported in 1987 that
"there is a sense that this 15-year-old policy is floundering."[3] Under the
Trudeau government, the policy remained a sideline of the activities of the
Secretary of State, especially when compared to the substantial effort invested
in official bilingualism.[4] Over time, policy emphasis moved away from preserving cultural heritage toward addressing the problems of race relations and
discrimination.[5] It was not until 1988, under the Mulroney administration,
that Parliament adopted a multiculturalism act, which created the short-lived
Department of Multiculturalism and Citizenship. In 1993, the department was
subsequently carved up, with multiculturalism functions being absorbed by
the Department of Canadian Heritage.

as i recall

The initial pressure for a federal multiculturalism policy arose in
English Canada among people of non-British, non-French descent
suffering what Raymond Breton calls "status anxieties": "The fear
of being defined as second-class citizens, marginal to the identity
system being redefined" by Quebec's push for dualism.[6] As multicultural programming developed, ethno-cultural groups across the
country became political stakeholders for multicultural grants programs, including heritage language education.[7]

The policy also took on a symbolic, nation-building role,
addressed to all Canadians, concerning the meaning of
"Canadianness." As the country has been transformed by waves of
immigration, many English Canadians have held that Canada's
respect for its multicultural "mosaic" is an important differentiating
factor *vis-à-vis* the United States and its "melting pot."[8]

But by many accounts multiculturalism has progressively fallen out of favour in English Canada.[9] For example, in 1991 the Citizens' Forum on Canada's Future noted:

> While Canadians accept and value Canada's cultural diversity, they do not value many of the activities of the multicultural program of the federal government. These are seen as expensive and divisive in that they remind Canadians of their different origins rather than their shared symbols, society and future.[10]

The Forum concluded: "The key goal of multiculturalism should be to welcome all Canadians into an evolving mainstream, of both Quebec and Canadian society alike." English-Canadian concern over the ongoing unity crisis and the perceived weakening of Canada's distinctiveness brought about by continental free trade has created a climate more favourable to integration than the promotion of diversity. Multiculturalism is often blamed for the lack of a clear national identity in English Canada.[11]

Interestingly, the western-based Reform Party has led criticism of government spending on multiculturalism.[12] While multiculturalism may have been initially embraced in western Canada as an antidote to the "French domination" implicit in bilingualism and biculturalism, this reaction has now been forgotten, according to University of Calgary political scientist Tom Flanagan.[13] Also, an increasing number of ethnic voices are being raised against multiculturalism policy in Canada. Best known among the critics is author Neil Bissoondath, whose 1994 essay *Selling Illusions: The Cult of Multiculturalism in Canada* argues that federal policy has gone too far, weakening the social fabric, and the divisions that multiculturalism celebrates as diversity in fact hinder the full acceptance of immigrants into the mainstream.[14]

Nevertheless, multiculturalism continues to enjoy the support of its key stakeholders, namely ethnic and cultural organizations.[15] In addition, polling data on multiculturalism show,
paradoxically, that support for the retention of minority cultures is
high among university-educated Canadians of British ancestry.[16] ◆

si je me souviens bien

In Quebec, the policy of multiculturalism has been widely perceived
as relegating Quebec's francophone majority to the status of one
ethnic group among many, with no claim to special political status.[17]
Consequently, the policy has been, in the words of Kenneth
McRoberts, "almost universally rejected in francophone Quebec" as
a vision of Canada.[18]

Quebecers' minority status within anglophone North
America makes the integration of immigrants into French-speaking
society a highly charged issue, and the linguistic practices of immigrants, who are traditionally drawn to English, have been an important concern since the 1960s.

It is not surprising, then, that at the outset Quebec
Premier Robert Bourassa wrote to Trudeau protesting the new
policy, warning that his province would not adopt multiculturalism. Since then, successive Quebec governments, both Parti
Québécois and Liberal, have defended pluralist policies which
place explicit emphasis on the integration of immigrants into an
over-arching common culture.[19] Federal multiculturalism is perceived as running counter to this objective because its cultural
relativism suggests to immigrants that it is legitimate for them
not to integrate into the francophone culture of the province. Its
association with official bilingualism conveys the sense that
choosing French is merely optional. The situation is even more
worrisome for a great many Quebecers who feel that the exis-

tence of two identity systems vying for the allegiance of immigrants in Quebec creates an ambiguity which effectively hinders
their integration into the francophone majority.[20]

Quebecers' rejection of the federal policy of multiculturalism
is a refusal not of pluralism itself, but of "a model of integration that
denies the existence of a political community already in place in
Quebec that must be the main focus of integration for members of
ethno-cultural minorities."[21]

Quebecers favour an alternative model, "interculturalism."
Articulated in a 1990 white paper, the policy lists three principles as
elements of the moral contract between immigrants and the state:
1) the use of French language as the everyday language of public
life, 2) a democratic society in which the participation and contribution of all are both expected and valued, and 3) a pluralistic society
open to a diversity of contributions, within the limits imposed by
democratic values, and the need for intercultural exchange.[22] ◆

In McRoberts assessment, multiculturalism has "intensified the constitutional conflict between Quebec and Canada" rather than aiding national unity as
Trudeau had planned.[23] In some respects, the multiculturalism policies of Quebec
and Ottawa have actually grown more alike, with both, for example, placing
emphasis on discrimination and race relations.[24] There now appears to be a convergence of opinion around the need to give greater priority to the integration of
ethnic diversity into the mainstream of Quebec and Canadian society. However, for
Quebec immigrants, this integration must take place against the backdrop of a
greater, unresolved identity dilemma: What is Quebec's place in Canada?

chapter 4

Beyond the Quiet Revolution

Introductions by
John Meisel
Guy Rocher

Essays prepared by
Alain Desruisseaux,
Sarah Fortin and
Nicholas Ignatieff

Beyond   the   Quiet
Revolution

T HE ESSAYS IN THIS CHAPTER DISCUSS THE QUIET REVOLUTION AND ITS AFTERMATH.
   They chronicle some key events that shaped opinion in Quebec and ROC
during and after the Quiet Revolution. English Canada was made aware of the
changes taking place in Quebec during the first half of the 1960s by a dramatic
phrase on the opening pages of the Preliminary Report of the B&B Commission:
"Canada, without being fully conscious of the fact, is passing through the greatest crisis in its history,"[1] a *cri de coeur* that would be received with a big yawn
today because everyone has heard it many times. In the mid-1960s, however, it
was shocking and deeply disquieting to most Canadians.

    Anglo-Canadian reaction to these episodes in Canadian history varied con-
siderably from one event to the next. Moreover, virtually no development elicited
a uniform reaction. Thus using the term ROC, while extremely convenient, poses
a great risk. While there often appears to be a dichotomy between Quebec and
other parts of the country, a closer look reveals that the views and interests of ROC
are anything but homogeneous or unanimous; there are always clusters of incompatible and conflicting positions. Generalizations can be made, but the fact remains
that different governments, regions, businesses, groups and individuals espouse
complex and sometimes dissenting voices *vis-à-vis* questions of national unity.

    But even when this rich fabric of interests and opinion is taken into
account, we still find certain common threads that permit us to cautiously identify positions around which opinions toward Quebec cluster. Adherents of three
basic positions stand out: "friends" (of Quebec), "foes" and "neutrals." Each group
normally reacts quite differently to incidents and events affecting French-English
relations, and each is, of course, subject to further differentiation.[2] The specific

group in which individuals find themselves depends on the case. Thus, ROC's reaction to "Vive le Québec libre!" was the same as its attitude to the 1980 referendum — unanimous and negative. Even "friends" were outraged by what seemed a totally improper intrusion by a head of state into the internal affairs of a friendly country. And the implication that Quebec was not free was offensive to those who valued Canada's democratic institutions and traditions.

Sometimes opinions change, though the volatility of opinion in ROC varies by issue. It tends to be fairly consistent on constitutional questions and assessments of the Quebec nationalist movement. On the other hand, "domestic" Quebec policies are usually met with initial hostility but come to be accepted once their rationale is made clear. Even the 1976 election of an *indépendantiste* Quebec government, which was initially received with horror, came to be accepted as an unfortunate reality.

The air traffic dispute similarly shows how public opinion can come around after an initial hostile reaction. Extreme, provocative positions are not always sustained and may give way to greater tolerance and understanding. One reason why opinion in ROC became so inflamed over the air traffic dispute was that powerful and determined interest groups (unions, in this case) succeeded in presenting their arguments in a manner that elicited great public support. Their access to influential members of the government did not hurt, but what really put the wind in their sails was an inflammatory press. This is not an isolated example. Any issue affecting relations between Quebec and ROC creates an instant opportunity for individuals and groups with vested interests, and an exploitative media, to turn the situation to their advantage. However, our country's political culture and political leadership help reduce the duration of these somewhat artificial crises. Unless we allow deeply irritating issues to fester, time usually attenuates many of the differences plaguing us.

The essay dealing with Quebec's efforts to grapple with the language question reinforces some of these points. ROC and Quebec Anglophones and Allophones at first expressed profound opposition to Bill 101 and its successors. The grounds for their opposition were numerous: the bill was deemed unfair, coercive, xenophobic, economically damaging and so on. Even many "friends" were dismayed: just when the rest of the country was embarking on a grand project of bilingualism, Quebec was turning itself into a unilingual province.

But despite these and other devastating criticisms, a very large number of observers were eventually persuaded that some of the adopted measures were necessary if Quebec was to maintain and strengthen its identity. The end result is that even the rancour caused by that intensely emotional issue has largely dissipated in an atmosphere of comprehension and accommodation, or at least acceptance of the inevitable.

ROC's perception of the October Crisis was quite different. Condemnation of the FLQ was universal, since resorting to terrorism under the conditions then prevailing in Canada was seen as totally indefensible. Numerous other avenues for dissent were available. Thus the imposition of the War Measures Act was initially welcomed by the vast majority of the public, though the political left expressed strong opposition. As often happens when governments overreact to a crisis, a cooler perspective slowly gained ground and important questions were raised about the civil-liberty implications of the intervention. Significantly, one of the first serious academic studies of the October Crisis, an attack against the Trudeau intervention, was written by a well-known English-speaking political scientist, Denis Smith.[3]

In its long-term impact, the creation of a "made in Canada" constitution in 1982 was by far the most significant event in the 15-year period covered by chapter 4. It strikingly revealed how far apart Quebec and ROC had moved since the 1960s. English Canada was generally buoyed by what it saw as the successful conclusion to many years of constitutional wrangling and the adoption of a law containing such innovative features as the Charter of Rights and Freedoms. But Quebec was dismayed by the way the final compromise was achieved and by some of the elements built into the new constitutional order, in particular the provisions affecting language rights and the amending formula that deprived Quebec of its traditional veto.

Although the public seemed to accept the outcome of the negotiations and was no doubt impressed by the Queen's ceremonial signing of the new document on Parliament Hill, not everyone was satisfied. The group we have labelled "friends" included many individuals who were knowledgeable about conditions and attitudes in Quebec; they realized that the denial of Quebec's demands could not endure and would ultimately cause considerable grief and instability. The highly respected Institute of Intergovernmental Relations at Queen's University, which had been tracking federalism and constitutional developments in Canada since the Quiet Revolution, published a series of bipartisan studies and commentaries, *And No One Cheered*.[4]

The foreboding generated by the events of 1981-82 stood in stark contrast to the optimism that had swept Canada in the mid-1960s. When Canada marked the Centennial of Confederation in 1967, the necessity of redefining Canada in the wake of the Quiet Revolution was beginning to be widely recognized. This

was the heyday of the dualist vision of Canada. Expo '67 captured the imagination of the whole country, as it seemed to offer a concrete example of how Anglophones and Francophones could work together successfully. The symbiosis of that event was seen as a harbinger of an imaginative and creative joint future. De Gaulle's visit during Expo grated on the nerves of many people partly because it contrasted so harshly with this upbeat mood.

A view of Expo '67, an event embodying the optimistic outlook of the 1960s both in Quebec and throughout Canada. (NAC, PA168602)

The optimism of the mid- and late 1960s was reinforced by other developments. In Quebec, the Union Nationale's 1966 return to power under Daniel Johnson's leadership prompted renewed demands for substantial constitutional change. In ROC, a strong urge to accommodate Quebec developed, and several steps were taken to deal with the constitutional situation. But to the great consternation of Ontario Premier John Robarts, who had developed a strong commitment to the national unity cause, the federal government was unresponsive. Despite Ottawa's reticence, Robarts organized the 1967 Confederation of Tomorrow Conference in Toronto, which brought most of the principal players together (Ottawa sent only observers). Although it did not produce any solutions, the conference did shame Ottawa into activating the search for a new national accommodation. Consequently, a series of constitutional conferences was held, culminating in the Victoria Charter of 1971.

The conferences considered many proposals for a more flexible federal system that would expand provincial freedom of action through such devices as opting out of federal programs with compensation. While these proposals would benefit all interested provinces, the impetus for them came largely from the wish to satisfy Quebec. The apparent success of the Victoria talks brought relief to those who worried about meeting Quebec's needs, while Robert Bourassa's ultimate rejection of the Charter caused considerable disappointment.

The initial optimism largely dissipated in the following years, but hope springs eternal. In 1977, the Trudeau government appointed the Pepin-Robarts Task Force on Canadian Unity to hold hearings throughout the land and make recommendations for constitutional change. Its report was a remarkably sensitive and far-sighted document urging, among other things, a substantial degree of decentralization.[5] But its tenor was totally unacceptable to the Trudeau government and it had little impact on events. It was, however, an important indication that some "friends" in ROC were willing to go a long way toward accommodating Quebec. That these initiatives led nowhere (in part, of course, because, as Anglophones saw it, Quebec normally refused to accept such olive branches as were tendered to it) does not change the fact that some in ROC were striving to respond to Quebec's needs, ill-informed or unrealistic as these efforts may have been on occasion.

These examples partially correct the impression left by our case histories, that it was always the ROC side that was unyielding and bloody-minded in instances involving a difference of opinion. Although the record contains plenty of evidence of incomprehension, miscomprehension and self-absorbed thoughtlessness on the part of English Canadians, there has been more goodwill in Canada than a concentrated reading of the essays would lead one to believe. This is particularly true of the constitutional issue, where the main players have been politicians and governments schooled in seeking accommodation and compromise. But Canada being what it is, regional bias and other factors have affected the attitudes of groups and individuals to changes in Quebec and to the resulting redefinition of its needs. Although there are exceptions, the western provinces generally have expressed greater scepticism than Ontario, and people in the higher income and educational brackets have usually exhibited greater interest in, and sympathy for, nationalist stirrings in Quebec.

In sum, the 15-year period covered in this chapter witnessed a series of major confrontations between Quebec and ROC. The basic position of the protagonists was simple: Quebec was restless and seeking to redefine its place in Canada and the world; ROC was reasonably satisfied with the status quo but ready to make adjustments, within limits. Those adjustments did not go far enough to satisfy successive governments of Quebec. While ROC was quite willing to adapt during this period, it came up short, leaving a legacy that will have to be confronted in the future.

Beyond the Quiet Revolution

I T IS IMPOSSIBLE TO LOOK BACK AT THE 1960S AND 1970S IN QUEBEC WITHOUT REFER-
ring to the Quiet Revolution. Contemporary Quebec history is often divided
into three periods: pre-Quiet Revolution, Quiet Revolution and post-Quiet
Revolution. And the Quiet Revolution casts just as long a shadow over contemporary Canadian history as it does over Quebec history: It changed the relationship between Quebec and the rest of Canada, as well as the perceptions
Quebecers and other Canadians have of each other.

Like almost any other revolution, whether violent or "quiet," Quebec's Quiet
Revolution was neither sudden nor spontaneous. It went through a period of incu-
bation — the pre-Quiet Revolution — the history of which is no less important
than subsequent periods to our understanding of Quebec's past and present. The
Second World War undoubtedly ushered in the pre-Quiet Revolution. That war
changed the horizons, environments and living conditions of those Quebecers who
served in the armed forces at home and abroad as well as those who remained civil-
ians. One of the more significant changes was that women were given the chance
to work outside the home, mostly in factories. Moreover, in 1940, women won the
right to vote in provincial elections, over the strong objections of the Catholic clergy, many intellectuals and other public figures.

In a more immediate sense, however, the Quiet Revolution was developing
in two interrelated settings: the trade union movement and intellectual circles.
Scorned and ridiculed by those in power, trade unionists and intellectuals interacted with and supported each other, developing a sort of symbiotic relationship.
Thus, when the war ended, the Laval University's faculty of social sciences began
training a new generation of union leaders concurrent with a new generation of

social science researchers, as well as a number of intellectuals who would play a major role in various sectors of Quebec and Canadian life throughout the second half of the 20th century. Certain media, particularly the newspaper *Le Devoir* and Radio-Canada, welcomed these dissenters and gave them a voice. This was an appreciable feat, since the Duplessis government, which remained in power by relying on an essentially conservative and backward-looking ideology and politics, ruled over Quebec during most of the period. The Quebec Liberal Party, then in opposition, also provided a forum for the promoters of more modern thinking.

Those who lived through this era will never forget what took place in 1959-60 following the death of Maurice Duplessis. Jean-Paul Sauvé, Duplessis' successor as premier and leader of the Union Nationale Party, had until then been known only as Duplessis' faithful lieutenant. People were therefore surprised when he quickly distanced himself from his former leader and showed an astonishing openness toward all the new currents of thought to which the party had been systematically closed. His repeated use of the words "from now on..." to mark each new change in direction has remained notorious. This was a great embarrassment to the Liberal Party as it watched its program being taken over, piece by piece, by the government. However, Mr. Sauvé's premature death, after only three months as head of the government, guaranteed victory for Jean Lesage's Liberal Party in the 1960 election. Had Mr. Sauvé lived, autumn 1959 would have been the undisputed beginning of the Quiet Revolution.

René Lévesque, minister of natural resources in the Jean Lesage cabinet, presents his hydro-electric nationalization project. (*La Presse*)

Jean Lesage governed from 1960 to 1966. Several major changes and achievements characterized those six years, notably the nationalization of electricity and the creation of Hydro-Québec, and the establishment of the Caisse de dépôt et placement (Deposit and Investment Fund). That period also saw the reform of the education system, from kindergarten to university. These actions were in line with the motto "Masters in Our Own House" adopted by the governing Liberal Party. Montreal was chosen as the site for the 1967 World Fair and construction of the Montreal subway system, the *métro*, also began. During those years, a climate of optimism and unprecedented collective self-esteem reigned in Quebec — anything seemed possible and the future held only promise.

The events of 1967 were part of that trend and, thus, still part of the Quiet Revolution. Quebecers took less notice of the centenary of Confederation than the rest of Canada. The success of Expo '67 and the opening of the *métro* received almost all of the attention. Charles de Gaulle's visit to Quebec and his triumphal procession from Quebec to Montreal, ending with his amazing declaration "Vive le Québec libre!," were part of that euphoric atmosphere. Although not everyone in the province approved of de Gaulle's gesture, there is no doubt that his visit, and perhaps even the federal government's rebuff of a man of de Gaulle's stature, rekindled and strengthened Quebecers' pride.

However, we should not paint an overly idyllic portrait of those years. Concurrent with Jean Lesage's Liberal team taking power and the beginning of the Quiet Revolution, a small group of young activists founded a Quebec independence movement, the Rassemblement pour l'indépendance nationale (RIN), which was destined to have an unexpected future. But that event went virtually unnoticed and gave no inkling of the coming political upheaval in Quebec which it was nevertheless announcing. Other young people founded *Parti pris*, an *indépendantiste* and socialist magazine intended to counterbalance *Cité libre*, which in their eyes was outdated. Still other young people — though far fewer — joined forces in a clandestine radical movement, the Front de libération du Québec (FLQ), which in 1963 started to set off bombs. Those first violent acts eventually led to the kidnapping of James Cross and Pierre Laporte, triggering what came to be called the 1970 October Crisis.

Thus, the Quiet Revolution was neither completely harmonious nor all encompassing. Some people were actively and enthusiastically involved in the changes taking place, while others, especially the young, thought the changes too slow, modest or even ill-conceived. Many people were so worried or bothered by the changes that they mounted effective resistance to them — so effective, in fact, it led to the 1966 defeat of the Lesage government. On the student scene, "baby boomers" entered the fray, protesting against anything to do with the "system," a term that was applied to practically anything established. Those young people provided a rich source of recruitment for supporters of an independent Quebec.

A final point: the Quiet Revolution was launched and led by francophone Quebecers; Anglophones did not take an active part. They might have been sympathetic, but they were also worried. They felt threatened, somewhat justifiably, by the motto "Masters in Our Own House" insofar as it was aimed at the anglophone economic establishment. Moreover, the creation of a Department of Education as part of the education reforms would reduce the substantial autonomy hitherto enjoyed by the network of both Catholic and Protestant English-language schools. The anglophone community's reaction to this major reform was more ambivalent than enthusiastic.

The 1970 October Crisis can be reasonably seen as the end of the Quiet Revolution. In the history of Quebec, the October Crisis — which was in reality brought on by a very small core of people — was an earthquake that shook the very foundations of Quebec society and sent shock waves through Canada. The crisis was aggravated by the panic and fear that took hold of political leaders, and by the climate of civil war created by the arrest and incarceration of nearly 500 leaders from various sectors of Quebec society.

The *indépendantistes* were generally embarrassed by the actions of the FLQ and kept their distance from it. They saw the FLQ as radical and violent, doing more harm than good to their cause both internationally and in Quebec. Moreover, the Trudeau government clearly used the kidnappings and general state of panic to discredit the independence movement by identifying it with violence, in an attempt to wipe it out for good.

But the Trudeau government's hopes were frustrated. The independence movement continued to grow, culminating in the 1976 election of the Parti Québécois. This is why Premier Bourassa conducted his entire political career, from start to finish, with his eyes riveted on the actions of nationalists and *indépendantistes*. Perhaps he was somewhat of a nationalist himself, but he was primarily driven by the objective of promoting the economic prosperity of Quebec and Quebecers. From time to time he had to take into account and, if need be, respond to the political pressures exerted by the nationalist movement.

His apparent reluctance with regard to the Victoria Charter can be understood in the light of those pressures, as can the 1974 language law that, for the first time, made French the official language of Quebec. The ministerial staff Bourassa recruited in 1970 included nationalist figures whose influence undoubtedly carried some weight.

It was in the post-Quiet Revolution period that the language issue came to play a dominant role in Quebec political life. It exploded violently under Union Nationale rule with the crisis in Saint-Léonard in 1968-69, and it was a constant thorn in the side of the Bourassa government from its election in 1970 to its defeat in 1976 — a defeat undoubtedly due in part to the language issue. The adoption of the Charter of the French Language, or Bill 101, in the summer of 1977 marked the high point of the Péquiste government's first mandate. The language issue even provoked a totally unexpected crisis among airline pilots, a group thought so "anglicized" as to be essentially oblivious to the widespread use of English in their profession.

Outside of Quebec, and in some circles within it, the language question was seen as an obsession. However, one must understand that French Canada's unique identity had been built, in the 19th century, on three pillars: French law, the Catholic religion and the French language. The first was eclipsed in the early 20th century and the decline of the Catholic Church's influence considerably weakened the second. Only language remained. Then, during the 1960s, that suddenly seemed threatened, not by Anglophones but by the ethnic minorities, nearly all of whom opted for English schools, the English language and integration into Quebec's English-speaking minority. The future of the French language thus became an issue of power. In the only province in which it formed a majority, the French-Canadian community was in imminent danger of losing its political power. Thus, *realpolitik* provides the ultimate explanation for the turmoil over Quebec language laws from 1969 until the present. It also explains the constantly expressed nationalist fear that Bill 101 is being eroded and weakened by the efforts of Anglophones to convince the courts and the government to eliminate what they see as "irritants."

For some, the Charter of the French Language has become a symbol of the new Quebec; for others, especially Anglophones and Allophones, it symbolizes social and political ostracism. But it must be recognized that without this law relations between Francophones and ethnic communities of Quebec would have been headed toward a confrontation that might very well have led to tragedy. In this respect, Bill 101, despite the dissension it may have created, has helped bring about relative social peace.

"Vive le Québec libre!" (1967)

I N THE SUMMER OF 1967, CANADA WAS IN THE MIDST OF THE CENTENNIAL CELEBRA-
tions and Expo '67 was in full swing in Montreal. Among the heads of state
expected for the occasion was Charles de Gaulle, President of the French
Republic. General de Gaulle's obvious sympathy for Quebec's nationalist aspirations and the privileged relations that were then developing between France and
Quebec increasingly annoyed the federal government and made it anxious about
his visit.[1] Moreover, the Quebec government had sent the French President a

General de Gaulle on the balcony of Montreal city hall during his controversial 1967 visit. (Malak, NAC, C6013)

personal invitation without first consulting the federal authorities. Not only did de Gaulle agree to come to Canada as a guest of Quebec, he had even insisted on starting his visit in Quebec City rather than Ottawa, a breach of diplomatic protocol.

The purpose of de Gaulle's trip was to formally celebrate the renewed ties between France and Quebec and to express friendship between France and Canada according to protocol.[2] But it did not work out that way. On July 23, 1967, when de Gaulle stepped off the Colbert cruiser at L'Anse-au-foulon near Quebec City, his reception was euphoric. The next day, the excitement continued to build as de Gaulle left Quebec City and headed for Montreal. His procession along the Chemin du Roi was greeted in each town along the way by loudly cheering crowds. As the General got closer to Montreal, his speeches grew warmer and the crowds more enthusiastic.[3] The day culminated with his arrival in Montreal, where he addressed the public from the balcony of city hall. Comparing the atmosphere he had encountered that day to that of the liberation of France, de Gaulle exclaimed before the excited crowd, "Vive le Québec libre!" (Long live a free Quebec)

as i recall

In the spring of 1967, the visit of the French president was already starting to attract attention. People questioned the true intentions of the General in coming to Canada.[4] Immersed in an atmosphere of national pride surrounding the Centennial celebrations, English Canada took de Gaulle's speech as an affront to Canada. The next day, Ottawa informed the General by communiqué that his words were "unacceptable to the Canadian people and its government...The people of Canada are free. Every province of Canada is free. Canadians do not need to be liberated."[5]

Lester B. Pearson, the prime minister at the time, described his reaction in his memoirs:

I could hardly believe my ears when I heard the words he uttered: "Vive le Québec libre." This was the

slogan of separatists dedicated to the dismember-
ment of that Canada whose independence de Gaulle
had wished to see assured only a few years before
when he proposed a toast to my health in Paris.[6]

De Gaulle's declaration brought a swift, angry reaction from
English Canadians. Within hours, the federal government was inun-
dated with telegrams and telephone calls denouncing de Gaulle's
behaviour and calling for his expulsion from the country.
"Monstrous! It is monstrous that anybody, let alone an invited and
privileged guest, should encourage any person at all 'to destroy
Canada'," raged *The Globe and Mail*.[7] The English-Canadian political
elite and press were unanimous in condemning the French
President's remarks. Editorialists called his speech misplaced and
viewed it as external interference in Canadian affairs.[8] ◆

si je me souviens bien

Many Quebecers perceived the French president's visit as the first
official visit from a "member of the family," comparable to a visit
from a member of the royal family for English Canadians. While not
all Quebecers shared the General's enthusiasm, most reacted
favourably to his famous declaration. Historian Jean-Claude Robert
observes, "Quebecers did not...disclaim the General's gesture; they
were rather pleased to see the cat being set among the pigeons in
Ottawa."[9] Premier Daniel Johnson, for his part, came to the defence
of his guest:

> Courageous and lucid, President de Gaulle indeed
> got to the bottom of the matter with us. Quebec was
> not offended...We will never forget that, in words
> touching the hearts of all Quebecers, the President
> of the French Republic raised the problem of the dis-
> tinct identity of Quebec and its immense effort to

assert itself. Quebec has never been a province like
the others, and while some Canadians still find this
basic fact difficult to accept, the whole world now
knows about it.[10]

On the other hand, Jean Lesage, leader of the Quebec
Liberal party, denounced de Gaulle's speech and blamed it on
Premier Johnson. This stance led to the departure of François
Aquin, one of his MNAs. The head of the Rassemblement pour
l'indépendance nationale (RIN), Pierre Bourgault, was jubilant over
what he saw as de Gaulle's endorsement of Quebec independence.
A CROP poll taken less than two months after the incident revealed
that a majority of Quebecers were happy with the General's visit
and with the "Vive le Québec libre" speech. That majority saw his
declaration as not so much an invitation to seek independence as to
"promote the freedom that Quebec already had within Canada."[11] It
was in that spirit, recalling the Canadian reality in which Quebec
was evolving, that the Montreal mayor, Jean Drapeau, chose to
respond to the General's intervention: "We are profoundly attached
to our vast country and for us this is the best way to serve French
culture and French life."[12] ◆

By proclaiming "Vive le Québec libre!," General de Gaulle threw Quebec
onto the international stage, making its name suddenly known all over the world.
The Quebec independence movement came out of the episode stronger, fortified
by its new-found visibility. Only months after the balcony speech, René Lévesque
left the Liberal Party of Quebec to found the Mouvement souveraineté-association
(MSA), which would later become the Parti Québécois. Ever since de Gaulle's
visit, Quebec sovereignists have fostered the hope that France would quickly recognize Quebec's sovereign status following a declaration of independence.

More than 30 years later, General de Gaulle's visit continues to arouse very
strong reactions in English Canada. Thus, in 1997, many indignant Canadians
denounced both the Quebec government's decision to erect a monument to de

Gaulle and France's announcement that it was to issue a stamp commemorating de Gaulle's controversial declaration.[13] On the other hand, General de Gaulle does not create the same fervour in Quebec as he did in 1967. In 1997, 51.5 percent of Quebecers were of the opinion that his speech changed Quebec's political destiny "little or not at all," compared to 39.2 percent who believed that it contributed "a lot or a fair amount" to the advancement of Quebec.[14]

The October Crisis
(1970)

I N OCTOBER 1970, THE FRONT DE LIBÉRATION DU QUÉBEC (FLQ) KIDNAPPED JAMES Cross and Pierre Laporte, an act that for the first time brought political terrorism to centre-stage in Canada. Inspired by Third World struggles for de-colonialization, the FLQ advocated an extreme left-wing vision of revolutionary "liberation" for Quebecers.

The FLQ was responsible for a bombing campaign, mainly in Montreal, which dated back to March 1963. They targeted sites such as government, army and corporate buildings, as well as letterboxes in anglophone Westmount. Although the bombings intensified in 1969-1970, the FLQ remained a marginal part of a widespread atmosphere of social protest in Quebec associated with labour and student unrest and the rise of the sovereignist movement.

The October Crisis began on October 5, 1970, with the kidnapping of British diplomat James Richard Cross. The FLQ cell holding Cross demanded that its political manifesto be broadcast and that 23 imprisoned FLQ members be set free; they also demanded $500,000 and safe passage to Cuba or Algeria. The manifesto, a diatribe against the capitalist exploitation of Quebecers, was broadcast on radio and television[1] and the kidnappers were offered safe passage out of the country, but federal and provincial authorities refused to meet the other conditions.

The crisis deepened on October 10 when a second cell kidnapped the Quebec minister of labour, Pierre Laporte. On October 15, the Bourassa government requested army reinforcements for the police and, that night, agreed to Ottawa's imposition of the War Measures Act.[2] The government's emergency powers would be allowed to lapse on April 30, 1971.

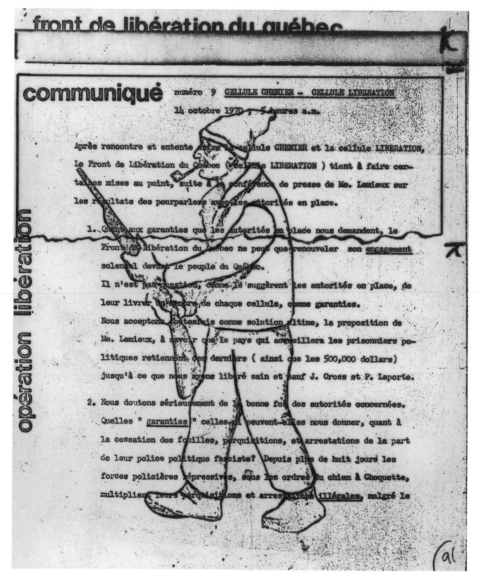

Communiqué No. 9 of the FLQ, dated October 14, 1970. The drawing depicts an 1837 rebel (a "Patriote") and is based on a painting by Henri Julien. (NAC, PA 129833, *Montreal Star* Fund)

The Act was invoked on the grounds that a state of "apprehended insurrection" existed in Quebec, and was justified by letters from Premier Bourassa and the Montreal city administration requesting that emergency measures be taken. Prime Minister Trudeau and his justice minister, John Turner, pointed to "the state of confusion that existed in the province of Quebec" and an "erosion of the public will" in justifying their actions in the House of Commons.[3]

Regulations issued under the Act banned the FLQ and made membership in the organization punishable by up to five years in prison. Approximately 500 persons were arrested under those regulations; most were freed without being charged after spending up to three weeks in detention.

On October 17, Pierre Laporte was found dead in the trunk of a car. Several weeks later, Cross was freed after his hiding place was discovered; his abductors negotiated safe passage to Cuba. Laporte's kidnappers were captured at the end of December, accused of murder and sequestration, found guilty and sentenced to up to life in prison.[4]

Canada was not prepared for the crisis caused by the FLQ. English Canadians viewed their country as a "peaceable kingdom." They were becoming familiar with the pressure for social and political change in Quebec, but had welcomed the April 1970 election of Robert Bourassa's Liberal government as a reaffirmation of Quebecers' commitment to federalism.[5]

Shocked by the appearance of terrorism in Canada, English Canadians generally supported the federal government's hard-line approach. On October 14, Premier Robarts of Ontario publicly rejected the idea of negotiating with the FLQ:

By Jove, this has got to be a law-abiding country where you can bring your children up without fear...the demands are wrong – morally wrong and socially wrong – we have to stand and fight. It's war – total war.[6]

The Canadian Institute of Public Affairs conducted a national poll on October 18 (just after the imposition of the War Measures Act) and found that 51 percent of Canadians felt the government's approach was "about right," while 37 percent believed the government was not "tough enough."[7] Most English-Canadian newspapers supported the imposition of the War Measures Act but acknowledged that it raised grave concerns about civil liberties.

Some members of the Canadian left, the most prominent of whom was New Democratic Party (NDP) leader Tommy Douglas, opposed the Act on the grounds of civil liberties. In the House of Commons, Douglas accused the government of "using a sledgehammer to crack a peanut."[8] Lorne Nystrom, one of 16 NDP members to vote against the Act, later recalled:

> The pressure was unbelievably intense. If you were against the act, you were made to feel un-Canadian. For months after I voted against it, I was tremendously unpopular in my riding. I would have been wiped out if there had been an election any time then. I think the polls showed that we dropped to nine per cent as a direct result of that vote.[9] ◆

si je me souviens bien

As in English Canada, Quebec opinion favoured harsh measures against the FLQ, with public opinion polls registering up to 85 percent support for the imposition of the War Measures Act.[10] As Raymond Garneau, then Quebec finance minister recalls,

> The whole population was very nervous and everybody wanted to see action taken; they wanted something to be done. It was a big shock. There was also

the fact that the premier was very young; besides
being young, he looked young, and a certain nervous-
ness had been created because of that.[11]

In the early stages of the crisis, some nationalists expressed
sympathy for the FLQ's objectives, if not its means. René Lévesque
took pains to distance the PQ from the FLQ's use of violence, while
pointing out that the crisis underscored the urgent need to address
social and economic injustices in Quebec.[12] Student rallies were held
in support of the FLQ. Sympathetic declarations were issued by the
Front d'action politique (FRAP), a municipal coalition contesting the
Montreal civic election, and by the executive committee of the
Conseil des syndicats nationaux (CSN), a trade union federation
headed by Michel Chartrand. A group of prominent intellectuals,
including René Lévesque and *Le Devoir* editor-in-chief Claude Ryan,
issued a much-discussed call for the government to meet the FLQ's
demand that political prisoners be freed.[13]

While most Quebec newspapers, including *Le Soleil* and *La
Presse*, backed the government's hard line, *Le Devoir* struck a more

Curious children gaze at Canadian soldiers deployed at the request of the mayor of
Montreal and the premier of Quebec. (NAC, PA129838)

ambiguous note that was more in line with the mixed feelings of
Quebec intellectuals. *Le Devoir* supported the Bourassa government's decision to call in the army for the purposes of reinforcing
the civil authorities but opposed the War Measures Act. Claude
Ryan would later write: "The scope of the War Measures Act...with
its potentially far-reaching powers, greatly exceeded the scale of
the problem the authorities were facing."[14] Ryan condemned
Bourassa's decision to "subordinate" his government to Ottawa as
contrary to the province's preceding 10 years of political evolution.[15]

These critiques did not find strong support among the
Quebec public, particularly after the murder of Laporte. The hard-
line Drapeau administration was re-elected in the November
Montreal civic election, winning 92 percent of the vote and every
seat on council. By March of 1971, a Laval University study showed a
more complex breakdown of Quebec opinion: 35 percent of those
polled expressed their complete approval for the actions of the federal government during the crisis, 31 percent partial approval and
23 percent complete disapproval.[16] ◆

The thesis that Quebec was in a state of insurrection was controversial
from the outset. Claude Ryan noted that despite the thousands of searches undertaken during the crisis, the sum total of weapons found was 33 firearms and 21
other weapons of various sorts.[17] Nor did the special powers speed the release of
the hostages: imposition of the War Measures Act appears to have led directly to
Laporte's execution[18] and may have slowed the search for Cross by diverting
resources away from police work.[19]

The federal government subsequently blamed the RCMP's Security Service
for having provided inadequate intelligence on Quebec separatism. Political scientist Reg Whitaker has shown that this inadequacy led directly to "a more aggressive and intrusive" form of surveillance of the sovereignist movement during the
1970s, including various illegal acts committed by the RCMP.[20] The ensuing public scandals caused the federal and provincial governments to establish commis-

sions of inquiry into RCMP wrongdoing. The upshot was the creation, in 1984, of the civilian Canadian Security Intelligence Service (CSIS).

While the Trudeau government may have hoped that its actions during the October Crisis would halt the rise of Quebec separatism,[21] the PQ's progression was not significantly reversed. In the February 1971 by-election to fill Laporte's seat, the PQ vote held at the April 1970 level, and in the 1973 general election its share of the popular vote rose by seven percent.[22] Three years later, the PQ would form a majority government.

The Victoria Charter (1971)

A T THE START OF THE 1970S, THE PATRIATION OF THE CANADIAN CONSTITUTION from Great Britain had been discussed in Canada for over 40 years. Federal-provincial agreement had previously been reached in 1964 (the Fulton-Favreau formula) but had fallen apart when Quebec's Premier Lesage withdrew his support in the face of strong opposition in his province.

In the wake of the momentum created by the Royal Commission on Bilingualism and Biculturalism, a new round of constitutional negotiations was undertaken in 1968 and, in June 1971, the First Ministers reached a tentative agreement known as the Victoria Charter.

The fruit of a three-year intergovernmental review, the process had been slowed down by provincial demands and, most importantly, by the fundamentally opposed visions of the country held by the Trudeau Liberals and by Quebec's Union Nationale Party.[1] Ottawa's priority in the Victoria round of constitutional negotiations was to achieve constitutional protection for basic human rights and linguistic minority rights. Questions concerning division of power were low on its agenda, whereas for the Union Nationale government, elected in 1966 under the slogan "Égalité ou indépendance" (Equality or Independence), they were of primary importance. The 1970 election of Robert Bourassa's Liberals in Quebec led to a breakthrough.

The Victoria Charter comprised 61 articles, covering: basic political and language rights; provincial participation in the nomination of Supreme Court justices; a commitment to work against regional disparities; an amendment to the distribution of powers in the social policy field providing for concurrent jurisdiction with provincial paramountcy over family, youth and occupational training allowances; and, most importantly, a formula for amending the Constitution, allocating vetoes over constitutional change on a regional basis, including a veto for Quebec. The latter proved to be a more flexible amending formula than the Fulton-Favreau formula proposed in 1964, which required provincial unanimity for any change affecting provincial jurisdiction.[2]

The agreement reached at Victoria included a proviso that each government would notify Ottawa of its acceptance of the Charter within 12 days. All provinces except Saskatchewan (which elected a new government in the intervening days) and Quebec complied. Premier Bourassa, under intense pressure from virtually all elite opinion in Quebec, and from within his own Liberal government, announced his rejection of the agreement, arguing that the Charter's language on social policy jurisdiction was too vague. Quebec's decision effectively ended this round of constitutional negotiations.

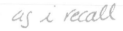
as i recall

The search for a new amending formula to permit patriation rallied broad support in English Canadian provinces but all rejected formal special status for Quebec.[3] During the negotiations leading to the Victoria agreement, their concerns tended to be economic in nature, mainly dealing with regional disparities and fiscal federalism. Even though Alberta adopted a stance similar to Quebec's, calling for full provincial control over social policy and advocating an end to shared-cost programs, the anglophone provinces remained "bystanders for the most part...[feeling] little pressure to come to agreement and incapable of mediating what was essentially a battle among Quebecers, in Quebec City and Ottawa, about their future."[4]

The prevailing attitude about constitutional reform in English Canada, clearly distinct from the situation in Quebec, was generally one of apathy.[5] But the possibility of entrenching minority language rights, which had been a recommendation of the Royal

Commission on Bilingualism and Biculturalism, ran into strong opposition from the western provinces, led by Alberta and British
Columbia.[6] The sense that the federal government's agenda was
being driven by "the Quebec question" was a source of western
alienation. Alberta's Premier Strom warned at Victoria that "the
West is particularly sensitive to the federal government's appearance of continually giving the concerns raised by certain provinces
top priority while ignoring concerns raised by others."[7]

The achievement of an agreement at Victoria was generally
hailed by the English-Canadian press as a breakthrough in Canada's
constitutional history[8]; eight provinces swiftly adopted it. Premier
Davis of Ontario, for example, told his legislature that the Victoria
agreement exemplified "the Canadian genius for compromise" and
the Canadian talent for forging unanimity from diverse opinions.[9]
The failure of the Victoria round was thus a bitter disappointment
for English Canadians:

> We have been foolish in Canada, and weak. With the
> best intentions, and feeling that Quebec has been
> short-changed in the past, we have submitted to
> round after round of gouging, hoping to salvage the
> country. But nothing grows strong by yielding indefi-
> nitely, wrote *The Globe and Mail*.[10] ◆

si je me souviens bien

Quebec's refusal to accept the Victoria Charter reflected its consistent demands for greater devolution of powers. In his opening statements at the February 1969 conference, Premier Jean-Jacques
Bertrand told his English-Canadian counterparts,

> What is important for French Canadians in Quebec is
> not to be able to speak their language anywhere in
> Canada, but to be able, collectively, to live in French,

to build a society in their image. That is possible
only if the Quebec government has the powers necessary for the tasks the population expects it to
carry out.[11]

From the outset, one of Quebec's priorities was to clarify the
matter of jurisdiction over social policy, both in the name of efficient service delivery[12] and because there was, in Claude Forget's
words, "a feeling that Quebec had a somewhat more enlightened
agenda than the rest of Canada."[13] Social Affairs Minister Claude
Castonguay, co-author of the Castonguay-Nepveu Report on Health
and Social Welfare (1967-1972), which called for "an integrated global policy" on income security,[14] was a key advocate of Quebec's gaining control over social policy formulation.

When the Victoria Charter produced only modest, and
ambiguous, reinforcement of Quebec's existing jurisdiction in social
policy — while confirming the federal government's right to legislate
in the area — it did not measure up to Quebec's expectations of
clear-cut devolution, which it had defended throughout years of
negotiation. Quebec premiers had traditionally refused to accept
patriation without concessions from Ottawa on the division of powers.[15] Boismenu and Rocher described the Charter as "a blunt
refusal, both on the question of recognizing Quebec's nationhood,
which was prized by Johnson and Bertrand, and on the question of
a partial and selective reorganization of jurisdictions, which could
have appealed, as a last resort, to Bourassa."[16]

In the days following the Victoria conference, a common
front of Saint-Jean-Baptiste societies and labour federations
announced a campaign against the Victoria Charter under the
provocative motto, "Proclamation to the People of Quebec: The
Days of Conscription are Back."[17] Quebec's opposition parties and
editorialists were unanimous in their condemnation of the
Charter. Even the English-language newspaper *The Gazette* joined
in the opposition:

Si je me souviens bien

> An affirmative answer...would signify the acceptance
> in principle of a revised Constitution that still fails to
> take account of the fact that Canada is, after all, a
> country composed of two distinct societies.[18] ◆

The failure of the Victoria Charter had long-lasting effects. The mobilization against its adoption in Quebec, followed by the backlash in the rest of the country, highlighted English Canada's and French Canada's divergent visions of federalism: "Not since the Second World War have the sociological and political differences between Quebec and English Canada been so pronounced."[19]

Bourassa's apparent about-face contributed to English Canada's cynicism about negotiating with Quebec, a reaction which had already surfaced in the wake of Premier Lesage's rejection of the 1964-1965 Fulton-Favreau agreement.[20]

Given the unfruitful constitutional episodes that followed Victoria, many Quebec federalists have since regretted Bourassa's decision.[21] The veto Quebec would have acquired in that agreement was lost in the 1982 constitutional round, and, while Jean Chrétien's Liberal government did extend a veto to Quebec in 1995, this has yet to be entrenched in the Constitution.

Quebec's Language Laws (1969-1994)

T HE LANGUAGE LAWS PROTECTING THE STATUS OF FRENCH IN QUEBEC HAVE BEEN AT the centre of the debates generated by Quebec nationalism for decades. During the 1960s, the declining fertility rate of Francophones and the continuing high rate of immigrant integration into the English-speaking community raised serious concerns among Quebec Francophones. At the same time, the traditional Anglophone domination of the Quebec economy was increasingly coming into question. Nationalist groups such as the Saint-Jean-Baptiste society and the Rassemblement pour l'indépendance nationale (RIN) articulated demands for state language policies in favour of French.[1] As early as 1961, the Quebec Liberal Party (QLP) created the French Language Bureau, now officially called the Office de la langue française (OLF)[2], and by 1966 the QLP promised to make French "the principal language of work and communication in Quebec."[3]

The first significant legislative intervention on language was spurred by a 1968-1969 controversy concerning access to English-language schools in Saint-Léonard, a Montreal suburb. Forced to act, the Union Nationale government proposed legislation guaranteeing parents freedom of choice between French and English schooling. The government also established the Commission of Inquiry on the Position of the French Language and on Language Rights in Quebec, also known as the Gendron Commission. In 1969, Bill 63, giving parents the right to send their children to English schools, while requiring graduates to possess a working knowledge of French, outraged many Francophones. Large protest rallies and student "teach-ins" in Montreal and Quebec City accompanied the bill's passage in the National Assembly.[4]

Demonstration in support of the French language in 1971. (ANQ, Québec-Presse Collection, P404, McGill-Front commun file)

The Gendron report, published in 1972, recommended that "the Quebec Government set itself the general goal of making French the common language of Quebecers."[5] The response of Robert Bourassa's Liberal government came in the form of Bill 22, passed in 1974. That legislation implemented the recommendation that French be made Quebec's official language but excluded the Commission's recommendation that English be granted the status of "national language." Thus, Bill 22 altered the implicit "equal status that French and English had held in Montreal and Quebec since Confederation."[6] The Bill also established the Régie de la langue française with the mandate to encourage the use of French in the private sector by requiring companies to obtain a "francization" certificate in order to obtain provincial government permits, licences or contracts. In the field of education, the Bill allowed for students to attend English public schools if they could demonstrate sufficient knowledge of the language in an entrance test.[7]

Bill 22 proved politically costly to Robert Bourassa's Liberals: many Anglophones switched their allegiance to the Union Nationale in the election of 1976 in protest of Bill 22, while francophone nationalists rejected it as insufficiently stringent.

Upon their victory in the 1976 election, the Parti Québécois, under the leadership of Camille Laurin, minister of state for cultural development, moved to strengthen Bill 22. Laurin's Charter of the French Language, adopted as Bill 101 in August 1977, was the result.

Bill 101 was broader than Bill 22, and firmer in its determination to make French "the language of government and the law" and "the normal and everyday language" in other domains. The preamble stated: "Being the distinctive language of a people that is French-speaking in its majority, the French language is the instrument by which that people has articulated its identity."[8] The status of French as Quebec's official language was strengthened in a variety of ways: French was the only language in which legislation would be written, presented and adopted in the National Assembly; it would be the sole language of most court proceedings; and local public institutions were to operate in French except where a majority of clients were non-francophones.

In the workplace, Bill 101 required that companies of 50 employees or more obtain a certificate of "francization." The Bill strengthened the right of individual employees to work in French and provided protection against linguistically based employer discrimination. In education, access to English-language schooling was restricted principally to children having at least one parent who had received primary school instruction in English in Quebec — the so-called "Quebec clause" — and children with a sibling already attending an English school. Immigrants arriving in Quebec would no longer have access to English schooling. Furthermore, in contrast to Bill 22, Bill 101's provisions applied to public schools *and* all private schools receiving subsidies from the province.[9] Finally, Bill 101 imposed French-only signage for commercial establishments. The law's enforcement was strengthened by the creation of a commission of surveillance, with a staff of inspectors, later named the Commission de protection de la langue française.

In 1983, following a lobbying campaign by members of the anglophone community, the PQ government amended the language legislation by way of Bill 57. These amendments protected the province's anglophone institutions and made concessions, such as allowing for English internal communications in those institutions. In 1986, the Liberal government adopted

Bill 142, which strengthened the rights of Anglophones to have access to English-language health and social services.

Most other modifications to the language regime have been responses to court decisions, generally in cases brought about by Anglo-Quebecers.[10] In 1979, the Supreme Court of Canada struck down as unconstitutional Bill 101's provisions regarding the use of French in the courts and legislature (contrary to section 133 of the Constitution Act, 1867, which guarantees the use of French and English in federal and Quebec courts, the Parliament of Canada and Quebec's legislative assembly). In 1984, after the Charter of Rights and Freedoms came into force, the Supreme Court of Canada determined that some of the provisions on education were inconsistent with section 23 of the Charter — the "Canada clause" — which protects official language minority rights. Children having at least one parent who had received primary instruction in English anywhere in Canada — not just Quebec — had the right to attend English schools.

The most controversial of the court decisions against Bill 101 were rendered on challenges to the sign law in the Ford and Devine cases of 1988. In those cases, the Supreme Court found obligatory unilingualism on signs to contravene the freedom-of-expression provisions of both the Quebec Charter of Human Rights and Freedoms and the Canadian Charter of Rights and Freedoms.[11]

The Bourassa government reacted by passing Bill 178, which upheld French unilingualism on external signs while permitting English on internal signs provided that French was predominant. These provisions were explicitly shielded from the Canadian Charter by invoking the "notwithstanding clause". When the five-year protection period ended, the Bourassa government enacted Bill 86 to amend the Charter of the French Language, adopting the compromise recommended by the Supreme Court in the Ford decision, which was that Quebec to require French predominance on signs while permitting other languages to be displayed as well. Bill 86 also brought Quebec's language laws into line with the 1979 and 1984 court decisions referred to above and abolished the Commission de protection de la langue française.

as i recall

Outside Quebec, Canadians have tended to view Quebec's language laws as a betrayal of the bilingualism project undertaken by the rest of the country. In 1974, after Robert Bourassa's Liberal government had adopted Bill 22, the *Globe and Mail* questioned the expeditious process used in adopting it and worried about its consequences for national unity: "Mr. Bourassa is tampering with Confederation in a most reckless way."[12]

Given the widely held perception that bilingualism was undertaken for Quebec's sake, the province appeared to English Canada to be "acting in bad faith" by "insisting on linguistic equality in the rest of Canada, but refusing to recognize it within its own territory."[13]

In 1977, with the adoption of the Charter of the French Language, politicians across the country expressed their regret and disappointment. Progressive Conservatives called on the government to test the constitutionality of the bill in the courts, while Liberal Senator David Steuart dubbed it a "shame."[14]

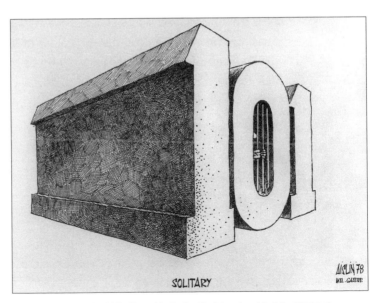

SOLITARY

Bill 101 as perceived by Aislin (Terry Mosher), editorial cartoonist at the Montreal newspaper *The Gazette*. (McCord Museum of Canadian History, M983.227.16)

For historian Donald Creighton, the law marked the end of an era:

A very well defined period in Canadian history has
come to an abrupt end. There is little point now in
waiting for the results of René Lévesque's promised
referendum. If Quebec's language bill is enacted in its
present form, Quebec will legally, as well as morally,
have declared its independence.[15]

The difference of opinion in Quebec and the rest of Canada
reflected contrasting visions of the country. Indeed, from 1982
onwards, the premise that the Quebec government had a mission to
promote the health of the French language, a collective good which
justified limitations on individual rights, contradicted the principle of
equality for all provinces which the rest of Canada largely adhered
and the new Charter culture, which holds that all Canadians have
identical rights.[16]

This difference in vision was crystallized in 1988 with the
adoption of Bill 178 by the Liberal government of Robert Bourassa, a
law that Stanley Hartt would later describe as "the virus that
destroyed Meech Lake."[17] Quebec's use of the notwithstanding clause
to exempt its sign law from the force of the Charter played a significant part in turning English-Canadian opinion against the Meech
Lake Accord and its recognition of Quebec as a "distinct society."[18] ◆

si je me souviens bien

For the francophone majority of Quebec, the stakes in the
province's language debates are very high. Their principal concern is their 240-year struggle against assimilation. Christian
Dufour argues that increased use of English in the province pro-
vokes an existential angst in Francophones, along the lines of
"There you go. Just what we have always feared — 'the unthinkable' — is happening after all."[19]

Thus, Bill 101 was of tremendous symbolic significance. Michel Plourde, former president of the Conseil de la langue française, recalls that it was greeted by nationalists, and indeed by most Francophones, as "the greatest moment in our history since the founding of Quebec."[20]

Sociologist Guy Rocher, a key contributor to the drafting of Bill 101, has remarked that the "francophonization" (the process of increasing the number of French speakers) and francization (the process of increasing the use of French) of the Quebec economy and work force were, in fact, the primary objectives of the legislation.[21] Language laws were not meant to stifle the expression of English culture in Quebec,"[22] as Camille Laurin explained when the Charter was adopted, but rather to ensure that French was the "common language that unites all Quebecers."[23] In 1996, the report of the Bélanger-Campeau Commission stated that Quebec's language laws reflected the natural wish of the majority to see its language used as the main means of communication in its territory.[24] Also, Quebecers view their language laws as a message to newcomers. In 1982, René Lévesque wrote,

> It is important that the face of Quebec be French at
> first sight, so as not to bring back the ambiguity that
> once prevailed, in the eyes of newcomers, as to the
> character of our society...In a way, each bilingual sign
> effectively says to the immigrant: "There are two lan-
> guages here, English and French, and you can choose
> the one you want."[25]

For a variety of reasons, then, the consensus among Quebec Francophones in support of state intervention to protect the French language is clear and has endured for over 20 years, through changes of government, negative court decisions and international disfavour. At the same time, there exist significant differences, even among nationalists, as to the degree of protection necessary; René Lévesque and Camille Laurin, for example, were not in perfect

agreement,[26] and over time public support for the language laws has
varied with the circumstance. Once the Charter of the French
Language was in place in the 1980s, for example, there was a certain
softening of support, with a sizeable group feeling that the PQ had
gone too far with its language legislation.[27] Polls showed that
Francophone support for French-only commercial signs dropped
from 66 percent in 1979 to 46 percent in 1985.[28]

Nonetheless, the essentials of the language laws have
enjoyed broad public support among Francophones, as well as
consensus among federalist and sovereignist politicians. This
support has been bolstered by perceived rebuffs, such as
Supreme Court decisions striking down elements of Bill 101 and
campaigns by English-rights groups in Quebec. In March 1996, a
poll conducted by Léger & Léger found that only 10 percent of
Francophones judged the current language laws too severe, compared to 60 percent who thought them "severe enough" and 25
percent "not severe enough."[29]

For Anglo-Quebecers, however, the language laws have significantly altered the political climate. For many Anglophones, the
adoption of the Official Language Act in 1974 represented a turning point; their traditional "majority psychology" – based on
belonging to the majority linguistic group of Canada – was shat-
tered, and a new sense of themselves as a threatened minority
took hold.[30] In their view, the scope of Bill 22 was disproportionate
to the objective intended:

> To promote French, as it needed to do, the Bourasssa
> government has gone further in inhibiting English in
> Quebec than any impartial study of the relative
> strengths of the two languages could justify. It has
> breached the customary language rights of the non-
> French-speaking in the province.[31]

The adoption of language laws in Quebec coincided with an
increase in Anglophone departures from the province. Between 1971

and 1986, the anglophone population of Quebec shrank by 13 percent, or approximately one percent per year.[32]

Many of those who stayed, however, opted for mobilization,
launching pressure groups, political parties and legal battles. For
instance, Bill 22 (1974) provoked intense opposition from Anglo-
Quebecers. George Springate and John Ciaccia broke with party discipline and voted against it – which cost them their place in the
Liberal caucus. A petition asking the federal government to disallow
the Bill garnered 600,000 signatures, and a court case was launched
against the constitutionality of the law.[33] Some say that, from then
on, the diverse elements of the anglophone population became
"united only by a sense of grievance regarding linguistic issues."[34]

Surveys show, however, that there has been an evolution in
anglophone attitudes toward the language laws. In 1971, SORECOM,
polling for the Gendron Commission, found that about one-third of
Anglo-Quebecers believed that the Quebec government should
intervene to promote the use of French[35]; in 1983, a poll found that
82 percent of Anglophones believed it was "legitimate" for the government to protect the French language.[36]

Still, when, in late 1988, Premier Bourassa invoked the
"notwithstanding" clause to uphold Bill 101's sign law, three of his
four anglophone cabinet ministers resigned in protest. In the 1989
provincial elections, many Anglophones switched their political allegiance to the new anglo-rights Equality Party, which elected four
members to the Assembly.[37] During this period the anglophone population was, in the words of historian Ronald Rudin, "in a churlish
mood, feeling that it had been given little credit for having finally
accommodated itself to the French fact."[38] ◆

In 1994, the newly elected PQ government retained Bill 86's compromise
on the language of signs. Premier Bouchard has weathered opposition by some
PQ members (particularly from the region of Montreal) over his government's

refusal to take an uncompromising stance on the language issue. To date, the government has limited itself to a few measures: it has tightened its policies on the use of French in its own ministries and agencies[39] and adopted Bill 40, a relatively modest initiative that focuses on increased enforcement; and it has revived the Commission de protection de la langue française and updated the consumer protection provisions of the Charter of the French Language to cover computer products such as software and electronic games.

Following the narrow federalist victory in the 1995 Quebec referendum, language policy returned to the Quebec political agenda when anglo-rights activist Howard Galganov launched a campaign in favour of bilingual signs to the extent per-

French-speaking demonstrators heckle English-speaking demonstrators demanding that department stores apply Bill 86 and post signs in both languages, in September 1998 in Montreal. (Ryan Remiorz, Canapress)

mitted by Bill 86. This initiative generated significant support in the English-speaking community and swayed retailers in anglo-dominated regions, such as Montreal's West Island, to put up more English on their signs, even when threatened with boycotts. A SOM poll in February 1996 found that 80 percent of Anglophones and 62 percent of Allophones (those having neither French nor English as their mother tongue) supported an easing of the French Language Charter provisions.[40]

In 1996, a Quebec government study of Quebec's French-language situation concluded that language legislation since 1977 had produced "clear progress" toward the general use of French in the province.[41] In the early 1970s, 80 percent of allophone students attended English-language schools; the proportion was now reversed, with nearly 80 percent of Allophones attending French-language schools.[42] Meanwhile, bilingualism among Anglo-Quebecers had risen from 37 percent to 59 percent in 20 years; and the wage differential that once existed between Anglophones and Francophones had almost disappeared.[43] Despite the progress achieved, however, the study concluded that the objective of making French the "the common language of public life" had not been achieved, particularly in Montreal. The province's metropolitan hub remains "ground zero" in Quebec's language conflict.

The Bilingual Air Traffic Control Crisis (1976)

U NTIL 1974, ENGLISH WAS THE ONLY LANGUAGE THAT COULD BE USED FOR AIR traffic control in Canada. During the 1960s, this policy of unilingualism was, however, increasingly called into doubt as francophone pilots, controllers and radio operators grew in number.[1] In 1973, the federal minister of transport appointed a task force to "determine the extent and nature of demand for the use of both official languages in the provision of air traffic control and other services provided to pilots through air-ground communications during flight time," and, in 1974, the federal government allowed the use of both English and French at five small Quebec airports.[2]

Bilingualism, however, was encountering opposition from anglophone pilots and air traffic controllers, who argued that English was the language of international aviation and safety considerations required that it also be used in Quebec.[3] But, at this time (1974) Quebec was making French its official language, and francophone pilots and air traffic controllers were becoming increasingly frustrated at limitations on their using French in carrying out their duties in Quebec. They therefore decided to form the Association des gens de l'air du Québec (AGAQ) to defend their viewpoint.[4]

The dispute quickly became the centrepiece of contract negotiations between the Canadian Air Traffic Control Association (CATCA), the Canadian Airline Pilots Association (CALPA) and the federal minister of transport, Otto Lang. The conflict exploded into a crisis in June 1976 when the pilots went on a strike to support the controllers who opposed bilingualism. The strike disrupted air service throughout Canada for nine days. On June 23, Prime Minister Trudeau went on television to address the nation. He stated that the safety and security of passengers, crew members and the public was the first priority of his government and promised that there would be no movement whatsoever toward implementing bilingual air traffic control at the Montreal airports until strict safety standards were met: "No other goal of public policy has ever or will ever take precedence over the goal of preserving and improving public safety in the air."[5]

On June 28, the strike was ended after the government had made three concessions: a third commissioner — approved by CATCA and CALPA — would sit on the committee mandated to study the air traffic security issue; the commissioners' recommendations would have to be unanimous; and their report would be subject to a free vote in the House of Commons.[6] This agreement between minister of transport Otto Lang, CATCA and CALPA unleashed a storm of protest in Quebec.

as i recall

At the outset of the crisis, English Canadians overwhelmingly supported the protest campaign mounted by the anglophone pilots and controllers. "English Canadians," writes John F. Conway, "took the view that the Québécois were again being hypersensitive and unreasonable in pressing the language issue in ways that jeopardized air safety."[7]

Over the following weeks, however, with more extensive media coverage, English Canadians began to see the other side of the issue and to show a willingness to compromise. Having initially accepted the CATCA-CALPA version of the story and having blamed the federal government for the strike – the *Toronto Sun,* for example, castigated the "bone-headed, bloody-minded federal government determined to shove French down our throats"[8] – the English print media began to publish a broader spectrum of opinion. Some journalists denounced the bigotry and francophobia of certain opponents of bilingualism and pointed out that it functioned at many European airports without any compromise in security.[9]

CANADIAN KAMIKAZI

Cartoon by Andrew Donato published in *The Toronto Sun* in 1976. (NAC, C146109)

Following Trudeau's address to the nation, *The Globe and Mail* and *The Toronto Star* endorsed the guarantees offered by the government and called for the strikers to get back to work.[10] However, the Commissioner of Official Languages, Keith Spicer, admitted to being troubled by the agreement between Lang, CATCA and CALPA, regarding it as a blow to the dignity of Francophones. Spicer even considered resigning his position,

because he did not see how he could defend the Official Languages
Act to Quebecers.[11]

Also contributing to the shift in English-Canadian opinion
was the 1976 Parti Québécois victory.

The change in climate became more evident after
the election of the Parti Québécois on November 15.
Prime Minister Trudeau's popularity increased dramatically and "national unity" became a major
political issue once again. English Canadians
appeared to feel some need to atone for their sins,
which had led Quebecers to vote for a separatist
government. Public support for CATCA and CALPA
dropped still further.[12] ◆

si je me souviens bien

In Quebec, the air traffic control crisis struck at the heart of the language issue, and quickly took on great importance. Kenneth
McRoberts explains this reaction:

Unlike virtually all other federal language policies
concerned with the role of French in the civil service
or the provision of French-language services outside
Quebec, this policy dealt with language practices
within Quebec itself. Ottawa was restricting the use
of French rather than extending it. Most significantly,
Ottawa appeared to have responded to pressure from
English-speaking Canadians. Thus, even though the
number of individuals directly affected by the decision was minuscule, it acquired high symbolic status
for many Québécois.[13]

Most of the francophone press interpreted the illegal pilots'
strike as an irrational act contemptuous of Francophones.[14]

Si je me souviens bien

Francophones were further disappointed by the agreement between
Lang, CATCA and CALPA, believing that it would prevent the use of
French in air traffic communications. The agreement was perceived
as a humiliating defeat that put into question the right to work in
French in Quebec: "It demonstrated that the federal government
[would] always yield to a determined English majority, even when
they [were] in violation of the law and regardless of the merits of
the case; only an independent Quebec [could] be relied on to protect French rights and interests."[15]

Quebec Premier Robert Bourassa publicly stated that if the
federal government proved incapable of respecting something as
"essential, fundamental and normal" as the use of French in
Quebec, then the Canadian Constitution should be changed.[16] Even
within the Trudeau cabinet there were rumblings of discontent.
Communications minister Jeanne Sauvé publicly denounced the
agreement, calling it capitulation to a bunch of fanatics, while environment minister Jean Marchand chose to resign.[17] ◆

Several months after the strike was ended, the federal government
appointed a commission to study the impact of bilingualism on air safety in
Quebec. After three years of work, the commission concluded that all Quebec airports could safely implement bilingual air traffic control. The Conservative government of Joe Clark accepted the commission's conclusions in August 1979 and
implemented its recommendations in 1980. Aviation services were, from that
point on, equally available in French and English in Quebec.

According to John Conway, the goodwill generated in Quebec by the
federal government's policy of bilingualism "was at least temporarily wiped
out" by the crisis.[18] The episode also appears to have had a direct impact on
the political fortunes of some of those involved. According to Robert Bourassa,
his defeat in the November 1976 election was partly due to the conflict over
bilingual air traffic control.[19]

The Election of
the Parti Québécois
and the Referendum
on Sovereignty-
Association
(1976-1980)

THE PARTI QUÉBÉCOIS (PQ) WON THE NOVEMBER 1976 QUEBEC GENERAL ELECTION with 41 percent of the popular vote, compared to 34 percent for the outgoing Bourassa government. The PQ campaigned on the theme of "good government," making sure voters understood that a vote for the PQ was not necessarily a vote for independence.[1] The party's unexpected success was largely due to widespread dissatisfaction with the Liberal government[2] and the anger provoked by the 1974 adoption of Bill 22.[3] It was the first time in Quebec history that a party advocating Quebec sovereignty had formed a majority government in the National Assembly.[4]

Following the PQ victory, which was seen as a rejection of the Canadian unity strategy advocated by the Liberals, the federal government undertook initiatives to meet the sovereignist challenge.[5] It held several federal-provincial conferences between 1976 and 1979, and appointed the Pepin-Robarts Task Force in July 1977. In June 1978, before the task force had submitted its report, the government went on to publish its white paper *A Time for Action*, which outlined a two-phase constitutional reform. During the first phase, a statement of Canada's fundamental objectives would be developed, federal institutions would be remodelled and a Charter of Rights — at first applicable only at the federal level — would be introduced. The second stage would include discussion of the division of powers and the amending formula. Bill C-60, declaring the government's intention to unilaterally proceed with the first phase, was tabled one week later.[6]

Busy with developing its own constitutional project, the government of Quebec was not prepared to conclude any agreement before it held a referendum on sovereignty-association.[7] However, Quebec was not the only province to block the federal government's initiatives. After the 1971 round of negotiations (the Victoria Charter), and especially after the 1973 oil crisis, the western provinces became more demanding, particularly with regard to the division of powers.[8] Moreover, in December 1979, the Supreme Court ruled that Ottawa could not unilaterally alter the essential characteristics of the Senate, particularly the representation of provincial and regional interests in the federal legislative process.[9]

Having pledged to hold a referendum during its first mandate, but mindful of unfavourable opinion polls,[10] the Lévesque government first sought to implement its economic and social program.[11] On the constitutional front, it set out to demonstrate the cost of federalism and the feasibility of sovereignty. This process culminated in November 1979 with the publication of a white paper on sovereignty-association, *The New Quebec-Canada Agreement*. The public announcement of a referendum date and the wording of the question came one month later.[12]

Officially launched on April 15, 1980, the referendum campaign lasted more than six weeks. As required by provisions of the law on popular consultations adopted in 1978, the campaign was fought by two referendum organizations: the No camp, led by Claude Ryan, and the Yes camp, led by René Lévesque. Supported by the federal government and Prime Minister Trudeau, the No camp stressed the economic risks related to sovereignty while also promising a renewal of the federation. On May 14, at Montreal's Paul Sauvé Arena, Pierre Trudeau gave his most memorable speech, declaring,

The length and complexity of the referendum question was much criticized. This Montreal *The Gazette* cartoon by Aislin (Terry Mosher) reminds us that this could well be perceived as a way to muddy the waters and "play it safe." (McCord Museum of Canadian History, M988.176.211)

I know that I can make a most solemn commitment that following
a no, we will start immediately the mechanism of renewing the constitution, and we will not stop until it is done. We are staking our
seats, we Quebec MPs. We want change, we are staking our seats to
have change.[13]

as i recall

Canadians were urged to remain calm in the days immediately following the PQ election. *The Globe and Mail,* following the lead of
most political leaders, wrote, "The election of René Lévesque and
the Parti Québécois does not mean that the people of Quebec have
decided to separate from Canada."[14] It also warned:

As Canada confronts the new reality of a Parti
Québécois election victory in Quebec, the greatest
cause for concern – apart from any immediate and
short-lived danger of wasteful and destructive panic
– is...the danger of straining too successfully to
assure ourselves that all is well.[15]

Shaken, Canadians started to take stock. Conferences were
held on the state of Confederation and books with evocative titles
were published.[16] For some, especially those on the left, this was an
opportune time to recognize Quebec's right to self-determination.[17]
However, supporters of this option were rather pessimistic about
the likelihood of its being officially endorsed in time to save
Canada.[18] Indeed, the general tendency in English-Canadian political
and intellectual circles was rather that the whole Quebec question
could somehow be resolved by the defeat of the sovereignist option
in the referendum.[19]

There were also hard-liners whose attitude was that Quebec
was a spoilt child perennially dissatisfied with the concessions made
by the rest of Canada. One unbending opponent was historian

Donald Creighton, for whom the election of the Parti Québécois was nothing more than an egregious manifestation of the politics of blackmail that Quebec had been practising since the days of Duplessis and to which Canadians should not submit yet again. He and some other Canadians pushed for a position that was as tough as possible on the sovereignists.[20] The federal and provincial governments adopted this line of thinking. Their refrain throughout the referendum campaign was that negotiating sovereignty-association was out of the question.[21]

Polls showed that Canadian public opinion was divided on the separation question. From 39 percent (in the Atlantic provinces) to 50 percent (in British Columbia) of Canadians outside Quebec were opposed to any concessions by the government to prevent Quebec from separating, while 38 percent agreed that Ottawa could make minor concessions. At the same time, a majority of respondents supported the idea of negotiating an economic agreement with Quebec if it achieved independence.[22] ◆

si je me souviens bien

Sovereignists saw the election of the Parti Québécois as the beginning of an era. It marked the first step in a project aimed at changing the unequal balance of power between the two founding nations of Canada.[23] Pierre Vadeboncoeur, a renowned sovereignist essayist wrote, "For the first time in my lifetime, there is a new government. This government wants to take action to try and get Quebecers out of the historical woods...Imagine — we were going to exist!"[24] For Vadeboncoeur and many others, sovereignty meant national liberation. It was an inescapable necessity. "In reality, we do not have any choice: the failure of the independence project can only mean the beginning of an interminable end...We must win now, or lose forever."[25]

But for a majority of Quebecers, the PQ victory simply
meant the arrival of a new and, they hoped, more competent government. For years, the PQ had been asking citizens to make the
distinction between its ability to govern and its constitutional
option, and it appeared that the people had grasped this nuance.
The PQ promise to hold a referendum guaranteed voters the opportunity to have a say on the independence issue.

A highly controversial event, the referendum itself provoked
an important public debate on the place of Quebec within Canada.
Federalists in Quebec staked out their own position, most notably in
the Quebec Liberal Party's beige paper, *A New Canadian Federation*,
which proposed a highly decentralized federation and which was
used during the campaign to counterbalance the PQ proposal.
Regardless of partisan allegiances, the referendum was seen as a
legitimate and democratic exercise that concerned only Quebecers,
firmly establishing their right to self-determination. In this sense, the
federal government's refusal to subject itself to the law on popular
consultations, and the inability of legislators to enforce it, was interpreted as an abuse of power:

> by shamelessly using taxpayers' money for partisan
> purposes, it...denied in practice what it agreed to in
> theory – that is, the right of Quebec to determine its
> political status by itself.[26]

For Anglo-Quebecers, the PQ election marked the end of
their illusions. Like many other English Canadians, they had continued to think that the aspirations of francophone Quebecers were
restricted to culture and language. The victory of the PQ was a
traumatic experience for them, and it accelerated the wave of emigration that had started during the Quiet Revolution.[27] For many
who stayed on, it also marked the beginning of a period of mobilization, with the formation of various anglophone pressure
groups.[28] The referendum provided a chance for them to express,
nearly unanimously, their opposition to the PQ option. ◆

On May 20, 1980, with a turnout of over 85 percent, 59.56 percent of Quebecers refused to give the government of Quebec "the mandate to negotiate the proposed agreement between Quebec and Canada." The victory of the No side was greeted with relief in English Canada, and many people interpreted it as an end to the sovereignist threat. The premier of Nova Scotia, Richard Hatfield, on hearing Quebec's demands during the constitutional negotiations that followed the referendum, remarked: "We don't have to listen to this anymore — this is over. There was a referendum which settled all that."[29] For many in English Canada, the referendum had resolved the Quebec question once and for all, and some analysts announced the end of Quebec nationalism.[30]

Premier René Lévesque, leader of the Yes forces, speaking on the evening of the referendum defeat: "À la prochaine fois" (Canapress)

Certainly there were reasons for such an interpretation. When René Lévesque acknowledged defeat on the evening of May 20, he concluded his speech with an emotional "à la prochaine" — until next time. In the months and years that followed, however, this promise became a mere illusion. After the referendum, support for sovereignty substantially declined; by 1984 only one-third of Quebecers were in favour of that option.[31] In the circles supporting independence and among militants, this period was one of demobilization and disenchantment.[32] In this changing landscape, the Parti Québécois was transformed into a traditional political party defending Quebec's traditional demands. Thus it was with his party in a weakened state, without any real negotiating power despite its re-election in 1981, that René Lévesque entered the constitutional negotiations that led to the 1982 patriation of the Canadian Constitution.

The Patriation of the Constitution (1982)

T HE FEDERAL GOVERNMENT RE-LAUNCHED CONSTITUTIONAL TALKS SHORTLY AFTER the 1980 Quebec referendum campaign. Its aim was to patriate the constitution and find an amending formula. By autumn, it was clear that an agreement with the provinces would not be possible. The Trudeau government consequently announced that it would act unilaterally, and it introduced a resolution asking the British Parliament to proceed, despite the objections of the provinces. The resolution provided for the patriation of the constitution, with a newly incorporated charter of rights and freedoms and an amending formula fashioned after the one in the Victoria Charter (1971). Also included in the resolution was a clause enabling the federal government to obtain provincial consent through a referendum, a mechanism that would allow it to bypass the provincial governments by going directly to the people. Only two provinces — Ontario and New Brunswick — supported Ottawa's initiative.

The other provinces, or the "Gang of Eight" as they became known, united to form a common front in opposition to Ottawa's unilateral action. Three of them, Newfoundland, Quebec and Manitoba, even challenged the federal initiative by referring it to the courts to assess the constitutionality of the unilateral process; considerable effort was also put into making the provincial objections known to the British government.

During the winter of 1980-1981, the Gang of Eight devised a counter-proposal, and in April made it public. The provincial right to opt out of national programs with financial compensation and an amending formula requiring the approval of seven provinces, comprising 50 percent of the Canadian population (the 7/50 formula), were two notable items in their proposal. In accepting this formula, Quebec renounced its historical right to veto.[1]

The legality of the federal resolution was challenged and after divided decisions from the three provincial courts of appeal, Ottawa asked the Supreme Court of Canada to settle the question before proceeding. In September 1981, the Supreme Court handed down its judgement. The majority held that it would be legal for the federal government to proceed unilaterally, but, contrary to constitutional convention; "substantial" provincial consent would be required for it to proceed with patriation.[2] Following this judgement, Prime Minister Trudeau called a First Ministers' conference for November 1981, where an agreement was reached with all provinces but Quebec.

This agreement paved the way for the patriation of the constitution with an amending formula modelled after the provinces' formula[3] and a charter of rights and freedoms. The signatory provinces, however, negotiated a "notwithstanding clause", applicable only to fundamental freedoms (section 2 of the Charter) and legal rights (sections 7 to 15). This allowed for the implementation of laws in contravention of these sections of the Charter for five years, renewable thereafter. The patriation package also enshrined the principle of equalization between richer and poorer provinces and strengthened provincial control over natural resources. Finally, the deal incorporated the "opting out" formula that Quebec had demanded, but without financial compensation.[4] The accord did not address the distribution of powers between the two levels of government nor the reform of federal institutions.

 *as i recall*

English Canada welcomed the patriation of the Constitution and was heartened by the announcement that the First Ministers had reached an agreement. The day after the announcement, *The Globe and Mail* commented that Canada was now a truly sovereign nation.[5] In June 1982, a Gallup poll showed that 57 percent of Canadians believed that the new Constitution would be a good thing for the country.[6]

A major source of satisfaction – aside from the fact that the Constitution had finally been brought home, effectively laying to rest Canada's last colonial relic — was Prime Minister Trudeau's decision to withdraw his threat of proceeding unilaterally with patriation. "Canada is still a political federation. That was the biggest achievement," rejoiced *The Globe and Mail*.[7] Moreover, polls revealed that most Canadians supported the entrenchment in the Constitution of the Charter of Rights and Freedoms.[8] The Charter firmly established the equality of all Canadian citizens and represented a gain for Canadian democracy, since it was likely to limit the dominance of government over the political life of the country in favour of individual citizens.[9]

This warm reception for the Constitution contrasted with the one reserved for the Quebec government. The sovereignist Parti Québécois was said to have neither the desire nor the will to sign any agreement: "Premier René Lévesque had to find a way out of any agreement. It would have been impossible for him to stand as one of the new Fathers of Confederation," commented *The Globe and Mail*, adding that with a Quebec contingent consisting of 74 of the province's 75 MPs, Prime Minister Trudeau — a Francophone himself — had all the legitimacy necessary to proceed.[10] In his memoirs, Trudeau took up this argument: "When you add up the National Assembly legislators in Quebec City and the members of Parliament from Quebec, a very clear majority of all elected members from Quebec voted for the patriation package."[11] The former prime minister continued to vigorously deny having plotted to isolate Quebec[12] or reneging on commitments made during the 1980 referendum: "On the whole, the Constitution Act largely enshrined the values I had been advocating since I wrote my first article in *Cité libre* in 1950."[13] Quebec's accusation that it had been abandoned by the other provinces was also rejected. Indeed, the other provinces claimed Quebec was the first province to scuttle the common front when René Lévesque accepted Trudeau's proposal to settle the constitutional issue through a referendum.[14]

Quebec's isolation nevertheless fed a lingering sense of lost opportunity.[15] Contrary to the views of Trudeau and his supporters,[16] a number of Canadian experts believed the Constitution Act of 1982 did not provide the kind of blueprint around which all Canadians could rally.[17] Others observed that the various governments' domination of the constitutional amendment process, their refusal to submit the package to a referendum and the inclusion of a "notwithstanding clause" were at odds with the democratic dimension of the Charter.[18] Many worried about questions left unanswered. In the West, notably, many people were disappointed because the Act did not address reform of federal institutions.[19] In many ways, there was not a great difference between the constitutional agenda before and after patriation. Overall, then, the Constitution Act of 1982 was seen as a reasonably successful compromise but not the final word, since it had left a number of questions unresolved, including the status of the First Nations and of Quebec.[20] ◆

si je me souviens bien

Reacting to the agreement reached between the nine provinces and Ottawa, René Lévesque declared, "I must say that I deeply regret that Quebec finds itself today in a position that has become one of the fundamental traditions of the Canadian federal system as it normally functions: Quebec finds itself alone."[21]

Though the Quebec government's chosen position divided public opinion in the province,[22] a large majority of Quebec's leaders found the November agreement unacceptable, because it failed to meet Quebec's historical demands and fell well below its expectations. Quebec Liberal Leader Claude Ryan wrote:

> Quebec has always stressed that the primary objective of any request for constitutional reform on its part was to arrive at a new distribution of legislative and fiscal powers that would do more justice to its evolving needs. Quebec has been calling for major

changes for more than twenty years now. So far, it
has obtained next to nothing.[23]

These disillusioned federalists saw the 1981 accord as a
renunciation of the federal government's referendum promises.[24]
Following publication of the Pepin-Robarts report (1979) and the
Quebec Liberal Party's beige paper (1980) – both of which called for
a decentralization of powers – and after Prime Minister Trudeau had
solemnly pledged to renew the federation,[25] many Quebecers were
astounded to see that patriation, rather than leading to greater
autonomy, would lead to a reduction of the National Assembly's
powers to administer justice and set language and education policy.[26] In 1989, Marcel Adam, an editorialist at the Montreal daily *La
Presse* and no friend of the sovereignist movement, wrote:

> Fraud is not too strong a word to describe this
> unprecedented imposition on Quebec of a reform that
> will result in the opposite of what was expected of the
> commitments made to keep it in the federation.[27]

Quebec negotiators maintain that the accord was put
together in their absence, to the detriment of Quebec:

> Two key requirements [financial compensation and
> the respect of provincial jurisdiction over lan-
> guage issues] were thereby flouted, in an incredi-
> bly contemptuous way, at the close of a process
> that was, or so we were promised, to lead to
> renewed federalism.[28]

Claude Morin adds that "each group of elected members
represents Quebecers in the spheres of jurisdiction that are under
the aegis of each order of government," and consequently the support of the Quebec government was needed to proceed with any
constitutional amendment which affected its powers.[29]

For many Quebecers, the November agreement was unacceptable not only for its content but also for the manner in which
it was reached. Quebec firmly believed that its historical veto on

constitutional amendments affecting its jurisdictions had been
denied and for this "ten signatures on a text of less than fifty
lines" had sufficed.[30] Opposition leader Claude Ryan, though
harshly critical of the Quebec government, would adopt the
same position:

> To use the separatist orientation of the Lévesque
> government as a pretext to justify the way in which
> it has been ignored these last few months is to
> demonstrate little concern for the legitimacy of
> political institutions.[31]

The position of these critics was that Quebec had agreed to
renounce its historical right of veto during negotiations with the
seven other dissident provinces, in exchange for the guarantee that
it would be able to withdraw from federal programs in which it did
not want to participate and receive full financial compensation.
When the November 1981 agreement watered down the financial-
compensation provisions along with other changes agreed to by the
provinces, Quebec was entitled to reclaim its right of veto.

Many observers in Quebec see the events of 1981-1982 as a
breach of trust and a rejection of the vision of Canada underlying
contemporary federalist thinking in Quebec. The entrenchment of
the Charter constitutionalized a certain vision of Canada – that of a
nation comprising of individuals who enjoy identical constitutional
rights – at odds with the "two founding nations" ideal dear to
Quebec federalists. "It must be concluded," wrote Jean-Louis Roy,
editorial writer at *Le Devoir*,

> that this "Two Nation" concept of Canada that Daniel
> Johnson evoked long ago, this Canada of constituent
> duality evoked by the Laurendeau-Dunton and Pepin-
> Robarts commissions, is fiction, a poetic, minority
> vision, a candle in full sunlight.[32]

Because patriation resulted in changes not approved by
Quebec, some experts go so far as to suggest that the Constitution

Si je me souviens bien

Act of 1982 is one of discontinuity and assimilation.[33] Without the consent of the people of Quebec, and in the face of Quebec government opposition, the constitutional reform of 1982 was, and remains, illegitimate in the eyes of many Quebecers. Guy Laforest writes:

> In 1760, New France was conquered by England through the use of arms. In 1982, Canada subjected Quebec to the same fate, through measures reflecting a narrow vision of rights and justice. The forms of legality may have been respected, but in defiance of the requisites of legitimacy.[34]

Since then, the night of November 4, 1981, when the agreement was reached, has remained woven in Quebec's political imagery as the "night of the long knives," recalling that the deal was reached while Quebec was not there. ◆

The Queen signs the new constitution of Canada, together with Prime Minister Pierre Elliott Trudeau, on April 17, 1982. (Robert Cooper, NAC, PA141503)

On November 25, 1981, the Quebec government adopted an order-in-council through which it symbolically used its right of veto against the resolution on the patriation of the Constitution,[35] and on December 1, 1981, the National Assembly adopted a motion laying out the conditions necessary for Quebec to accept the patriation project.[36] Furthermore, Quebec announced that it would not participate in any further constitutional conferences and undertook legal action to have its right of veto recognized.[37] Finally, until the election of the Liberals in 1985, the "notwithstanding" clause was invoked on all pieces of legislation introduced in the Quebec National Assembly, thus exempting them from the Canadian Charter of Rights and Freedoms.

On April 17, 1982, the Constitution Act of 1982 was proclaimed in the presence of the Queen while some 30,000 people gathered to watch the ceremony: "Masters in our own house," proclaimed the *Toronto Sun*.[38] Meanwhile, the Quebec flag was flown at half-mast on all government buildings and a protest march was held in the streets of Montreal, drawing some 25,000 participants. For many Quebecers, patriation remained an unjust act. The quest for reconciliation would be taken up with the Conservative win in the 1984 federal election.

chapter 5

The Economic
Debates

Introductions by
John Meisel
Guy Rocher

Essays prepared by
Patricia Bittar and
Alain Desruisseaux

The Economic
Debates

T HERE ARE NOT MANY AREAS OF OPINION WHERE ALL CANADIAN REGIONS AGREE, BUT there are some. One is the way each sees itself treated by the federal government, other regions and the Canadian political and economic system as a whole. Every part of the country, with the possible exception of Newfoundland, believes it is short-changed and that the other parts are favoured. The essays in this chapter examine events that have manifested these sentiments.

Quebecers believe that the West's severe under-representation in federal Liberal governments has led to generous compensatory policies designed to attract western votes, while westerners are convinced that their weak presence in the federal government has led to serious neglect of their interests. Western feelings of alienation have a long history. They go back to the days when the largely agrarian population of the West felt shamelessly exploited by the East. Eastern bankers based in Montreal and Toronto were demonized as blood-sucking capitalists incapable of comprehending the needs of a remote, agrarian population; westerners saw them as holding all political and economic power to the near catastrophic detriment of the West.

That sense of isolation and neglect was so widespread and profound that social movements and political parties repeatedly emerged to seek redress. In no other region have so-called "third parties" (the Progressives, the Reconstruction Party, United Farmers of Alberta, the United Farmers of Manitoba, the Co-operative Commonwealth Federation (CCF), Social Credit and the New Democratic Party) been so successful in challenging the economic and political establishment. The rise of the Reform Party, strongly linked to the animus against the East, is only the most recent manifestation of the West's deep sense of estrangement.

The 1970s saw the most virulent manifestation of anti-eastern feeling because of the Trudeau government's economic nationalism, particularly its National Energy Policy. In western eyes, that initiative compelled the oil industry to subsidize the East by forcing it to price its black gold substantially below world levels, at a colossal economic loss. That episode left westerners with a strong sense of victimization that has been exacerbated by other policies viewed as exclusively addressing eastern concerns, such as the decision to award the CF-18 contract to Quebec. This was received with dismay and served to reinforce the belief that Ottawa continually mollycoddles Quebec. Many in the West and elsewhere felt that such decisions resulted from two main factors: Quebec's disproportionate voice at the federal level and the desire to create what Premier Bourassa called "un fédéralisme rentable," a profitable federalism for Quebec. These factors were seen as predisposing Ottawa to decisions favouring Quebec's economy at the expense of other regions.

The essays here, and in some other sections of this book, show that economic factors may exert both positive and negative influences on politics. On the down side, commercial and industrial organizations pursue profits — the "bottom line" is everything. In chapter 3, we saw that a private radio station in Montreal, CKAC, opposed the creation of a public broadcasting system because it would threaten French service in Canada. The station clearly had a vested interest in the matter, and it was patently wrong, since Radio Canada has been a pillar of French radio and television. Similarly, the powerful voice of Canadian Pacific in the Bill S-31 issue pitted corporate interests against what might have been a positive development for Canadian federalism, and private economic interests contributed to tensions over the CF-18 contract and legislation affecting pharmaceuticals.

On the positive side, economic self-interest can serve to facilitate accommodation among the three main players in the Canadian economic game: Quebec, Ottawa and the other provinces. Quebec's defensive posture in federalism does not always place it in opposition to the federal government or ROC. This may have positive results, because the literature on conflict resolution tells us that crosscutting cleavages are more amenable to satisfactory resolution than situations in which two congealed camps repeatedly confront one another.

In defending greater autonomy for itself, Quebec more often than not allies itself with other governments seeking to enhance their freedom of action. While these efforts at province-building often have political motivations, they also reflect economic interests like taxation, social policy, immigration and the regulation of economic activities. The Churchill Falls contract also reminds us that it is not always the conflict between Quebec and Ottawa that causes distress. On some occasions, Ottawa may side with Quebec. At other times, alliances among the provinces result in agreements that link Quebec to other Canadian jurisdictions.

Although the evidence here is tenuous, it seems probable that Quebec enterprises, at least those that are indigenously owned, are more likely to consider "national" — i.e., Quebec —, interests than enterprises situated in other provinces are likely to heed Canada's interests. This is probably because Quebec nationalism tends to be stronger than Canadian nationalism. Other Canadians have a real enough attachment to Canada, but it is usually less intense and less clearly defined than the attachment of Quebecers to their province. The presence of multinational corporations and branch plants also reduces the likelihood that the Canadian national interest is given much weight when economic decisions are made.

This is one reason why concern over the Free Trade Agreement (FTA) was much greater in ROC, particularly Ontario, than in Quebec. Many outside Quebec feared that the agreement would lead to further attenuation of Canadian economic autonomy, the exodus of many Canadian firms and thus loss of jobs and, ultimately, a profound Americanization of Canada. Feelings toward the FTA among Canadian nationalists ran very high. The strong reaction of a well-known friend of Quebec, Philip Resnick, is indicative of the emotional impact of the issue in ROC. There was much less anxiety over these matters in Quebec, although the unions certainly shared some of the uncertainties of their colleagues in other parts of Canada.

This was, of course, a reversal of the traditional situation. Usually, Quebec is intensely watchful over its cultural interests. Compared to other regions, Quebec prizes its culture highly and often accords it primacy over economic interests. In ROC, economic benefits are usually considered first, societal and cultural interests getting secondary consideration. In the late 1980s Quebec for once appeared to be less vigilant on the cultural front, whereas many in ROC feared the cultural consequences of the FTA.

Many Canadian nationalists thought that the dominant North American language would facilitate assimilation; they worried that increasing numbers of

Canadians would become integrated into US economic and social networks and thus become de-nationalized. Francophones, however, tended to assume, quite rightly, that the French language and the strong Quebec culture would protect Quebecers from assimilation.

Compared to the profound national impact of many of the events outlined in other chapters, such as the adoption of Medicare, the Official Languages Act or the Victoria Charter, the cases considered in chapter 5, with the exception of the FTA, may seem to be of secondary importance. Yet, their impact should not be underestimated. Because of their relevance to the lives of many people, economic decisions can arouse considerable passion; their impact often reaches well beyond the merely economic. The cases in this chapter demonstrate how economic disputes can easily spill over into the political realm. Hence, the CF-18 decision may well have played a part in Manitoba's stance toward the Meech Lake Accord and, along with other irritants to the west, helped prepare the ground for the emergence and growth of the Reform Party.

The cases selected for examination are excellent examples, because they reveal how economic self-interest can exacerbate relationships. But they are also somewhat one-sided, because all focus on the negative consequences of economic interaction. There is another, more positive, side. Since the Second World War, the Canadian federation has developed an elaborate program of income redistribution. The arrangements are currently undergoing substantial revision and are much too complex to be considered here in detail, but one important component of the program involves conditional grants and equalization payments, administered by the federal government, which ensure that low-income provinces receive assistance. The details of the program have been subject to intense, often acrimonious, negotiations between Ottawa and the provinces, but, and this is a crucial but, a system that provides economic assistance to those who need it most *has* evolved. Canadians have accepted some collective economic responsibility for one another. This suggests that economic concerns do not produce a Hobbesian "war of everyone against everyone." The economic dimension of Canadian society involves not only self-interest, but also the creation of tolerable conditions for human co-existence.

The Economic
Debates

QUARRELS OVER ECONOMIC INTERESTS OFTEN UNDERLIE POLITICAL BATTLES. MONEY emerges when we read between the lines of political discourse, and, very often, financial relationships are also power relationships.

This interrelationship is not always apparent in the media coverage of political events. The underlying money/power link usually comes to light only in specific crisis, and even then only for a relatively short period. Political life is often played out and interpreted in public opinion as if the economy was not part of the scene. However, closer examination of a drama often reveals that economic interests are indeed at play, but have manage to remain in the background, attracting little attention even though they are almost constantly on stage. Unlike the political realm, the business world is not obliged to be "transparent." Entrepreneurs deal and negotiate out of the spotlight — on golf courses, in hotel suites or in private clubs.

When an economic debate comes to public attention, its relationship to the political realm is generally ambiguous and confusing. Is it generated by political interests, exaggerated and stirred up by conflicting interests, or does it serve to divert political confrontation? The answer is not always clear.

Fortunately, the economic interests of a country often converge. However, they may also diverge and directly contradict each other, especially in a huge country like Canada with its many diverse regions, each pursuing its own interests. Every region will at some point think, rightly or not, that it has been wronged by decisions made without its consent, even when it has been part of the debate. In a country with two official languages and home to Aboriginal peoples and various other minorities, occasions for economic debate with a political flavour are numerous and crop up when least expected.

As in most diverse countries, mutual suspicion is a constant if dormant fact of political life in Canada, always likely to suddenly appear. Some debates reveal old rivalries, always ready to be rekindled by any event or decision. Economic issues in which many different political authorities are called upon to participate in decision-making are particularly likely to have an underlying political dimension. Suspicions are therefore aroused. Non-economic reasons, it is believed, interfere with the neutrality, objectivity and economic rationality that should govern decision-making. Political authorities are suspected of being partial, biased, motivated by political opportunism, subject to economic blackmail, or, worse still, corrupt.

The scenario described above was at work in the economic issues dealt with in this chapter. But the phenomenon is nothing new. Quebec has long been suspicious of federal economic decisions. Quebecers believe that the federal government has always systematically favoured Ontario to the detriment of Quebec, and western Canada over eastern Canada. Since Canada's founders did not give the national capital the status of a state or "district," as was the case in the United States, Ottawa is part of Ontario. This fuelled suspicions of favouritism right from the start. Moreover, for a long time, a large part of the federal bureaucracy was recruited from Ontario, and Quebecers are convinced that this is still the case. From Quebec's vantage point, the federal bureaucracy's natural tendency is to act in complicity with Toronto at the expense of Montreal and Quebec, to be more receptive to lobbying by Toronto than by Montreal, all the more so because it is carried out in the language of the majority of civil servants. Quebecers can always find examples of federal bias in favour of Ontario. Construction of the St. Lawrence Seaway, which robbed Montreal of its role as the hub of Canadian economic activity, and the placement of the majority of federal research centres in Ontario are just two examples.

When it comes to the West, it is more the impartiality of politicians that Quebecers suspect. The federal political parties have often lacked electoral support in the West, their strength traditionally lying in Quebec and Ontario. It is therefore easy to reason that politicians concerned about remaking or maintaining their image in the West would want to win over a rebellious electorate by offering it compensations at the expense of Quebec. Quebecers perceive the problem as not so much the influence of western politicians in the federal government as the absence of politicians from the West. Ottawa, they believe, must compensate for this by offering economic advantages to the West.

Viewed from Quebec, the West seems a far off, unfamiliar place — a kind of "other Canada" — filled with people who do not understand Quebec or appreciate its interests. So it is natural enough to reason that westerners might defend and promote their own interests to the detriment of the East, particularly Quebec. How then, Quebecers ask, when Quebec is so badly served, can those same westerners who have long been favoured by the federal government, suspect that Ottawa shows favouritism toward Quebec?

The slogan of the Quiet Revolution, "Maîtres chez nous" (Masters in Our Own House), helps us better understand this reasoning. During the Quiet Revolution, every francophone Quebecer understood that this referred to control over economic life, something that Quebecers had not yet enjoyed. Quebec had too long been the *porteur d'eau* (water carrier), as was said at the time. In the decades following the Quiet Revolution, a francophone entrepreneurial class emerged and has made major breakthroughs in high-tech industries, particularly aerospace, biotechnology and data processing. As a consequence, the traditional economic structure has collapsed, resulting in a severe employment crisis. At the same time, however, a new economic structure, focused on the future, has emerged. Thus there are two contradictory images of Montreal, one as a city in decline, hard hit by the departures of firms and head offices, the other as a city whose economic and employment structure is renewing itself through young, technically oriented entrepreneurs whose businesses hold the key to Quebec's future.

Although Quebecers may have some reservations about these entrepreneurs, clearly they are proud of their successes. Quebecers may also feel that this new entrepreneurship is fragile precisely because it is still new, having barely laid down roots. It must prove itself and make its mark in an Anglo-Saxon world that is not always welcoming. Quebecers therefore react strongly to decisions or actions that appear to threaten Quebec's francophone entrepreneurship. Bill S-31, for example, seemed an unacceptable obstacle to the initiative of francophone directors of that most Québécois of financial institutions, the Caisse de dépôt et placement (Deposit and Investment Fund). The Canada-U.S. Free Trade Agreement may not have received unanimous support, but the great majority of Quebecers thought it would be good for the market opportunities of young Quebec firms, without understanding fully how it could harm the interests of Ontario and western Canada.

It is because of these issues and others that Quebecers wonder how Ontario or Manitoba can accuse the federal government of favouring Quebec, when Quebec is barely getting its fair share of Canada's economic pie. In that sense, it can probably be said that Quebec is *not* a distinct society within Canada, for it seems to share with the other provinces a mistrust of the federal government's allocation of resources, benefits and investments. Suspicions about lack of impartiality are solidly rooted in Canadian political culture.

The Churchill Falls Contract (1969)

W HEN THE CHURCHILL FALLS PROJECT WAS CONCEIVED IN THE EARLY 1950S, JOEY Smallwood's Newfoundland government had its sights set on the markets of New England and Ontario.[1] In order to get the electricity from Labrador to those destinations, Newfoundland had to cross Quebec territory or go around it. Studies showed the second option to be technically feasible but much too expensive.[2] So Newfoundland started negotiations with the Quebec government, which eventually agreed to have the electricity from Labrador cross its territory provided that the energy was sold to Quebec beyond a certain "point A," a euphemism for the border between Quebec and Labrador.[3]

In May 1969, three years after a first agreement-in-principle had been signed, Hydro-Québec reached a final agreement with the British Newfoundland Company (Brinco), the company given a monopoly on the exploitation of Labrador's natural resources by the Newfoundland government. Quebec reserved the right to buy all electricity produced by Churchill Falls for a period of 65 years and committed itself to doing so. The contract provided for a fixed price of three cents per kilowatt-hour for the first 40 years and a slightly lower price for the remaining 25 years; Newfoundland retained the right to use up to 300 of the project's approximate output of 5200 megawatts. In order to offset financial difficulties, Hydro-Québec subscribed for $15 million in common shares and $100 million in bonds, which ensured completion of the project and advanced the necessary funds. Hydro-Québec also guaranteed interest and exchange rates.

Four years later, the oil crisis completely changed the situation and the price of hydro-electric power started to climb. In 1976, the Newfoundland government asked Hydro-Québec to grant it 800 additional megawatts, but without success. It then brought the dispute before the Superior Court of Newfoundland but lost the case.

In 1980, the government of Newfoundland under Premier Brian Peckford passed the Upper Churchill Water Rights Reversion Act. This legislation gave Newfoundland complete ownership and control of the waters of the Churchill River by cancelling the lease, dating back to 1961, by which the Churchill Falls Labrador Company (CFLCo) — a subsidiary company of Brinco — had the right to exploit the waters of the Churchill River.[4] The Act would result in the appropriation of hydro-electric plants with no compensation to Hydro-Québec and would terminate the 1969 contract. The government of Quebec contested the Peckford plan, in vain, before the Newfoundland courts. In March 1982, the Superior Court of Newfoundland recognized the constitutionality of the Reversion Act.

The Quebec government took the case all the way to the Supreme Court of Canada.[5] The governments of Newfoundland and Quebec twice asked the Supreme Court to delay its decision in order to try to reach an out-of-court settlement, but those talks failed.[6] On May 3, 1984, the Supreme Court ruled the Reversion Act *ultra vires* (beyond Newfoundland's constitutional authority). In 1988, the Newfoundland government had its case dismissed again when it asked the Supreme Court to force the CFLCo to give 800 megawatts of power to the province.

LE PLAN TOBIN...

HÉ! HÉ! HÉ!

In 1996, Brian Tobin threatened to pull the plug on Hydro-Québec at the Churchill Falls complex. (Serge Chapleau, McCord Museum of Canadian History, M997.52.248)

In September 1996, Newfoundland Premier Brian Tobin rekindled the controversy by demanding, yet again, that the contract be re-opened. The Quebec government and Hydro-Québec refused to give in to the demand but said they would consider undertaking new hydro-electric projects in Labrador.[7]

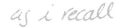

Until the 1973 energy crisis, the Churchill Falls contract had not drawn any opposition. "When approved in 1966, the contract provided Newfoundland with $20-million a year, or about one-tenth of provincial revenues."[8] It was only with the oil crisis that the idea of unjust negotiation of the contract began to circulate: the burden of financial difficulties, it was claimed, had forced Newfoundland to accept Hydro-Québec's offer. The price paid by Hydro-Québec, which was ridiculously low in hindsight, and the lengthy duration of the contract were harshly denounced.

Although the federal government intervened on Quebec's behalf,[9] Newfoundland's position found sympathy in other regions of Canada. Thus in 1982 the governments of British Columbia, Saskatchewan and Manitoba supported Newfoundland before the Supreme Court of Canada.

Newfoundland's Premier Brian Peckford was deeply disappointed by the Supreme Court's 1984 decision and worried that it would fan the "separatist" fires in his province.[10] "There must be some sense of natural justice and fairness. And when it's weighted so heavily against one province and so heavily in favour of another province, surely there's some way of resolving it,"[11] he asserted.

In 1996, Brian Tobin, Peckford's successor, chastized Quebec Premier Lucien Bouchard for recognizing the legitimacy of Canadian courts only when it suited him. Declaring that he was cornered, Tobin began a media blitz across Canada, denouncing the contract as "unjust" and threatening to cut off Hydro-Québec from the Churchill Falls project:

Honestly, what choice do I have? Am I going to
explain to the province that we're losing money and
for the next 40 years we'll borrow, tax or close down
hospitals and schools in the province to pay for the
privilege of pumping power to Quebec so they can
make a billion-plus a year?[12]

At the same time, *The Globe and Mail* editorialized:

Everyone close to the deal knew exactly how rough
Quebec was playing: a 65-year contract for vast
amounts of energy at ridiculously low prices with no
price-adjustment clause...All evidence showed
[Premier Smallwood] was aware that he had been
backed into a corner: He faced the choice of a deal
on Quebec's terms or no development at all.[13]

The Globe and Mail considered, however, that it would be
preferable for Newfoundland to work out a new deal with Quebec
rather than cut off Hydro-Québec's power. On the federal scene,
opinion was somewhat divided. The Reform Party was fully behind
Premier Tobin,[14] whereas Prime Minister Jean Chrétien would only
say that the dispute was a problem between two provinces and that
the federal government was not involved.[15] ◆

si je me souviens bien

At the time the contract was signed, some in Quebec were concerned about the lack of prior consultation and issues surrounding
the Labrador border.

Why is Mr. Lessard [Hydro-Québec's President] rushing
to sign a contract that involves five billion dollars for a
110,000-square-mile territory of which we were fraudu-
lently deprived in Oct.-Nov. 1926, before the National
Assembly could have a say in the matter?...That con-

tract could be, if signed for 65 years, particularly
embarrassing on the day of reckoning with
Newfoundland over the Labrador border issue.[16]
Nevertheless, the agreement aroused little controversy. Newfoundland's complaints got a cool reception during the 1970s. Quebec's
perception was that the construction and hydroelectric development of Churchill Falls were carried out in accordance with a contract that had been signed in good faith. At the time, the negotiated
prices had satisfied both parties and there had been no hint of the
impending 1970s oil crisis. Obviously, Quebec City was pleased with
the Supreme Court's 1984 decision. Premier René Lévesque commented, "It's the first time in a long while that the court has leaned
in favour of Quebec's interests."[17]

In 1996, the French-speaking media in Quebec were unim-
pressed by Tobin's attempt to revisit the deal. Alain Dubuc, editorialist at *La Presse*, made this observation:

> [Hydro-Québec] signed a contract with Newfoundland
> which reflected the cost structure of its own power
> plants, their very long-term, fixed costs. These low, sta-
> ble prices were not the result of some kind of trap set
> for Newfoundlanders. If Quebec had imagined that these
> prices might one day be open to challenge, the deal with
> Newfoundland would never have been signed.[18]

Following Premier Tobin's threats, Eric Kierans, a minister in the
Lesage government from 1963 to 1966, defended the validity of the
1969 contract:

> Churchill Falls was not an unfair agreement nor did
> the Newfoundland government think so five years
> later when it bought out Brinco's share for $160 mil-
> lion. The oil crisis and subsequent surging world
> inflation benefited the buyers of the power more
> than the sellers, but that is not a reason for breaking
> the contract.[19] ◆

For a long time, the contract binding Hydro-Québec and the CFLCo remained an obstacle to the development of other hydro-electric projects in Labrador. Bernard Lamarre, president of SNC-Lavalin, one of the largest engineering firms in Canada, recently remarked, "There is enormous potential there. But that potential is frozen because of a debate [over Churchill Falls]."[20] The Quebec government and Hydro-Québec were prepared to look at developing other hydro-electric projects in Labrador, but flatly rejected a re-opening of the 1969 contract, a persistent demand of the Newfoundland government.

It was not until March 1998 that the two governments finally came to an agreement aimed at completing the hydro-electric development of the Churchill River.[21] Soon after being re-elected on February 9, 1999, Brian Tobin agreed to a meeting with Lucien Bouchard on the issue of the Lower-Churchill Falls.[22] However, the desire of the Innu of Nitassinan (Quebec and Labrador) to be part of the development of what they consider to be their territory may modify the development of the project.[23]

Bill S-31 and
Quebec Deposit and
Investment Fund
(1982)

T HE CAISSE DE DÉPÔT ET PLACEMENT (DEPOSIT AND INVESTMENT FUND) WAS CRE-
ated in 1965 to administer the assets of the Régie des rentes du Québec, or
Quebec pension plan, which was set up by Quebec in parallel to the Canada
Pension Plan. From a mere administrator of the pension plan, the Caisse became
an aggressive actor on the Canadian equity market following the appointment of
Jean Campeau as its head in 1979. The Caisse rapidly acquired many large blocks
of shares in major Canadian companies such as Alcan (5.3 percent), Dofasco (4.5
percent), Dominion Textile (19 percent), Nova Corporation (8 percent), Nabu
Manufacturing (20 percent), Sceptre Ressources (23.4 percent) and Canadian
Pacific (CP) (9.4 percent).[1] The Caisse soon approached several of those firms
seeking representation on their boards of directors. Thus, towards the end of
1981, the Caisse asked for two seats on the board of CP. Worried about the keen
interest shown by the Caisse, CP reacted by asking for Ottawa's help. The company's president, Fred Burbidge, declared:

> CP was deliberately created as a private company by the federal
> government and now a province that wants to separate from the
> rest of Canada is buying into a company that was meant to bind the
> country together.[2]

On November 2, 1982, the government of Canada tabled Bill S-31, the
Corporate Shareholding Limitation Act. This legislation was meant to restrict
provincial governments and their Crown corporations — the Caisse de dépôt et
placement, but others too, such as the Alberta's Heritage Fund, created in 1976
— to ownership of no more than 10 percent of the voting shares of any company involved in interprovincial or international transportation. It should be

recalled that Ottawa had already taken numerous steps to restrict the economic manoeuvrability of provincial governments.[3]

The arguments put forward by the federal government to justify its bill related to: maintaining the integrity of federal jurisdiction over interprovincial and international transportation; protecting the Canadian common market against "balkanizing" provincial interventions; and returning the Caisse to its role as a passive investor, which it had abandoned to embark on the "socialist" path, as André Ouellet, the federal minister of consumer and corporate affairs charged.[4]

To avoid debate in the House of Commons and speed up the process, the interests of the Caisse in CP having reached 9.9 percent, the cabinet invoked an extraordinary parliamentary procedure and submitted the Bill straight to the Senate. The Bill therefore became enforceable on the day it was tabled.

as i recall

As a result of its attempts to acquire seats on the boards of Canadian companies, the traditional bastions of Canadian power regarded the Caisse as a bridgehead for Quebec's offensive on Canadian capital. For businesspeople, Bill S-31 was a means to counter nationalization scenarios that institutions like the Caisse de dépôt et placement might consider.

The Canadian establishment therefore rallied around CP chairman Fred Burbidge, who claimed to be opposed not to the francophone presence on his board of directors, but to government intrusion into the affairs of private corporations. The Canadian Chamber of Commerce, Power Corporation of Canada, Bell Canada, Stelco, Dominion Textile, the Bank of Montreal and many other corporations joined CP in putting pressure on Ottawa. For the Business Council on National Issues, a business lobby group, the Bill did not go far enough. Minister André Ouellet stated that at least one hundred businesspeople, Francophones and Anglophones, had

expressed fears about the initiative of the Caisse de dépôt et placement, but he refused to give names so as not to spark a witch-hunt.[5]

The federal opposition parties, on the other hand, immediately protested against the Bill. The New Democratic Party declared
it a useless and unacceptable restriction on provincial entrepreneurship, and the Progressive Conservative Party reproached the government for pursuing fundamentally centralizing policies and
neglecting to consult the provinces.[6] The pivotal role of Canadian
capital and the importance of the transportation industry in Canada
gave the bill an added dimension, with broad consequences for
many provincial Crown corporations. Thus the government of
Alberta immediately protested against the Bill, and the governments of Ontario, British Columbia, Saskatchewan and
Newfoundland soon expressed their uneasiness with it as well.[7]

Even though many recognized the Quebec Caisse de dépôt
et placement as the main target of Bill S-31, not everyone saw the
reactions to it as based merely on linguistic or partisan lines. For
some, whether or not corporations had business links with governments explained the divergent reactions.[8] Allan Tupper writes:

> [T]he driving force behind S-31 is an alliance between
> the federal government and certain large Canadian
> corporate and financial interests, notably Canadian
> Pacific Ltd. Ottawa's primary interest was to reduce
> the provincial governments' capacity to influence
> economic activity beyond their borders, while the
> corporations concerned attempted to preserve their
> decision-making prerogatives by blocking, through
> federal legislation, provincial government investment
> in firms.[9] ◆

si je me souviens bien

There was no doubt in Quebec that the real purpose of Bill S-31 was to block the Caisse from taking control of CP. The federal government's argument that provincial investment in a firm would politicize its decision-making process was rejected.[10] Alain Dubuc of *La Presse* saw the Trudeau government as "hostile toward any manifestation of regional nationalism," and the Bill as intended "to concentrate all economic levers in Ottawa."[11]

In a rare demonstration of unanimity ,the Quebec protest brought together the government, the opposition, the labour movement and the financial community — including the Montreal Stock Exchange, where the Caisse accounted for more than half of the business transactions.[12] Serge Saucier, president of the Montreal Chamber of Commerce, summed up the situation:

> Canadian unity will be viable only if French
> Canadians feel they play a role in the Canadian
> economy, in the upper levels of the private sector,
> corresponding to their numerical importance in
> Canada...Concentration of government power is an
> evil, we agree. But the absence of French
> Canadians in key decision-making centres is an
> even worse evil. Our support goes to the lesser of
> two evils, the Caisse.[13]

Bill S-31 was seen as a plot of the anglophone elite against financial interests based in Quebec, and more precisely against rising francophone entrepreneurship and the Parti Québécois itself.[14] Quebec finance minister Jacques Parizeau accused Ottawa of trying to prevent Francophones from taking CP away from the anglophone business establishment.[15] He asserted that a deal had been made between the federal government and Ian Sinclair, president of CP: in exchange for the assurance that the Caisse de dépôt et placement would never take control of CP, Sinclair had supposedly given his support to a federal policy placing a ceiling on salary increases.[16]

Si je me souviens bien

Accompanied by a dozen prominent Quebec businessmen
including the president of the Montreal Stock Exchange, Pierre
Lortie, and the president of the Chamber of Commerce, Serge
Saucier, Jacques Parizeau made the following statement in front of
the Senate Justice and Constitutional Committee, which was hold-
ing hearings on the Bill: "I fail to understand why those who love
Canadian unity are so afraid of seeing Francophones succeed in
business."[17] Parizeau maintained that under the terms of the Bill
Quebec would be treated in ways that the Foreign Investment
Review Agency never treated foreign investors.[18]

For its part, the Liberal Party of Quebec, which had been
silent for a month following the tabling of the Bill in the Senate,
took everyone by surprise when Gérard-D. Lévesque, the party's
interim leader, criticized the Bill for attacking the Caisse de dépôt et
placement and for having ill-defined objectives. He also complained
that no one had been consulted in advance.[19]

Besides *The Gazette* which pronounced the Bill to be in the
national interest,[20] one of the few Quebec organizations to support
it was the Conseil du patronat (Employers' Council), which suggested the Caisse stick to its fiduciary role.[21] Another dissenting voice
was that of Michel Vastel of *Le Devoir*:

> A compilation...of data available at the Toronto
> Stock Exchange and at the federal ministry of
> consumer and corporate affairs indicates that
> either the finance minister, Mr. Jacques Parizeau,
> and the president of the Caisse de dépôt et place-
> ment have grossly exaggerated the financial
> impact of the federal law, or the Quebec govern-
> ment [has] taken the political decision to take
> control of CP.[22] ◆

While the Liberal caucus was increasingly divided over the issue, the Senate committee studying the Bill submitted its report on December 17, 1982. It concluded that Bill S-31 exceeded the federal government's jurisdiction. Bill S-31 was thus shelved at the end of the autumn session.

On November 3, 1983, a slightly amended version of the Bill appeared. Faced with public protest in Quebec, the Liberal caucus demanded that the bill be withdrawn. On November 30, Bill S-31 died for a second time — and for good. Political analysts Yves Bélanger and Pierre Fournier maintain that "even if the bill was never passed, it was a clear warning to the Caisse to keep its ambitions for pan-Canadian companies in check."[23] The Caisse did not increase its holdings in Canadian Pacific.

The CF-18
Maintenance
Contract (1986)

O N APRIL 10, 1980, A FEW WEEKS BEFORE THE REFERENDUM ON SOVEREIGNTY-association, the Canadian government announced its decision to award the contract to build new Canadian fighter planes to McDonnell Douglas (F-18) instead of General Dynamics (F-16).

Five years later, in 1985, three consortiums submitted bids in response to the government's call for tenders for the maintenance contract of the new fleet of CF-18s: the Canadair Group of Montreal, the Bristol Group of Winnipeg and the IMP Group in Halifax.[1]

The government set up an evaluation committee of 75 experts to study those bids. The bid from IMP was soon found to be technically inadequate. Then, in June 1986, the committee recommended that the cabinet choose the bid from Bristol, which earned 926 points out of a maximum of 1000 for technical merit (compared to 841 points for Canadair) and was $3.5 million lower than Canadair's.[2] Bristol had lowered its price without being asked to do so by Ottawa, in order to make its bid more attractive.

Despite the committee's recommendation and the lower price, on October 31, 1986, the government announced its decision to award the contract to Canadair. Ottawa justified its decision by declaring that as a Canadian firm Canadair would be better able to ensure the transfer of technology in Canada. "This decision is based on sound financial and economic criteria,"[3] said Treasury Board president Robert de Cotret in announcing the decision, brushing aside the idea that regional or political considerations had influenced the choice of firm.

as i recall

The federal decision provoked a strong reaction in Manitoba, and the CF-18 issue became a symbol of western alienation. Political analysts Robert M. Campbell and Leslie A. Pal sum up the issue:

> In 1985 the contract had been about jobs; by 1986 it was about the nature of Canada. The decision engendered a depth of bitterness not seen in the west since the energy wars over the National Energy program.[4]

In reply to Prime Minister Brian Mulroney's assertion that the decision taken was in the national interest, Don Braid of *The Gazette* wrote: "This implies that central Canada's interest is national, but western Canada's interest is not."[5]

Political parties in Manitoba unanimously protested the decision. The New Democratic Party premier, Howard Pawley, sharply denounced the political favouritism shown by the decision: "I have, until frankly a few days ago, considered that a strong central government protecting the smaller provinces was the best way. I have had to reluctantly re-examine that premise."[6] He went so far as to threaten to pull out of the constitutional talks that would result in the Meech Lake Accord. Each of the western premiers was approached by Pawley to lend their support to Manitoba, but only BC's Social Credit premier, Bill Vander Zalm, responded; neither of the Tory premiers – Don Getty of Alberta and Grant Devine of Saskatchewan – rallied behind Manitoba.[7]

Tories from the West rejected the explanations advanced by the federal government to justify its decision and maintained that it was politically motivated. The Conservative Party of Manitoba, led by Gary Filmon, even considered changing its name to distance itself from its federal "big brother." Party members tore up their cards, while Liberals and New Democrats saw their popularity sky-rocket in the polls.[8] Felix Holtmann, one of nine Conservative MPs from Manitoba, used particularly colourful language: "We were confident that Bristol had a very good bid. I'll have to scream and holler a little louder. The squeaky wheel gets more grease."[9]

The business world also criticized the decision. "Brian Mulroney has committed political suicide," said John Doole, president of the Winnipeg Chamber of Commerce. Using strong terms, he admitted feeling sorry for Manitoba federal Tories, who "have been left to hang and dry in the sun...for the vultures to pick their eyes out."[10] ◆

Si je me souviens bien

Many in Quebec had pressured Ottawa to select Canadair: the Quebec government, the Montreal Chamber of Commerce, the City of Montreal and the Montreal Urban Community, to name only a few bodies. Canadair also received the "unconditional" support of federal Liberals in Quebec.[11]

In Quebec, the CF-18 decision was presented as Quebec versus Ontario.[12] The maintenance contract would reinforce Montreal's aerospace industry and was seen merely as the share of industrial benefits to which Quebec was entitled: "Ontario has the automobile industry and we want the aerospace industry consolidated here," said Yvon Marcoux, president of the Montreal Chamber of Commerce.[13]

Premier Robert Bourassa called Brian Mulroney's decision courageous, declaring it justified by the higher unemployment rate in eastern Canada.[14] René Lévesque pointed out that Ottawa had promised Quebec the CF-18 maintenance contract to make up for the 1980 decision to award the contract to build the new fleet to McDonnell Douglas instead of General Dynamics.[15] In short, the federal decision was warmly welcomed. Campbell and Pal aptly sum matters up:

Montrealers felt that giving the CF-18 maintenance contract to Bristol would have been a "political decision." In

their view, Montreal was the site of 50 percent of
Canada's aerospace industry, Montreal had been given
promises in 1980, Montreal was competing with British
and American owned firms who would do the work in
Ontario, and Montreal, through Canadair, had played by
the rules while Bristol submitted unsolicited bids to
undercut its competitors.[16] ◆

As a sort of consolation prize, the government announced in December
1986 that the maintenance contract for the CF-5 fleet would go to Bristol, not to
Canadair as originally planned. Additionally, the federal minister, Jake Epp,
awarded his home province of Manitoba a major health-research project.[17] In
1988, also to make amends, the Tories announced new investments in the
province: two laboratories, an environmental research centre and a national park
in the north of Manitoba. They also assured the province that maintenance of the
new Air Canada Airbus planes would be carried out in Winnipeg.[18]

Nonetheless, as pointed out by political analysts Alain-G. Gagnon and
Brian Tanguay, the Conservative government's decision to favour Montreal
over Winnipeg for the CF-18 contract was a catalyst for the establishment of
the Reform Party:

> This decision outraged most Westerners and convinced them that
> the Conservatives were no better than the Liberals at defending the
> interests of the West, especially when votes in Quebec were at stake.
> An entirely new party, many felt, was necessary to act as the voice
> of Western protest... [19]

Some analysts believe that this incident also contributed to the victory of
many western Liberals in the 1988 election[20] and according to the *Winnipeg Free
Press*, to the defeat of the Meech Lake Accord in 1990:

> Manitoba's resentment against that contract award was one back-
> ground factor in the Manitoba legislature's refusal to endorse the
> Meech Lake Accord. In winning the CF-18 contract, Mr. Bourassa
> lost more than he won.[21]

Canadair's CF-18 maintenance contract was renewed in July 1996 for a period of three years. The Reform Party, strong in the West, criticized the Chrétien government for having failed to publish a new call for tenders and acting discreetly to favour Canadair, once again, at the expense of western firms.[22]

Bill C-22 on Drug Patents (1987)

T HERE HAS BEEN A MAJOR DEBATE IN CANADA OVER THE PRICE OF DRUGS SINCE the 1950s. In March 1969, Parliament adopted Bill C-102, which guaranteed compulsory licensing for the manufacture and import of drugs. This law compelled the patent holder to allow generic drug manufacturers to make a product similar to the patent version — from the fourth year of its entry in the market — in exchange for a four-percent royalty on the net price of the product. More favourable to consumers than to patent-holders, this policy kept prices low, encouraged the emergence of a Canadian generic drug industry and enjoyed strong public support. But toward the end of the 1970s, some began to question the policy. The questions reflected new economic conditions and translated into an issue of Quebec versus the rest of Canada because the manufacturers of patented drugs, mostly foreign-owned, were largely located in Quebec.[1]

The Progressive Conservative Party had promised as early as July 1984 to amend the Patent Act to extend patent protection, as an incentive for innovative firms to increase their investment in Canada; that meant creating an environment in which firms involved in research and development could make the most of their investments, while Canadian consumers would be able to purchase medicine at competitive prices.[2]

In its September 1984 report, the Royal Commission of Inquiry on the Pharmaceutical Industry (the Eastman Commission) recommended that the protection already granted to patents not be extended, on the grounds that the measure would be detrimental to healthy competition and lead to increased prices.[3] Brian Mulroney's Conservative government ignored that advice and tabled Bill C-22 in the House of Commons on November 6, 1986. This amendment granted patent-holders protection against compulsory licences for a period of seven to 10 years, created a price review board and advanced $100 million to the provinces to cover additional costs of drugs. At the same time, generic drug manufacturers committed themselves to investing $1.4 billion in research and in the manufacture of new drugs.

Contrary to its expectations, the government had to spend a great deal of time and effort in having the bill passed. There were heated debates at all stages of the legislative process. The Liberal Party of Canada and the New Democratic Party fought fiercely against the Bill, and the Senate, with a Liberal majority, twice refused to pass it. Bill C-22 brought into conflict opposing philosophies of the role of the state: the welfare state versus a policy of laissez-faire; the interests of the sick, poor and elderly versus those of business. It also pitted the economic interests of multinational drug companies against those of the generic drug industry and the interests of Quebec against those of the other provinces. Not until November 19, 1987, did the Senate finally give up the battle and pass Bill C-22. Fearing for the unity of the Liberal Party and the creation of a regional grievance following defeat of the Bill, members of the Quebec Liberal caucus insisted that the Senate allow it to pass — after having themselves opposed the bill to conform to the party line.[4]

as i recall

English Canada was much divided over Bill C-22. Generic drug manufacturers, concentrated in the Toronto region, firmly opposed it because it favoured patented drugs, and many consumer groups opposed it because they feared it would lead to increased prices. In a Gallup poll conducted in August 1986, 57 percent of those interviewed felt that a new drug should be immediately available at a low cost.[5] Robert Kerton, a professor at the University of Waterloo and adviser to the Consumers' Association of Canada, doubted that the price review board would be able to restrict the price of new drugs effectively: "The message the law sends to the multinationals is, 'When you set your entry price in Canada, set it high'."[6]

This fear was cleverly stoked by generic drug manufacturers, who predicted that patented drugs, being more expensive than generics, would end up costing the Canadian taxpayer billions of dollars.[7]

A large coalition of interest groups, the National Coalition on Patent Act Changes, soon emerged to oppose the bill, mounting an intense campaign in Ottawa.[8] But not everybody was against Bill C-22. Patented drug manufacturers, concentrated in the Montreal region but also present in Ontario, strongly supported it, as did the medical establishment and the entire biomedical research community.

However, other issues soon overshadowed the debate on patent protection: free trade, the power of multinationals, the role of the Senate, the role of the state in the economy and Quebec's position within the federation. The view of most provinces was that the Drug Patent Act should favour an approach based on prices (to the advantage of the generic drug manufacturers) rather than investment (which benefits drug patent-holders).[9] Prince Edward Island and Manitoba even passed motions against the bill.

Many considered the bill favourable mainly to Quebec, and, as time went by, the regional dimension of the issue gained prominence. The Mulroney government did little to discourage this view – on the contrary, it used it to silence its opponents:

> The fortuitous concentration of the industry in
> Quebec allowed the government to portray oppo-
> nents of C-22 as being "anti-Quebec," which effec-
> tively neutralized the class and price dimensions of
> the issue...Whether Bill C-22 would lead to higher or
> lower prices became increasingly irrelevant. Bill C-22
> was good for Quebec – period.[10] ◆

si je me souviens bien —

Since patented drug manufacturers were concentrated in
Quebec, it was only natural that Bill C-22 would enjoy a lot of
support there. The National Assembly, the unions, the Montreal
Chamber of Commerce, the Montreal Urban Community and the
universities backed it. Michel Bergeron, director of the department of physiology at the University of Montreal, described the
opinion of the bill's advocates: "The issue is simple: Mrs.
Tremblay might have to pay more for her valium, but her son
will have a job."[11]

The Conservative government's approach, which was
focused on investment, was perfectly compatible with Quebec's economic interests. The Liberal government of Robert Bourassa vigorously condemned the Senate's obstructionism, for imperilling a
$600-million investment in R&D in Quebec. Twice, the National
Assembly passed a resolution in favour of the bill.[12]

In Quebec, Bill C-22 had the effect of threatening the unity of
the federal Liberal caucus. The Quebec Liberal MPs publicly supported the bill, and when time came to vote, several, along with Liberal
senators, broke with the party and voted in favour (among them
Senator Pierre de Bané and MP Jean-Claude Malépart).[13] Quebec
opponents advanced arguments similar to those used elsewhere in
Canada, but they were less numerous and remained marginal compared to their counterparts in other provinces. ◆

Bill C-22 came into effect on December 7, 1987. The disaster predicted
by the generic drug companies never occurred. The rate of increase in patented drug prices remained lower than the inflation rate, and the Ontario drug
industry thrived.[14]

Because legislation on drug patents must be amended every five years,
the government of Canada revised the Act in 1993, with Bill C-91, which
brought an end to the compulsory licensing system and extended the patent-
protection period to 20 years, despite ongoing opposition from generic drug

manufacturers and consumer groups.[15] The result of the new protection measures has been a multiplication of biotechnology firms, mainly in Quebec and Ontario.[16]

The government of Canada initiated another review of the Patent Act in 1997. There was no confrontation this time, due to the support of the Greater Montreal and Metropolitan Toronto chambers of commerce for the current version of the Patent Act.[17] Modifications to Bill C-91 came into effect in March 1998.

The Canada-U.S.
Free Trade
Agreement (1988)

I N 1982, AT THE TAIL END OF A DEEP RECESSION, THE TRUDEAU GOVERNMENT appointed the Royal Commission on the Economic Union and Development Prospects for Canada. Chaired by Donald S. Macdonald, the Commission tabled its report on September 5, 1985, recommending that Canada negotiate a free trade agreement with the United States. Prime Minister Brian Mulroney wasted little time in taking up the cause, despite the fact that the previous year he had opposed free trade during his campaign for the leadership of the Progressive Conservative Party.

Canada reached an agreement with the United States on October 3, 1987, after many months of tough negotiations. That December, the text of the proposed agreement was tabled in the House of Commons, and on January 2, 1988, Prime Minister Mulroney and President Ronald Reagan, of the United States signed the Free Trade Agreement. All that remained was approval by the Canadian Parliament and the American Congress.

This was not the first time the issue of free trade had been debated in Canada. The first agreement between Canada and the United States, the Reciprocity Treaty, was signed in 1854. For Canada, this had compensated for the end of its trade relationship with Britain in 1846, when the system of imperial preferences was dismantled. Canada had tripled its exports after 10 years of free trade with the United States. In 1866, following pressures from the American fishing and lumber industries and the antagonism resulting from the Canadian actions during the American Civil War, the United States abrogated the Reciprocity Treaty. Confederation in 1867 established a new political community and a new Canadian common market, this time based on an east-west axis. In

1879, Prime Minister John A. Macdonald's National Policy, with its high tariffs, came into effect in reaction to the US refusal to re-establish reciprocity.[1]

Free trade between Canada and the United States was once again seriously considered in 1911 but an arrangement failed to materialize. The Auto Pact, negotiated in 1965 and establishing free trade in automobiles and automobile parts, was the last serious attempt, before 1988, at forming a free trade relationship — albeit limited — between the two countries.[2]

On May 24th 1988, Bill C-130, the legislation implementing the Free Trade Agreement, was introduced for first reading in the House of Commons. The Liberals and New Democrats opposed it. In committee, members of these two parties presented over 50 amendments, two of which were accepted. The bill was sent for a third reading in the Commons on August 4. Knowing that his party and the NDP could do nothing to defeat the Bill, Liberal leader John Turner asked the Liberal majority in the Senate to withhold its approval of the Bill until an election was held.[3]

As the Liberal Senators proceeded to systematically delay the adoption of the agreement, Prime Minister Mulroney was forced to call an election on the issue of free trade, for November 21, 1988.

as i recall

Free trade touched off a passionate debate in Canada outside Quebec. In contrast to Quebec, the debate in the rest of Canada went beyond the mere economics of free trade.

> Canada is disintegrating,... wrote Mel Hurtig, in 1991. We have allowed inept political leadership and manipulative, greedy, and selfish corporate leaders to destroy the labours and accomplishments of generations – the work and dreams of millions of Canadians from every political background and from every part of Canada...Never before in my lifetime have I encountered a situation that so threatens the existence of our country.[4]

Like Hurtig, many Canadians viewed free trade as a threat to
Canada's future. Opponents of free trade believed it would threaten
Canadian identity and sovereignty, imperil the Canadian social safety net and lead to an outflow of jobs to the United States. A Decima
poll conducted in December 1985, surveying 1500 people, found
that 45 percent of Canadians thought that the "risks to Canada's
political and economic independence outweigh[ed] any potential
benefits" of free trade.[5] Opponents of free trade were little interested in the potential benefits of an integrated economy and very worried by the perception that Canada would be weakened politically.[6]

Demonstration against free trade on Parliament Hill in Ottawa. (University of
Ottawa, French Canadian Civilization Research Centre, *Le Droit* Collection, C76,
Ph92-7/2188MAN; photographer Gilles Benoît)

The Liberal Party of Canada and the NDP shared those
fears. In the election campaign of 1988, Liberal leader John
Turner maintained that Canadian social programs, especially the
health-insurance programs run by the provinces, would be threatened by free trade. He argued that competition from American
manufacturers would jeopardize the Canadian economy and its
ability to pay for social programs.[7] Opposition also came from the

labour movement, the artistic community and farmers, who formed a number of coalitions against free trade. Delegates to the 1986 annual meeting of the Canadian Labour Congress approved a policy paper stipulating that free trade would mean "abandonment of the Canadian tradition of using government to promote a caring and sharing society."[8]

The most favourable reaction to the agreement came from senior federal and provincial civil servants (80 percent in favour) and business leaders (almost 70 percent in favour).[9] The provincial premiers largely supported free trade, the only exceptions being the Liberal premiers of Ontario and Prince Edward Island.

Public opinion, however, was divided. Support for the agreement was lower in the other provinces than in Quebec, but opinion polls revealed significant regional variation: a majority of Albertans were in favour, a majority of Ontarians opposed.[10] Alberta Premier Don Getty had harsh words for the opponents of free trade:

> I am warning those who would damage Alberta's
> future, by taking positions against free trade, that we
> will never forget it...We cannot have those who want
> to dominate Alberta and the West continue to fight
> this free trade agreement in order that they can pur-
> sue that domination."[11] ◆

si je me souviens bien

Bolstered by the support for free trade in the business world and among civil servants in the ministry of industry, trade and technology, the Liberal government of Robert Bourassa, elected in 1985, supported the Free Trade Agreement.

The Parti Québécois also backed the agreement. Several years earlier, the party had decreased its support for state intervention in favour of a more market-based approach to the economy, as

Si je me souviens bien

evidenced by the documents *Bâtir le Québec* (1979) and *Le virage technologique* (1982). Thus at the beginning of 1985, prior to the announcement of the Macdonald Commission recommendation in favour of free trade, PQ ministers Jacques Parizeau and Pierre-Marc Johnson were already working on a new commercial strategy for Quebec. Directed toward free trade, this strategy was aimed at overcoming the growing problem of American protectionism, transforming the Quebec economy to make it more competitive and securing an economic association with the United States.[12]

A poll conducted between January and June 1986 by the Canadian Federation of Independent Business also revealed optimism in the private sector regarding free trade with the United States: four out of five Quebec small and medium-sized enterprises did not feel threatened by it.[13]

As it did elsewhere in Canada, the labour movement in Quebec was opposed to free trade. As early as 1986, many unions united to form the Coalition québécoise d'opposition au libre-échange (Quebec Anti-Free Trade Coalition), on the grounds that free trade it threatened national identity, as well as for social and economic reasons:

> A free trade agreement between Canada and the
> United States represents perhaps the greatest threat
> to Quebec identity since the Conquest...Sovereignty
> itself and Canadian and Quebec cultural integrity
> could slowly disappear.[14]

The Coalition feared the loss of social programs, as a result of the levelling effect of the American model, and a reduction in Quebec industrial autonomy.[15]

A majority of Quebecers, however, saw free trade as a means of opening up to the world and preventing ill effects of American protectionism. Being of a distinct linguistic community, Francophones felt that their culture, unlike that of English Canadians, was protected. Benoît Bouchard, minister of transport in the Mulroney government, remarked, "The fear aspect of free trade plays less well in Quebec because Quebecers have been living with cultural fears for 300 years."[16] Historian Jacques Portes offers another explanation:

> Since the 19th century, French Canadians have always
> viewed the Americans as their friends. Thus they
> have always been more positively disposed to
> American investments than other Canadians...never
> having suffered at the hands of [the Americans] and
> having much reason to criticize [the English].[17] ◆

After a rough-and-tumble campaign, the Conservatives won 170 of 295 seats and 43 percent of the popular vote, and the House of Commons approved the Free Trade Agreement on December 31, 1988; it came into effect on January 1, 1989. Many English-Canadian opponents of free trade were angered that the government proceeded to implement the Agreement given that a majority of Canadians had voted for parties opposed to it.[18] The overwhelming support for the Conservative Party in Quebec has also been interpreted as evidence of the profound insensitivity of Quebecers to the national aspirations of English Canada.[19]

Two years later, the Mulroney government began trilateral negotiations with the United States and Mexico, with the goal of reaching a North American Free Trade Agreement. That agreement was signed on December 17, 1992, and adopted by the House of Commons on June 23, 1993. Following the crushing defeat of the Conservatives in the October 1993 federal election, the Liberals left the North American Free Trade Agreement untouched, even though they had suggested, during the election campaign they would do otherwise. The North American Free Trade Agreement came into effect, as planned, on January 1, 1994.[20]

chapter 6

Failed
Reconciliation

Introductions by
John Meisel
Guy Rocher

Essays prepared by
Alain Desruisseaux
and Sarah Fortin

Failed
Reconciliation

D URING MOST OF THE 20TH CENTURY THE LIBERAL PARTY OF CANADA PLAYED THE leading role in mediating the interests of English and French Canada. Both its electoral base and its leading cadres reflected Canada's dualism, as exemplified by its longstanding practice of alternating Québécois and non-Québécois party leaders: And since the Liberals have been, in the words of Reginald Whitaker, "the Government Party,"[1] Quebecers have regularly occupied the prime minister's office. Their principal rivals, the Conservatives (the Progressive Conservatives after 1942), have historically been the party of the Anglo establishment, a pattern that started to change only in the 1950s when John Diefenbaker, a western populist, became its leader and subsequently our prime minister. It is therefore somewhat paradoxical that the Progressive Conservatives were behind the effort to undo the grievous damage inflicted on Quebec-ROC relations by the substance and method of the 1981 constitutional accord.

Brian Mulroney, a bilingual Quebecer, was the principal agent in the effort to bring Quebec back into the constitutional fold. However, it is important to note that his two Anglo predecessors, Robert Stanfield from Nova Scotia and Joe Clark from Alberta, diligently sought to build bases in, and bridges to, Quebec and to seriously address the issues plaguing Quebec-Canada relations during their terms in office. To some extent, they laid the groundwork for Mulroney. Outside Quebec, the work of these two anglophone leaders facilitated the party's acceptance of the initiatives launched and orchestrated by Mulroney, which led to the Meech Lake and Charlottetown accords.

A major reason for the failure of those major and sustained efforts at redress, particularly the Meech Lake Accord, is that many non-Quebecers have difficulty agreeing that Quebec's status as a distinct society should be enshrined in the Constitution. Much of ROC is animated by a visceral provincial egalitarianism that finds it repugnant that one province should be treated any differently from another. The fact that differential treatment has been the norm since Confederation in 1867 carries little weight, as the constitutional position of Preston Manning currently attests.

However, opposition to special treatment for Quebec does not reflect simply a benign preference for equality. Since it is patently obvious that Quebec is not a province like the others and does, indeed, constitute a distinct society, it is clear that some veiled concerns underlie Anglo rejections of special arrangements for Quebec. These preoccupations run deep and largely explain why accommodation has been so difficult. Vestiges of anti-Catholic and anti-French sentiments rooted in Canadian history fans opposition to special status. There is also perennial resentment over a perceived favouring of Quebec by a central government that is, as we are frequently reminded, more often than not presided over by a Quebecer. And some Canadians, particularly westerners, see the whole Canada-Quebec issue as a dispute among Quebecers who hold power in both Ottawa and Quebec City.

Within the so-called multicultural groups, many fail to understand or empathize with Quebec's passionate commitment to the French language, since they themselves, particularly if they or their forebears arrived in Canada long ago, willingly abandoned their mother tongue, usually in favour of English. Similarly, some "ethnic" Canadians argue that they *are* bilingual, speaking English and their group's original language, like Ukrainian or Icelandic. Why can't the Québécois do likewise? These critics fail to differentiate between language retention in a diasporic situation and in a society with a critical cultural mass.

A largely subconscious but powerful obstacle to the acceptance of distinct status for Quebec is the fear that this "concession" would open the door to the ultimate separation of Quebec from Canada. Some view the history of Quebec since the Quiet Revolution as a continuous, escalating series of demands that never seem to be satisfied. To accord the province unique status is thus seen as a step toward the breakup of Canada.

Another impediment to finding a *modus vivendi* between Francophones and Anglophones, and between Quebec and ROC, arises from the evolving vision and definition of Canada among newly mobilized "entitlement groups," those based on characteristics unrelated to ethnicity or language. Some of these groups, notably advocates of aboriginal and women's rights, succeeded in obtaining recognition in the final stages of the constitutional negotiations of 1980-81. These groups, known as "Charter groups" because much of their clout arises from the Charter of Rights and Freedoms, have tended to play down regional and inter-ethnic accommodation in favour of meeting the needs of their members. Since these were not addressed in the constitutional adjustments proposed during the "Quebec round" leading up to the Meech Lake Accord, that agreement found little resonance among the Charter groups. Worse, they saw in the Accord a dangerous threat to concessions they had wrung from the architects of the 1982 Constitution and its Charter. Elijah Harper's critical vote in the Manitoba legislature, which, with the wave of a feather, sank the Accord, has received widespread publicity; but the negative stance of the National Action Committee on the Status of Women under the leadership of Judy Rebick, though less widely appreciated, also played a major role in weakening ROC support for Meech.

The increasing importance of the Charter groups, whose influence seems to be greater in ROC than in Quebec, complicates the process of finding a suitable basis for the creative co-existence of Anglophones and Francophones. This is illustrated by the way ROC perceives Quebec's treatment of minorities. There is a widespread sense in ROC that Quebec is not as tolerant of its minorities as other parts of the country. In the case of the Oka crisis involving the Kanesatake Mohawks, some interpreted the situation as an indication of Quebec's lack of understanding of, or sympathy for, its aboriginal population. This perceived insensitivity was seen as characteristic of French Quebec's attitude to all "foreign" or "alien" groups. The reasons for this belief are difficult to document but can be traced to several factors.

One is the distrust that has developed between many Francophones and Quebec's aboriginal population in general, the Cree in particular. Some Anglophones believe that the government of Canada has certain legal and moral obligations to Quebec Aboriginals that conflict with the plans of Quebec *indépendantistes*. In certain quarters, there is a view that the emphasis in Quebec on the shared history, language and community ties of Francophones somehow discriminates against the Innu and Indians, as well as other non-Québécois *de souche*. The term *de souche*, widely used in Quebec to distinguish "old stock"

Quebecers from newcomers, is seen by some as a telling indication of the deep chasm that exists between "we" and "they" in Quebec. Similarly, the provincial motto displayed on car licence plates, "Je me souviens", is sometimes seen as an exclusivist gesture. This partly explains why the English media coverage of the Kanesatake disturbances tended to be favourable to the Mohawks: there was an inclination to see them as victims. The francophone press did not start with that assumption.

Another reason for English Canada's suspicions concerning attitudes towards minorities in Quebec is that Quebec's language and education policies have to some extent restricted freedom of choice for Quebec's non-Francophones, disconcerting them and many people in ROC. In some quarters, particularly those far removed from the situation in Quebec, these measures have been interpreted as xenophobic. Additionally, there is the knowledge that the Quebec nationalist movement, at least in its early days, displayed anti-Semitic tendencies and some think vestiges of these still persist.

The Oka crisis, the constitutional initiatives and other divisive episodes reveal that it is easier to mobilize Quebec's diverse "foes" than it is to animate its "friends." Yet in spite of this, the decade starting in the mid-1980s did give birth to a prodigious number of initiatives by "friends," studying the question of ROC-Quebec relations and seeking to find solutions to outstanding problems. That development was partly an outgrowth of the consciousness-raising started by the Quiet Revolution and the B&B Commission, built upon by the 1980 referendum and its aftermath. A tangible expression of this changing state of mind is the growth of French immersion schools in ROC.

The numerous activities designed to address Canadian unity fall into two groups: academic and scholarly exercises and citizen projects intended to build closer contacts and relations with Quebecers. The former usually consist of conferences or seminars followed by the publication of related studies or research programs addressing various aspects of the unity question. The latter include thousands of projects to enhance contacts and express goodwill: visits and exchanges, the twinning of municipalities, and projects like the billboard and bumper-sticker campaign launched by a trucker to spread the message "My Canada Includes Quebec." These grassroots efforts have been undertaken by existing organizations and by bodies established specifically for the purpose. Big

During the 1995 sovereignty-partnership referendum, several grass-root initiatives were undertaken to try to avert a Yes victory. Here, students of Owen Sound High School in Wiarton, Ontario, show postcards they intend to send to francophone families in Quebec. (James Masters, Canapress)

business, professional and occupational groups, volunteer groups and private individuals all have had a hand in them.

These citizen and voluntary-association efforts have been partly triggered by a concern over the fate of the country, by a belief in the idea that a critical defining feature of Canada is the co-existence of the Quebec and ROC communities, or just by a fondness for Quebec. There were and are many among Quebec's "friends" who believe that the country and their own lives are greatly enriched by the presence of two Canadian entities — Quebec and ROC.

But there was another motive, engendered by the Chrétien government's attitude to the national unity question, which grew in strength as the 1995 referendum approached. When elected in 1993, Chrétien declared that Canada was tired of constitutional wrangling; he and his colleagues essentially ignored the national unity file and the still unrepaired damage of patriation. Many in ROC were alarmed by what they saw as dangerous government inaction. They sought to compensate for this abdication of responsibility by supporting various private initiatives to engage Quebecers in dialogue and enhance the social and community infrastructure of the Canadian federation. The immense pro-Canada demonstration in Montreal on the eve of the 1995 referendum was, in a sense, the culmination of much of that effort, though it benefited from the last-minute involvement of the federal government.

During the period leading up to the referendum, a fundamental change in the country's political culture affected relations between Quebec and ROC. Its roots lay in the remarkable decline in Canada of deference,[2] a growing disillusionment with politicians and the political class (at least outside Quebec), and an ever deepening anti-elitism, particularly concerning the management of the federal system. This distrust of "top-down" federalism received impetus from the 1982 Constitution, with its rights-bestowing Charter and an amending formula requiring the consent of provincial legislatures. The transformation was further aided by the decision to submit the Charlottetown Agreement to a national referendum.

The parliamentary tradition based on the Westminster model, in which the cabinet plays a the central role, has given way to a much more diffuse political process in which entitlement groups, the courts and the electorate seriously challenge the supremacy of political elites. The long-established system of elite accommodation,[3] in which political leaders have the tacit or express support of the public for bridging differences between the principal groups comprising ethnically-divided or religiously-cleaved society, no longer applies in Canada. Democratization of decision-making and greater public participation considerably lengthen and complicate the process of finding solutions to the problems confronting heterogeneous societies.

Failed

Reconciliation

T HIS PERIOD OPENS WITH A DREAM, A WAKING DREAM. WOULD QUEBEC AND ROC
finally reach an *entente cordiale* (a cordial agreement), to borrow an expression used at the beginning of the century in discussing relations between France and England?

Quebecers were traumatized by the events of 1980 and 1981: the tough referendum campaign had seen families divided and friendships destroyed. Francophone Quebecers found themselves in painful conflict with one another, both winners and losers left feeling wounded. Then, the 1981 negotiations failed and Quebec emerged more isolated than ever, having opted out of an agreement that it deemed unacceptable. Quebec still remembers the "Night of the Long Knives" despite all the denials by some of the actors in that drama that Quebec was deliberately excluded.[1] During the first part of the 1980s, there was much discussion about the prevailing "bad mood" in Quebec.

Another very important political reality should also be recalled: by imposing conscription in 1917, the Conservative Party lost francophone Quebec, and it never regained it. The Conservative Party even disappeared from the provincial scene, to be replaced by the nationalist Union Nationale. The federal election of September 1984 saw this pattern reversed and marked the beginning of a short but exceptional love affair between the Progressive Conservative Party and Quebecers. The Conservatives borrowed the proven Liberal Party strategy of choosing a leader from Quebec, in this case Brian Mulroney.

Quebecers have always had somewhat ambivalent relations with federal party leaders from Quebec. They remain loyal to them at election time, but they are never entirely sure they will be loyal in return. So, from time to time Quebec feels let down by these leaders, in some quarters actually developing an antipathy — almost a hatred — toward them, something that it never feels toward anglophone leaders. Such was the fate of Wilfrid Laurier, King's lieutenant Ernest Lapointe and, more recently, Pierre Elliott Trudeau, not to mention the case of Réal Caouette as head of the federal Social Credit Party.

And such was the fate of Brian Mulroney, though he was not subject to the degree of resentment reserved for Trudeau and, more recently, Jean Chrétien and Stéphane Dion. Mulroney enjoyed an advantage the others denied themselves: He openly pleaded Quebec's cause and made himself the champion of reconciliation by attempting to bring Quebec out of isolation to resume its place within Canada and erase the memory of the "Night of the Long Knives." Not since Lester Pearson had a prime minister used language so pleasing to Quebecers' ears.

Mulroney's triumph was his success in persuading René Lévesque to join him in the quest for an honourable compromise. Lévesque made this commitment to Mulroney knowing it would provoke a deep split within his party and cost him his staunch lieutenants — Jacques Parizeau, Camille Laurin and a good many others. Never before had Quebecers' ambivalent feelings toward their compatriots in the federal government been more clearly and dramatically illustrated than by that conciliatory gesture on the part of René Lévesque and the condemnation that it provoked.

Quebecers also transferred their ambivalence toward Mulroney to what was seen as his creation: the Meech Lake Accord. Although it was quickly ratified by the Quebec National Assembly, the Accord received a fair amount of criticism, even from its supporters, and was strongly opposed by those in the nationalist camp. There was considerable fear in nationalist and sovereignist circles that, despite strong opposition among a significant number of Canadians, the provincial legislatures would adopt the Accord, in an attempt to put an end to interminable constitutional debates and thus prevent the worst from happening. More than anything, sovereignists feared that recognition of Quebec as a "distinct society" would be enough to convince a majority of Quebecers, even some sovereignists, to postpone the indépendantiste project forever, leaving it to die a slow death.

The way in which Quebecers took the news of the Accord's demise in Winnipeg speaks volumes about the complexity of their feelings. They took it as a slap in the face, one that had been eagerly awaited by sovereignists and feared by federalists. For nationalists and sovereignists, rejection of the Accord confirmed their conviction that Quebec was different from the rest of Canada and that ROC would never understand or accept this fact, and would certainly never recognize it in the Constitution. It had finally been demonstrated to them that it was time they left this inhospitable country. On the other hand, supporters of the Accord felt humiliated, even betrayed, by its failure and the inability of ROC to accept conditions that Quebec saw as minimal. So great was the disappointment among federalists that the sovereignist option even won favour with some prominent Quebec Liberal Party members. For a moment it appeared that through an astonishing turn of events, Robert Bourassa rather than René Lévesque would undertake to negotiate Quebec independence and become the first president of the new republic. Never before had Quebec public opinion, even in circles where the sovereignist option had barely penetrated before, been more ready to opt for independence. If Bourassa had wanted to, he could have done the deed.

Compared to the hopes raised by the Meech Lake Accord, the Charlottetown Accord and the referendum of 1992 had little emotional impact in Quebec. Popular thinking could not have been simpler or clearer: if Quebec was unable to secure agreement for the minimal conditions of the Meech Lake Accord, the Charlottetown Accord must be offering still less. The Yes campaign could do nothing to shake this common-sense logic. In the end, Quebec and ROC voted the same way, but for reasons that were diametrically opposed: the former, because the Accord offered too little; the latter, because it promised too much. This difference of opinion dramatically and symbolically epitomized the opposition of the two political cultures: one asserted Quebec's uniqueness; the other asserted equality, within diversity, for all the provinces. It might even be said that it summed up the balkanization of Canada, for between Meech and Charlottetown something very important occurred: Aboriginal peoples began to receive political recognition in Canada. Excluded from Meech, aboriginal peoples won a place for themselves in the Charlottetown negotiations and had their rights written into the Accord. Their dissatisfaction with the result and their subsequent support for the No side added to the complexity of the Canadian puzzle, whose pieces, more than ever before, seemed unwilling to fit together.

The complexity created by the presence of aboriginal peoples' on the political scene perhaps appeared even greater in Quebec than elsewhere. René Lévesque became aware of the aboriginal issue very early on. His stint as minister of natural resources in the Lesage government in the early 1960s had given him firsthand knowledge of Inuit and Amerindians, and when he became premier he kept that Cabinet portfolio for himself. Under Lévesque's tenure Quebec could claim to have gone further than ROC in recognizing the legitimate rights of the country's first inhabitants.

Despite these accomplishments, relations between Inuit, Amerindians and French Quebecers, particularly sovereignists, remained strained. First Peoples' attachment to a federal government that had never exactly overindulged them and their continual refusal to support a sovereign Quebec have always seemed incomprehensible to many French Quebecers: How could these first inhabitants demand autonomy for themselves yet not understand Quebecers' desire for self-determination? The international campaigns mounted by some Chiefs to denounce Quebec have done nothing to improve the climate. Quebecers felt humiliated and betrayed by the bad reputation they have received at the hands of aboriginal peoples, both in ROC and abroad. These feelings have become particularly acute since the Oka crisis, the wounds from which have not yet healed, on either side. For those in the nationalist camp, the widespread negative attitude among natives toward sovereignty appears to be yet another obstacle to achieving their aims. Some have not hesitated to take this one step further and conclude that natives and English Canadians are conspiring to block the sovereignty project.

Blame directed at francophone Quebecers for their strained relations with Aboriginals they see as part of a defamatory wave victimizing Quebec. Quebecers see themselves as democratic, tolerant citizens. They sometimes even think of themselves as too tolerant. Since enactment of the 1970s language legislation, Quebecers believe their reputation has been tarnished in the Anglo-Saxon world, where Quebec's language requirements for immigrants are interpreted as xenophobic, racist and occasionally anti-Semitic. Quebecers, who pride themselves on having a Charter of Rights and Freedoms that predates Canada's, have been accused, unjustly in their own eyes, of neglecting fundamental rights. They find that the English-Canadian press treats them very unfairly. The negative coverage carries over to reports in the American and European press. And Quebecers who listen to English-language open-line radio shows quickly understand that it is not only members of the media who hold such negative opinions of Quebecers, but a good number of Canadians in other provinces as well.

To Quebecers, these developments indicate that Canadian attitudes have hardened even though Quebec's demands are minimal. More than ever, they feel they are an "irritant" in Canadian society, and will not be accepted unless they get into line, abandon their demands, rescind Quebec's language laws and accept bilingualism in Quebec and Canadian multiculturalism. What they see, in short, is imposition of the "Trudeauist" vision of Canada and Quebec's place within it.

"Trudeauism" emerged during the 1940s and 1950s, under the regime of Maurice Duplessis, whose nationalism was mixed with, and occasionally used to legitimize and justify, his retrograde conservative policies. Those who had the courage to denounce Duplessism, particularly the team at *Cité libre* magazine, which included Pierre Elliott Trudeau, did not draw a distinction between the two ideologies. In their view, French-Canadian nationalism by its very nature was conservative and retrograde, and thus posed an obstacle to the democratization and modernization of the Quebec they sought to promote. Indeed, French-Canadian nationalism was at that time generally conservative, at least as expressed in *L'action nationale* magazine, one of its quasi-official organs, and in the Ordre de Jacques Cartier, a widespread secret society. This characteristic went a long way towards reinforcing *Cité libre's* opinion of French-Canadian nationalism.

In 1989, anti-Quebec demonstrations and the decision by some Ontario municipalities to declare themselves English-only contributed to the deterioration of the political climate surrounding the Meech Lake constitutional agreement. Here a group of demonstrators trample the Quebec flag in Brockville, Ontario. (Deanna Lysko, Canapress)

Trudeau's conception of Canada eventually became part of the official program of the Liberal Party of Canada and quickly found favour in the rest of Canada. Its promoters considered this "Canadian project" anti-nationalist while affirming the equality of all cultures, none superior to another. It gave priority to human rights, a reminder of its "personalist" roots.[2] In constitutional terms, the Trudeau doctrine affirmed equality within diversity for all the provinces, and the need for a strong federal government with the means to initiate and guarantee national policies. While claiming to draw on a philosophy that was universalist, Trudeauism encouraged, fostered and flattered Canadian nationalism as it condemned Quebec nationalism.

Trudeauism survived Trudeau's departure from active political life. The refusal to recognize Quebec as a distinct society, or to give the provinces room to manoeuvre either within or outside national policies, is based on a centralizing, equalizing vision that has been the hard core of the "Trudeau vision." The events that have marked Canadian history from Meech to the 1995 Quebec referendum can be explained by the fact that Trudeauism has become the main current of thought in Canada outside Quebec.

In Quebec, unlike in ROC, the popularity of Trudeau and his vision of Canada dropped after the 1980 referendum even though he surely contributed to the victory of the No side. Even his referendum allies were alienated by Trudeau's lack of action in fulfilling his solemn commitments to renew the Constitution in a manner satisfactory to Quebec. By contributing to the failure of both the Meech and Charlottetown accords, Trudeau and Trudeauism fanned the flames of Quebec nationalism and had a hand in the Yes side coming within an inch of victory in the 1995 referendum.

Two Canadian prime ministers from Quebec, Trudeau and Mulroney, fervently wished to integrate Quebec into Canada and mould this country into a united and strong nation. They tackled the job in two very different ways, according to two different visions of the country and using different processes. While Mulroney used extended negotiations sanctioned by legislatures or the public, Trudeau took strong positions unilaterally and imposed his vision. They both had a mission to unify Canada, but they have left behind a country that has never been so divided and balkanized and a Quebec that is more wounded than ever.

The Meech Lake Accord (1987)

O N SEPTEMBER 4, 1984, THE PROGRESSIVE CONSERVATIVE PARTY LED BY BRIAN Mulroney won the federal general election with 49.9 percent of the popular vote and 211 seats. During the election campaign, Mr. Mulroney had promised to bring Quebec back into the constitutional family "with honour and enthusiasm"[1]; for although Quebec was legally bound by the Constitution of Canada, it had not yet endorsed it. Mr. Mulroney's commitment thus heralded the beginning of a new round of constitutional talks known as the "Quebec round."

In May 1985, taking advantage of Ottawa's new conciliatory attitude, René Lévesque's Parti Québécois government agreed to enter into negotiations (a strategy Lévesque dubbed a "beau risque," a great risk) and published its *Constitutional Accord Program*. When the Liberals were elected in December 1985, they took over this strategy; in May 1986, intergovernmental affairs minister Gil Rémillard set out the five conditions necessary for his government to recognize and sign the 1982 Constitution Act.[2] In August 1986 the 10 provincial premiers met in Edmonton and committed themselves to giving priority to the issue of Quebec and negotiating on the basis of those five conditions. Issues not dealt with in the Quebec round would be addressed in a subsequent round of negotiations. Less than a year later, Quebec's conditions were met as all the premiers and Prime Minister Mulroney signed the 1987 Constitutional Accord, better known as the Meech Lake Accord.

Parliament and the provincial legislatures had to approve the agreement within three years of its ratification by any one of the signatories. On June 23, 1987, Quebec established the ratification deadline when it became the first province to endorse the Accord, by a vote of 95 to 18.[3]

The Meech Lake Accord proposed: 1) adding an interpretative clause (section 2) to the 1867 Constitution Act recognizing that Quebec constitutes a distinct society within Canada and giving the legislature and the government of Quebec the mandate to preserve and promote its distinct identity[4]; 2) increasing the number of fields in which unanimous approval was required to amend the Constitution[5]; 3) requiring the government of Canada to provide fair compensation to provincial governments that opted out of any new, national, shared-cost program in an area of exclusive provincial jurisdiction, providing the province implemented a similar program or measure that met the national objectives; 4) giving constitutional recognition to the Supreme Court, allowing provinces to submit candidates for vacant positions and reserving three seats for judges from the Quebec Bar while leaving intact Ottawa's power to select and appoint judges; and 5) amending the Constitution to incorporate administrative agreements relating to immigration. In addition to these five proposals, the Accord provided for provincial participation in the appointment of senators, as well as a yearly First Ministers' conference on the economy and the Constitution.

Over the three years allowed for the ratification of the Accord (1987 to 1990), there were a number of calls to amend the initial agreement to take various criticisms into account. The positions taken by former Prime Minister Pierre Elliott Trudeau and, later, Frank McKenna of New Brunswick and Clyde Wells of Newfoundland were particularly influential in this regard. For instance, the committee responsible for consulting the citizens of New Brunswick recommended that the equality of that province's two linguistic communities be recognized[6]; others demanded that the meaning of the distinct society clause be clearly defined and its impact on the Charter of Rights and Freedoms specified.[7]

On March 21, 1990, Premier McKenna tabled a resolution in the New Brunswick legislature proposing that his province ratify the Meech Lake Accord only if the other provinces accepted a parallel accord including seven amendments to the original agreement. The very next day, on March 22, 1990, Prime Minister Mulroney created a special House of Commons committee (the Charest Committee) to study these proposals. Meanwhile, on April 6, 1990, the Newfoundland legislature cancelled the previous administration's favourable vote and Premier Wells tabled his own recommendations for changes to the Accord.

In May 1990, the First Ministers met to try to find a solution to the constitutional deadlock. On June 9, they signed the 1990 Constitutional Accord. (Fred Chartrand, Canapress)

The 1990 Constitutional Accord was the outcome of these efforts to revisit the pact. Signed on June 9, it was presented as a supplement to the Meech Lake Accord. In particular, it included a legal opinion drafted by six constitutional experts specifying the impact of the distinct society clause on the application of the Charter of Rights and Freedoms, as well as a commitment to proceed with Senate reform. The three provinces that had not yet approved the Meech Lake Accord — New Brunswick, Manitoba and Newfoundland — committed themselves to pulling out all the stops in order to do so before the June 23, 1990, deadline.

The Meech Lake agreement's initially favourable reception reflected a feeling of satisfaction that Quebec was voluntarily re-entering the Canadian constitutional framework. *The Globe and Mail* commented, It was a moving and historic moment after years of uncertainty during which the very existence of the

Canadian union was challenged. Canada has finally
lived up to its word, offered during the 1980
Quebec referendum campaign, to renew federalism
in a way that satisfies Quebec's modern sense of
place within Confederation.[8]

Public opinion polls showed strong support for the Meech Lake
Accord if it would allow Quebec to sign the Canadian Constitution.[9]

But others found the price of correcting the 1982 mistakes
too high: "*The Star* has supported efforts to bring Quebec into the
constitutional accord of 1981. But not at any price. The price
agreed to at Meech Lake is too high."[10] A movement of protest and
discontent, fed by the news events of the day, took hold and grew.[11]
Anglophone public opinion, which had been evenly divided in 1988
(26 percent for, 27 percent against, 47 percent undecided), moved
against the Accord; by March 1990, 51 percent of the people polled
thought the Meech Lake Accord a bad thing for Canada, 19 percent
a good thing, and 30 percent were undecided.[12]

Experts and public figures who supported the 1987 agreement argued its merits and tried to quell the public's fears.[13] But it
was clearly the opponents of Meech who set the tone of the
debate. Pierre Elliott Trudeau started the ball rolling and was soon
joined by women's groups, linguistic minority groups, human
rights groups, aboriginal peoples and ordinary citizens. These
groups used public hearings[14] and the Liberal Party,[15] as well as the
New Brunswick, Manitoba and Newfoundland governments, as
their main vehicles of protest.

Many observers interpreted the mobilization against the
Meech Lake Accord as an expression of English Canada's evolving
political culture. Increasingly, English Canadians wanted to participate in the constitutional process not just as observers but as active
players alongside government authorities. Those opposed to the
agreement denounced its elitist nature and the secrecy surrounding
the negotiations.[16]

But it was the distinct society clause that provoked the greatest hostility and gradually rallied opposition to the Accord.[17] Opponents of this clause sang four different choruses, all to the same tune: 1) supporters of the Trudeauist vision said the clause went against the principle of equality of individuals and the provinces[18]; 2) women's groups feared the clause would weaken their hard-won right to equality, obtained in 1982, and introduce a hierarchy of rights that would work against their interests[19]; 3) the First Nations, disappointed and frustrated by the failure of the 1982-1983 conferences on aboriginal matters, denounced what they saw as privileged treatment of Quebecers; the Meech Lake Accord seemed to deny their own distinctiveness: "What are we? Chopped liver?" asked an infuriated Inuit spokesperson[20]; and, finally, 4) linguistic minorities harshly criticized the weak mandate given to Parliament and the provincial legislatures to protect minority languages as compared to the Quebec government's obligations to protect Quebec's distinct society.[21]

Most opponents also reproached Prime Minister Mulroney for having given up federal powers to the provinces. Introduced as the "Quebec round," the Meech Lake Accord was soon re-baptized "the round of the provinces," because it put all the provinces on the same footing as Quebec. It was criticized as an attempt to buy off Quebec nationalism at the price of Canadian unity.[22] According to Clyde Wells, the limits imposed on federal spending power would unduly restrict the government's ability to implement national programs, thereby imperilling the principles of redistribution of wealth and equality of opportunity that ensure the welfare of all Canadians.[23] Pierre Elliott Trudeau sums up the viewpoint of English-Canadian opponents to the Accord:

> In addition to surrendering to the provinces important parts of its jurisdiction (the spending power, immigration), in addition to weakening the Charter of Rights, the Canadian state made subordinate to the

provinces its legislative power (Senate) and its judicial power (Supreme Court). And it did this without
hope of ever reversing the process (a constitutional
veto granted to each one of the provinces).[24] ◆

si je me souviens bien

Although the Meech Lake Accord was not unanimously supported
in Quebec, the level of opposition there never approached that
seen in the other provinces. Throughout the ratification period,
less than 20 percent of French speakers thought that the Accord
was a bad thing for Canada. In March 1990, it was supported by
41 percent of Quebecers; the percentage of undecided remained
high (in early 1990, 40 percent of Quebecers could not say
whether the Accord was a good or bad thing for Canada).[25] The
Accord was also greeted favourably by the press. *La Presse* editorialist Michel Roy wrote:

> Brian Mulroney and Robert Bourassa have expressed,
> rightly, their pride and deep satisfaction...Here is an
> accord...which attests to the maturity of the country
> and recognizes the political reality of the Canadian
> federation. This is what Quebec has asked for.[26]

Le Devoir added that since: "Eleven Canadian first ministers
have recognized these basic facts [Canadian duality and Quebec
specificity] and the obligations that they create, our support and
encouragement are justified."[27] Even *The Gazette* concurred: "The
agreement on a renewed deal for Quebec within Confederation is a
massive achievement."[28]

> Thus Premier Robert Bourassa could rightly claim:
> Quebec has won one of the biggest victories in its
> history, one of the greatest historical victories in
> two centuries...We are for the first time winners in

a constitutional debate: all the provinces accept
our conditions.[29]

Experts who studied the Accord, such as Léon Dion, agreed
with Bourassa, although their enthusiasm was tempered and their
support equivocal.[30] It was generally agreed that the substantial
gains for Quebec compensated for the Accord's shortcomings. For
many, the recognition of Quebec's distinct identity in a specific provision rather than in the preamble of the Constitution was an unexpected gain. Daniel Latouche, René Lévesque's former advisor,
noted that "no Quebec government had ever prepared the groundwork so well, nor so skilfully put to use all the handshakes the rest
of the country was offering."[31]

Opposition to the Accord nevertheless emerged in sovereignist circles. In spring 1987, the new Parti Québécois leader,
Pierre-Marc Johnson, asked the members of his party to mobilize against "the Meech Lake monster" and force the Quebec
government to withdraw.[32] His position was supported by nationalist groups, unions and artists. In an advertisement published
on April 30, 1987, the St-Jean-Baptiste society and the
Mouvement national des Québécois denounced the Accord as
alienating and unacceptable.[33]

Nationalist criticism was especially directed toward the distinct society clause and the federal government's spending power.
The wording of the distinct society clause worried most observers,
who questioned its meaning and expressed doubts about its real
impact in terms of additional jurisdiction. Even moderates such as
Léon Dion and Fernand Dumont were concerned about the lack of
precise definition, and for the most radical it was a meaningless
phrase: "We are a people! It is a dark day when a people is reduced
to an insignificant sociological reality such as a distinct society."[34]
Pierre Fournier aptly summed up Quebecers' reservations:

Beyond the petty squabbles and the contradictory
analyses, the distinct society provision was meaning-

less because it granted no new powers to Quebec, did
not refer to the French language and culture as being
essential components of that distinctiveness, and
would have been rendered null and void by the other
measures contained in the accord.[35]

While there were doubts about the distinct society clause,
there were none over the spending power clause. The terms of
that clause were so precise and restrictive that they would have
allowed Ottawa to do indirectly what it could not do directly, "to
acquire the constitutional authority to invest and control, to all
intents and purposes, all the fields of exclusive provincial jurisdiction."[36] While the Accord stipulated that a province could opt out
of new federal programs in areas of provincial jurisdiction, it
added the proviso that the province would have to offer a similar
program in order to get compensation – an important limitation,
in the eyes of many Quebecers.

But opposition was short-lived. Following public hearings
held in June 1987 and the hasty ratification of the Accord on June
23, public debate in Quebec was essentially closed. Support solidi-
fied when increasing opposition to the distinct society clause in
ROC prompted Quebecers to close ranks behind the Accord. Despite
its shortcomings, Meech was seen as making amends for the injustice inflicted in 1982[37] and as an irreducible minimum that met the
least exacting conditions ever set by a Quebec government. The
Accord took on symbolic value in the eyes of Quebecers; its ratification became a crucial test of ROC's good faith.

Premier Bourassa faced strong pressure to hold firm
when McKenna, Wells and others moved to revisit the Accord,
and he initially resisted any attempt to amend the agreement,[38]
saying no to "federalism on our knees." But in the end Bourassa
agreed to the amendments included in the 1990 Constitutional
Accord, presenting this as a demonstration of Quebec's good
faith toward its partners.[39] ◆

On the eve of the June 23 deadline, Manitoba and New-foundland still had not approved the Meech Lake Accord. Though, on the face of it, it was the procedural obstruction of Elijah Harper, an aboriginal member of the Manitoba Legislature, that caused the agreement to collapse, no one in Quebec was taken in by that turn of events: "Nobody could have blocked the Accord...without broad support, not only from these two provinces but from English Canada as a whole," wrote Lucien Bouchard.[40]

A majority of Quebecers took the collapse of the Accord as a rebuff of their aspirations. Renewed federalism, the most popular option since 1985, lost much support:

By preventing the adoption of the Meech Lake Accord, Manitoba MLA Elijah Harper has shown that aboriginal issues could no longer be ignored as they had during the 1987 negotiations and has become a symbol of First Nations' assertiveness. (Canapress)

"The failure of the Meech Lake Accord has highlighted the illusionary character of the bi-national vision maintained by Quebec federalist elites for generations...and it has confirmed the *indépendantiste* thesis."[41] In the following months, support for sovereignty reached an all-time high of 58 percent.[42] Disappointed, supporters of the *beau risque* strategy created a new federal party, the Bloc Québécois, with Lucien Bouchard — who had resigned from the Mulroney government to protest the report of the Charest Committee — as leader. This sovereignist party was intended to bring greater consistency to Quebecers' actions and offer a real political alternative to the existing parties.

Even the Quebec Liberal Party could not remain indifferent, and, for a while, its militants toyed with the idea of sovereignty. On June 22, 1990, reca-pitulating the events that led to the adoption of the Meech Lake Accord, Premier Bourassa concluded with these now famous words: "English Canada must understand very clearly that, whatever one might say or do, Quebec is, now and forever, a distinct society, free and capable of assuming control of its future and its development."[43]

In order to sketch out this future, the premier launched the Commission on the Political and Constitutional Future of Quebec (the Bélanger-Campeau Commission). This led to a new round of constitutional negotiations, which culminated in the signing of the Charlottetown Accord and a Canada-wide referendum in October 1992.

The Oka Crisis (1990)

ON MARCH 10, 1990, THE KANESATAKE MOHAWKS (RESIDING ON THE NORTH shore of Lac des Deux Montagnes, near Montreal) put up a roadblock to protest the planned expansion of the Oka municipal golf course, which was situated on land they claimed as sacred. On July 11, 1990 (just after the collapse of the Meech Lake Accord), the Sûreté du Québec (Quebec provincial police) intervened in force to take down the barricade. A police officer, corporal Marcel Lemay, was killed in the operation. The same day, Quebec's minister responsible for native affairs, John Ciaccia, started negotiations with the Mohawks. On August 8, faced with a deadlock in negotiations, the government of Quebec mandated the Canadian armed forces to take over from the Sûreté du Québec.

Aboriginal peoples from all regions of Canada showed their support to the peoples of Kanesatake[1]; in Quebec, on July 12, 1990, in a gesture of solidarity, the Kahnawake Mohawks (residing on the south shore of the St. Lawrence River, near Châteauguay) blocked the Mercier bridge, which connects the Island of Montreal to the south shore. This forced thousands of people to drive several additional hours every day in order to get to work in the city.

It was not until September 6 that the Mercier bridge was reopened to traffic, and not until September 26, after several weeks of tense negotiations, that the last band members finally agreed to surrender in Oka. About 50 men, women and children entrenched behind the last blockade left Kanesatake aboard military buses headed for the Farnham military base. The stand-off had lasted 78 days.[2]

as i recall

English Canadians were generally sympathetic to the Mohawks. Many saw them as victims, while viewing Quebecers, the Quebec government and the federal government as the aggressors. On July 29, a delegation of about 1000 Canadians went to Oka to demonstrate their support for the aboriginal peoples,[3] and on September 6 a petition signed by nearly 150 Canadian public figures and addressed to Prime Minister Mulroney demanded an end to all military action and a return to the negotiating table. It read:

> We as Canadians felt anger and shame about your handling of the crisis at Kanesatake and Kahnawake. As the world watched, you chose silence over leadership, brutality over negotiation, guns over talk...We stand with the aboriginal people of Canada, and with their leaders who have advocated non-violent and just resolutions of their disputes.[4]

From the mid-1980s, aboriginal demands had received more and more attention, to effect: An Angus Reid poll taken toward the end of the Oka crisis (September 19 to 27) revealed that more English Canadians were favourable to the recognition of Aboriginals as a distinct society than to the recognition of Quebec as a distinct society.[5]

According to some analysts, however, anti-Quebec sentiments stirred up in English Canada over Meech Lake contributed greatly to English-Canadian perceptions of the Oka crisis. Native journalist Paul Ogresko wrote:

> The crisis at Oka likely brought a sly smile to the faces of those who are less than supportive of the special rights of Quebec. Never mind the undeniable fact that if the Mohawks had been blockading, say the 401 in Toronto, the backlash and ugliness would have been as great, if not greater than that in Châteauguay. Just as it would be naive to assume in the year 1990, in the wake of the failure of the Meech Lake Accord and the

popular movement toward Quebec independence, that the Oka crisis did not afford a chance to do a little francophone bashing.[6] ◆

Si je me souviens bien

In Quebec, public opinion was divided over the legitimacy of the Mohawk demands: 35 percent of people asked believed that they were justified, 37 percent unjustified. However, more than 80 percent of those polled thought the means used to make the demands were unacceptable.[7] In November 1990, 34 percent of Quebecers claimed to be less favourable to the aboriginal cause since the crisis.[8]

Over the course of the summer, gatherings of angry residents sometimes had overtones of racism and violence, and these images were sent all across the country on television: "The closure of the bridge, the inconvenience it caused, and their perception that the civil authority was weak and outflanked, together were enough to induce [usually law-abiding citizens] to riot."[9] The mutual lack of understanding was no doubt aggravated by inflammatory remarks made by some aboriginal leaders denying the existence of a Quebec nation, and the connection between the Mohawk opposition and the Warriors Society, whose illegal activities in gambling and contraband cigarettes were well known, did little to raise sympathy.[10]

Nevertheless, demonstrations of support for the Mohawks were held regularly on the streets of Montreal, though they never received the same media coverage as the crowds burning effigies near the blockades.[11] In fact, the English-language media's treatment of events caused much dissatisfaction. The Sûreté du Quebec publicly denounced the English press for fostering a bad image of Quebec for political reasons.[12]

Other observers took up that accusation. Robin Philpot wrote: "Harper, Erasmus, Fontaine and Mercredi were thus given a platform as well as a hand, not in helping to further the cause of Amerindians and the Inuit but in attacking Quebec and Quebecers."[13] According to Philpot, the Oka crisis came along at just the right time: with nationalist sentiments in Quebec at an all-time high, the crisis demonstrated to the opponents of Quebec sovereignty the racist nature of Quebec society and its inability to manage its own affairs.

Robert Bourassa felt the need to defend Quebecers against criticisms expressed by many international public figures and organizations that had taken up the native cause:

> There have been many international protests. The way the situation is perceived outside Quebec is far from realistic, particularly by some European representatives of international organizations. I have been striving to point out to them that if bridges in Paris were blocked off for several weeks, and Parisians were forced to drive several hours to get to work, their reaction would be exactly the same as that of the people of Châteauguay.[14] ◆

Although the crisis ended without any further loss of life, the incident left its mark on the Canadian political scene. One year after the Oka crisis, the federal government set up the Royal Commission on Aboriginal Peoples, which was given the task of examining relations between aboriginal peoples and Canadian society.

Kenneth McRoberts asserts that the Oka crisis transformed the attitude of English Canadians toward the constitutional question:

> [It] convinced many English Canadians that any constitutional revision would have to meet the demands of the aboriginal peoples. Indeed, a good number of English Canadians argued that aboriginal demands were far more urgent than Quebec's.[15]

More than ever, Quebec's demands and aboriginal claims have become inseparable; this is why the Charlottetown Accord, in addition to recognizing

Quebec as a distinct society, also included provisions for Aboriginal peoples, the most important being recognition of their inherent right to self-government.

The specific dispute that had caused the Oka crisis, however, remains unsettled, although negotiations are ongoing and the federal government has bought some land to give back to the Mohawks.

The
Gagnon-Tremblay-
McDougall
Agreement on
Immigration (1991)

Q UEBEC AND OTTAWA SIGNED THE GAGNON-TREMBLAY-McDOUGALL AGREEMENT
on Immigration on February 5, 1991. Officially called the Canada-
Quebec Accord Relating to Immigration and Temporary Admission of Aliens, this
agreement is the fourth of its kind. It follows the 1971 Cloutier-Lang Agreement,
the 1975 Bienvenue-Andras Agreement and the 1978 Couture-Cullen Agreement.[1]

Since the creation of the first Quebec department of immigration in 1968,
Quebec has strived to increase its decision-making power in this field, particularly control over the selection and integration of immigrants. Since the
mid-1960s, successive Quebec governments have considered immigration a useful means to reinforce the Quebec economy and counterbalance the fall in the
birth rate without putting the French character of Quebec society in danger.[2]

Following the examples of its predecessors, the government of Robert
Bourassa asked for greater control over immigration matters during the Meech
Lake Accord negotiations. The Meech Lake Accord itself contained only general
principles intended as guidelines for a parallel accord on immigration that the
federal government would negotiate with Quebec or any other province. After the
failure of Meech, this parallel accord was subsequently negotiated and used as the
main part of the Gagnon-Tremblay-McDougall administrative agreement. The difference between this agreement and the principles in the Meech Lake Accord was
that the former would not be constitutionalized.

The distinct identity of Quebec is at the heart of the agreement. Among its
objectives are "the preservation of Quebec's demographic weight within Canada
and the integration of immigrants to that province in a manner that respects the
distinct identity of Quebec."[3] It mainly deals with three issues: determining

immigration levels, selecting immigrants and providing settlement and integration services. The agreement grants the Quebec government the exclusive right to select all independent immigrants bound for Quebec. For its part, the government of Canada is obligated to admit any immigrant destined for Quebec who meets Quebec's selection criteria.[4] The government of Quebec undertakes to annually admit a percentage of immigrants equal to Quebec's percentage of the Canadian population, plus five percent if so desired, whereas the government of Canada undertakes to establish immigration levels for the country as a whole that are compatible with this objective.[5] Finally, the agreement provides for the transfer to Quebec of all services related to the reception of new arrivals and their linguistic, social and economic integration, with financial compensation. The government of Canada provided Quebec with $332 million in the 1991-1995 period. The agreement provides a formula for calculating the financial compensation to be paid to Quebec for 1995-1996 and the following years.[6]

as i recall

Unlike francophone Quebecers, English Canadians tend to view immigration primarily as within federal jurisdiction. Joseph H. Carens points out that no other province has attempted to control immigration policy to the extent that Quebec has. According to Carens, the reason is quite simple.

> Quebec is different. The other provinces do not worry that immigrants to their provinces will choose to learn French rather than English and thereby contribute to doubts about the status of English as the language of common life in their territories. They can assume without thinking about it much that the immigrants will send their children to English schools.[7]

The signing of an agreement between Quebec and Canada granting Quebec more powers over immigration provoked little reaction in English Canada. Examination of newspaper reports at the time suggests that it did not shock English Canada. The agreement's subsequent application, however, gave rise to harsh criticism about the financial compensation that Ottawa was providing to Quebec.

English Canadians were upset that the Quebec government was admitting far fewer immigrants than it had claimed it would, with no adjustment of financial compensation.[8] This inequity was denounced by the governments of British Columbia, Alberta and Ontario, which maintained that Quebec, because of the Gagnon-Tremblay-McDougall Agreement, was receiving much more than its fair share of federal support.[9]

The Globe and Mail columnist Jeffrey Simpson summed matters up:

> This year [1995], Quebec will take about 12 percent of Canada's immigrants, but receive 37 percent of the federal funds for resettlement. Next year, Quebec might accept even fewer than 12 percent of immigrants, but will still take about 37 percent of federal funds. The result, by definition, is that other parts of Canada with many more immigrants, many of whom do not speak English, receive much less per immigrant…Indeed, Quebec's share of national immigration has been falling while its share of funding has been rising.[10] ◆

si je me souviens bien

Many Quebecers had long "perceived immigration as a means used by the federal government to increase the percentage of Anglophones in Canada and thus decrease the percentage and influence of Francophones."[11] According to Kenneth McRoberts, this perception was the reason behind the creation of the Quebec department of immigration. "Claiming that historically Ottawa had made no

effort to attract francophone immigrants, and that indeed the opposite had been the case, the Quebec government had established its
own department of immigration in 1968."[12]

Identity is a key concern for Quebecers when it comes to
immigration. Indeed, the future of the French culture and language
is inextricably linked to this issue. In 1990, the Quebec minister of
cultural communities and immigration, Monique Gagnon-Tremblay,
explained why the Quebec government negotiated a new agreement
on immigration: "The distinct character of Quebec society and the
particular issues that immigration represents for this society have
dictated the amendments to be made to the Couture-Cullen Agreement in order to update and complete it."[13]

Quebecers were generally happy with the agreement, seeing
it as a step in the right direction. Even before it was signed, the editor of *Le Devoir*, Lise Bissonnette, came to its defence: "Not only is
there no reason to deny Quebec what was granted by Meech without
reservation, but if federalism is incapable of recognizing Quebec's
key role on a matter where its "distinct" demographic and economic
destiny is at stake, then we might as well just get out now."[14]

For federalist Quebecers, the agreement was an encouraging
development after the failure of Meech, allowing them to believe in
the renewal of the Canadian federation. For intergovernmental
affairs minister Gil Rémillard, it constituted

> a first step towards a new vision of our federalism.
> This is an extremely interesting case which will allow
> us to seek this kind of efficiency in other fields such
> as labour...This agreement shows that Quebec has
> the capacity and powers to express what we are and
> protect the federal link.[15]

According to the sovereignists, on the other hand, the agreement did not grant enough powers to Quebec. René Marleau, international affairs and immigration advisor to the Leader of the
Opposition, Jacques Parizeau, wrote at the time:

Si je me souviens bien

We do not control our immigration. We do not even
exercise true shared power with the federal government. We administer, within the overall framework of
Canadian policy, administrative responsibilities that
are specific and limited in scope.[16]
Others deplored the fact that the agreement had not been
constitutionalized as provided for in the Meech Lake Accord and were
concerned about the precarious nature of future Quebec-Canada
agreements on immigration.[17] ◆

In 1997, the government of Canada began discussions with the other
provinces to consider the possibility of renouncing certain controls on immigration and to address the financial grievances of Ontario, British Columbia
and Alberta.[18]

The Charlottetown Accord (1992)

THE FAILURE OF THE MEECH LAKE ACCORD (1990) USHERED IN A NEW ERA IN Canadian constitutional history. The legacy of the Quebec Round was democratization of the amending process, culminating in a Canada-wide referendum.

In September 1990, following the failure of Meech, there began a period of public consultation that was unequalled in Canadian history. In Quebec, the goal of the consultations was to weigh the advantages of sovereignty *versus* the status quo; in the rest of the country, the aim was to reconcile Quebec's minimal demands with the goals of English Canadians and the aspirations of the First Nations. Those consultations and the negotiating round that followed, now known as the "Canada Round," were embodied in the Charlottetown Accord, signed in August 1992 and submitted to Canadians for approval on October 26, 1992.

In Quebec, this period was dominated by the hearings of the Bélanger-Campeau Commission and the tabling of the report of the Constitutional Committee of the Quebec Liberal Party entitled *A Quebec Free to Choose* (also known as the Allaire report). Released in January 1991, the report made an ambitious proposal: a new division of powers and a new Quebec-Canada confederal structure.[1] The report of the Bélanger-Campeau Commission, tabled two months later, put forward two alternatives to the constitutional impasse: 1) a new, final attempt to redefine Quebec's status within the federal system, or 2) Quebec independence. Like the Allaire report, the Bélanger-Campeau report proposed that a Quebec referendum on sovereignty be held if constitutional negotiations with the rest of Canada failed.[2] In June 1991, the Quebec government adopted Bill 150, which specified the deadline of October 26, 1992, for a referendum and established two committees: one to examine issues related to Quebec sovereignty, the other to examine any constitutional offer from ROC.

On the federal side, the Canadian government announced, in November 1990, the creation of the Citizens' Forum on Canada's Future, or Spicer Commission, with a mandate to "sound out the hearts and minds of common citizens." In December, Ottawa also established a Special Joint Committee of the House of Commons and the Senate (the Beaudoin-Edwards Committee) to examine the process of constitutional amendment.[3] With the reports of these two bodies in hand, the federal government formulated its constitutional package in the document *Shaping Canada's Future Together*. That package presented an ambitious program of reform including constitutional recognition of the fundamental characteristics of Canada (common values and the distinctiveness of First Peoples and Quebec), along with alterations to federal institutions (the Senate, the House of Commons and the Supreme Court), the economic union and the distribution of powers.[4]

Cautious after the Meech Lake experience, Prime Minister Mulroney made sure he clarified that this was a proposal only and could be amended. To that end, the government created a travelling committee chaired by Claude Castonguay (who would be replaced by Gérald Beaudoin) and Dorothy Dobbie to make its proposals known and record the opinions of the public. Additionally, during the winter of 1992, five public conferences were held to seek consensus on the distribution of powers, institutional reform, economic union and Canadian identity and values. A sixth forum, on aboriginal matters, was organized at the insistence of the aboriginal peoples. During 1991 and 1992, all the provinces and territories established their own public hearings as well.

Those consultations paved the way for the spring 1992 negotiations. Headed by Joe Clark, these multilateral talks brought together nine provincial premiers plus territorial and aboriginal leaders. The presence of the First Peoples' representatives was unprecedented in the history of constitutional negotiations, and consequently their demands took on greater importance than they had in previous rounds. In keeping with his commitment to negotiate only on a bilateral basis, Premier Bourassa refused to take part in these meetings, 12 of which were held between March 12 and July 7, 1992. By the end of that period, the 17 participants had agreed on a set of constitutional proposals including Senate reform, a "Canada clause," a review of the distribution of jurisdictions, spending power and recognition of aboriginal peoples' inherent right of self-government. Only once this offer was finalized did Robert Bourassa join the negotiations. He attended the last four meetings, which ended with the signing of the Charlottetown Accord on August 28.

With 60 provisions set out under five main themes, the Charlottetown Accord was much more complex than the Meech Lake Accord. Among its key provisions were: the Canada clause, including a statement of shared Canadian values and recognizing Quebec as a distinct society; a guarantee that Quebec would always have a minimum of 25 percent of the seats in the House of Commons; an elected Senate with equal representation from each province; recognition of the inherent right of self-government of aboriginal peoples, and recognition of aboriginal government as one of the three orders of government in Canada; controls on federal spending power and provisions for provincial opting out of new shared-cost programs, with financial compensation; and tighter constitutional amending procedures that would make more of the Constitution subject to unanimity.

The Consensus Report on the Constitution was fragile. Several proposals could not generate the consensus needed (in particular, the distribution of jurisdictions and matters related to aboriginal government) and were thus subject to changes during subsequent intergovernmental discussions.

On September 10, 1992, the House of Commons approved legislation for a pan-Canadian referendum on the question "Do you agree that the Constitution of Canada should be renewed on the basis of the agreement reached on August 28, 1992?" The referendum campaign was officially launched on September 21, 1992.

as i recall

At the start of the campaign, the Yes forces seemed to enjoy a clear lead. Not only did the Yes side enjoy the support of the prime minister, all the premiers and territorial and aboriginal leaders, but it was backed by the three main federal political parties, the business community and the major unions. Public support was also running in favour of the Accord at around 60 percent.[5] A senior advisor to the prime minister said, "The referendum seemed like a formality. It looked as if it would be 'Come and sing in the street with us'."[6]

The main argument for the Accord was that it represented the best compromise possible under the circumstances. *The Globe and Mail* remarked, "Ratification is in the national interest, despite disappointments for virtually all players from some angles on some issues."[7] Prime Minister Mulroney said the Accord was key to keeping Quebec in Canada, and he painted his opponents as enemies of Canada: "If there are people who want to tear down this deal, they will be battling against their own nation."[8] Themes of reconciliation and national unity dominated at the beginning of the campaign.

But despite this initial promise, the Yes side experienced problems very early on in the campaign. In the first part of October, Yes support dropped 20 points; in mid-October, this setback was confirmed, especially in the West; it never recovered to get back over the 50 percent mark from then on.[9]

There were important organizational handicaps and blunderings on the Yes side. Bringing three rival parties together on the same team gave rise to tensions over proposed strategy and led to a slow start to the campaign.[10] Moreover, fragile support and lack of enthusiasm on the part of some signatories of the Accord hurt the credibility of the Yes side.[11] The legal text of the agreement was not released to the public until October 13, a month after House of Commons approval; this only served to exacerbate the Yes campaign's problems.

Just as in the debate surrounding the Meech Lake Accord, there were many groups opposed to the Charlottetown Accord and just as many motives for opposing it. The package was a hard sell because it was too complex, its consequences too uncertain: concessions made to satisfy everybody ended up satisfying no one.[12] This was especially true of Senate reform, the element of the Accord designed to seduce non-aboriginal and non-francophone

voters, especially in the West, which did not play its expected mobilizing role within its constituency.[13]

But if any number of concerns defeated the Accord, they fell
under two themes. The first was the idea that Quebec had received
too much: The distinct society clause was unpopular, but guaranteeing
Quebec 25 percent of the seats in the House of Commons provoked
even more opposition.[14] "This latest deal confirms Quebec's desire for
superiority," stated Phil Fontaine, Grand Chief of the Assembly of
Chiefs from Manitoba.[15] His view was widely shared by voters outside
Quebec; a poll published in *The Globe and Mail* on October 9 showed
that 87 percent of respondents who intended to vote No and 61 percent of those who intended to vote Yes thought the Accord made too
many concessions to Quebec.[16] Former prime minister Trudeau
encouraged this view in an essay published in *Maclean's,* in which he
denounced the insatiable demands of Quebec's elites, and in a much-
publicized speech at a *Cité libre* dinner on October 1.[17]

The second principal concern related to the impact of the
Canada clause on the interpretation of the Charter of Rights and
Freedoms and on equality. Groups that were not explicitly recognized in this clause were concerned that they would have fewer
rights than groups — such as women and ethnic minorities — that
were,[18] whereas groups recognized in the Charter feared that their
constitutional rights might be weakened. Pierre Trudeau's assessment — "This mess deserves a resounding NO" — summed up the
views of many Canadians.[19] ◆

si je me souviens bien

Unlike the campaign in the rest of Canada, there was no significant
turnaround in voting intention in Quebec: even in the days following
the signing of the agreement, the No side was in the lead. It stayed
there, increasing its support from 41 to 52 percent between August

and October, while support for the Yes side dropped from 37 to 31 percent during the same period.[20]

Driven by the need to amend Bill 150, adopted in the fall of 1990, which provided for a referendum on sovereignty, the Quebec referendum campaign took off rapidly. And the stakes were better defined here than in the rest of Canada, since Quebec's Yes and No forces were clearly identified with the Parti Québécois and the Quebec Liberal Party, respectively. Additionally, the referendum campaign was held under the auspices of the Quebec Act Respecting Consultations with the People, which restricted the number of referendum committees to two, thus helping to consolidate a two-player-only debate.

On August 24, even before the final agreement had been signed, Jacques Parizeau publicly questioned Premier Bourassa's negotiating skills, arguing that "Robert Bourassa caved in and came back empty-handed."[21] The argument that Quebec had obtained little from the negotiations dominated the campaign. Numerous experts maintained that the Charlottetown Accord failed to meet Quebec's traditional demands and, indeed, would lead to the enshrinement of centralizing federalism.[22] Lise Bissonnette wrote in *Le Devoir,* "The little that Quebec did obtain – this line of defence – is in fact a maximum, an absolute limit, a ceiling, a wall."[23] Several Liberal dissidents publicly stated that the substance of the agreement fell far short of the Quebec Liberal Party's constitutional program, the Allaire report, adopted in March 1991. The architect of that policy, Jean Allaire, stated: "At best, we have just marked time, and we have tried to avoid the worst...but all this does not constitute gains for Quebec, which has worn itself out running after the essence of Meech."[24]

This interpretation was widely supported by the general population, including francophone non-sovereignists, who felt that Quebec had come out the loser in yet another constitutional round.[25] Suspicions were reinforced by the fact that the authorities were slow in making the official documents public, leading people to believe that vital information was being withheld and that the Accord was being watered down.[26] Moreover, the "Wilhelmy Affair" – which involved an intercepted cellular phone conversation in which the premier's negotiating abilities were questioned by two close associates – seemed to confirm Jacques Parizeau's misgivings about Bourassa's bargaining skills.[27]

A court injunction prevented the Quebec media from reporting the content of the conversation between two close advisers of Premier Robert Bourassa in the "Wilhelmy Affair". Serge Chapleau summarized it in a cartoon: "The injunction does not cover the visual..." (McCord Museum of Canadian History, M996.10.103)

Even the distinct society clause, which was supposed to be one of the main concessions to Quebec, did not find favour with opponents: a banality without legal value according to some, a political insignificance according to others.[28] Opponents also challenged Robert Bourassa's claims that a vote for the Accord would bring political stability and an end to the climate of constitutional uncertainty. In the National Assembly, Jacques Parizeau denounced what he called the constitutionalization of bickering. During the campaign, the Accord was described as a draft: "Far from achieving national unity, we are perpetuating administrative intrigues [and] squabbles about figures and jurisdictions," affirmed Jean Allaire.[29] ◆

On October 26, 1992, with a national participation rate of 74.7 percent (82.8 percent in Quebec), Canadians rejected the Charlottetown Accord: 54.3 percent of Canadians outside Quebec were opposed, as were 56.7 percent of Quebecers and 62.1 percent of aboriginal people.[30]

The referendum result was interpreted in two distinct ways: as a mandate to move on to other things, such as the economy,[31] or, in Quebec, as a prelude to the next step. Alain Dubuc of *La Presse* observed: "Rightly or wrongly, Quebecers have in fact perceived this referendum as an inconclusive stage. They are already getting ready for the next stage."[32]

The No victory left all the federal political parties without a project for renewal at the very time when expectations in Quebec were greater than ever. The constitutional status quo seemed to have become the only possible alternative to sovereignty. In terms of both the process (public consultation and participation) and the substance (distinct society, triple-E Senate, self-government for the First Peoples and the Canada clause), the Charlottetown agreement appeared to have left a legacy of contradictory and irreconcilable demands. The federal government did consider an administrative path to achieve certain goals or effecting constitutional change step-by-step,[33] but it was the October 1993 federal election, when 54 Bloc Québécois candidates were elected to the House of Commons and formed the official Opposition, followed by the PQ victory in the 1994 Quebec election, that re-opened the constitutional debate.

The Referendum on
Sovereignty-
partnership (1995)

THE PARTI QUÉBÉCOIS WON THE SEPTEMBER 1994 QUEBEC ELECTION with 77 SEATS to the Quebec Liberal Party's 47. That PQ victory marked "round three" in a political match that began with the 1992 defeat of the Charlottetown Accord and continued with the 1993 federal election, which saw 54 nationalist Bloc Québécois members elected to the House of Commons.

From its 1994 election to the October 30, 1995, referendum, the PQ government engaged in a pre-referendum campaign whose objective was to broaden support for sovereignty. In December 1994, Premier Jacques Parizeau unveiled the draft bill on Quebec sovereignty, which stated, "Quebec is a sovereign country." In addition to addressing the major issues related to sovereignty (constitution, territory, citizenship, currency, continuity of law, apportionment of property and debts, etc.), the draft bill envisioned an economic association with Canada. After hearings were held, the Quebec National Assembly was to adopt the draft bill and submit it to Quebecers in a referendum.

A turning point in the referendum process came in the spring of 1995 when Lucien Bouchard, Bloc Québécois leader and Leader of the Opposition in the House of Commons, suggested that Premier Parizeau change his strategy by adding to his sovereignty project a proposal for partnership with the rest of Canada. On June 12, the Parti Québécois, Bloc Québécois (BQ) and Action Démocratique du Québec (ADQ) signed a tripartite agreement reflecting this change. The government of Quebec committed itself to proposing and negotiating a new economic and political partnership with Canada following a Yes victory.

During the lead-up to the referendum, federal politicians refused to discuss the consequences of a Yes vote. Their silence served to heighten the uncertainty about the viability of partnership with Quebec in the event of a sovereignist victory, which played well in the rest of Canada.[1] Until just before the referendum, Prime Minister Chrétien also refused to make any commitment whatsoever to appease the people of Quebec. Instead, Ottawa directed its efforts toward demonstrating that the sovereignty project was outworn and that Canadian federalism was constantly evolving. It also attempted to reinforce Quebecers' sense of belonging to Canada through initiatives such as commemoration of the 30th anniversary of the adoption of the Canadian flag.[2]

> The referendum writ was issued on October 1, 1995, with this question: Do you agree that Quebec should become sovereign, after having made a formal offer to Canada for a new economic and political partnership, within the scope of the Bill respecting the future of Quebec and of the agreement signed on June 12, 1995? Yes or No.

During the campaign, the No camp followed an essentially negative strategy, emphasising the costs associated with sovereignty. The federal government was not alone in this undertaking; it was assisted by corporate leaders,[3] financial institutions, research institutes[4] and politicians in other provinces. However, the slow but sure increase in support for the Yes side, which became especially marked after Lucien Bouchard's appointment as chief negotiator for a sovereign Quebec, prompted the No strategists to put aside their "bank manager" discourse and try to give their campaign what it was lacking: "a soul."[5] Thus, on October 25, Prime Minister Chrétien addressed the nation, stating that he was ready to recognize the distinct identity of Quebec and promising that no change would be made to the Constitution without Quebec's consent: "If Canada were to break up, it would be the end of a dream..." he declared.[6]

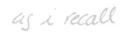

as i recall

Since the Parti Québécois garnered only 44.7 percent of the popular vote in the 1994 provincial election, compared to the Liberal Party's 44.4 percent, English Canada interpreted the PQ victory as simply a desire for a change of government and indeed as a moral defeat for the sovereignist option. As Jean Chrétien put it, "It's a good indication that Canada is here to stay."[7] Whether because a sovereignist defeat was seen as inevitable or because it was feared that any attempted intervention might have a negative effect, ROC's initial response to the PQ challenge was to play a waiting game. Even the English-Canadian left, which had supported Quebec's right to self-determination in 1980, showed less interest this time round. Instead, the Charter of Rights and Freedoms, First Nations issues and the threat to Canadian sovereignty posed by free trade held the attention of the left.[8]

The university community was the main forum for studying and discussing the challenges raised by the sovereignty debate. Such reflection had begun after the failure of the Meech Lake Accord and was stimulated by the election of the PQ. Something new emerged from those studies: more concern was expressed about the future of Canada without Quebec than about the renewal of the federation. English Canadians had begun to "think the unthinkable."[9]

Many Canadians, weary of the never-ending Quebec question, remained indifferent to the new version of that familiar tune – that is, "the imminent breakup" of Canada.[10] In fact, the majority (73 percent) felt that Quebecers would reject "sovereignty-association."[11] Media coverage of dissension within the sovereignist camp and polls indicating that support for sovereignty was softening reinforced the belief that the sovereignist option was on its way to a sound defeat.[12]

For the most part, the change in direction in the Yes camp's drive for sovereignty, which took place in the spring of 1995 at the instigation of Bloc Québécois leader Lucien Bouchard, was denounced as a means of deceiving the people of Quebec.[13] In general, Canadians outside Quebec believed that Quebecers had to make a choice – they could not have their cake and eat it too. A number of political players outside Quebec took the opportunity to point out that Canada would not be inclined to negotiate with a sovereign Quebec: "You are either in the family or you are out," said the premier of Saskatchewan, summing up the position of his colleagues and the majority of his fellow citizens.[14] Their argument: The Canadian economic union already exists, so why risk losing it?

Thousands of people answered the invitation to come to Montreal on October 27, 1995, in a last-minute effort to avert a Yes victory. (Ryan Remiorz, Canapress)

While few were willing to offer concessions to Quebec to ensure that it would stay in the family, Canadians generally hoped that Quebecers would reject the Péquiste option.[15] But polls indicating that the Yes side was gaining ground gave rise to concern. Tens of thousands of Canadians from across the country responded to politicians' calls to assemble in Montreal three days before the referendum in a massive "national unity" rally. This gathering provided people with the chance to take part in a debate that greatly affected them and from which they had so far been excluded. A demonstrator from Nova Scotia commented: "We came here to tell Quebecers in the only way we know how that we don't want them to leave us."[16] A survey conducted after

the referendum revealed that 61 percent of Canadians felt that
the rally had had a positive impact on how the No camp fared in
the referendum.[17] ◆

si je me souviens bien

Quebec federalists saw the narrower than expected 1994 PQ provincial election victory as a positive sign. For Quebec Liberal leader
Daniel Johnson, the results indicated that Quebecers did not want
to set out on the path to separation.[18] In fact, sovereignist fervour
had been declining steadily after reaching its peak in 1990. Polls
conducted in 1994 revealed that sovereignist support had dropped
to 44 percent.[19]

However, with 45 percent electoral support and a leader
with deep and clear convictions, the political atmosphere was more
encouraging for sovereignists in 1994 than in 1976 when they had
formed a majority government for the first time.[20] Sovereignists
were further heartened by the fact that the party Action Démocratique du Québec, which proposed a renewal of Quebec-Canada relations patterned after the European Union, had won 6.5 percent of
the provincial vote in the 1994 election and by the presence in
Ottawa of a sovereignist party, the BQ, elected with almost 50 percent of the vote in 1993.

For sovereignists, it was thus a matter of recreating the
momentum of 1990-1991 and, in the words of Jacques Parizeau,
convincing "those Quebecers who have the will and the desire to
control their destiny that the only way to become more autonomous
is to become sovereign."[21] BQ leader Lucien Bouchard sensed the
need for caution and suggested that the new premier call a referendum only if he was sure of winning.[22]

Held during the winter of 1994-1995, the regional Commissions on the Future of Quebec, the largest public hearings in the

history of the province, established that nearly all Quebecers were dissatisfied with the status quo. While the Quebec Liberal Party denounced them as focused only on sovereignty, the hearings did reveal that many people did not identify with the PQ project. Indeed, in the spring of 1995 support for sovereignty remained stalled well below the 50 percent level.[23] Despite the fact that a copy of the draft bill had been distributed to all Quebec households, over half of the population felt that they still did not know enough about the PQ project to make a decision. This sentiment was indicative of how little attention many Quebecers had given the issue and how weary they were of constitutional discussions.[24]

Two major concerns appeared to have dampened their enthusiasm. First, the lack of concrete justification for sovereignty was an Achilles' heel of the government project. A frequently asked question was, "Sovereignty? What for?" The majority of Quebecers believed that sovereignty needed to be supported by a societal blueprint, or *projet de société*. In its report, the national commission noted that witnesses addressed subjects such as decentralization, jobs, the economy and education in spite of the tenuous links of such topics with the Commission's mandate.[25]

However, with ongoing changes to the Canadian welfare state – unemployment insurance and old age pension reform, the new Canada Health and Social Transfer – the sovereignist project enjoyed the benefit of the doubt: "With a Yes, we have no guarantee of improvement, but with a No, we can be sure that things will get worse," explained an activist during the referendum campaign.[26] The impression that small business, ordinary workers and the less fortunate had a stronger affinity with the Yes than the No side was reinforced by the fact that almost all high-profile business leaders – the "arrogant privileged," in Jacques Parizeau's words – supported the No side.[27]

It was also apparent that the support of many Quebecers for the Yes side was conditional on economic ties being maintained

with ROC.[28] Thus, the signing of the tripartite agreement by
Parizeau, Bouchard and Dumont was warmly received and
advanced the Yes camp's position in the polls by a few percentage
points. However, only 46 percent of those polled believed that ROC
would agree to negotiate a new partnership with Quebec if the Yes
side won the referendum,[29] and the Yes side continued to trail
before the launch of the campaign. During the referendum campaign, the ability of the Yes side to convince Quebecers that its
offer of economic partnership was serious and realistic would
prove to be a determining factor to the Yes performance. The nomination on October 5 of the first members (including Jean Allaire, a
dissident Liberal) of the committee that would negotiate a new
partnership, and the announcement two days later that Lucien
Bouchard would act as chief negotiator for a sovereign Quebec,
enhanced the credibility of the Yes side.[30]

Although Quebecers expressed concern about the economic
future of a sovereign Quebec, they paid little heed to what businesspeople had to say or to their catastrophic pronouncements concerning the economic risks associated with sovereignty; many found
such statements exaggerated. Some analysts believe those prophe-
cies actually helped the Yes side:

> It would appear that the businesspeople who were
> positioned – like scarecrows – at the forefront of
> each referendum campaign (1980, 1992, 1995) suf-
> fered a credibility loss. The crows were no longer
> scared by them.[31]

Other analysts have noted that Quebecers had become less
fearful about the economic impact of sovereignty and that "the
Yes gains resulted mainly from either a greater degree of optimism
or a lesser degree of pessimism...about the economic consequences of sovereignty."[32]

The politics of identity also played a part in the outcome.
According to a poll conducted at mid-campaign, the people of

Si je me souviens bien

Cartoon by Serge Chapleau depicting the relationship between Quebec and the rest of Canada as a conjugal situation and showing the irritation felt by many Quebecers for the demonstration of national unity: "We love you...Not now, I've got a headache." (McCord Museum of Canadian History, M998.51.207)

Quebec were most sensitive to arguments related to identity.[33] And they were not easily swayed. The "demonstration of love" that brought together thousands of Canadians in downtown Montreal three days before the referendum probably did not have the expected results:

> the love expressed by those visitors can be understood not so much as love for Quebec, but as love for Canada expressed in a panic at the thought that it may be living its last days, and harbouring an unexpressed threat against those who would dare tamper with it.[34]

For many, the collapse of the Meech Lake Accord was still too fresh in their minds for them not to question the sincerity of this last-minute outpouring of affection.[35] ◆

On the evening of October 30, during the live broadcast of the referendum results, the atmosphere was electric. Quebec and Canada held their breath until 10:20 p.m., at which time the No side was declared the winner. The No camp had garnered 50.6 percent of the vote, the Yes camp, 49.4 percent — only 54,288 votes separated them. Voter turnout was close to 94 percent, the greatest in the history of Canadian politics.[36]

A bitter Jacques Parizeau declared: "It's true that we were beaten, but by what? Money and ethnic votes."[37] The next day, he stepped down as premier of Quebec, to be replaced, in January 1996, by Lucien Bouchard. Parizeau's declaration and the referendum results highlighted as never before the linguistic split in the province.[38] The political climate that prevailed after the referendum, characterized by the militancy and anger of Anglo-Quebecers,[39] or "Angryphones," prompted some politicians and ordinary citizens to call for calm and dialogue. Lucien Bouchard, in particular, expressed the need for reconciliation.[40]

Unlike Parizeau, most sovereignists reacted to the referendum outcome with dignity and took satisfaction from the nine-percentage-point gain over the 1980 referendum result, which gave the defeat an air of victory. René Lévesque's "see you next time" became "see you soon": "Don't lose hope, because the next time will be the right one, and it could come faster than we think," Lucien Bouchard announced.[41]

For most Quebec observers and politicians, the decision of Quebecers was to be interpreted as a vote for change rather than the status quo. "The referendum resulted in a mandate; otherwise the whole process would have been an out and out exercise in futility...There is a mandate for changes to Canadian federalism," commented Quebec Liberal Party leader Daniel Johnson.[42]

English Canada's response took two forms: plan A and plan B. Under plan A, Ottawa would see to it that Quebecers preferred to remain within Canada.[43] To that end, the Chrétien government passed two resolutions during the months following the referendum. The first recognized Quebec as a distinct society within Canada and encouraged the federal government's legislative and executive branches to take this into account in their deliberations and decisions. The second resolution granted a right of veto to Quebec, Ontario, British Columbia, the Prairie provinces and the Atlantic provinces. Proposals for the devolution of

Federalists demonstrate in front of the Supreme Court, alongside sovereignists, after the nine judges handed down their decision on a unilateral secession by Quebec. One side's sign says "Supreme Court Rules on Canada's Legitimacy;" the other reads: "Nine wigs against seven million tuques [wool caps]." (Jonathan Hayward, Canapress)

power were also considered.[44] For their part, the provinces started public consultations on the 1997 Calgary declaration, which recognized the "unique" character of Quebec while affirming the equality of all provinces. All the provinces except Quebec ratified it by 1998.[45]

After the 1995 referendum victory for the No side, however, a growing number of Canadians favoured taking a hard-line approach toward separatists. A November 1996 opinion poll revealed that 63 percent of Canadians outside Quebec preferred plan B, Ottawa's "so-called 'tough love' approach," to efforts at reconciliation.[46] Increasingly, it seemed impossible to accommodate Quebec without alienating ROC or one of its components.[47] Yet the referendum result did stun Canadians, who realized more than ever that the breakup of Canada was indeed possible. This led to new efforts to shore up plan B, which involved laying out the conditions for another referendum and the rules governing secession.[48] In this vein, the partitionist view — that if Canada was divisible, so was Quebec — became the object of renewed attention, and the Supreme Court of Canada was called on to rule on the legality of a unilateral declaration of independence. On August 20, 1998, the Supreme Court ruled that Quebec could not unilaterally secede from Canada, whether according to the Canadian Constitution or international law.[49]

Re-elected in 1998, the PQ promised to hold another referendum if winning conditions could be found.

Conclusions

by John Meisel
by Guy Rocher

Conclusion

B OTH FRENCH AND ENGLISH CANADIANS BELIEVE THEY CONSTITUTE CRITICAL COM-
ponents of the Canadian state. They evaluate incidents and developments
like those covered in this book by applying a rough cost/benefit analysis. This
weighing of the situation is undertaken more or less subconsciously and involves
not only rational judgement but also emotions. Of course, both advantages and
disadvantages accrue from cohabitation in one country. The case studies show
that both partners have frequently had to adapt to the presence of the other and
to modify their point of view.

Many debates have centred on the balance sheet for the two groups. The
final tally usually depends on who is making the calculations. The causality
here is very complex, but it is safe to assume that the evaluation of costs and
benefits differs for the various groups identified in chapter 4 ("friend," "foe" or
"neutral" among Anglophones; *indépendantiste*, federalist or "in between"
among Quebecers).

While useful insights accrue from applying cost/benefit analysis to the way
in which groups interact with one another, there are also liabilities. This "plus or
minus" approach encourages black-and-white thinking. This is normally accompanied by the assumption that what is good for one party must be bad for the
other, that one is dealing with a zero sum game in which for every winner there
must be a loser. But this is not necessarily the case.

It is quite possible that a particular event can have a positive impact on
both parties; likewise, both can suffer baleful consequences. The October Crisis
of 1970, unceasing constitutional wrangling and the disruptions caused by the air
traffic controllers' dispute had negative consequences for both Francophones and

Anglophones. Expo '67, joint federal and provincial support for the Quebec aerospace industry and the founding of the CBC, however, proved salutary for both.

Still, imbalances are not uncommon. The Conquest and the subsequent decline of the French-speaking population relative to the English-speaking population have meant greater benefits for the latter. Over time, the disparity has substantially diminished, though a lively debate still rages. Some argue that the imbalance has essentially been eliminated; others claim that the gap is still considerable. That and related topics are sources of considerable disagreement and receive extensive discussion in numerous forums, publications and the electronic media.

It is true that Francophones and Quebecers, as a minority, have often had to give way to the majority: witness the conscription crisis or the patriation of the Constitution. But ROC has also paid a price, particularly in modern times. Canadian policies have frequently been modified to bring them more in line with the wishes and interests of Quebecers and Francophones. Examples include the CF-18 contract, pharmaceutical policies and immigration policies.

While extremists dwell on the preponderance of costs over benefits, majorities on each side recognize that each community has benefited from their association. The legacy of the Westminster parliamentary model and our British political culture have helped create a Canadian political framework that encourages civilized and generally productive discourse between Francophones and Anglophones and between Quebec and ROC. Although it has flaws, that framework has permitted the development of political, social and economic institutions that enable most Canadians to enjoy an enviable standard of living. More important, perhaps, Canadians have developed an admirable style of conflict resolution; a way of doing things that is civilized and attractive to citizens of other countries.

This political framework conducive to accommodation has led to policies advantageous to both linguistic groups, and benefits that might not have been realized in a smaller state or two smaller states. Though this view is not shared by everyone, many feel that the French language and culture have been strengthened by Quebec being part of Canada, although the same cannot be said of French minorities, particularly in the West. And whatever frustrations some Quebecers experience as a result of their links with Canada, Quebec has, since the end of the Second World War, developed a cultural, entrepreneurial, technological and social dynamism matched by few other communities in the

Francophonie or the world. At the same time, Canada as a whole has benefited from the energy generated by the interaction of Francophones and Anglophones and has become a major world player because of the size and rich variety of its constituent communities.

Yet despite these mutual benefits, the essays demonstrate that Canada has been and continues to be a fragile political entity. Insofar as national unity is concerned, Canada is in poor health. But, like many sickly individuals, the country has shown an impressive capacity to endure and survive its ailments. Nevertheless, it seems that almost any event, even a seemingly harmless and innocent one, can ignite a crisis or at least a dust-up in the relations between some elements of the francophone and anglophone communities.

The vast majority in ROC wish to see the country survive these shocks and find appropriate ways of reconciling its differences. Accordingly, the need to minimize friction and, if possible, promote harmony should be high on the policy agenda for governments as well as private organizations and individuals. But much more than harmony is at issue; it is essential that we devise ways to facilitate mutual satisfaction and enrichment in the interactions between Quebec and ROC (not to mention other groups and regions of Canada). A chemistry must be fashioned at the collective and individual levels that can generate creativity and fulfilment for all of Canada's principal constituents.

The 27 post-Second World War cases examined in chapters 2 through 6 provide a reasonably accurate cross-section of incidents and events aggravating relations between Quebec and ROC. No fewer than 15 deal with federal-provincial relations or cultural and language policy. It is these areas that preoccupy the so-called chattering classes — writers, academics, artists, journalists and politicians. Members of these groups have unparalleled access to media and policy circles. In my introduction to chapter 6, we saw that in Quebec this group, which consists of mostly intellectuals, tends to be much more nationalistic and separatist than the rest of the population. In ROC, however, it tends to be the segment of the population most conciliatory toward Quebec. Furthermore, intellectuals are more highly esteemed in Quebec than elsewhere in Canada and are therefore better placed to set the public agenda.

It is partly because of these differences that issues likely to provoke inter-ethnic and inter-regional conflict more often than not originate in Quebec. And when contentious points are raised Quebec vociferously presses them, whereas the reaction in ROC is usually rather muted and diffuse. The pattern of conflict and the manner in which the protagonists comport themselves are partly shaped by the societal contours of each side. These configurations have deep roots and are not readily amenable to change. Therefore, we can expect that differences and conflicts will persist and will produce more vigorous and articulate reactions from Quebec than ROC.

But intellectuals are not the only important actors. Both governments and the private sector influence relations between diverse regions and ethnic communities. As we have seen, official acts can precipitate and sustain crises. Likewise, economic steps taken by blinkered decision-makers obsessed with the bottom line, or disputes fanned by sometimes irresponsible and inflammatory media, can also ignite or exacerbate dissension. Canadians hoping to achieve harmony among Francophones, Anglophones and other groups, must therefore recognize that perpetual vigilance is required to forestall unnecessary and costly rifts. Governments and private decision-makers must acquire the habit of systematically and rigorously examining all new initiatives, for any direct or indirect impact on the cohesion of Canada. Similar observations can be made about issues affecting the environment, health and other areas. It may be necessary to devise a system of more effectively scrutinizing proposed initiatives from the viewpoint of their ultimate consequences. How are they likely to affect not only Canadian unity but also the way in which Canadians manage their human and physical resources? For one important factor in our cost/benefit analysis must be the capacity of the Canadian state to meet the social, economic and cultural expectations of its population.

The above comments speak to the "public" perspective — the viewpoints of the state and the public interest. This is appropriate at one level, but it can also dangerously diminish the role of the individual. In the final analysis, the individual is pivotal — the state is, after all, there to serve various communities and their citizens. The public and the private are, in short, linked and mutually dependent. We must consider not just government action but also personal experiences.

As an academic who has worked for governments and been active in the voluntary sector, I have frequently interacted with colleagues in the francophone community. Such contact is perhaps easier in the world of academia, but it is common in other circles too. Participation in business, voluntary associations, cultural and sports activities, public affairs and other areas of human endeavour often throws Francophones and Anglophones together. As the two groups pursue ends unrelated to their ethnic backgrounds, they learn from one another, form friendships, become more proficient in the other's language and gain insight into the values of those living on the other side of the linguistic divide.

... a future together   ... un avenir ensemble

English and French have lived   Au Canada, le français et l'anglais
side by side in Canada   se côtoient depuis
for over 230 years.   plus de 230 ans.

In 1992, the Commissioner of Official Languages launched a series of three posters – "Vision, Tradition, Perspective" – to celebrate both official languages. They were intended to foster understanding between the two language groups and promote Canadian unity. (NAC, C145712; Office of the Commissioner of Official Languages)

These experiences are not only intrinsically valuable; they also enhance the capacity of both groups to live together creatively. It is not easy to measure the benefits accruing from the intermingling of two or more language and cultural groups. It is, however, plausible to assume (and my personal experiences, as well as my close friendships with numerous Quebec colleagues, strongly support this assumption) that sustained contacts enlarge the universe of both groups and encourage their members to compare their views and performance, giving each side the benefit of a new, external perspective. Furthermore, by occasionally engendering competition and rivalry, interaction between two communities is likely to spur each to greater ingenuity and effort. Most important perhaps, in associating with individuals possessing different characteristics, and particularly in speaking another language, horizons and knowledge are expanded. One's persona assumes an additional dimension and exceeds its bounds. It is a most pleasant and enriching process. And even when tensions and stresses arise, the lasting benefits of the contact offset many of its short-term inconveniences and frustrations.

The experience of two cultures broadens understanding. The French saying *comprendre c'est pardonner* (to understand is to forgive) may exaggerate the point, but it contains, as proverbs often do, a kernel of truth: intimate knowledge of another person brings insight into his or her motivation and behaviour. Familiarity with the background and context of a particular person or group helps us understand how they see the world. While we may not always share their point of view, we at least see the path they have taken to arrive at their conclusions. It is the purpose of this book to enhance mutual understanding between Francophones and Anglophones by showing how and why they have differed in their perspectives on various divisive issues and developments.

But if personal contact and enhanced understanding have a beneficial effect on relations between our two communities, these processes do not normally occur spontaneously. Deliberate efforts are often required to encourage members of the two groups to meet and undertake joint endeavours. In Canada, it is largely in the political realm that such efforts have been made. Pan-Canadian institutions like federal commissions of inquiry, governmental or quasi-governmental bodies and organizations like the IRPP, throw Canadians of diverse backgrounds into each other's arms, so to speak. Without such institutions pursuing shared ends and linking linguistic, cultural and regional communities, many people would simply not have cause or opportunity to become acquainted or work together.

The positive consequences of sustained interaction between Francophones and Anglophones are also apparent in relations between other groups, be they linguistic, national or territorial. As the populations of ROC and Quebec become increasingly heterogeneous, they will have ever more varied and mutually enhancing experiences. The increasing diversity of the Canadian population is profoundly changing the country and altering the context of French-English relations. This does not change the fact that the French presence in Canada will always bestow unique characteristics on our political and social arrangements. Because of its culture, geographical concentration and a highly efficient and popular political base in Quebec, the francophone presence is assured of a special place in Canada to which the majority — whatever its composition — must accommodate. The irreducible and primordial importance of Canada's French component survives despite the increasing heterogeneity of Canada and Quebec and, in particular, of more realistic and just attitudes developing — however late — toward Aboriginal Canadians.

I have noted how I have personally benefited from contacts with my ethnic opposites and how these have broadened and deepened my experiences. My colleagues and I were fortunate to have such opportunities — ones that cannot, alas, be shared by all Canadians. This does not mean that those who have led more isolated lives have not indirectly benefited from the experiences of the luckier ones. While these interactions touch only a small section of society, they are vitally important. The groups exposed to rewarding contacts play a mediating role in society and contribute to its capacity for accommodation, which benefits everyone. But these important tasks would be performed better if the opportunities for cross-cultural contact were available to larger numbers of people in all walks of life. It is one of the challenges facing Quebecers and other Canadians to devise means of interacting more with one another in a wide variety of common pursuits.

In sum: while considerable emphasis has traditionally been placed on political accommodation, and while this is of colossal importance, it must be remembered that the political sphere touches only some aspects of human experience. There are other, more meaningful facets of life, far removed from government, public policy and matters of state. Politics, while indispensable, is only a means of attaining things we value for their own sake; these are the *raison d'être* of politics; in the final analysis, politics must be subservient to them. Consequently, in seeking opportunities for interaction and mutual enrichment, Canadians must use both political and non-political means and institutions.

When thinking about how they might best adapt their cultural, educational, economic and political processes and institutions, Canadians should remember this: if we wish to preserve a unique, precious and richly rewarding partnership, built up over the last century and a half, we should keep in mind some of the serendipitous features of the framework elaborated so far. Whatever changes are introduced in the future, they will be the richer if they embody some of the institutional incentives — public and private, coercive and voluntary — now in place for the intermingling of Francophones and Anglophones. For our two communities must continue to work together in formal and informal settings even if such interaction produces friction and the raw material for a future collection of essays resembling those in this book.

Conclusion

A S WE BRING THIS BOOK TO A CLOSE, THREE QUESTIONS COME TO MIND. FIRST, WHAT CON-clusions can be drawn from these essays as a whole? Second, what can be predicted for the future? And third, what trust should we put in history and what weight should we grant it? The answer to the last question will help us answer the others.

This entire book relates to Canadian history, from the Conquest of New France by the British Empire up to events of the past few years. This raises two questions: What is the sociological and political significance of history? And how reliable is it?

Ernest Renan, the French philosopher, included the possession of common memories in his well-known description of the nation.[1] If there is a Canadian culture common to Anglophones and Francophones, one must recognize that it includes memories of conflicts, struggles and misunderstandings. The question, then, is whether we should forget history if we want to continue to live together in some political framework. The answer appears obvious: History is a collective memory, and it can no more be obliterated from a society than it can from a person's mind. The attempt to conceal memory always ends up giving someone or some group the opportunity to dredge it up and use it in an often-unexpected way. The Franco regime in Spain believed it could crush the memories of Basques and Catalans forever, but they were preserved and have emerged with renewed force in recent decades. The socialist regimes of central and eastern Europe thought they had stamped out any nationalist longings. We now know how quickly nationalist groups in these countries rediscovered and revitalized their national histories.

History often serves to unite the members of a collectivity and engender a common identity by attaching a symbolic meaning to events and public figures.

Collective memory sometimes takes unexpected forms. This graffito, "Je me souviens" (I remember), which is also the slogan of the province, recalls some of the major events that feed the Quebec collective memory, from the 1760 Conquest to the Patriots' Rebellion (1837), the referendum on sovereignty-association (1980), the patriation of the Constitution (1982), and the failures of the Meech Lake Accord in 1990, the Charlottetown Accord in 1992 and the referendum in 1995. (Robert Galbraith, Canapress)

The "founding myths" of peoples are built from materials provided by the great "chroniclers" of old, materials that today are provided, if reluctantly, by historians. The image of King Clovis, for example, leader of the first Frankish Christian kingdom in the sixth century and considered the first king of France, owes everything to the somewhat romanticized history of his life, a mixture of truth and imagination written by Bishop Gregory of Tours in his *Historia Francorum* nearly a century after Clovis' death. Fortunately, this work was preserved and still serves as a reference for historians of Gregory of Tours — despite the reservations they are quick to express about its description of the King. At the same time, the founding myth of the origins of France as both homeland and the "eldest daughter of the Church" was built on the work. Similarly, American nationalism, which has fulfilled a unifying function in the "melting pot," was born of images of the Revolution of 1776 and the mythologized figure of George Washington.

The history of ancient Greco-Roman civilization, the decline of the Roman Empire, the Middle Ages and the beginnings of the Modern Age — at least that

which can be reconstructed today — are based on the writings of certain historiographers whose work has been preserved. Occasionally, as in Caesar's account of
the Gallic Wars, the hero told his own story. More often, men from the sovereign's
entourage told the story. They either took it upon themselves to recount the sovereign's life and exploits, or, as in the case of several Roman emperors, the sovereign
gave them the task of writing his story. Such writings obviously served to preserve
and embellish the memory of the sovereign, but they also helped to create and
maintain a common collective conscience. It is readily acknowledged, for example,
that depictions of the English nation can be found in a succession of historical
works, from the writings of Saint Bede the Venerable (731), Bishop Geoffrey of
Monmouth (1136), Edward Hall (1548), William Harrison (1577) and Edmund
Spenser (1590-96), through to the great English tragedies of Shakespeare. It is with
examples like these that Renan was able to claim that the national "soul" is, at least
in part, made up of "the common possession of a rich heritage of memories."[2]

But the works of these historiographers suffered from a host of method-
ological flaws. Some time ago, history left the age of "chronicles"; it is now a genuine scientific discipline that relies on a rigorous, critical methodology, an
increasing variety of sources and increasingly broad horizons. However, because
the past still acts on the present, historians face an infinitely delicate task. They
strive to understand the past by freeing themselves from contemporary ideological
frameworks, but the present continually intrudes, because current political, social
and cultural movements seek to make use of their work or the historians themselves are not entirely impervious to the dominant ideologies of their age and environment. This explains, in part, the existence of competing "historical schools,"
referred to by Arthur Silver in some of the essays contained in chapter I.

It is more likely now than ever that the work of historians will be used, with
or without their approval, by social movements, dominant or subordinate groups
and in contemporary currents of thought. Of all the humanities and social sciences, history is involved in more minor and major disputes in which divergent
political parties, religions, interests, ideologies, values and options clash, and disputes between historians of different schools spill into the public arena. History
informs political disputes and enters the arsenal of contemporary struggles.
Witness, for example, the lively historical debates over the Celtic origins of the
Scots in the United Kingdom, the interpretation of Nazism in Germany or the

meaning of multiculturalism in the United States, to say nothing of the use made of a sometimes distant past in violent conflicts such as those in Ireland and Kosovo. Thus, while history can unite, it can also divide. A society has to learn to live with its memory, to absorb it and to fashion its present and future accordingly.

This answer to the question concerning history — its truth, its limits, its sociological impact — allows us to consider our first question: What conclusions can be drawn from these essays as a whole?

A beginning observation: The focus of this book is historical events that featured pronounced differences of opinions between francophone Quebec and anglophone Canada. One could criticize this approach for neglecting what these two communities have in common, the things that despite everything have held them together in the past and continue to do so. Although such a criticism would not be unfounded, it would nevertheless be unjust, because the central purpose of this book is to examine, with courage and candour, the differences in the perception of Francophones and Anglophones that have existed since the Conquest. This phenomenon cannot be denied, even if we might wish to balance it with some recognition of the convergence of perspectives that has also taken place. Indeed, it must be acknowledged that these differences are deeply embedded in the history, culture and institutions of Canada and that we must not lose sight of them as we seek solutions or compromises, whatever they may be.

A second observation we can draw from these essays has to do with the increasing complexity of Canadian political life. The rifts of the 19th century were relatively simple. They divided and sometimes pitted Francophones against Anglophones and Protestants against Catholics. But the differences multiplied as many new ethnic or cultural groups arrived and integrated, first in the western provinces, then in Ontario and then, increasingly, in Quebec. To this was added the growing political activism of native communities. These developments have raised a series of important questions across Canada, and have greatly increased the complexity of the Canadian political landscape. Majority-minority relations had already greatly influenced Canadian history; these new facets have simply increased the scope and complexity of the situation.

That said, the relations and rifts between Francophones and Anglophones remain the central axis of Canadian history. Some might wish to deny the reality of "two founding peoples," but the relationship of Francophones and Anglophones continue to occupy centre stage in Canadian political, social and cultural life.

To that we must add another reality: This is not a confrontation between two homogeneous, monolithic blocs. As is revealed in many of the essays in this book, and as noted by John Meisel in his introductions, there is neither a single English Canada nor a single French Canada. English Canadians make up a complex whole, one that is rarely unanimous in its opinions, attitudes and behaviours regarding Quebec and Francophones.

For its part, French Canada is made up of the francophone minorities of the western provinces and Ontario, the Acadians of the Maritime provinces and Quebec francophones, to which could be added, if they agreed, French-speaking natives. These groups often have divergent interests, concerns and preferences. And, within Quebec, the differences between federalist and sovereignist francophones are well known, even though their opposition is overlaid with a shared French-Canadian or Quebec nationalism. These divisions just add to the complexity of the Canadian scene.

And, finally, what of our question concerning the future? Will the divergence of viewpoints between Francophones and Anglophones remain steady, grow or diminish? Only the very smart or the very bold dare predict the future with any certitude. In fact, answers to this question depend more on preferences or aspirations than any well-grounded prediction. Realistically, we must first recognize that any route is possible. There is no determinism in the unfolding of human history and thus no predetermined future. Political and social life depends on a variety of factors that condition the existence of all. These factors have to do with structure and events, the activity or activism of groups and the emergence of public figures and leaders.

One factor that appears to be particularly decisive for the present, and in all likelihood for the future, is increasing polarization of Anglophones and Francophones. This trend has been highlighted throughout this book and has become more pronounced during the last two or three decades. Two new nationalisms, Canadian and Québécois, have emerged, and they have become increasingly explicit; they are pitted against each other. Paradoxically, immigration has greatly contributed to this rise of two nationalisms.

Outside Quebec, all immigrants adopt the English language and English-Canadian culture via school and the media. These new Canadians have played an active role in pushing aside the ideas of "two founding peoples" and bicultural-ism in favour of the image of a uniform, egalitarian Canada. Thus paradoxically, Canadians of non-British and non-French origin have strongly contributed to both the definition of a multicultural Canada and the development of a Canadian neo-nationalism founded on the equality of all citizens and the eclipsing of dif-ferences. It is they who have insisted that the hyphenated identities of Canadians be abandoned: Why should people continue to identify themselves as French-Canadian or English-Canadian when there is no need to identify as German-Canadian, Ukrainian-Canadian or Vietnamese-Canadian?

Through their decisions to integrate into the anglophone community, which is a minority in Quebec and a majority in Canada, or the francophone com-munity, which is a majority in Quebec and a minority in Canada, the arrival of new cultural groups in Quebec since the Second World War has raised the question of Quebec's identity. The history of Quebec's linguistic laws and cultural policy ini-tiatives since the late 1960s stems from the desire to answer this question. It is the ground in which Quebec neo-nationalism has taken root and developed.

The two nationalisms are dynamic and interactive. The more ROC affirms its Canadian nationalism, the more Quebec nationalism grows. The more the lat-ter expresses itself, the more the former swells in response. So much so that while the rest of the world discusses the crisis of the nation-state, Canada and Quebec appear to be swimming against the current, building themselves a new Canadian nation-state on the one hand and a new Quebec nation-state on the other. In both cases, the idea of the nation is evolving away from the traditional ethnic vision and moving closer to a pluralist definition.

It would appear then that the country is not up to the challenge of mov-ing "beyond the impasse." In all that is said and written about trying to find a way forward, the solutions range from a redefinition of Canada, which is unlike-ly for the moment, to a search for a new partnership, which is equally unlikely. What this book teaches us is that the "impasse" has existed for a very long time, that it is built on divergent and contradictory perceptions and that what ails Canada is therefore much more profoundly cultural than constitutional, more societal than political. It is for us to draw conclusions from this lesson.

General introduction

1   See, for example, François Moreau, *Le Québec, une nation opprimée* (Hull: Éditions Vents d'Ouest, 1995); François Rocher and Michel Sarra-Bournet, "La longue quête de l'égalité," in Michel Sarra-Bournet (ed.), *Manifeste des intellectuels pour la souveraineté* (Montreal: Fides, 1995), pp. 43-57. Federalist Quebecers are also aware of the historical dimension of Quebec's discontent. See André Burelle, *Le mal canadien: essai de diagnostic et esquisse d'une thérapie* (Montreal: Fides, 1995); Christian Dufour, *Le défi québécois: essai* (Montreal: L'Hexagone, 1989).

2   Fernand Dumont, *Genèse de la société québécoise* (Montreal: Boréal, 1993), pp. 333-34. [Translation] Recent studies suggest that sovereignists and nationalists are striving to free themselves from this legacy and to rethink Quebec identity in broader terms. See Michael Elbaz, Andrée Fortin and Guy Laforest (eds.), *Les frontières de l'identité: modernité et postmodernisme au Québec* (Sainte-Foy: Les Presses de l'Université Laval, 1996); Michel Sarra-Bournet (ed.), *Le pays de tous les Québécois: diversité culturelle et souveraineté* (Montreal: VLB, 1998); Gérard Bouchard, *La nation québécoise au futur et au passé* (Montreal, VLB, 1999).

3   Some have been more sympathetic to the Quebec perspective. See, for example, John F. Conway, *Debts to Pay: A Fresh Approach to the Quebec Question*, rev. ed. (Toronto: James Lorimer, 1997); Kenneth McRoberts, *Misconceiving Canada: The Struggle for National Unity* (Don Mills, ON: Oxford University Press, 1997); Ray Conlogue, *Impossible Nation: The Longing for Homeland in Canada and Quebec* (Stratford, ON: Mercury Press, 1996). However, in general, Quebec occupies a place of secondary importance in Canadian history textbooks. On this subject, see the review by Brian Young, "New Wine or Just New Bottles?",

Journal of Canadian Studies, Vol. 30, no. 4 (Winter 1995-1996), pp. 194-99. For a study of older textbooks, see Daniel Francis, *National Dreams: Myth, Memory and Canadian History* (Vancouver: Arsenal Pulp Press, 1997), pp. 88-110.

4   John A. Dickinson, "Canadian Historians: Agents of Unity or Disunity?", *Journal of Canadian Studies*, Vol. 31, no. 2 (Summer 1996), p. 148.

5   Marcel Trudel and Geneviève Jain, *Canadian History Textbooks: A Comparative Study* (Ottawa: Queen's Printer, 1970), p. 133. In 1943, the Canadian and Newfoundland Association for Education struck a committee to study history textbooks used by the various provinces. The committee was to propose reforms to encourage national unity by suggesting means of ensuring greater harmony in the viewpoints presented in textbooks. See documents at the Fondation Lionel-Groulx, dossier P1/618.

6   J.L. Granatstein, *Who Killed Canadian History?* (Toronto: HarperCollins, 1998), pp. 148-49. See also Michael Bliss, "Privatizing the Mind: The Sundering of Canadian History, the Sundering of Canada," *Journal of Canadian Studies*, Vol. 26, no. 4 (Winter 1991-1992), pp. 5-17; Thomas S. Axworthy, "Curing the Historical Amnesia That Is Killing Canada," *Canadian Speeches*, Vol. 11, no. 6 (October 1997), pp. 19-24.

7   John Ralston Saul, *Reflections of a Siamese Twin: Canada at the End of the Twentieth Century* (Toronto: Viking, 1997), pp. 12, 505. In 1968, Paul G. Cornell, Jean Hamelin, Fernand Ouellet and Marcel Trudel published a history book entitled *Canada: unité et diversité* (n.p.: Holt, Rinehart and Winston, 1968) whose objective was precisely to neutralize this trend by providing a history common to all Canadians: "...if history has the effect of dividing people by recalling bad memories," they wrote, "it can also help to bring

them together, if it reminds them of what they have in common." (foreword) [Translation]

8   See Paul Watson, "We Flunk Badly on Basic History Test," *The Toronto Star*, August 13, 1988, p. A1; Brad Evenson, "Canadians Clueless," *The Gazette*, June 30, 1998, p. A1; Granatstein, *Who Killed Canadian History?*, pp. 1-17; Micheline Lachance, "L'école: zéro en histoire," *L'actualité*, March 1, 1996, pp. 33-38.

9   Nancy Huston, *Pour un patriotisme de l'ambiguïté: notes d'un voyage aux sources* (Saint-Laurent, QC: Fides, 1994), p. 24. [Translation] For an academic discussion of this phenomenon, see Bliss, "Privatizing the Mind," and Desmond Morton, "History and Nationality in Canada: Variations on an Old Theme," *Historical Papers* (1979), pp. 1-10.

10   Dominique Moisi, "Confront the Past," *Financial Times*, August 26, 1997.

11   Pierre Nora quoted in Jacques Mathieu and Jacques Lacoursière, *Les mémoires québécoises* (Sainte-Foy, QC: Les Presses de l'Université Laval, 1991), p. 20. [Translation] Mathieu and Lacoursière add: "Collective memory is society's knowledge about itself...It is the reference point through which one recognizes oneself and identifies oneself." [Translation]

12   Two specialized journals devoted to national and political history have recently appeared in Quebec and Canada. See *Bulletin d'histoire politique* and *National History: A Canadian Journal of Enquiry and Opinion*. In Fall 1996 (Vol. 5, no. 1), the *Bulletin* devoted a special issue to the teaching of national history.

13   See the issue of the *Bulletin d'histoire politique* devoted to this question, Vol. 4, no. 2 (Winter 1995), pp. 7-74. Kenneth McRoberts explored the ins and outs of this debate in "La thèse de la tradition-modernité: l'historique québécois," in Elbaz, Fortin and Laforest (eds.), *Les frontières de l'identité*, pp. 29-45.

14   The annual speeches of the chair of the Historical Society of Canada are often instructive regarding the debates provoked by this question of the historical construction of a national identity. See for example, Margaret Prang, "National Unity and the Uses of History," in Peter Gillis and Marcel Caya (eds.), *Historical Papers 1997* (Ottawa: Historical Society of Canada, 1997); Veronica Strong-Boag, "Contested Space: The Politics of Canadian Memory," *Canadian Historical Review*, new series, Vol. 5, 1994.

15   Although neglect of the First Nations has been corrected in recent history textbooks, the story of Canada is still a European story first and foremost. See Gérald Friesen, "New Wine or Just New Bottles? A Round Table on Recent Texts in Canadian History," *Journal of Canadian Studies*, Vol. 30, no. 4 (Winter 1995-96), pp. 179-80. Examples of history from an Aboriginal perspective can be found in Georges E. Sioui, *Pour une auto-histoire amérindienne* (Sainte-Foy, QC: Les Presses de l'Université Laval, 1989); see also Royal Commission on Aboriginal Peoples, *Report: Looking Forward, Looking Backward, volume 1* (Ottawa: Minister of Supply and Services, 1996).

16   For more on this topic, see Roger Gibbins and Sonia Arrison, *Western Visions: Perspectives on the West in Canada* (Peterborough, ON: Broadview Press, 1995); David J. Bercuson (ed.), *Canada and the Burden of Unity* (Toronto: Macmillan, 1977); Robert C. Vipond, *Liberty and Community: Canadian Federalism and the Failure of the Constitution* (Albany: State University of New York Press, 1991).

Chapter 1 : The first steps

John Meisel's introduction

1   Throughout my introductions to chapters 2 through 6, I frequently distinguish between Quebec and the rest of Canada (ROC) and between francophone Quebecers and their non-francophone compatriots. I often refer to the latter as well as to the inhabitants of ROC as "Anglos." This is, strictly speaking, not correct. Often, they are not of British origin and may not even speak English, but the meaning is always clear from the context. Recourse to these abbreviations avoids more tedious descriptions.

2   For a classic illustration and exploration of this phenomenon, see Arthur Koestler's *Darkness at Noon* (London: Jonathan Cape, 1940).

3   This description is only a rough approximation of reality, of course. It obviously does not apply to everyone. A recent immigrant from Asia, for instance, naturalized shortly after arrival here, will not have been exposed to the Canadian environment long enough to be affected by the forces described above. Likewise, Aboriginal Canadians, mindful of their own history, bring a unique set of "inarticulate major premises" to their evaluation of current developments. And one should remember that French-English co-existence is only one of Canada's attributes. The consciousness of the presence of other groups — ethnic, regional or occupational — is also important.

The Conquest (1760)

1   See Guy Frégault, *Canada: The War of the Conquest* (Toronto: Oxford University Press, 1969), part 5.

2   Quoted in Fernand Ouellet, *Economic and Social History of Quebec, 1760-1850* (Toronto: Macmillan; Ottawa: Institute of Canadian Studies at Carleton University, 1980), p. 96.

3   The British found no French document at Quebec to indicate exactly what part of New France had been designated by the name Canada. Defining a province called Quebec avoided ambiguity. French regime censuses went as far west as Les Cèdres, about seven km. past the Ottawa River. See Vol. 4 of the 1871 census: *Censuses of Canada, 1665-1871* (Ottawa: Taylor, 1876).

4   See Cornelius Jaenen, "French Sovereignty and Native Nationhood during the French Regime," in *Native Studies Review*, Vol. 2, no. 1 (1986).

5   See Pierre Tousignant, "The Integration of the Province of Quebec into the British Empire," in *Dictionary of Canadian Biography*, Vol. IV (Toronto: University of Toronto Press, 1979). On competition from Albany, see Ouellet, *Economic and Social History*, pp. 75-77.

6   One exception to the use of French laws in Lower Canada was that public land could now be granted in freehold tenure.

7   Quoted in Mason Wade, *The French Canadians, 1760-1967* (Toronto: Macmillan, 1968), p. 88.

8   Allan Greer's study of habitant life, *Peasant, Lord, and Merchant: Rural Society in Three Quebec Parishes, 1740-1840* (Toronto: University of Toronto Press, 1985), p. 230, shows a "basic continuity of the structure of rural life prior to 1840" as the traditional feudal relationships and peasant economy remained in place. Even rural merchants who arrived after 1760 operated within "the existing order." There were attempts to revive conscription in 1777 and after, but they were confused and generally produced more corvée labour than military service.

9   Fernand Ouellet, *Economy, Class, and Nation in Quebec* (Toronto: Copp Clark Pitman, 1991), p. 71.

10 Ouellet, *Economy, Class, and Nation in Quebec*, pp. 74, 107-08.

11   A well-known example is Michel Brunet, "La conquête anglaise et la déchéance de la bourgeoisie canadienne," of which an abridged English translation, "The British Conquest and the Decline of the French-Canadian Bourgeoisie," appears in Dale Miquelon (ed.), *Society and Conquest* (Toronto: Copp Clark, 1977).

12   Ouellet, *Economic and Social History*, p. 79.

13   Ouellet defends the first explanation in *Economic and Social History*, pp. 142-45. For the third, see José Igartua, "A Change in Climate: The Conquest and the 'Marchands' of Montreal," in *Historical Papers* (Ottawa: Canadian Historical Association, 1974).

14   Marcel Trudel, "La servitude de l'Église catholique du Canada français sous le régime anglais," in *Report* (Ottawa: Canadian Historical Association, 1963).

15   Quoted in Michel Brunet, *Les Canadiens après la conquête* (Montreal: Fides, 1969), p. 36. [Translation]

16   Louis-François Laflèche, *Quelques considérations sur les rapports de la société civile avec la religion et la famille* (Montreal: Senécal, 1866), p. 73.

17   Ramsay Cook, "Some French-Canadian Interpretations of the British Conquest: Une quatrième dominante de la pensée canadienne-française," in *Historical Papers* (Ottawa: Canadian Historical Association, 1966), pp. 76-77, mentions Laurier, Mercier and Henri Bourassa.

18   Quoted in Serge Gagnon, *Le Québec et ses historiens de 1840 à 1920: la Nouvelle-France, de Garneau à Groulx* (Sainte-Foy, QC: Les Presses de l'Université Laval, 1978), p. 314. [Translation]

19   Quoted in Wade, *The French Canadians*, p. 89.

20   Maurice Séguin, *L'idée d'indépendance au Québec: genèse et historique* (Trois-Rivières, QC: Boréal Express, 1971), p. 12. [Translation]

21   See Philip Lawson, *The Imperial Challenge: Quebec and Britain in the Age of the American*

Revolution (Montreal/Kingston: McGill-Queen's University Press, 1989), chap. 2.

22   "How happy, then, ought the Canadians to be," wrote William Smith in an 1826 history of the country, that they had been separated from France, and made subjects of the British king, for whom Conquest was merely "the means of extending his beneficence." Quoted in J. K. McConica, "Kingsford and Whiggery in Canadian History," in *Canadian Historical Review* (1959), p. 112.

23   A.R.M. Lower, *Colony to Nation* (Toronto: McClelland and Stewart, 1975; first published 1946), p. 65; Susan Trofimenkoff, *The Dream of Nation* (Toronto: Macmillan, 1982), p. 31.

24   In P. B. Waite (ed.), *The Confederation Debates in the Province of Canada, 1865* (Toronto: McClelland and Stewart, 1963), p. 59.

25   William Foster, *Canada First* (Toronto: Hunter Rose, 1890; originally published in 1871), pp. 18-20, 39.

26   Samuel LaSelva, *The Moral Foundations of Canadian Federalism* (Montreal: McGill-Queen's University Press, 1996), p. 157.

27   This argument was made by Michel Brunet in his essay *Canadians et Canadiens* (Montreal: Fides, 1954). It is developed by Christian Dufour, *A Canadian Challenge/Le défi québécois* (Lantzville, BC: Oolichan Books; and Halifax, NS: IRPP, 1990).

28   "Notre dépendance coloniale," *Le Courrier de St-Hyacinthe*, November 22, 1864.

29   Quoted in Wade, *The French Canadians*, p. 870.

30   Michel Brunet, "Une autre manifestation du nationalisme 'canadian'," in *Canadians et Canadiens*.

31   Eric Schwimmer, *Le syndrome des Plaines d'Abraham* (Montreal: Boréal, 1995), p. 102.

32   Dufour, *The Canadian Challenge*, chap. 2.

The Rebellion of 1837-1838

1   On the spread of intellectual influences
    from other North Atlantic countries, see
    Jean-Pierre Wallot, "Frontière ou fragment
    du système atlantique: des idées étrangères
    dans l'identité bas-canadienne au début du
    XIXe siècle," *Historical Papers* (Ottawa:
    Canadian Historical Association, 1983). For
    a study emphasising the influence of British
    constitutional principles and practices, see
    Lawrence Smith, "'Le Canadien' and the
    British Constitution, 1806-1810," *Canadian
    Historical Review*, Vol. XXXVIII, no. 2 (June
    1957), pp. 93-108.
2   The assembly voted repeatedly to exclude
    judges, who held their judicial positions
    through the governor's patronage, and to
    expel Ezechiel Hart, who held patronage
    offices and was a personal friend of Governor
    Sir James Craig. Such men were seen as rep-
    resenting the governor's views rather than
    those of voters. Craig dissolved the assembly
    and called elections in three successive years;
    in 1810 he closed down the reformers' news-
    paper, *Le Canadien* (Quebec), and arrested
    several reform leaders.
3   See David Gagan, *Hopeful Travellers*
    (Toronto: University of Toronto Press,
    1981), pp. 20-37.
4   The lower estimate comes from Elinor
    Senior, *Redcoats and Patriotes* (Stittsville,
    ON: Canada's Wings in collaboration with
    the Canadian War Museum, National
    Museum of Manitoba, National Museums
    of Canada, 1985), p. 213; the higher num-
    ber is from Jean-Paul Bernard, *The
    Rebellions of 1837 and 1838 in Lower
    Canada*, no. 55 (Ottawa: Canadian
    Historical Association Historical Booklet,
    1996), p. 9.
5   Quoted in Allan Greer, "1837-38 Rebellion
    Reconsidered," *Canadian Historical Review*,
    Vol. LXXVI, no. 1 (1995), p. 14.
6   On this aspect of the rebellion, see Allan
    Greer, *The Patriots and the People: The
    Rebellion of 1837 in Rural Lower Canada*
    (Toronto: University of Toronto Press,
    1993), especially chap. 9.
7   Gilles Paquet and Jean-Pierre Wallot,
    Patronage et pouvoir dans le Bas-Canada
    (Montreal: Presses de l'Université du
    Québec, 1973), p. 109: "Of the public
    offices and pensions reserved for French
    Canadians, the seigneurial and military
    nobility got the greatest number and espe-
    cially those of the greatest value," but (p.
    114) "the British minority obtained the
    majority of positions at all levels of the
    administration." [Translation]
8   Historians are not agreed on the degree to
    which this French-English conflict influ-
    enced the rural population. Fernand Ouellet
    has argued that a growing agricultural crisis
    and rural impoverishment created bitterness
    among the habitants, which Patriote politi-
    cians were able to turn against the English,
    converting it into a sort of popular national-
    ism. But Allan Greer finds no
    French-English conflict in the countryside
    before the crisis of 1837. It was only, he
    argues, when constituted authority and gen-
    eral security seemed threatened that ner-
    vous English settlers, many of whom were
    recent immigrants not yet fully adapted to
    their new environment, rose up in defence
    of the Constitution and against their
    French-Canadian neighbours. See Fernand
    Ouellet, *Lower Canada* (Toronto: McClelland
    and Stewart, 1976); Greer, *The Patriots and
    the People*, especially chap. 6.
9   Mason Wade, *The French Canadians, 1760-
    1967* (Toronto: Macmillan, 1968), p. 88.
10 "Projet de M. L. J. Papineau," in papers of
    the Mouvement Anti-Unioniste, Bas
    Canada, 1822-1825, in National Archives
    of Canada (MG24 B 22). [Translation]
11 *Le Canadien* (Quebec), August 13, 1831.
    Quoted in Maurice Séguin, *L'idée d'indépen-
    dance au Québec: genèse et historique* (Trois-
    Rivières, QC: Boréal Express, 1971), p. 19.
    [Translation]

12 See, in this volume, the essay "The union of the Canadas."

13 Séguin, L'idée d'indépendance au Québec, p. 33. [Translation]

14 Pierre Vallières, Les héritiers de Papineau (Montreal: Québec/Amérique, 1986), p. 11. [Translation]

15 See F. Murray Greenwood, Legacies of Fear (Toronto: The Osgoode Society, 1993).

16 In Jean-Pierre Wallot and John Hare (eds.), Ideas in Conflict; a Selection of Texts on Political, Economic and Social Questions in Lower Canada, 1806-1810 = Confrontations; choix de textes sur des problèmes politiques, économiques et sociaux du Bas-Canada, 1806-1810 (Trois-Rivières, QC: Boréal Express, 1970), pp. 219-22.

17 Greer, The Patriots and the People, p. 138.

The Union of the Canadas (1840)

1   Gerald Craig (ed.), Lord Durham's Report (Toronto: McClelland and Stewart, 1963), pp. 127, 140.

2   Craig, Lord Durham's Report, pp. 37-38.

3   On this development see William Ormsby, The Emergence of the Federal Concept in Canada (Toronto: University of Toronto Press, 1969).

4   As things stood in the 1860s, Upper and Lower Canada each had 65 MLAs. If representation had been based on population, Upper Canada would have had 72 MLAs and Lower Canada 58. See Maurice Giroux, La pyramide de Babel (Montreal: Éditions de Sainte-Marie, 1967), part 1.

5   On the new approach of French-Canadian politicians toward business development after 1840, see Fernand Ouellet, Economic and Social History of Quebec, 1760-1850 (Toronto: Macmillan; Ottawa: Institute of Canadian Studies at Carleton University, 1980), p. 448. For a case study of one Patriote who found common cause with Montreal business after 1840, see Brian

Young, George-Étienne Cartier: Montreal Bourgeois (Montreal: McGill-Queen's University Press, 1981). On mutual influences of the legal systems, see David Howes, "From Polyjurality to Monojurality," McGill Law Journal, Vol. 32 (July 1987); G. Blaine Baker, "The Reconstruction of Upper Canadian Legal Thought in the Late-Victorian Empire," Law and History Review, Vol. III (1985), pp. 234-42.

6   For a good survey of the ultramontane movement and its increasing influence in Lower Canada after 1840, see the first chapter of Marta Danylewycz, Taking the Veil (Toronto: McClelland and Stewart, 1987).

7   Jacques Monet, "French-Canadian Nationalism and the Challenge of Ultramontanism," in Historical Papers (Ottawa: Canadian Historical Association, 1966).

8   The most coherent expression of this view is Louis-François Laflèche, Quelques considérations sur les rapports de la société civile avec la religion et la famille (Montreal: Sénécal, 1866), especially articles VII-X.

9   Jacques Monet, The Last Cannon Shot (Toronto: University of Toronto Press, 1969).

10 Maurice Séguin, L'idée d'indépendance au Québec: genèse et historique (Trois-Rivières, QC: Boréal Express, 1968), p. 47. [Translation]

11 Michel Brunet, "L'Église catholique du Bas-Canada et le partage du pouvoir à l'heure d'une nouvelle donne (1837-1854)," in Historical Papers (Ottawa: Canadian Historical Association, 1969).

12 "The Union as It Affects Lower Canada," The Monthly Review: Devoted to the Civil Government of Canada (January-February 1841), p. 21.

13 Janet Ajzenstat, The Political Thought of Lord Durham (Montreal/Kingston: McGill-Queen's University Press, 1988), or Janet Ajzenstat, "Liberalism and

Nationality," *Canadian Journal of Political Science*, Vol. XIV, no. 3 (September 1981).

14   Samuel LaSelva, *The Moral Foundations of Canadian Federalism* (Montreal: McGill-Queen's University Press, 1996), p. 157.

Confederation (1867)

1   *The Globe* (Toronto), quoted in W.L. Morton, *The Critical Years: The Union of British North America* (Toronto: McClelland and Stewart, 1964), p. 71.

2   Prince Edward Island, for example, had only one-eighteenth the population of Upper Canada.

3   The delegates were not unaware of the ambiguity they were putting into their plan. The division of powers between federal and provincial governments, for example, could have been made clearer than it was if the powers of one had been specified in a list, with all remaining, unspecified, powers going to the other. Yet Cartier insisted, and the conference accepted, that there would be two separate lists of powers. There were no formal minutes of the Quebec conference, but two sets of notes are contained in G.P. Browne (ed.), *Documents on the Confederation of British North America* (Toronto: McClelland and Stewart, 1969).

4   *Le Moniteur Acadien* (Shediac), July 8, 1867. [Translation]

5   Louis-François Laflèche, *Quelques considérations sur les rapports de la société civile avec la religion et la famille* (Montreal: Senécal, 1866), p. 43. [Translation]

6   *Le Pays* (Montreal), July 23, 1864. [Translation]

7   C.S. Cherrier *et al.*, *Discours sur la confédération* (Montreal: Lanctot, Bouthillier & Thompson, 1865), p. 13. [Translation]

8   *Le Pays* (Montreal), March 27, 1867. [Translation]

9   Browne, *Documents on the Confederation of British North America*, pp. 42-43.

10   P.B. Waite (ed.), *The Confederation Debates in the Province of Canada, 1865* (Toronto: McClelland and Stewart, 1963), p. 22.

11   Joseph Cauchon, *L'Union des provinces de l'Amérique britannique du Nord* (Quebec: Côté, 1865), p. 45. [Translation]

12   *La Minerve* (Montreal), July 1st, 1867. [Translation]

13   Étienne-Pascal Taché, who praised Confederation, had promised some years before that "the last cannon which is shot on this continent in defence of Great Britain will be fired by the hand of a French Canadian." Quoted by Andrée Désilets, *Dictionary of Canadian Biography*, Vol. IX (Toronto: University of Toronto Press, 1976), p. 776.

14   The historian J.-C. Bonenfant described Cartier as having "an almost morbid fear of the United States." [Translation] Jean-Charles Bonenfant, "Le Canada et les hommes politiques de 1867," *Revue d'histoire de l'Amérique française*, Vol. XXI, no. 3a, p. 579. Cartier himself put the matter bluntly when he said, "The matter resolved itself into this: either we must obtain British American Confederation or be absorbed in an American Confederation." Waite, *The Confederation Debates in the Province of Canada*, p. 50. In the first federal cabinet, Cartier would choose the defence portfolio.

15   See Cartier's speech to Quebec City businessmen in Joseph Tassé (ed.), *Discours de Sir Georges Cartier* (Montreal: Senécal & fils, 1893), p. 642.

16   Some five or six hundred thousand French Canadians left Quebec for the US between 1850 and 1900. By the turn of the century, the American census showed almost as many French Canadians living in that country as in Quebec.

17   Reported in *L'Union des Cantons de l'Est* (Arthabaskaville), May 23, 1867. [Translation]

18   In *Parliamentary Debates on the Subject of the Confederation of the British North American*

Provinces, 3rd session, 8th Provincial
Parliament of Canada (Quebec: Hunter,
Rose, Parliamentary printers, 1865), p. 60.

19   Le Courrier de St-Hyacinthe, October 28,
      1864. [Translation]

20   Le Courrier de St-Hyacinthe, October 28,
      1864 [Translation]; also Le Courrier du
      Canada (Quebec), November 7, 1864;
      Joseph Cauchon, Discours...sur la question de
      la Confédération (n.p., n.d.), p. 8. These
      argued that each government would receive
      its powers directly from the ultimate source
      of sovereignty, the imperial parliament.

21   L'Union des Cantons de l'Est
      (Arthabaskaville), July 4, 1867.
      [Translation]

22   Waite, The Confederation Debates in the
      Province of Canada, p. 44.

23   Letter to M.C. Cameron, December 19,
      1864, in National Archives of Canada,
      Macdonald papers.

24   Macdonald commented that "there was as
      great a disinclination on the part of the var-
      ious Maritime Provinces to lose their indi-
      viduality, as separate political organizations,
      as we observed in the case of Lower
      Canada herself." Brown agreed that not
      only French Canadians were against legisla-
      tive union: "so were most of the delegates
      from the Maritime Provinces." (In Waite,
      The Confederation Debates in the Province of
      Canada, pp. 41, 74.) The Atlantic provinces
      had a long history, distinct from that of
      Canada, and there was still very little com-
      munication between them on the eve of
      Confederation. Their isolation from Canada
      meant that they had no significant sense of
      common identity with English Canadians.

25   See Phillip Buckner, "The Maritimes and
      Confederation: A Reassessment," in G.
      Martin (ed.), The Causes of Canadian
      Confederation (Fredericton: Acadiensis
      Press, 1990).

26   The Globe (Toronto), August 30, 1864, and
      June 20, 1867, quoted in Robert Vipond,
      Liberty and Community: Canadian

Federalism and the Failure of the Constitution
(Albany: State University of New York
Press, 1991), pp. 32-33. In general, see
chap. 2 on this point.

27   Waite, The Confederation Debates in the
      Province of Canada, pp. 48, 40.

28   See Ralph Nelson et al., "Canadian
      Confederation as a Case Study in
      Community Formation," in Martin (dir.), The
      Causes of Canadian Confederation, pp. 50-85.

29   Waite, The Confederation Debates in the
      Province of Canada, p. 50.

30   The "Canada First" story is told by one of
      the members, George Taylor Denison, The
      Struggle for Imperial Unity (London:
      Macmillan, 1909), pp. 10-12.

31   In that same period, anglophone historians
      would look back on Confederation itself
      from the point of view of Canadian nation-
      alism, emphasizing the centralizing tenden-
      cies and playing down the elements of
      provincial autonomy, paying more attention
      to centralizers like John A. Macdonald than
      to those with opposing views. The best
      known representative of this historiographi-
      cal tendency is Donald Creighton, whose
      interpretation was presented in British North
      America at Confederation (a study done for
      the Rowell-Sirois Commission, Ottawa,
      1939), in his biography of John A.
      Macdonald, Vol. 1 (Toronto: Macmillan,
      1955), and The Road to Confederation
      (Toronto: Macmillan, 1964).

The Hanging of Louis Riel (1885)

1   This seemed necessary, since Riel's take-
     over had effectively destroyed the authority
     of the Hudson's Bay Company.

2   Ritchot apparently believed he had been
     promised amnesty. See his impressions in
     W.L. Morton (ed.), Manitoba: The Birth of a
     Province (Winnipeg: Manitoba Record
     Society, 1965). But federal and imperial
     officials felt that "We can only wait and do

nothing for the present." (Lord Kimberley to Sir John Young, August 10, 1870, in *Public Archives of Canada*, Lord Lisgar papers: MG27, I, B2.)

3 Riel's message is in *Epitome of Parliamentary Documents in Connection with the North-West Rebellion, 1885* (Ottawa: Maclean, Roger, 1886), p. 226.

4 *Le Courrier de St-Hyacinthe*, January 11, 1870; [Translation] *La Gazette de Sorel*, April 20, 1870.

5 *Le Pays* (Montreal), March 29, 1870; [Translation] *Le Journal des Trois-Rivières*, April 18, 1870.

6 *Le Courrier de St-Hyacinthe*, April 16, 1870. [Translation]

7 Frits Pannekoek, *A Snug Little Flock* (Winnipeg: Watson and Dyer, 1992), claims the English Métis were strongly opposed to Riel, even willing to fight in a "civil war" against him, and only seemed to remain passive because of a lack of arms and effective leadership.

8 *Le Journal de Québec*, April 11, 1870. [Translation]

9 *L'Union des Cantons de l'Est* (Arthabaskaville), April 14, 1870. [Translation]

10 A.-A. Dorion to A. Mackenzie, Montreal, June 10, 1874, in PAC, Mackenzie papers on microfilm (M-197), pp. 529-30.

11 *La Minerve* (Montreal), February 11, 1875. [Translation]

12 *L'Événement* (Quebec), February 10, 1875; *Le National* (Montreal), February 9-10, 1875.

13 Archbishop A.-A. Taché of St-Boniface wrote to Bleu MP L.R. Masson, October 20, 1875, that the "fake amnesty" had ended violence against the Métis. (Typed transcripts of Taché-Masson correspondence are kept in the Montreal municipal library.)

14 *Le Nouveau Monde* (Montreal), March 28, 1885. [Translation]

15 Accounts in memoirs of French-Canadian volunteers: C.R. Daoust, *Cent-vingt jours de*

service actif (Montreal: Senécal, 1886), pp. 21-22; Arthur Eventurel, diary entry for April 2, 1885, in *Archives Nationales du Québec*, Fonds Levasseur-Eventurel (PO152-0001).

16 *Le Pionnier de Sherbrooke*, April 9, 1885. [Translation]

17 *L'Union des Cantons de l'Est* (Arthabaskaville), April 11, 1885. [Translation]

18 *La Minerve* (Montreal), March 30, 1885.

19 *La Patrie* (Montreal), May 18, 1885; [Translation] *L'Union des Cantons de l'Est* (Arthabaskaville), May 30, 1885.

20 *L'Union des Cantons de l'Est* (Arthabaskaville), November 14, 1885. [Translation]

21 Although Riel's own lawyer told reporters at the end of the appeals process that the trial had been fair, and although the 1874 Lépine trial had shown that francophone jurors were as prepared to convict as anglophones were, the composition of the jury was bound to strike the public at the time as confirmation of their conviction that Riel was being discriminated against because he was French.

22 *La mort de Riel et la voix du sang* (n.p., n.d.), p. 15. [Translation]

23 Quoted in Mason Wade, *The French Canadians, 1760-1967* (Toronto: Macmillan, 1968), p. 417.

24 *The Canadian Statesman* (Bowmanville, ON), December 2, 1869.

25 *The London Advertiser*, January 28, 1870.

26 *The Gazette* (Montreal), April 5, 1870. Riel's supporters would later argue that Ottawa had in effect recognized his provisional government by negotiating with the three delegates in May. But, at the time, Sir John A. Macdonald described the three not as delegates of a government but as men sent by "a meeting of the people from the different localities" and carrying "a statement of grievances...to lay them at the foot of the throne" — i.e., as

simple petitioners to the Governor General. (Ottawa: *House of Commons Debates*, 1870, cols. 894, 1082.)

27 *The London Advertiser*, September 19, 1870.

28 *The Ottawa Citizen*, October 18, 1873.

29 *The Ottawa Free Press*, November 4, 1874.

30 *The London Advertiser*, January 19, 1875.

31 *The Telegram* (Toronto), July 23, 1885; *The Montreal Star*, July 20, 1885.

32 *The Ottawa Citizen*, August 3, 1885.

33 C. A. Boulton, *Reminiscences of the North-West Rebellions* (Toronto: Grip, 1886), p. 408. See the testimony of Father André and of Charles Nolin in *The Queen v. Louis Riel* (Toronto: University of Toronto Press, 1974), pp. 233, 294-95.

34 *The Irish Canadian* (Toronto), August 6, 1885.

35 *The Northern Advance* (Barrie, ON), November 5, 1885.

36 J. A. Teskey to Sir John A. Macdonald (Appleton, ON, September 16, 1885), in PAC, Macdonald papers, Vol. 108.

37 *The Hamilton Spectator*, August 3, 1885; *The Northern Advance* (Barrie, ON), November 19, 1885.

38 *The London Advertiser*, September 3, 1885.

39 *The Telegram* (Toronto), November 24, 1885.

40 *The London Advertiser*, September 8, 1885.

41 *The Hamilton Spectator*, February 24, 1890.

42 Charles Castonguay, *Le Devoir* (Montreal), January 7 and 23, 1980; Gerald Godin, *La Presse* (Montreal), January 21, 1980.

43 *L'Express de Toronto*, October 18-25, 1983.

44 A 1997 Angus Reid poll showed that only 40 percent of young Canadians (35 percent in Quebec) knew the name of the Métis leader who had been hanged in 1885.

45 In Desmond Morton's introduction to *The Queen vs. Louis Riel*, p. xxviii.

46 See Doug Owram, "The Myth of Louis Riel," *Canadian Historical Review*, Vol. LXIII, no. 3 (September 1982); J.R. Miller, "From Riel to the Métis," *Canadian Historical Review*, Vol. LXIX, no. 1 (March 1988). In 1998, MPs from all parties and parts of

Canada sponsored a private members' bill in the House of Commons that would exonerate Riel, declaring him a Father of Confederation and founder of Manitoba.

The Minority Rights Disputes (1871-1916)

1 Louis-François Laflèche, *Quelques considéra-tions sur les rapports de la société civile avec la religion et la famille* (Montreal: Sénécal, 1866), art. XX-XXI; or, on New Brunswick schools, *Le Journal des Trois-Rivières*, May 27, 1872.

2 C. B. Sissons, *Bi-Lingual Schools in Canada* (Toronto: Dent, 1917), pp. 17-22. This tol-erance did not in itself guarantee that fran-cophone children would actually have French-language schools. That only hap-pened when Francophones were numerous enough in a school district, and on the local school board, to influence the lan-guage of the local school. See Chad Gaffield, *Language, Schooling, and Cultural Conflict* (Montreal: McGill-Queen's University Press, 1987).

3 Report of the Royal Commission on Bilingualism and Biculturalism, Book II: *Education* (Ottawa: Royal Commission on Bilingualism and Biculturalism, 1968), p. 44; Maud Hody, "The Anglicising Common Schools Act of 1871: A Study in Folklore," *Les Cahiers - Société Historique Acadienne*, Cahier no. 19 (April-June 1968), pp. 347-49.

4 Report of the Royal Commission on Bilingualism and Biculturalism, Book II: *Education*, p. 45.

5 Official equality in these 19th-century texts applied only to the legislatures and courts, not to government services.

6 He was helped by an 1897 encyclical from Pope Leo XIII, who agreed that Laurier had done as well as possible, considering that Catholics were a minority in Canada.

7 Regulation 17 was withdrawn in 1927, but

it was not until the 1960s that significant French language rights were secured.

8   Hector to Jean and Edmond Langevin (London, November 19, 1866), *Archives Nationales du Québec*, Collection Chapais, Langevin papers, box 4. [Translation]

9   Joseph Tassé (ed.), *Discours de Sir Georges Cartier* (Montreal: Senécal, 1893), pp. 734-75. [Translation]

10   *Le Pays* (Montreal), November 17, 1866. [Translation]

11   *Le Courrier de St-Hyacinthe*, May 1, 1872. [Translation] *Le Courrier du Canada*, January 30, 1872.

12   Tassé, *Discours de Sir Georges Cartier*, pp. 752-53. [Translation]

13   *La Minerve* (Montreal), April 24, 1873; Hector Langevin, telegram to the Bishop of Rimouski (Ottawa, May 19, 1873), in *Archives Nationales du Québec*, Langevin papers. [Translation]

14   *Le Courrier de St-Hyacinthe*, March 12, 1870. [Translation]

15   *Le Nouveau Monde* (Montreal), January, 30 and February 3, 1875; *La Minerve* (Montreal), February 15, 1875. [Translation]

16   *Le Canadien* (Quebec), February 3, 1875. [Translation]

17   *La Revue Canadienne* (Montreal), Vol. XXVI-II (1892), p. 471. [Translation]

18   *La Patrie* (Montreal), February 21, 1890. [Translation]

19   Henri Bourassa, *Pour la justice* (Montreal: Imprimerie du Devoir, 1912), p. 12. [Translation]

20   *The Globe* (Toronto), March 6, 1865.

21   *The Toronto Leader*, November 12, 1864.

22   *The Hamilton Spectator*, February 4, 1870; *The London Advertiser*, February 22, 1870.

23   *The Varsity* (Toronto), June 10, 1885.

24   Cited by O. D. Skelton, *Life and letters of Sir Wilfrid Laurier, Vol. 1* (Toronto: McClelland and Stewart, 1965), p. 129.

25   Equal Rights Association for the Province of Ontario, *Address by the Provincial Council to the People of Ontario Dealing Mainly with Separate Schools* (Toronto: n.d.). It will be noted that while in the 1850s and 1860s the argument against separate schools was usually based on the liberal principle of separation of Church and State, the most common argument in the 1890s was based on the idea of national unity.

Imperialism and World War (1884-1917)

1   Desmond Morton, "French Canada and War, 1868-1917: The Military Background to the Conscription Crisis of 1917," in J.L. Granatstein and R. D. Cuff (eds.), *War and Society in North America* (Toronto: Nelson, 1971), p. 93.

2   Jean Pariseau and Serge Bernier, *French Canadians and Bilingualism in the Canadian Armed Forces*, Vol. 1 (Ottawa: Directorate of History, Department of National Defence, 1988), p. 64.

3   R. C. Brown and Donald Loveridge, "Unrequited Faith: Recruiting the CEF, 1914-1918," *Revue internationale d'Histoire militaire*, no. 51 (1982), pp. 56-59.

4   One Unionist of French origin was elected in Ontario. Of 152 Unionist MPs, 148 were of British origin. See John English, *The Decline of Politics* (Toronto: University of Toronto Press, 1977), pp. 199-201.

5   *The News* (Toronto), January 31, 1885.

6   When the Liberals ran on a free trade (reciprocity) platform in 1891, Conservatives branded their proposal "veiled treason" and won the elections.

7   See Stephen Leacock, "Greater Canada: An Appeal," *The University Magazine* (April 1907), pp. 134, 137.

8   Sir Charles Tupper, *Bart and the Unification of the Empire* (Halifax: T. C. Allen, 1896).

9   Leacock, "Greater Canada," p.133.

10   For this view of imperialism as an expression of Canadian nationalism, see Carl Berger, *The Sense of Power: Studies in the Ideas*

of Canadian Imperialism, 1867-1914 (Toronto: University of Toronto Press, 1970).

11 D'Alton McCarthy, *Speech...Delivered on Thursday, 12 Dec. 1889, at Ottawa, under the Auspices of the Ottawa Branch of the Equal Rights Association* (n. p., n. d.), pp. 28-30.

12 Reported in *Le Journal des Trois-Rivières*, January 27, 1890. [Translation]

13 Reported in *La Presse* (Montreal), September 16, 1889. [Translation]

14 Quoted in Robert Page, *The Boer War and Canadian Imperialism* (Ottawa: Canadian Historical Association, 1987), p. 13.

15 George Taylor Denison, *The Struggle for Imperial Unity* (London: Macmillan, 1909), p. 266.

16 Quoted in Laurier LaPierre, "Politics, Race, and Religion in French Canada: Joseph Israel Tarte." Unpublished Ph.D. thesis, University of Toronto, 1962, p. 374.

17 *The News* (Toronto), September 20, 1899, p. 12.

18 Reported in *Le Nouveau Monde* (Montreal), October 26, 1899.

19 Quoted in Robert Craig Brown, "Sir Robert Borden, the Great War and Anglo-Canadian Relations," in J. S. Moir (ed.), *Character and Circumstance* (Toronto: Macmillan, 1970), pp. 203-04.

20 On the link between the war and social reform, see J. H. Thompson, "The Beginning of Our Regeneration: The Great War and Western Canadian Reform Movements," *Historical Papers*, Canadian Historical Association (1972).

21 In J.L. Granatstein and J.M. Hitsman, *Broken Promises: A History of Conscription in Canada* (Toronto: Oxford University Press, 1977), pp. 27, 82.

22 Quoted in Desmond Morton, "The Limits of Loyalty: French-Canadian Officers and the First World War," in Edgar Denton III (ed.), *Limits of Loyalty* (Waterloo, ON: Wilfrid Laurier University Press, 1980), p. 96.

23 On this affinity between French-Canadian ultramontane influences and late-19th cen-

tury imperialism, see A.I. Silver, "Some Quebec Attitudes in an Age of Imperialism and Ideological Conflict," *Canadian Historical Review*, Vol. LVII, no. 4 (December 1976), pp. 440-60.

24 *La Patrie* (Montreal), November 20, 1884. On the French-Canadian press coverage of the Sudan expedition, see A.I. Silver, "Quelques considérations sur les rapports du Canada français avec l'impérialisme britannique au XIXe siècle," *Revue canadienne des études africaines*, Vol. XV, no. 1 (1981), pp. 60-66.

25 A. B. Routhier, *La Reine Victoria et son jubilé* (Quebec: Darveau, 1898), p. 82. [Translation]

26 *L'Union des Cantons de l'Est* (Arthabaskaville), October 27, 1899, and February 23, 1900; *Le Nouveau Monde* (Montreal), November 2, 1899.

27 *Le Nouveau Monde* (Montreal), September 21, 1899.

28 *L'Union des Cantons de l'Est* (Arthabaskaville), October 20, 1899; [Translation] *Le Nouveau Monde* (Montreal), October 26, 1899.

29 Henri Bourassa, "Duties to England," from *Le patriotisme canadien-français, ce qu'il est, ce qu'il doit être* (1902) as translated in Ramsay Cook (ed.), *French-Canadian Nationalism* (Toronto: Macmillan, 1969), p. 119.

30 Quoted in René Durocher, "Henri Bourassa, les évêques et la guerre de 1914-1918," in *Historical Papers* (Ottawa: Canadian Historical Association, 1971), p. 248. [Translation]

31 Durocher, "Henri Bourassa, les évêques et la guerre de 1914-1918," p. 253. [Translation]

32 *Le Devoir* (Montreal), August 18, 1918. [Translation]

33 Quoted in Mason Wade, *The French Canadians, 1760-1967* (Toronto: Macmillan, 1968), p. 660.

34 Quoted in Wade, *The French Canadians, 1760-1967*, p. 681.

35 The most publicized was the motion of

J.-N. Francoeur in the Quebec legislature, that if the rest of Canada considered Quebec an obstacle to its national development, then Quebec would be disposed to leave confederation. Though it never came to a vote, it drew attention to the impasse that French and English Canadians had reached.

36 Some journalists estimated that the actual number of wounded was double the 35 officially reported by Quebec's doctors. See Jean Provencher, *Québec sous la loi des mesures de guerre* (Trois-Rivières, QC: Boréal Express, 1971), pp. 123-24.

37 E.g., a recent television program entitled "Vimy: The Birth of a Nation." (Vimy Productions, Vancouver, BC, 1996)

38 Quoted, with approval, in *Le Devoir* (Montreal), December 20-21, 1917.

39 Lionel Groulx, "Ce Cinquantenaire" and "Les Canadiens français et l'établissement de la confédération," both reprinted in *Revue d'histoire de l'amérique française*, Vol. XXI, no. 3a (1967); *Notre avenir politique* (Montreal: Action Française, 1923).

40 See H.B. Neatby, "Mackenzie King and National Unity," in H. L. Dyck and H. P. Krosby (eds.), *Empire and Nations* (Toronto: University of Toronto Press, 1969).

41 For an exposition of this French-Canadian view, see André Laurendeau, "The Conscription Crisis," in Philip Stratford (ed.), *André Laurendeau, Witness for Quebec* (Toronto: Macmillan, 1973), especially pp. 55-57.

42 Marcel Chaput, *Pourquoi je suis séparatiste* (Montreal: Éditions du Jour, 1961), pp. 13, 28. [Translation]

Chapter 2: The making of the welfare state

Unemployment Insurance (1940)

1 The 1921 federal election ended in the formation of a Liberal minority government. In order to govern, Prime Minister King needed the support of Progressive members, who, for the most part, represented rural areas. At that time, farmers were opposed to unemployment insurance, which they believed would encourage workers to stay in the city, thereby reducing the amount of cheap labour available for agricultural work. King, ever prudent, did not follow through on his party's promise. However, this contributed to his defeat in the 1930 general election, which ended in a victory for R. B. Bennett's Conservatives. During the election campaign, Bennett had promised to implement a national unemployment insurance program. Allan Irving, *The Development of Income Security in Canada, Britain and the United States, 1908-1945: A Comparative and Interpretive Account*, (Working Papers on Social Welfare in Canada, Toronto: Faculty of Social Work, University of Toronto, 1980), p. 43.

2 Dennis Guest, *The Emergence of Social Security in Canada*, 2nd ed. (Vancouver: University of British Columbia Press, 1985), p. 89. Indeed, British Columbia had had an unemployment insurance program since 1928, Alberta since 1930, Saskatchewan and Manitoba since 1931. Alvin Finkel, *Business and Social Reform in the Thirties* (Toronto: James Lorimer, 1979), p. 87,

3 Jean-Guy Genest, *Godbout* (Sillery, QC: Septentrion, 1996), p. 159.

4 It should also be remembered that Adélard Godbout owed his victory to the support of the federal Liberals. Paul-André Linteau *et al.*, *Histoire du Québec contemporain: le Québec depuis 1930* (Montreal: Boréal, 1986), p. 152.

5　In failing to consult the Legislative Assembly before agreeing to the constitutional amendment, Godbout was following the convention adopted by his predecessors in Quebec and by the premiers of the other provinces. Genest, *Godbout*, p. 161.

6　Genest, *Godbout*, pp. 160-61. [Translation]

7　James Struthers, "Canadian Unemployment Policy in the 1930s," in R. Douglas Francis and Donald B. Smith (eds.), *Readings in Canadian History: Post-Confederation*, 3rd ed. (Toronto: Holt, Rinehart and Winston, 1990), p. 436.

8　Struthers, "Canadian Unemployment Policy in the 1930s," p. 433.

9　James Struthers, *No Fault of Their Own: Unemployment and the Canadian Welfare State 1914-1941* (Toronto: University of Toronto Press, 1983), p. 209.

10　Leslie A. Pal, "Relative Autonomy Revisited: The Origins of Canadian Unemployment Insurance," *Canadian Journal of Political Science*, Vol. XIX, no. 1 (March 1986), p. 91.

11　Yves Vaillancourt, *L'évolution des politiques sociales au Québec, 1940-1960* (Montreal: Les Presses de l'Université de Montréal, 1988), pp. 311-18; Finkel, *Business and Social Reform in the Thirties*, pp. 84-91.

12　Leslie A. Pal, *State, Class and Bureaucracy* (Montreal: McGill-Queen's University Press, 1988), p. 150.

13　Pal, "Relative Autonomy Revisited"; François-Albert Angers, "Assurance-chômage," *L'actualité économique* (August-September 1940), p. 370.

14　Guest, *The Emergence of Social Security in Canada*, p. 90.

15　André Laurendeau, "Alerte aux Canadiens français," *L'action nationale*, Vol. XVI (1940), pp. 202-03. [Translation] "This is a centralizing measure, designed to increase the powers of the federal government to the detriment of the provincial legislatures," added Léopold Richer, "Préliminaires d'une loi d'assurance-chômage," *Le Devoir*, June 26, 1940, p. 1. [Translation]

16　Angers, "Assurance-chômage," p. 369. [Translation] Léopold Richer wrote that

　　as long as Canada remains as it is — that is, a country with ample arable land that can easily be made available and of abundant natural resources able to provide employment to a large number of people — a proposal of this kind is a staggering admission of incompetence on the part of our governments.

　　Richer, "Préliminaires d'une loi d'assurance-chômage." [Translation]

17　Genest, *Godbout*, p. 161. [Translation]

18　Léopold Richer, "Les travailleurs catholiques à Ottawa," *Le Devoir*, June 17, 1940, p. 1.

19　Genest, *Godbout*, p. 160.

20　Pal, *State, Class and Bureaucracy*, pp. 152-58.

21　Pal, *State, Class and Bureaucracy*, p. 157.

22　For a brief overview of Quebec initiatives in this field, see Diane Bellemare and Lise Poulin Simon, *Le défi du plein emploi* (Montreal: Éditions Saint-Martin, 1986), pp. 235-38, 249-60.

23　On April 14, 1994, the National Assembly unanimously adopted a motion requesting "Mr. Jean Chrétien and the federal Liberal government to respect the consensus of all those concerned regarding the need for Quebec to exercise all of the powers connected to labour market training." [Translation] Furthermore, according to a *Le Devoir*-Sondagem poll, 74.5 percent of respondents believed that the unemployment insurance program would be better administered by Quebec and 70 percent supported the Quebec government's desire to manage all labour market training programs. Pierre O'Neill, "75 p. 100 des Québécois pour le rapatriement de l'assurance-chômage," *Le Devoir*, May 14, 1995, p. A1. See also Alain Dubuc, "Formation: à quelques pas du fil d'arrivée," *La Presse*, June 1, 1996, p. B2; and Lise Bissonnette, "L'échine raide," *Le Devoir*, June 1-2, 1996, p. A14.

24 For a critical analysis, see François Rocher
    and Christian Rouillard, "Using the
    Concept of Deconcentration to Overcome
    the Centralization/Decentralization
    Dichotomy: Thoughts on Recent
    Constitutional and Political Reform," in
    Patrick Fafard and Douglas M. Brown
    (eds.), *Canada: The State of the Federation
    1996* (Kingston: Institute of
    Intergovernmental Relations, 1996), pp.
    117-18. It might be noted that even in
    Godbout's time, when the federal minister
    of labour proposed in 1942 to provide
    apprenticeship courses and to confer cer-
    tificates of study, the issue of labour market
    created jurisdictional conflict between
    Ottawa and Quebec. See Genest, *Godbout*,
    pp. 246-47.

25 However, Ottawa retains management
    responsibility for the unemployment insur-
    ance fund. For further information, see
    Gérard Boismenu, "Les relations fédérales-
    provinciales: la formation de la main-d'œu-
    vre," in Denis Monière (ed.), *L'année
    politique au Québec 1993-1994* (Montreal:
    Fides and *Le Devoir*, 1994), pp. 55-62;
    Herman Bakvis, "Federalism, New Public
    Management, and Labour-Market
    Development," in Fafard and Douglas
    Brown (eds.), *Canada: The State of the
    Federation 1996*, pp. 135-65.

Tax Rental Agreements (1947-1954)

1   The Rowell-Sirois Commission recommend-
    ed a redistribution of revenues between the
    provinces and the federal government and
    among the provinces themselves. Personal
    and corporation income taxes and succes-
    sion duties were to be utilized solely by the
    federal government. A. Milton Moore, J.
    Harvey Perry and Donald I. Beach, *The
    Financing of Canadian Federation: The First
    Hundred Years* (Toronto: Canadian Tax
    Foundation, 1966), p. 12.

2   Réal Bélanger, Richard Jones and Marc
    Vallières, *Les grands débats parlementaires,
    1792-1992* (Sainte-Foy, QC: Les Presses de
    l'Université Laval, 1994), p. 166.

3   Richard Simeon and Ian Robinson, *State,
    Society, and the Development of Canadian
    Federalism* (Toronto: University of Toronto
    Press, 1990), p. 107.

4   Gérard Boismenu, *Le Duplessisme: politique
    économique et rapports de force, 1944-1960*
    (Montreal: Les Presses de l'Université de
    Montréal, 1981), p. 271.

5   These proposals are contained in what is
    known as the Green Book, published in
    1945, in which the federal government
    proposed setting up several social security
    programs (family allowance, old age securi-
    ty and a health insurance plan).

6   Boismenu, *Le Duplessisme*, p. 272.

7   New Brunswick was the first province to
    sign such an agreement. See Robert
    Rumilly, *L'autonomie provinciale* (Montreal:
    Édition de l'Arbre, 1948), p. 260.

8   For the Quebec government, the absence of
    tax agreements meant a loss of revenue of
    $150 million between 1947 and 1954. In
    1954, even with the provincial tax on per-
    sonal income, the Quebec government's
    loss was evaluated at $20.7 million.
    Boismenu, *Le Duplessisme*, pp. 273-74.

9   R. M. Burns, *The Acceptable Mean: The Tax
    Rental Agreements, 1941-1962* (Toronto:
    Canadian Tax Foundation, 1980), p. 108.

10 Léon Dion, *Québec 1945-2000 (tome II): les
    intellectuels et le temps de Duplessis* (Sainte-
    Foy, QC: Les Presses de l'Université Laval,
    1993), p. 109. [Translation]

11 For more details, see Burns, *The Acceptable
    Mean*, pp. 107-12.

12 Burns, *The Acceptable Mean*, p. 106.

13 It is worth recalling that in the immediate
    postwar period Quebec, Ontario and British
    Columbia paid 85.5 percent of all fiscal rev-
    enues in Canada, whereas the other
    provinces paid only 14.5 percent. Boismenu,
    Le duplessisme, footnote 20, p. 272.

14 Simeon and Robinson, *State, Society and the Development of Canadian Federalism*, p. 112.

15 Moore and Perry, *The Financing of Canadian Federation*, pp. 27-28; Roland Parenteau, "Québec et le partage des impôts," *L'actualité économique*, Vol. XXX, no. 2 (July-September 1954), pp. 325-26.

16 Cited by Rumilly, *L'autonomie provinciale*, p. 270.

17 Quoted in John Grube, "M. François-Albert Angers et l'indépendance fiscale," *L'action nationale*, Vol. 70 (1980-1981), p. 801.

18 Quoted in Grube, "M. François-Albert Angers et l'indépendance fiscale," p. 803. See also Rumilly, *L'autonomie provinciale*, p. 178-88. [Translation]

19 Burns, *The Acceptable Mean*, p. 105.

20 See in particular François-Albert Angers, "À quelle sauce veut-on nous manger?", *L'action nationale*, Vol. XVI, no. 4 (December 1940), pp. 289-306; Anonymous, "Centralisation démocratique," *Relations*, Vol. I, no. 1 (January 1941), pp. 2-3; and the many articles which appeared in *Le Devoir* at the time, particularly those by André Laurendeau. Rumilly's *L'autonomie provinciale* is also an excellent example of this kind of discourse.

21 Quoted by Bélanger, Jones and Vallières, *Les grands débats parlementaires*, p. 167. [Translation]

22 Cited by Rumilly, *L'autonomie provinciale*, p. 186. [Translation] The election results were nonetheless mixed, with the Quebec Liberal Party getting 40 percent of the vote but only 37 seats and the Union nationale getting 38.2 percent of the vote but 48 seats. Once in opposition, the Liberals maintained that a federal income tax did not, in itself, undermine provincial autonomy.

23 Pierre Trépanier, "L'opinion publique anglo-québécoise et l'autonomie provinciale (1945-1946)," *L'action nationale*, Vol. 67, no. 1 (1977), p. 42. [Translation]

24 Michael D. Behiels, *Prelude to Quebec's Quiet Revolution: Liberalism Versus Neo-Nationalism* (Montreal: McGill-Queen's University Press, 1985), pp. 200-02.

25 René Durocher and Michèle Jean, "Duplessis et la Commission royale d'enquête sur les problèmes constitutionnels, 1953-1956," *Revue d'histoire de l'Amérique française*, Vol. 25, no. 3, December 1971, p. 338. [Translation] The tax agreements negotiated by Ottawa and the provinces authorized the provinces to levy a personal income tax of five percent without subjecting taxpayers to double taxation.

26 François-Albert Angers, "Le tour de M. Duplessis," *L'actualité économique* (July 1946), pp. 364-65.

27 Dion, *Québec 1945-2000*, p. 109. [Translation]

28 Durocher and Jean, "Duplessis et la Commission royale d'enquête sur les problèmes constitutionnels, 1953-1956," p. 346. [Translation]

29 Quoted in Durocher and Jean, "Duplessis et la Commission royale d'enquête sur les problèmes constitutionnels," p. 348. [Translation]

30 Cited by Rumilly, *L'autonomie provinciale*, p. 267. [Translation]

31 Parenteau, "Québec et le partage des impôts," p. 323.

32 Behiels, *Prelude to Quebec's Quiet Revolution*, p. 199.

33 Burns, *The Acceptable Means*, pp. 111-12.

Federal Grants to Universities (1951)

1 Michel Brunet, *Canadians et Canadiens: études sur l'histoire et la pensée des deux Canadas* (Montreal: Fides, 1954), p. 60.

2 Richard Simeon and Ian Robinson, *State, Society, and the Development of Canadian Federalism* (Toronto: University of Toronto Press, 1990), p. 148.

3 The same situation developed in 1997 when the Quebec government threatened to reduce grants to any educational or

research institution that accepted money from the Canadian Foundation for Innovation established by the federal government. Lysiane Gagnon, "Toujours le même vieux contentieux," *La Presse*, December 16, 1997, p. B3; Don Macpherson, "Quebec Right to Feel Leery Over Research Fund," *The Gazette*, December 17, 1997, p. B3.

4   Robert Bothwell, Ian Drummond and John English, *Canada Since 1945: Power, Politics, and Provincialism* (Toronto: University of Toronto Press, 1981), p. 167.

5   Robert Rumilly, *Maurice Duplessis et son temps tome II (1944-1959)* (Montreal: Fides, 1978), p. 402.

6   Frank R. Scott, "Areas of Conflict in the Field of Public Law and Policy," in *Essays on the Constitution: Aspects of Canadian Law and Politics* (Toronto: University of Toronto Press, 1977), p. 317.

7   Brunet, *Canadians et Canadiens*, p. 61. [Translation]

8   Pierre Elliott Trudeau, *Federalism and the French Canadians* (New York: St. Martin's Press, 1968), p. 87.

9   Cited in Rumilly, *Maurice Duplessis et son temps*, p. 492. [Translation]

10 Louis Maheu and Marcel Fournier, "Nationalisme et nationalisation du champ scientifique québécois," *Sociologie et Sociétés*, Vol. 7, no. 2 (November 1975), pp. 89-114.

11 Cited in Rumilly, *Maurice Duplessis et son temps*, p. 469. [Translation]

12 Jean-Claude Robert, *Du Canada français au Québec libre: histoire d'un mouvement indépendantiste* (Paris: Flammarion, 1975), p. 188. [Translation]

13 This was the University Finance Agreement, signed in 1959. Kenneth McRoberts, *Quebec: Social Change and Political Crisis*, 3rd ed. (Toronto: McClelland and Stewart, 1988), p. 141. This financing formula was extended to all the provinces as of 1967.

14 See David B. Perry, *Financing the Canadian Federation, 1867 to 1995: Setting the Stage for Change* (Toronto: Canadian Tax Foundation, 1997), pp. 207-24; and, in this volume, the essays on "Hospital Insurance and Health Insurance" and on "The Canada and Quebec Pension Plans."

Canada and Quebec Pension Plans (1965)

1   In 1951, the federal government had undertaken a review of old age income support and had adopted three new laws establishing a universal old age security program. These laws included a benefit program for persons aged 70 and over, a program of assistance to persons between the ages of 65 and 70 and a program of assistance to blind persons aged 21 and over. The new section 94A reads:

> It is hereby declared that the Parliament of Canada may from time to time make laws in relation to old age pensions in Canada, but no law made by the Parliament of Canada in relation to old age pensions shall affect the operation of any law present or future of a Provincial Legislature in relation to old age pension.

2   On August 23, 1963, the Quebec legislature unanimously adopted a resolution by which the Quebec government indicated its intention to create its own plan. "L'union nationale a dit NON jusqu'au bout," *Le Devoir*, August 23, 1963, p. 1.

3   Peter C. Newman, *The Distemper of Our Times* (Ottawa: McClelland and Stewart and Institute of Canadian Studies of Carleton University, 1978), p. 309.

4   "'Quebec's insistence on its own plan came as an unpleasant surprise' said one official. Even after Premier Lesage had said Quebec would have its own plan, Ottawa planners were unconcerned" Richard Simeon, *Federal-Provincial Diplomacy: The Making of*

Recent Policy in Canada (Toronto: University of Toronto Press, 1972), p. 45, note 7. Tom Kent's memoirs nevertheless showed that some senior federal officials did take Quebec's intentions seriously. According to Kent, Pearson was even prepared to create a funded scheme from which a substantial amount of revenue would be invested in provincial projects. However, political considerations pushed back negotiation of this agreement to spring 1964. See Tom Kent, *A Public Purpose* (Montreal: McGill-Queen's University Press, 1988), pp. 260-63.

5   The conference also dealt with the question of federal-provincial taxation arrangements (since 1960, the Quebec government had been demanding more tax points) and joint federal-provincial programs. At that time, the federal government was toying with the idea of extending family allowances and was planning to set up a federal student loan program. See Richard Simeon and Ian Robinson, *State, Society and the Development of Canadian Federalism* (Toronto: University of Toronto Press, 1990), pp. 194-202.

6   Cited in Newman, *The Distemper of Our Times*, p. 310; Peter Desbarats, *The State of Quebec* (Toronto: McClelland and Stewart, 1966), p. 125.

7   Cited by Simeon, *Federal-Provincial Diplomacy*, p. 56. "Never at such a high and public level has Confederation seemed so threatened," [Translation] wrote Mario Cardinal in "Le climat à Québec: un résultat qui remet en cause la Confédération," *Le Devoir*, April 3, 1964, p. 1. According to Tom Kent, a senior federal official, the conclusion of the conference "threatened a chain of events that would probably submerge Lesage and could well make the separation of Quebec from Canada a serious likelihood." Kent, *A Public Purpose*, p. 276.

8   Through this compromise, Quebec agreed to a constitutional amendment that would allow Ottawa to develop an income supplement program. The exemption of

social contributions it had initially contemplated for workers earning less than $1000 per year was granted to persons earning less than $600. The transition period was cut from 20 years to 10. In exchange, Ottawa adopted the capitalization formula advocated by Quebec and agreed that revenues would be administered by the provinces. For a detailed presentation of these negotiations, see Kent, *A Public Purpose*, pp. 276-83.

9   Simeon, *Federal-Provincial Diplomacy*, p. 46. See also John S. Morgan, "Welfare," in John Saywell (ed.), *Canadian Annual Review for 1963* (Toronto: University of Toronto Press, 1964), pp. 398-99; and Gordon Milling, "Labour's Interest in Pension Planning," in Laurence E. Coward (ed.), *Pensions in Canada* (Don Mills, ON: CCH Canadian Limited, 1964), p. 192. However, the federal government did submit several redrafted versions of the plan in an attempt to respond to Ontario's objections. As Ontario was the most populous province, its support for the federal plan was essential. See Kent, *A Public Purpose*, pp. 258-66.

10   Simeon, *Federal-Provincial Diplomacy*, p. 59.

11   Cited in Peter Stursberg, *Lester Pearson and the Dream of Unity* (Toronto: Doubleday, 1978), p. 196. Ontario won two concessions in exchange for its adherence to the national plan: a province could pull out of the plan when it wanted, and agreement would be required for future changes in the plan. Simeon, *Federal-Provincial Diplomacy*, p. 61.

12   See "Réactions favorables," *Le Devoir*, April 21, 1964, p. 1. [Translation] In Diefenbaker's opinion, Quebec's original proposal would have been "a step forward," contrary to the "hybrid" scheme finally adopted.

13   Quoted in Pierre Desbiens, "Perspectives sur l'État québécois," in Pierre Fournier (ed.), *Le capitalisme au Québec* (Laval: Les Éditions coopératives Albert Saint-Martin, 1978), p. 129. [Translation]

14 Jacques Parizeau recalled this period in the following terms:

> It was amazing the power those guys had...The usual practice was to dump $50 million worth of Quebec bonds onto markets after a provincial election and frighten stiff new governments. They would be in a panic, in 1962, 1966 and 1970. In the first few months of any provincial government, the spreads between Ontario and Quebec bonds would be usually 35 to 40 basis points [a difference in interest rates of .35 to .4 percent].

Cited by Diane Francis, *Controlling Interest* (Toronto: Macmillan, 1986), p. 207. Duplessis had succeeded in preserving the Quebec government's financial autonomy by recuperating tax points unilaterally and restricting public borrowings. He also tried to set up a rival investment banking syndicate but without success. See François Moreau, *Le capital financier québécois* (Laval: Les Éditions coopératives Albert Saint-Martin, 1981), p. 55; Mario Pelletier, *La machine à milliards: histoire de la caisse de dépôt et placement du Québec* (Montreal: Québec/Amérique, 1989), pp. 23, 52-54 and 56-60.

15 Pelletier, *La machine à milliards*. Quebec finally found the necessary sums in the United States.

16 Pelletier, *La machine à milliards*, pp. 25-26.

17 Cited by Newman, *The Distemper of Our Times*.

18 Claude Ryan, "Une victoire pour les personnes âgées et pour le vrai fédéralisme," *Le Devoir*, April 21, 1964, p. 4. [Translation]

19 Figure estimated by Pierre Arbour, *Québec Inc. and the Temptation of State Capitalism* (Montreal: Robert Davies Publishing, 1993), p. 84. Today, besides administering the Quebec Pension Fund, the Caisse also administers funds paid into 10 or so organizations including the Commission de la santé et de la sécurité du travail (Workers' Compensation Board), the Fonds d'assurance-prêts agricoles du Québec (Farm Loan Board) and the Régie de l'assurance automobile du Québec (Auto Insurance Board). The Caisse constitutes one of the largest capital reserves in North America. In 1981, its investment projects in Canadian Pacific provoked an angry outcry in English Canada. On this subject, see the essay on Bill S-31 in this book.

20 Thus, in June 1966,

> millions of dollars of Quebec bonds were put on sale by the Saint-Jacques Street brokers in a blatant attempt to intimidate the new government by ruining its credit. But the attempt failed, because the Caisse intervened and bought back the bonds. [translation]

Moreau, *Le capital financier québécois*, p. 58. After Quebec decided to borrow $38 million from a foreign bank consortium in 1968, the president of the Caisse observed that Quebec's financial soundness was better recognized outside Canada. See "C'est le reste du Canada plutôt que les États-Unis qui boude les obligations de la province de Québec," *Les Affaires*, March 25, 1968, p. 3. At the time of the Parti Québécois 1976 election victory, owing to the Caisse's intervention, massive resales were avoided, and in 1995 the Caisse helped prepare for the post-referendum period. Pelletier, *La machine à milliards*, pp. 135-40; and Presse canadienne, "Référendum: le PQ avait 37 milliards 'en réserve'," *La Presse*, May 18, 1996, p. A31.

21 Jean Lesage said:

> During the past month I have lived a terrible life. I worked for my province as no man has ever worked before. I used all the means that Providence has given me so that Quebec, in the end, would be recognized as a province with a special status in Confederation. And I have succeeded.

Cited by Newman, *The Distemper of our Times*. See also testimonies from political actors of the time is Stursberg, *Lester Pearson*, p.198; and Desbarats, *The State of Quebec*, pp. 132-33

22   Claude Morin, *Le pouvoir québécois...en négo-ciation* (Montreal: Boréal Express, 1978), pp. 22-24. For a critique of cooperative federalism, see also Jean-Marc Léger, "Le 'fédéralisme coopératif' ou le nouveau visage de la centralisation," in J. Peter Meekison (ed.), *Canadian Federalism: Myth or Reality* (Toronto: Methuen, 1968), pp. 317-20; and Donald V. Smiley, "Canadian Federalism and the Resolution of Federal-Provincial Conflict," in Frederick Vaughan (ed.), *Contemporary Issues in Canadian Politics* (Scarborough, ON: Prentice Hall, 1970), pp. 48-66.

Hospital Insurance and Health
Insurance (1957-1968)

1   Robert Bothwell, Ian Drummond and John English, *Canada Since 1945: Power, Politics, and Provincialism* (Toronto: University of Toronto Press, 1981), p. 162.
2   Yves Vaillancourt, *L'évolution des politiques sociales au Québec, 1940-1960* (Montreal: Les Presses de l'Université de Montréal, 1988), p. 196. The federal cabinet later made clear that this "substantial majority" meant at least six provinces, including either Quebec or Ontario. However, after the defeat of the Liberals in 1957, the new prime minister, John Diefenbaker, dropped this condition and agreed to implement the program with any province that was eligible, no matter how few there were. Gwendolyn Gray, *Federalism and Health Policy: The Development of Health Systems in Canada and Australia* (Toronto: University of Toronto Press, 1991), p. 37.
3   Gray, *Federalism and Health Policy*.
4   The discussion of social policy was stimulated by a number of reports, including the 1943 *Report on Social Security for Canada* (the Marsh report), the 1943 *Health Insurance Report* (the Heagerty report) and the 1945 Green Book Proposals produced

by Mackenzie King's Liberal government. Over the decade leading up to the adoption of the hospital insurance program, a number of government policies revealed the emergence of a new attitude about the role of the state in social policy matters. Of importance in this regard were the unemployment insurance program (1940), family allowances (1944) and the national health grants program (1948). Dennis Guest, *The Emergence of Social Security in Canada* (Vancouver: University of British Columbia Press, 1985), pp. 104-41.
5   In 1928, British Columbia had already appointed two commissions of inquiry on this issue. Donald Swartz, "The Politics of Reform: Public Health Insurance in Canada," *International Journal of Health Services*, Vol. 23, no. 2 (1993), p. 222. See also Gray, *Federalism and Health Policy*, pp. 26-30.
6   Gray, *Federalism and Health Policy*, p. 32.
7   Douglas Francis, Richard Jones and Donald B. Smith, *Destinies: Canadian History Since Confederation* (Toronto: Holt Rinehart and Winston, 1988), p. 321. See also Vaillancourt, *L'évolution des politiques sociales au Québec*.
8   Bothwell, Drummond and English, *Canada Since 1945*.
9   In a poll conducted by the Canadian Institute of Public Opinion in September 1965, 52 percent of respondents preferred a voluntary program, while 41 percent supported a mandatory program. Malcolm G. Taylor, *Health Insurance and Canadian Public Policy* (Montreal: McGill-Queen's University Press, 1987), p. 367.
10   Cited in Taylor, *Health Insurance and Canadian Public Policy*, p. 375.
11   Taylor, *Health Insurance and Canadian Public Policy*, pp. 161-238. See also Swartz, "The Politics of Reform," pp. 219-26.
12   The Ontario premier had launched a public campaign to pressure the federal government into implementing a national hospital insurance program. Bothwell, Drummond and English consider that the Ontario pre-

mier was a "key player" on this issue: "It was Frost who made national hospital insurance in Canada politically inevitable." Bothwell, Drummond and English, *Canada Since 1945*.

13 Jacques Paul Couturier, in collaboration with Wendy Johnston and Réjean Ouellette, *Un passé composé: Le Canada de 1850 à nos jours* (Moncton: Éditions d'Acadie, 1996), p. 293. Prime Minister Saint-Laurent only agreed to go along after Martin threatened to resign if he was not authorized to respond to the challenge of the Ontario premier.

14 Gray, *Federalism and Health Policy*, pp. 43-44. According to Malcolm G. Taylor, the chief supporters of health insurance in the cabinet were Judy LaMarsh, Walter Gordon, Allan MacEachen, Maurice Lamontagne and Jean Marchand. Taylor, *Health Insurance and Canadian Public Policy*, p. 353. It should be noted, however, that the Liberals were in a minority position and had to count on the support of a third party, in this case the NDP, to stay in power. This situation undoubtedly did much to make the expansion of social programs a government priority. A. W. Johnson, "Social Policy in Canada: The Past as It Conditions the Present," in Shirley B. Seward (ed.), *The Future of Social Welfare Systems in Canada and the United Kingdom* (Halifax: Institute for Research on Public Policy, 1987), p. 41.

15 Vaillancourt, *L'évolution des politiques sociales au Québec*, p. 200.

16 Réal Bélanger, Richard Jones and Marc Vallières, *Les grands débats parlementaires, 1792-1992* (Sainte-Foy, QC: Les Presses de l'Université Laval, 1994), p. 354. [Translation]

17 Cited in Taylor, *Health Insurance and Canadian Public Policy*, p. 365.

18 Deena White, "La santé et les services sociaux: réformes et remises en question," in Gérard Daigle (ed.), *Le Québec en jeu* (Montreal: Les Presses de l'Université de Montréal, 1992), pp. 232-33.

19 On the Quebec approach, see Pierre Bergeron and France Gagnon, "La prise en charge étatique de la santé au Québec," in Vincent Lemieux *et al.* (eds.), *Le système de santé au Québec* (Sainte-Foy, QC: Les Presses de l'Université Laval, 1994), pp. 16-28; and White, "La santé et les services sociaux," pp. 225-47.

20 Taylor, *Health Insurance and Canadian Public Policy*, p. 391.

21 The opting out formula was used for the first time in 1959 to settle the question of federal grants to universities. The right to opt out was recognized by the Liberal Party of Canada in 1961 and institutionalized in 1965 with the adoption by the federal government of the Established Programs (Interim Arrangements) Act. Quebec was the only province to have taken advantage of the interim arrangements by signing agreements to opt out of the hospital insurance program in return for 14 tax points on personal income tax. At the same time, it would withdraw from the Special Social Welfare Program (a program that included unemployment assistance, old age assistance, and allowances for blind and disabled persons) in return for four tax points, from a vocational training program (one point) and from a health grants program (one point). The opting out formula was also used for youth allowances in 1964 (four points). Yves Vaillancourt, "Un bilan de l'opting out du Québec des programmes fédéraux à frais partagés dans le domaine social (1964-1992)," in François Rocher (ed.), *Bilan québécois du fédéralisme canadien* (Montreal: VLB Éditeur, 1992), pp. 348-53; David B. Perry, *Financing the Canadian Federation, 1867 to 1995: Setting the Stage for Change* (Toronto: Canadian Tax Foundation, 1997), pp. 208-19.

22 Quoted by Taylor, *Health Insurance and Canadian Public Policy*, p. 392.

23 The objections raised against opting out are outlined in Yves Vaillancourt, *Le régime*

d'assistance publique du Canada: perspective québécoise (Ph.D. thesis, Université de Montréal, 1992), pp. 165-225. Vaillancourt points out that, during the 1964 negotiations over the opting out formula, the Quebec government had to agree to a five-year provisional period at the end of which the right to opt out would become permanent. This transition was never achieved, with the result that the special status Quebec had fashioned for itself still remains provisional, although it has been renewed up to the present. See also Kenneth McRoberts, *Misconceiving Canada: The Struggle for National Unity* (Toronto: Oxford University Press, 1997), chap. 3.

24　For more on the Canadian social union see Keith G. Banting, "The Past Speaks to the Future: Lessons from the Postwar Social Union," in Harvey Lazar (ed.), *Canada: The State of the Federation 1997: Non-Constitutional Renewal* (Kingston: Institute of Intergovernmental Relations, 1998), pp. 39-69; François Rocher and Christian Rouillard, "Décentralisation, subsidiarité et néo-libéralisme," in *Canadian Public Policy*, Vol. 24, no. 2 (June 1998), pp. 233-58; and the special issue of *Policy Options*, Vol. 19, no. 9 (November 1998).

Chapter 3: Definition of Canadian Identity

John Meisel's introduction

1　Hector Charlesworth, *I'm Telling You* (Toronto: Macmillan, 1937), p. 99.

The Creation of the Canadian Broadcasting Corporation (1932)

1　See Frank W. Peers, *The Politics of Canadian Broadcasting, 1920-1951* (Toronto:

University of Toronto Press, 1969), p. 49. It was Augustin Frigon, the French-speaking member of the Aird Commission, who had insisted that the provinces be given responsibility for programs. This would have guaranteed French-language service for Quebecers. This aspect of the report was ignored by the federal government following the decision of the Privy Council in London to recognize its jurisdiction over radio broadcasting.

2　On the role of Canadian nationalism in this decision, see Graham Spry's testimony, "The Origins of Public Broadcasting in Canada: A Comment," *Canadian Historical Review*, Vol. 46, no. 2 (June 1965), p. 136; and the study by Mary Vipond, "The Nationalist Network: English Canada's Intellectuals and Artists in the 1920s," *Canadian Review of Studies on Nationalism*, Vol. 7, no. 1 (Spring 1980), pp. 32-52; as well as Marc Raboy, *Missed Opportunities: The Story of Canada's Broadcasting Policy* (Kingston: McGill-Queen's University Press, 1990), pp. 17-47.

3　Raboy, *Missed opportunities*, p. 42; Peers, *The Politics of Canadian Broadcasting*, pp. 51-55, for reactions to the Aird report and pp. 75-77 for support for a public broadcasting system in 1931.

4　Comments reported by Michel Filion, *Radiodiffusion et société distincte* (Montreal: Méridien, 1994), p. 33. On the League's role, see Raboy, *Missed Opportunities*, pp. 31-45; and Peers, *The Politics of Canadian Broadcasting*.

5　Comments reported by Raboy, *Missed Opportunities*, pp. 45-46.

6　"It would be English as a rule," he said. Comments reported in Filion, *Radiodiffusion et société distincte*, p. 32.

7　E. Austin Weir, *The Struggle for National Broadcasting in Canada* (Toronto: McClelland and Stewart, 1965), p. 149; Peers, *The Politics of Canadian Broadcasting*, pp. 128-30; Raboy, *Missed Opportunities*, pp. 50-54.

8   Weir, *The Struggle for National Broadcasting
     in Canada*, p. 150.

9   Weir, *The Struggle for National Broadcasting
     in Canada*, p. 151.

10   Hector Charlesworth, *I'm Telling You*
     (Toronto: Macmillan, 1937), p. 99.

11   Peers, *The Politics of Canadian Broadcasting*,
     p. 159.

12   Peers, *The Politics of Canadian Broadcasting*,
     p. 140. There were 700 respondents in
     the sample.

13   Quoted by Peers, *The Politics of Canadian
     Broadcasting*.

14   Filion, *Radiodiffusion et société distincte*, p.
     31; and Peers, *The Politics of Canadian
     Broadcasting*, p. 52.

15   Raboy, *Missed Opportunities*, pp. 33-36.

16   Raboy, *Missed Opportunities*, pp. 20, 31, 44.

17   However, the language factor, combined
     with a lower radio reception rate than else-
     where in Canada, appeased any fears that
     Francophones might have had about this.
     Moreover, it should be noted that a recent
     study by Michel Filion shows that, even at
     that time, the listening habits of
     Francophones were "distinct" and that
     Francophones listened less than
     Anglophones to American programs. The
     main hope was that public broadcasting
     would make up for deficiencies in broad-
     casting equipment in French Canada (num-
     ber of transmitters or the strength of the
     signal). See Filion, *Radiodiffusion et société
     distincte*, pp. 65-86; Elzéar Lavoie, "L'évo-
     lution de la radio au Canada français avant
     1940," *Recherches sociographiques*, Vol. XII,
     no. 1 (January-April 1971), pp. 2-49.

18   On this subject, it is useful to read Arthur
     Laurendeau's comment, "La radio," *L'action
     nationale*, Vol. 4, no. 2 (October 1934), pp.
     117-34, in which he expressed his fears
     about the democratization of culture: "I
     would like the ordinary people to get a
     taste of what is beautiful provided that they
     are guided, led by an elite that militates,
     stirs and leads, especially an elite that has a

taste for intellectual charity." (p. 126)
[Translation]

19   Raboy, *Missed Opportunities*, p. 54. See also
     Omer Héroux, "Le français et la radio," *Le
     Devoir*, March 20, 1933, p. 1.

20   Murray said:
     > Broadcasting can help to make
     > the whole of Canada bilingual,
     > to make available to the
     > Canadian citizen of the future
     > the culture, literature and
     > thought of the two parent lan-
     > guages. This is not a vague aspi-
     > ration, it reflects a definite and
     > carefully considered policy.

     In 1936, the Chairman of the Canadian
     Broadcasting Corporation had announced
     his intention of turning radio into an instru-
     ment of national reconciliation: "If the radio
     is not a healing and reconciling force in our
     national life it will have failed of its high
     purpose. If Canadian radio makes no lasting
     contribution to a better understanding
     between the so-called French-Canadian and
     the so-called English-Canadian, between the
     East and the West...then we shall have fal-
     tered our stewardship." Comments reported
     in Peers, *The Politics of Canadian
     Broadcasting*, p. 250, 199.

21   Thanks to a private station called *Radio-
     Ouest-Française*, affiliated with Radio-
     Canada, Francophones in the Prairies were
     able to hear programs in their own language
     from 1942 onwards. It was not until 1952
     that Franco-Ontarians were able to receive a
     radio signal in French, and Radio-Canada
     would be established only in 1958. The
     Maritimes and the Prairies would not have
     access to French radio until 1956. Greg M.
     Nielsen, "L'impasse Canada-Québec et le sort
     de Radio-Canada : l'autonomie culturelle ou
     la mort," *Cahiers de recherche sociologique*,
     Vol. 25 (1995), p. 203. See also Lavoie,
     "L'évolution de la radio au Canada français
     avant 1940," p. 40, who observes that in the
     early 1940s "the regionalist option left more
     than 700,000 Francophones, or over 20 per-
     cent of this linguistic community, out of the
     transmission range of the French network."

[Translation] The frustration with this situation is made clear in "La litanie pour l'unité nationale," *L'action nationale*, Vol. 17, no. 6 (June 1941), p. 507.

22　Lavoie, "L'évolution de la radio au Canada français avant 1940," pp. 40-41.

23　See *Le Devoir* of May 19 and May 27, 1936.

24　Whether in terms of content or audience, the French network has succeeded much more than its English counterpart in promoting a Canadian product. Michel Filion, *Radiodiffusion et société distincte,* chaps. 7 and 8; Richard Collins, *Culture, Communication and National Identity: The Case of Canadian Television* (Toronto: University of Toronto Press, 1990), pp. 190-204.

25　It should be recalled that English and French programs were broadcast by the CBFT television network from its inauguration in September 1952 until January 1954. Gérard Laurence, "La naissance de la télévision au Québec 1949-1953," *Communication et information*, Vol. 2, no. 3 (1979), pp. 55-60; Jean-Pierre Desaulniers, "Television and Nationalism: From Culture to Communication," in Phillip Drummond and Richard Paterson (eds.), *Television in Transition* (London: BFI Books, 1986), pp. 112-22; Pierre Laporte, "La 'justice pour les deux parties' à la télévision," *Le Devoir*, May 29, 1953, p. 1; André Laurendeau, "Sur la télévision et les Canadiens français," *Le Devoir*, June 13, 14, 15, 1956, p. 1.

26　Raboy, *Missed Opportunities*, pp. 68-72.

27　Michel Roy, "La grève des réalisateurs de Radio-Canada," *Relations industrielles*, Vol. 14, no. 2 (April 1959), p. 276; Frank W. Peers, *The Public Eye: Television and the Politics of Canadian Broadcasting, 1952-1968* (Toronto: University of Toronto Press, 1979), pp. 181-93.

28　In 1968, the federal government adopted a new radio broadcasting act in which the CBC's mandate was clearly defined to include promoting national unity. Raboy, *Missed Opportunities*, pp. 204-08.

29　Raboy, *Missed Opportunities*, pp. 246-58.

30　Claude Marsolais, "Le référendum et les médias: le 'mea culpa' de Radio-Canada," *Bulletin d'histoire politique*, Vol. 4, no. 3 (Spring 1996), pp. 19-22; "The Media and Constitutional Reform in Canada," in David E. Smith et al. (eds.), *After Meech Lake: Lessons for the Future* (Saskatoon: Fifth House, 1991), pp. 147-203.

31　Esther Désilets, "Le canal d'information unilingue anglais: les francophones s'avoueraient-ils vaincus?", *Le Devoir*, January 7, 1988.

32　The conflict started in 1929 with the Quebec government's decision to contest federal jurisdiction over radio broadcasting and was settled, for a time, by the ruling of the Privy Council in London in favour of Ottawa. It flared up again in the 1960s with the establishment of Radio-Québec in 1968 and the creation of the Quebec *ministère des Communications* in 1969. Alain Laramée, "Le dossier des communications au Québec: historique des relations entre Québec et Ottawa," *L'action nationale*, Vol. 81, no. 9 (November 1991), pp. 1165-83; Marc Raboy, "Vers une politique québécoise de télévision : les leçons de l'histoire," *L'action nationale*, Vol. 81, no. 9 (November 1991), pp. 1313-25.

The Royal Commission on Bilingualism and Biculturalism (1963-1970)

1　Lester B. Pearson, *Mike: The Memoirs of the Right Honourable Lester B. Pearson*, Vol. 3 (Toronto: University of Toronto Press, 1975), p. 23.

2　Cited in Pearson, *Mike*, pp. 67-69. Pearson's speech was drafted by his Quebec adviser, Maurice Lamontagne.

3　André Laurendeau, editor of *Le Devoir*, had published an editorial in January 1962 entitled "Pour une enquête sur le bilinguisme," from which the idea of an inquiry arose.

4   From the Commission's terms of reference, in
    *A Preliminary Report of the Royal Commission
    on Bilingualism and Biculturalism* (Ottawa:
    Queen's Printer, 1965), Appendix 1, p. 151.
5   *A Preliminary Report*, p. 13
6   *A Preliminary Report*, p. 125. For Laurendeau,
    the regional meetings were dispiriting. He
    wrote: "A separatist who went through what
    we are experiencing at present would emerge
    with even greater conviction. A young
    nationalist would certainly be tempted by
    separatism." André Laurendeau, *Journal tenu
    pendant la Commission royale d'enquête sur le
    bilinguisme et le biculturalisme* (Outremont,
    QC: VLB Éditeur, 1990), p. 67. [Translation]
7   Laurendeau, *Journal tenu pendant la
    Commission royale d'enquête sur le bilinguisme
    et le biculturalisme*, p. 70.
8   Quoted in Peter Stursberg, *Lester Pearson
    and the Dream of Unity* (Toronto:
    Doubleday, 1978), p. 149.
9   *Preliminary Report*, p. 126. Commissioner
    Neil Morrison later recalled:
    > I remember vividly one meeting
    > the Commission had with rep-
    > resentatives of some of the
    > "other ethnic groups" in the
    > north end of Winnipeg, my
    > home town, when I became so
    > angry and embarrassed by the
    > attacks on André Laurendeau
    > and other French Canadians
    > that I almost walked out of the
    > meeting. I was only persuaded
    > to stay by a calmer and more
    > rational Dave Dunton.

    Neil Morrison, "Bilingualism and
    Biculturalism," in *Language and Society:
    Special Report on the 25th Anniversary of the B
    and B Commission and the 20th Anniversary of
    the Official Languages Act: English and French
    Canada* (Ottawa: Commissioner of Official
    Languages for Canada, 1989), p. R-7.
10 Laurendeau, *Journal tenu pendant la
    Commission royale d'enquête sur le bilinguisme
    et le biculturalisme* (entry for January 21,
    1964), p. 52. The Commission's *Preliminary
    Report* noted that westerners tend to prefer
    the vision of multiculturalism or "the
    Canadian mosaic," and discussed the

notion of a "third force" in Confederation,
composed of Canadians from other ethnic
backgrounds. *Preliminary Report*, p. 51.
11 *Preliminary Report*, p. 59
12 John Porter, "Bilingualism and the Myths of
    Culture," *Canadian Review of Sociology and
    Anthropology*, Vol. 6, no. 2 (1969), p. 116.
13 *House of Commons Debates*, October 17,
    1968, p. 1487.
14 *Preliminary Report*, p. 109, 114, 115, 118.
15 Denis Monière, *André Laurendeau et le destin
    d'un peuple* (Montreal: Québec-Amérique,
    1983), pp. 324-25. Trudeau was not a sig-
    natory to the *Cité libre* piece, but Marc
    Lalonde has confirmed his participation in
    its drafting. See Robert Bothwell, *Canada
    and Quebec: One Country, Two Histories*
    (Vancouver: University of British Columbia
    Press, 1995), p. 125.
16 From Lacoste's introduction in Laurendeau,
    *Journal tenu pendant la Commission royale
    d'enquête sur le bilinguisme et le
    biculturalisme*, p. 39. [Translation]
17 René Lévesque, *Option Québec* (Montreal:
    Éditions de l'Homme, 1968), p. 115.
    [Translation]
18 At the Constitutional Conference of
    February 1968, Johnson quoted extensively
    from the General Introduction to Volume I
    of the Commission's final report, the so-
    called "blue pages," in support of what he
    referred to as the "political dimension of
    cultural equality." See *Constitutional
    Conference Proceedings*, February 5-7,
    1968, p. 62.
19 Guy Rocher, "Le Canada: Un pays à
    rebâtir?", *Canadian Journal of Sociology and
    Anthropology*, Vol. 6, no. 2 (1969), p. 124.
20 Kenneth McRoberts, "English-Canadian
    Perceptions of Quebec," in Alain-G.
    Gagnon (ed.), *Quebec: State and Society,* 2nd
    ed. (Scarborough, ON: Nelson, 1993),
    pp. 116-17. See also Michael Oliver, "The
    Impact of the Royal Commission on
    Bilingualism and Biculturalism on
    Constitutional Thought and Practice in

Canada," *International Journal of Canadian Studies*, Vol 7-8 (Spring-Fall 1993), p. 23.

21 See, in this volume, the essays on "Federal Multiculturalism Policy" (1971) and "Official Bilingualism" (1969).

The Canadian Flag (1965)

1 George F. G. Stanley, *The Story of Canada's Flag: A Historical Sketch* (Toronto: Ryerson, 1965), p. 35.

2 Canadian Heritage, Canadian Identity Division, *The National Flag of Canada: A Profile* (Ottawa: Supply and Services Canada, 1995), p. 10. The Red Ensign was created in 1707 as the flag of the British Merchant Marine. Various forms of the Canadian Red Ensign, as well as the Union Jack, were flown from approximately 1870 to 1965.

3 Blair Fraser, *The Search for Identity: Canada, 1945-1967* (Toronto: Doubleday, 1967), pp. 238-39.

4 This committee was composed of 15 members: seven Liberal, five Conservative, one New Democrat, one Créditiste and one Social Credit MP. See Stanley, *The Story of Canada's Flag*, p. 67.

5 Ratified by 152 votes to 85, the motion was supported by 12 Créditiste, seven Social Credit and four Conservative MPs. On the opposing side, 73 Conservative, nine New Democrat, two Social Credit and one Liberal MP came down against the motion.

6 Stanley, *The Story of Canada's Flag*, p. 64.

7 John G. Diefenbaker, *One Canada: Memoirs of the Right Honourable John G. Diefenbaker: The Tumultuous Years, 1962-1967* (Toronto: Macmillan, 1977), p. 223.

8 "With Responsible Haste," *The Globe and Mail*, February 16, 1965, p. 6.

9 Fraser, *The Search for Identity*, p. 243.

10 J. M. Bumsted, *The Peoples of Canada: A Post-Confederation History* (Toronto: Oxford University Press, 1992), p. 327.

11 Léon Balcer, *Léon Balcer raconte* (Sillery, QC: Septentrion, 1988), p. 131. [Translation]

12 Claude Ryan, "Le drapeau du Canada," *Le Devoir*, February 16, 1965, p. 4. [Translation]

13 "Lesage: le Canada passe de l'adolescence à l'âge adulte," *Le Devoir*, February 16, 1965, p. 1. [Translation]

14 "Lesage: le Canada passe de l'adolescence à l'âge adulte." [Translation]

15 Hugh Winsor, "Ottawa Warned Against Promoting Maple Leaf," *The Globe and Mail*, September 25, 1996, p. A7.

16 Winsor, "Ottawa Warned Against Promoting Maple Leaf."

Official Bilingualism (1969)

1 Maurice Héroux, *A Chronicle of the Office of the Commissioner of Official Languages. 1970-1991* (Ottawa: Office of the Commissioner of Official Languages, 1991), p. 1.

2 Section 133 of the British North America Act stipulated that:
    Either the English or the French Language may be used by any Person in the Debates of the Houses of the Parliament of Canada and of the Houses of the Legislature of Quebec; and both those Languages shall be used in the respective Records and Journals of those Houses; and either of those Languages may be used by any Person or in any Pleading or Process in or issuing from any Court of Canada established under this Act, and in or from all or any of the Courts of Quebec.

3 Office of the Commissioner of Official Languages, *Our Two Official Languages Over Time*, revi. ed. (May 1994), pp. 3-9. Bilingual family allowance cheques were introduced in Quebec in 1945 and extended to all of Canada in 1962.

4 W. Seymour Wilson, "Language Policy," in G. Bruce Doern and W. Seymour Wilson (eds.), *Issues in Canadian Public Policy* (Toronto: Macmillan, 1974), pp. 256, 259; Kenneth McRoberts, "English-Canadian

Perceptions of Quebec," in Alain-G. Gagnon (ed.), *Quebec: State and Society*, 2nd ed. (Scarborough, ON: Nelson, 1993), p. 109; Paul-André Linteau *et al.*, *Histoire du Québec contemporain: Tome 1: De la Confédération à la crise (1867-1929)* (Montreal: Boréal, 1989), p. 600.

5   Eric Wadell, "State, Language and Society: The vicissitudes of French in Quebec and Canada," in Alan C. Cairns and Cynthia Williams (eds.), *The Politics of Gender, Ethnicity and Language in Canada* (Toronto: University of Toronto Press, 1986), pp. 78, 83.

6   Office of the Commissioner of Official Languages, *Our Two Official Languages Over Time*, pp. 15-16.

7   See in this book the essay on the creation of the Canadian Broadcasting Corporation. On the decision to print bilingual paper money, see *House of Commons Debates* (1936). On the situation of French in the armed forces, see Jean Pariseau and Serge Bernier, *French Canadians and Bilingualism in the Canadian Armed Forces, Vol. I, 1763-1969: The Fear of a Parallel Army* (Ottawa: Directorate of History, Department of National Defence, 1988).

8   See Wadell, "State, Language and Society," pp. 75-76; see the article in this book on "The minority rights disputes."

9   Wilson, "Language Policy," p. 255.

10   Kenneth McRoberts, *Misconceiving Canada: The Struggle for National Unity* (Toronto: Oxford University Press, 1997), p. 80. In the early 1960s, the Glassco Commission recommended again that special efforts be made to increase bilingualism among public servants. Wilson, "Language Policy," p. 260. See also Émile Gosselin, "L'administration publique dans un pays bilingue et biculturel," *Canadian Public Administration*, Vol. VI, no. 4 (December 1963), pp. 407-33.

11   Milton J. Esman, "The Politics of Official Bilingualism in Canada," *Political Science Quarterly*, Vol. 97, no. 2 (Summer 1982), p. 248.

12   McRoberts, "English-Canadian Perceptions of Quebec," p. 120.

13   Cliff Downey (Battle River), *House of Commons Debate*, May 21, 1969, p. 8918; and H. A. Moore, *House of Commons Debate*, May 27, 1969, p. 9104. See also J. T. Thorson, *Wanted: A Single Canada* (Toronto: McClelland and Stewart, 1973), pp. 123-34.

14   Downey, *House of Commons Debate*.

15   Michael O'Keefe, *An Analysis of Attitudes Towards Official Languages Policy Among Anglophones* (Ottawa: Office of the Commissioner of Official Languages, 1990), p. 10. In 1993, Scott Reid wrote:

> Designed to correct historic wrongs, official bilingualism has created new injustices. Intended to help create a new national identity in which all Canadians could share, it has become instead a symbol of sectionalism, elitism and division.

Scott Reid, *Lament for a Nation: The Life and Death of Canada's Bilingual Dream* (Vancouver: Arsenal Pulp Press, 1993), p. 251.

16   McRoberts, *Misconceiving Canada*, p. 113; O'Keefe, *An Analysis of Attitudes Towards Official Languages Policy Among Anglophones*, p. 6.

17   In to the 1971 Census, Francophones made up only 1.7 percent of the population in Saskatchewan, 1.4 percent in Alberta and 0.5 percent in British Columbia. They made up 31.4 percent of the population in New Brunswick and 4.6 percent in Ontario. McRoberts, *Misconceiving Canada*, p. 86.

18   Jean-Louis Roy, *Le choix d'un pays: le débat constitutionnel Québec-Canada* (Ottawa: Leméac, 1978), p. 170.

19   Davidson Dunton, "Majority Must Bend to Québec," in S. D. Berkowitz and R. K. Logan (eds.), *Canada's Third Option* (Toronto: Macmillan, 1978), p. 96.

20   On the reactions of the provinces, see McRoberts, *Misconceiving Canada*, pp. 95-97; Esman, "The Politics of Official Bilingualism in Canada," p. 237.

21 Esman, "The Politics of Official Bilingualism in Canada," p. 243.

22 Cited in Lewis Seale, "Language Bill's Loss is Separatist Gain, Fournier Contends," *The Globe and Mail*, July 9, 1969, p. 3.

23 *House of Commons Debate*, October 17, 1968, p. 1484, for Trudeau's statement; p. 1486 for Lewis' statement.

24 Lorne Nystrom, *House of Commons Debate*, May 23, 1969, p. 9010.

25 For examples of negative reaction to this policy, see Sam Allison, *French Power: The Francization of Canada* (Richmond Hill, ON: BMG Publishing, 1978); and J. B. Andrew, *Bilingual Today, French Tomorrow: Trudeau's Master Plan and How It Can Be Stopped* (Richmond Hill, ON: BMG, 1977).

26 O'Keefe, *An Analysis of Attitudes Towards Official Languages Policy Among Anglophones*. The number of students enrolled in French immersion increased from 37,835 in 1977-78 to 313,084 in 1995-96. Office of the Commissioner of Official Languages, *Annual Report 1995* (Ottawa: Supply and Services Canada, 1996), Table V.1, p. 100. The association Canadian Parents for French was founded in 1977.

27 Linteau *et al.*, *Histoire du Québec contemporain*, p. 69.

28 Renaude Lapointe, "Les Canadiens deviennent adultes," *La Presse*, July 9, 1969, p. 4. [Translation]

29 Jean-François Cardin and Claude Couture, *Histoire du Canada: Espace et différences* (Sillery, QC: Les Presses de l'Université Laval, 1996), p. 180. [Translation]

30 Jacques P. Couturier (in collaboration with Wendy Johnson and Réjean Ouellette), *Un passé composé: le Canada de 1850 à nos jours* (Moncton: L'Acadie, 1996), p. 333.

31 In 1974, Robert Bourassa's Liberal government adopted Quebec's Official Language Act (Bill 22), which made French the only official language of the province. On this, see the essay on "Quebec's Language Laws" in this book.

32 Wadell, "State, Language and Society," pp. 78, 85; Esman, "The Politics of Official Bilingualism," p. 246.

33 Charles Castonguay, "Chrétien, Durham, même combat," *Le Devoir*, August 22, 1996, p. A7.

34 Pierre Fournier, *A Meech Lake Post-Mortem. Is Quebec Sovereignty Inevitable?* (Montreal: McGill-Queen's University Press, 1991), p. 102.

35 Héroux, *A Chronicle of the Office of the Commissioner of Official Languages. 1970-1991*, p. 26.

36 The representation of Francophones has vastly improved. This change is seen not only in the number of positions held but also in the prestige and importance of the posts. Office of the Commissioner of Official Languages, *Annual Report 1995*, pp. 2-3. For a critical analysis, see Michel Sarra-Bournet, "'French power, Québec power': la place des francophones québécois à Ottawa," in François Rocher (ed.), *Bilan québécois du fédéralisme canadien* (Montreal: VLB, 1992), pp. 199-225.

37 An audit by the Commissioner of Official Languages in 1994 revealed that services were available in both languages in 98.8 percent of the two-language service points of Quebec and in 72 percent of those in the rest of the country. Office of the Commissioner of Official Languages, *Annual Report 1995*, p. 2.

38 "It is fair to say that minority language instruction is now more available in all provinces and territories and that more than half have adopted Education Acts that fully meet the requirements of the Charter [article 23]," wrote the Commissioner of Official Languages. Office of the Commissioner of Official Languages, *Annual Report 1995*, p. 6.

39 Office of the Commissioner of Official Languages, *Annual Report 1995*, p. 1.

40 Charles Castonguay, "Vérité et mensonge sur la langue," *Le Devoir*, April 1, 1996, p. A7; McRoberts, *Misconceiving Canada*, pp. 103-06.

41 In 1981, the rate of bilingualism among the
    Anglophone population outside Quebec was
    five percent. It was 6.4 percent in 1991 and
    seven percent in 1996. However, according
    to the 1996 Census, 62 percent of Anglo-
    Quebecers were bilingual. Among francoph-
    one Quebecers, the rate of bilingualism
    increased from 28.7 percent to 31.5 percent
    between 1981 and 1991 and had climbed to
    34 percent by 1996. Outside Quebec, 81.1
    percent of Francophones were bilingual in
    1991 and 84 percent in 1996. McRoberts,
    Misconceiving Canada, p. 108; Chantal
    Hébert, "Le bilinguisme qui s'essouffle," *La
    Presse*, December 4, 1997, p. B7.

42 In a Multi réso/*Le Devoir* poll conducted
    in April 1991, 53 percent of respondents
    identified themselves first as Quebecers,
    23 percent as French Canadians and
    19 percent as Canadians. Édouard
    Cloutier, "L'opinion politique québécoise
    en 1990-1991," in Denis Monière (ed.),
    L'année politique au Québec 1991 (Montreal:
    Québec/Amérique, 1992), p. 230. For
    more recent data confirming this trend,
    see Antoine Robitaille, "L'insondable âme
    américaine des Québécois," *Le Devoir,*
    May 9, 1998, p. A4. Nevertheless, many
    Quebecers still feel moderately or strongly
    attached to Canada, according to an April
    1998 poll, but this feeling remains far less
    widespread in Quebec than in the rest of
    Canada (54 percent of respondents *versus*
    88 percent). See Paul Wells, "Sovereignty
    Star Fading: Poll," *The Gazette*, April 2,
    1998, p. A1.

Federal Multiculturalism Policy (1971)

1   Raymond Breton, "Multiculturalism and
    Canadian Nation-Building," in Alan Cairns
    and Cynthia Williams (eds.), *The Politics of
    Gender, Ethnicity and Language in Canada*,
    Vol. 34 of the Royal Commission on the
    Economic Union and Development

    Prospects for Canada (Toronto: University
    of Toronto Press, 1986), p. 51.

2   House of Commons, *Debates*, October 8,
    1971, p. 8545.

3   Standing Committee on Multiculturalism,
    Multiculturalism: Building the Canadian Mosaic,
    Report of the Standing Committee on Multi-
    culturalism, Executive Summary (Ottawa:
    Supply and Services Canada, June 1987).

4   Kenneth McRoberts, *Misconceiving Canada:
    The Struggle for National Unity* (Oxford:
    Oxford University Press, 1997), p. 128.

5   Leslie A. Pal, *Interests of State: The Politics of
    Language, Multiculturalism, and Feminism in
    Canada* (Montreal: McGill-Queen's University
    Press, 1993).

6   See Breton, "Multiculturalism and Canadian
    Nation-Building," p. 49.

7   See Pal, *Interests of State*, p. 128.

8   According to sociologists Jeffrey Reitz and
    Raymond Breton, the actual differences
    between outcomes for immigrants to the
    United States and to Canada are much less
    significant than the "mosaic" and "melting pot"
    metaphors would suggest. See Jeffrey G. Reitz
    and Raymond Breton, *The Illusion of Difference*
    (Toronto: C.D. Howe Institute, 1994).

9   See, for example, Yasmeen Abu-Laban and
    Daiva Stasiulis, "Ethnic Pluralism under
    Siege: Popular and Partisan Opposition to
    Multiculturalism," *Canadian Public Policy*,
    Vol. 18, no. 4 (1992), pp. 365-86; Gina
    Mallet, "Multiculturalism: Has Diversity
    Gone Too Far?", *The Globe and Mail*, March
    15, 1997, p. D1.

10 Citizens' Forum on Canada's Future (Chair:
    Keith Spicer), *Report to the People and
    Government of Canada* (Ottawa: Supply and
    Services Canada, 1991), p. 128.

11 See, for example, Patricia E. Roy, "The Fifth
    Force: Multiculturalism and the English
    Canadian Identity," *Annals of the American
    Academy of Political and Social Science*, no.
    538 (March 1995), pp. 199-209.

12 See Abu-Laban and Stasiulis, "Ethnic
    Pluralism under Siege," p. 373. In 1989,

the Reform Party adopted a platform on multiculturalism that upheld the responsibility of the state to promote and preserve national culture and to "encourage ethnic cultures to integrate into the national culture."

13   Cited in Robert Bothwell, *Canada and Quebec: One Country, Two Histories* (Vancouver: University of British Columbia Press, 1995), p. 235.

14   Neil Bissoondath, *Selling Illusions: the Cult of Multiculturalism in Canada* (Toronto: Penguin, 1994), pp. 133-34.

15   See for instance the speech to the 57th Annual Conference of the Ukrainian Canadian Congress (UCC) given by Bohdan Kordan, Co-Chair, UCC Government Relations Committee, entitled "Multiculturalism, Citizenship and the Canadian Nation," Toronto, April 5, 1997.

16   Reitz and Breton, *The Illusion of Difference*, p. 127.

17   Daniel Salée, "Espace public, identité et nation au Québec: mythes et méprises du discours souverainiste," *Cahiers de recherche sociologique*, no. 25 (1995), p. 142. The 1991 report of Quebec's Bélanger-Campeau Commission explicitly denounced the entrenchment of multiculturalism in the Charter of Rights and Freedoms for the implicit rejection of Canadian duality. See *Rapport de la Commission sur l'avenir politique et constitutionel du Québec* (Quebec: National Assembly, March 1991), p. 33.

18   McRoberts, *Misconceiving Canada*, p. 135.

19   McRoberts, *Misconceiving Canada*, p. 130.

20   See for example Micheline Labelle's submission to the Bélanger-Campeau Commission, "Politique d'immigration: Politique d'intégration: identité du Québec," in *Les avis des spécialistes invités à répondre aux huit questions posées par la Commission*, Commission sur l'Avenir politique et constitutionel du Québec, Working Paper no. 4 (1991), pp. 491-506.

21   Micheline Labelle, François Rocher and

Guy Rocher, "Pluriethnicité, citoyenneté et intégration: de la souveraineté pour lever les obstacles et les ambiguités," *Cahiers de recherche sociologique*, no. 25 (1995), p. 218. [Translation]

22   *Au Québec pour bâtir ensemble: énoncé de politique en matière d'immigration et d'intégration* (1990) cited in Labelle, Rocher and Rocher, "Pluriethnicité, citoyenneté et intégration," p. 224.

23   McRoberts, *Misconceiving Canada*, p. 135.

24   McRoberts, *Misconceiving Canada*, p. 130. Daniel Latouche takes up this point in *Plaidoyer pour le Québec* (Montreal: Boréal, 1995), p. 200.

Chapter 4 : Beyond the Quiet Revolution

John Meisel's introduction

1   *A Preliminary Report of the Royal Commission on Bilingualism and Biculturalism* (Ottawa: Queen's Printer and Controller Stationery, 1965), p. 13.

2   Similarly, three basic positions stand out in Quebec: *indépendantistes*, federalists and an intermediary group dissatisfied with both options.

3   Denis Smith, *Bleeding Hearts...Bleeding Country: Canada and the Quebec Crisis* (Edmonton: Hurtig, 1971). Similarly, the most insightful analyses of RCMP misconduct in dealing with alleged illegal activities by Quebec nationalists are those by Reginald Whitaker, a professor at York University in Toronto. See "Canada: The RCMP Scandals," in Andrei S. Marcovits and Mark Silverstein (eds.), *The Politics of Scandal: Power and Process in Democracies* (New York: Holmes & Meyer, 1988), pp. 38-61. For a revisionist piece by the same author, see "Apprehended Insurrection? RCMP Intelligence and the October Crisis,"

Queen's Quarterly, Vol. 100, no. 2 (Summer 1993), pp. 383-406.

4   Keith Banting and Richard Simeon (eds.), *And No One Cheered: Federalism, Democracy and the Constitution Act* (Toronto: Methuen, 1983). This was the third in a series of insightful analyses by the Institute on the Canadian Union. The others were *One Country or Two?* (1972) and *Must Canada Fail?* (1977).

5   Jean-Luc Pépin and John Robarts (co-chairs), *The Task Force on Canadian Unity: A Future Together* (Ottawa: Supply and Services Canada, 1979).

"Vive le Québec libre!" (1967)

1   From 1960 onwards, the Quebec government had been strengthening its ties with France. The lavish 1961 inauguration of Quebec's Délégation générale in Paris was followed by agreements concerning work-study programs for young people, an educational exchange program and a cooperation program. As the power to sign treaties resides solely with the federal government, these international initiatives by the Quebec government were very closely watched by the federal government.

2   Renée Lescop, *Le parti québécois du général de Gaulle* (Montreal: Boréal Express, 1981), p. 51.

3   Jacques Portes, *Le Canada et le Québec au XXe siècle* (Paris: Armand Colin, 1994), p. 123.

4   Michel Sarra-Bournet, "De Gaulle et la mémoire collective du Canada anglais," *L'action nationale*, Vol. 88, no. 10 (December 1998), p. 93-95.

5   Quoted in Robert Bothwell, *Pearson: His Life and World* (Toronto: McGraw-Hill Ryerson, 1978), p. 202.

6   L. B. Pearson, *Mike: The Memoirs of the Right Honourable Lester B. Pearson*, Vol. 3 (Toronto: University of Toronto Press, 1972), p. 267.

7   "A Time to Go Home," *The Globe and Mail*, July 26, 1967, p. 6.

8   The French and international press generally echoed this view. Historian Jacques Portes recalls the reception reserved for the president upon his return from Canada: "No one really understood the President's initiative; many attributed it to his advanced age, others to 'the solitary exercise of power.' Most commentators deplored this interference in the affairs of a friendly country." Portes, *Le Canada et le Québec au XXe siècle*, p. 124. [Translation]

9   Jean-Claude Robert, *Du Canada français au Québec libre: histoire d'un mouvement indépendantiste* (Paris: Flammarion, 1975), p. 251. [Translation]

10   *Le Temps* (Montreal), July 29, 1967. Quoted in *De Gaulle au Québec* (Montreal: Éditions Actualité, 1967), pp. 83-84. [Translation]

11   Dale C. Thompson, *De Gaulle et le Québec* (Saint-Laurent, QC: Éditions du Trécarré, 1990), p. 297. [Translation]

12   Pierre O'Neill, "Drapeau: Notre attachement au Canada sert la vie française," *Le Devoir*, July 27, 1967, p. 1. [Translation]

13   On these controversies see Charles Grandmont, "Un timbre du général de Gaulle fait couler beaucoup d'encre: Québec se réjouit, Ottawa refuse de commenter," *La Presse*, March 1, 1997, p. A30; Gilles Lesage and Gilles Rhéaume, "Qui sont les timbrés?", *Le Devoir*, March 19, 1997, p. A1; Josée Legault, "Les apôtres de l'amnésie," *Le Devoir*, July 23, 1997, p. A6; Michel Venne, "Guerre des clans pour le général," *Le Devoir*, July 24, 1997, p. A1.

14   Pierre O'Neill, "De Gaulle n'a plus la cote," *Le Devoir*, November 21, 1997, p. A1.

The October Crisis

1   The manifesto is reproduced in Louis Fournier, *FLQ: histoire d'un mouvement clandestin* (Montreal: Québec/Amérique, 1982),

p. 306. The following passage is illustrative
of the text:

> The FLQ wants nothing less
> than total independence for
> Quebecers, united in a free soci-
> ety, purged once and for all of
> its band of voracious sharks,
> those "big boss" types and their
> footmen who have made
> Quebec their private preserve of
> cheap labour and unscrupulous
> exploitation... [Translation]

2   The federal War Measures Act, enacted during the First World War, gave the cabinet
unrestricted authority to issue orders and
regulations in dealing with a security emergency. It was invoked by order-in-council,
without the requirement of parliamentary
sanction. The Act was repealed in 1988 and
replaced by the Emergencies Act, which
also authorizes restrictions on civil liberties.
Peter Hogg, *Constitutional Law of Canada*,
4th ed. (Scarborough, ON: Carswell, 1996),
p. 706.

3   Denis Smith, *Bleeding Hearts, Bleeding
Country: Canada and the Quebec Crisis*
(Edmonton: Hurtig, 1971), pp. 42, 47.

4   Germain Dion, *Une tornade de 60 jours: La
crise d'octobre 1970 à la chambre des communes*
(Hull: Éditions Asticou, 1985), pp. 175-76.

5   *The Globe and Mail* commented on April 30,
1970, "Today this feels like a splendid
country," for "the province of Quebec is
alive and well in Canada." Cited in John
Saywell, *Quebec 70: A Documentary
Narrative* (Toronto: University of Toronto
Press, 1971), p. 22.

6   Cited in Smith, *Bleeding Hearts, Bleeding
Country,* p. 33.

7   Saywell, *Quebec 70,* p. 94.

8   Saywell, *Quebec 70,* p. 91. However, some
civil libertarians, such as J. C. McRuer and
Frank Scott, endorsed the War Measures
Act as a "necessary evil." Also, it is interesting to note that the Canadian Civil Liberties
Association waited until December 10 —
by which time the notion of an apprehended insurrection had lost credibility — to
demand that a royal commission be

appointed to investigate the government's
actions. Saywell, *Quebec 70,* p. 128.

9   "The end of innocence," *Maclean's*, October
15, 1990, p. 27.

10 Saywell, *Quebec 70,* p. 118.

11 Cited in Robert Bothwell, *Canada and
Quebec: One Country, Two Histories*
(Vancouver: University of British Columbia
Press, 1995), p. 129.

12 Fournier, *FLQ,* p. 314.

13 This declaration became the subject of a
controversy when it was alleged in Ottawa
that the group sought to overthrow the
Bourassa government, which was refuted
by Ryan in an editorial of October 30,
1970, entitled "Un complot qui n'a jamais
existé." See Claude Ryan, *Le Devoir et la
crise d'octobre 70* (Montreal: Leméac, 1971),
pp. 113-18.

14 Cited in Ryan, *Le Devoir et la crise d'octobre 70,*
p. 59; [Translation] see also Guy Lachapelle,
"The Editorial Position of *Le Devoir*," *Québec
Studies*, no. 11 (1990/1991), p. 3.

15 From Claude Ryan's October 17 editorial,
"Les mesures de guerre: trois questions," in
Ryan, *Le Devoir et la crise d'octobre 70,* p. 58.

16 Michel Bellavance and Marcel Gilbert,
L'opinion publique et la crise d'octobre
(Montreal: Éditions du jour, 1971), p. 47.
The authors found that 74 percent of
respondents indicated they had not felt a
direct threat from the FLQ during the crisis, and that the number of those who had
felt threatened by the security forces (34
percent) was greater than the number who
had felt threatened by the FLQ (22 percent). Bellavance and Gilbert, *L'opinion
publique et la crise d'octobre*, pp. 63, 67.

17 Ryan, *Le Devoir et la crise d'octobre 70,* p.
17. See also Reg Whitaker, "Insurrection?
RCMP Intelligence and the October Crisis,"
Queen's Quarterly, Vol. 100, no. 2 (Summer
1993), pp. 383-406.

18 Louis Fournier referred to Laporte's death as
"...[the] FLQ's response to the authorities'
refusal to negotiate." Fournier, *FLQ,* p. 351.

19 Whitaker, "Insurrection? RCMP Intelligence and the October Crisis," p. 401. Whitaker cites Joseph Ferraris, a Security Service veteran, as having claimed that the Act "delayed our finding Mr. Cross by about two or three weeks, or maybe a month," due to the time spent pursuing people not directly connected to the kidnappings.

20 Whitaker, "Insurrection? RCMP Intelligence and the October Crisis," p. 385. These acts included burning a barn, stealing dynamite, intercepting mail and stealing the PQ membership list. See Richard French and André Béliveau, La GRC et la gestion de la sécurité nationale (Montreal: IRPP, 1979), p. 1.

21 This explanation was advanced by Smith, Bleeding Hearts, Bleeding Country, and more recently by Whitaker, "Insurrection? RCMP Intelligence and the October crisis," p. 404.

22 John F. Conway, Debts to Pay: English Canada and Quebec from the Conquest to the Referendum (Toronto: James Lorimer, 1992), p. 90.

The Victoria Charter (1971)

1 Donald V. Smiley, Canada in Question: Federalism in the Seventies (Toronto: McGraw-Hill Ryerson, 1976), pp. 43-44.

2 See Constitutional Conference Proceedings, Victoria, June 14, 1971, Appendix B, Part IX. The Victoria formula required the assent of the legislatures of a majority of the provinces, including "each province that at any time...had, according to any previous general census, a population of at least 25 percent of the population of Canada" (i.e., Ontario and Quebec) as well as at least two of the Atlantic provinces and two of the Western provinces. The western veto could be exercised by any two provinces having combined populations of at least 50 percent of the total population of the western provinces. See James Ross Hurley, Amending Canada's Constitution: History, Processes, Problems and Prospects

(Ottawa: Minister of Supply and Services, 1996), Appendix 3, pp. 37-40.

3 See Jean-Louis Roy, Le choix d'un pays: Le débat Québec-Canada, 1960-1976 (Montreal: Leméac, 1978), p. 182; Gérard Boismenu and François Rocher, "Une réforme constitutionnelle qui s'impose," in Yves Bélanger, Dorval Brunelle et al., L'ère des Libéraux: Le pouvoir fédéral de 1963 à 1984 (Sillery, QC: Les Presses de l'Université du Québec, 1988), p. 87.

4 Richard Simeon and Ian Robinson, State, Society, and the Development of Canadian Federalism (Toronto: University of Toronto Press, in conjunction with the Royal Commission on the Economic Union and Development Prospects for Canada, 1990), p. 208.

5 Roy, Le choix d'un pays, p. 268

6 Roy, Le choix d'un pays, p. 184.

7 See Premier Strom's opening remarks to the Victoria conference, in Constitutional Conference Proceedings, p. 42.

8 John Saywell (ed.), Canadian Annual Review of Politics and Public Affairs, 1971 (Toronto: University of Toronto Press, 1972), p. 60. The newly elected government of Saskatchewan, in view of Quebec's decision not to proceed with the Charter, took no action to confirm or reject it.

9 Roy, Le choix d'un pays, p. 267.

10 "No Victoria Charter and no more yielding," Globe and Mail, June 24, 1971, p. 6. See also "Bourassa's 'no' is ominous for Canada," Toronto Star, June 23, 1971, p. 6.

11 Government of Quebec, Québec's Traditional Constitutional Positions, 1936-1990, Secrétariat aux Affaires intergouvernementales canadiennes, Working Paper (November 1991), p. 30. [Translation]

12 A paper presented by the Quebec government to the February 1968 conference suggested that the co-existence of the two governments in the social domain prevents "efficient planning in the area of social security, permits certain contradictions between the various programs and leads to

administrative overlapping and waste."
Cited in Roy, *Le choix d'un pays*, p. 200.
[Translation]

13 Robert Bothwell, *Canada and Quebec: One
Country, Two Histories* (Vancouver:
University of British Columbia Press,
1995), p. 134.

14 On the influence of the Castonguay-
Nepveu report on Quebec's bargaining
stance in Victoria, see a memo obtained by
Le Devoir addressed to Prime Minister
Trudeau by federal Privy Council Clerk
Gordon Robertson, "Le memorandum du 4
février 1971," *Le Devoir*, October 24, 1991,
p. B10.

15 Robert Bourassa, *Gouverner le Québec*
(Montreal: Éditions Fides, 1995), p. 128.

16 Boismenu and Rocher, "Une réforme constitutionnelle qui s'impose," p. 91. [Translation]

17 Roy, *Le choix d'un pays*, p. 269. [Translation]

18 From *The Gazette's* editorial of June 19, 1971,
cited in Roy, *Le choix d'un pays*, p. 271.

19 Roy, *Le choix d'un pays*, p. 268. [Translation]

20 Roy, *Le choix d'un pays*, pp. 53, 273.
Bourassa had left himself room to manoeuvre by not committing himself without consulting his government, but was perceived
as having essentially given his approval to
the Charter. See the recollections of Gordon
Robertson, in Bothwell, *Canada and Quebec*,
p. 134. However, in his memoirs, Bourassa
emphatically denies having given his agreement. Bourassa, *Gouverner le Québec*, p. 92.

21 See for example Claude Forget and Gérald
Beaudoin's recollections in Bothwell,
Canada and Quebec, pp. 134-35.

Quebec's Language Laws (1969-1994)

1 See Marc Levine, *The Reconquest of Montreal*
(Philadelphia: Temple University Press,
1990), chap. 3.

2 Paul-André Linteau *et al.*, *Histoire du Québec
contemporain: le Québec depuis 1930* (Montreal:
Boréal, 1986), p. 547. Initially, the OLF concentrated on promoting the correct use of the
language and updating terminology.

3 Cited in Alain-G. Gagnon and Mary Beth
Montcalm, *Quebec: Beyond the Quiet
Revolution* (Scarborough, ON: Nelson,
1990), p. 177.

4 This period is documented in Levine, *The
Reconquest of Montreal*, pp. 73-82.

5 See Jean-Denis Gendron (President), *Report
of the Commission of Inquiry on the Position of
the French Language and on Language Rights
in Québec, Book I* (Quebec: Government of
Quebec, 1972), p. 291. Other recommendations included recognition of French as
the official language of Quebec (English
was to be considered a "national language"
of Quebec, along with French); the adoption of a language law to, among other
things, "ensure the pre-eminence of French
in public language use (signs, billboards,
labels, etc.) without preventing the use of
English or any other language"; and the
establishment of "the consumer's right to be
served in French, without infringing on his
right to service in English."

6 Levine, *The Reconquest of Montreal*, p. 99.

7 William D. Coleman, "From Bill 22 to Bill
101: The Politics of Language under the
Parti Québécois," *Canadian Journal of
Political Science*, Vol. 14, no. 3 (September
1981), p. 467. Kenneth McRoberts has
argued that this technicality, which could
be interpreted as ensuring the conditions
for effective education, was in reality
designed to channel children of non-anglo-
phone immigrants into the francophone
education system. See Kenneth McRoberts,
Quebec: Social Change and Political Crisis,
3rd ed. (Toronto: McClelland and Stewart,
1988), p. 228.

8 From the preamble of Bill 101, cited in
Michel Plourde, *La politique linguistique du
Québec, 1977-1987* (Quebec: Institut québé-
cois de recherche sur la culture, 1988), p. 22.
[Translation] For a comparison of Bills 22 and
101, see Coleman, "From Bill 22 to Bill 101."

9 Coleman, "From Bill 22 to Bill 101," p. 469.

10 See "Évolution de la législation linguistique," in *Le Français langue commune: enjeu de la société québécois: bilan de la situation de la langue française au Québec en 1995: rapport du Comité interministériel sur la situation de la langue française* (Québec: Direction des communications du ministère de la Culture et des Communications, 1996), pp. 39-42.

11 Complaints concerning the sign law were subsequently filed with the United Nations Human Rights Committee, which concluded that the Charter of the French Language violated the minority language rights protection of the International Covenant on Civil and Political Rights (Article 27). See Peter W. Hogg, *Constitutional Law of Canada*, 4th abr. student ed. (Scarborough, ON: Carswell, 1996), Appendix VI, p. 1079.

12 "Mr. Bourassa: High-Handed and Reckless," *The Globe and Mail*, August 1, 1974, p. 6.

13 Kenneth McRoberts, "English-Canadian Perceptions of Québec," in Alain-G. Gagnon (ed.), *Québec: State and Society*, 2nd ed. (Scarborough, ON: Nelson, 1993), p. 127

14 "Quebec House passes controversial Bill 101," *The Globe and Mail*, August 27, 1977, p. 11.

15 Donald Creighton, "No More Concessions: If Quebec Does Go, Let It Not Be With Impunity," *Maclean's*, Vol. 90, no. 13 (June 1977), p. 24.

16 McRoberts, "English-Canadian Perceptions of Québec," pp. 124-25.

17 Cited in Robert Bothwell, *Canada and Québec: One Country, Two Histories* (Vancouver: University of British Columbia Press, 1995), p. 199.

18 For example, this point is made in Patrick Monahan's study, *Meech Lake: The Inside Story* (Toronto: University of Toronto Press, 1991), p. 253.

19 Christian Dufour, *Le défi québécois* (Montreal: L'Hexagone, 1989), p. 96. [Translation]

20 Plourde, *La politique linguistique du Québec, 1977-1987*, p. 26. [Translation] More

recently, on the 20th anniversary of the adoption of Bill 101, Quebec culture minister Louise Beaudoin referred to it as "a statute of constitutional scope." Louise Beaudoin, "French Language Charter Is Here to Stay," *The Gazette*, August 26, 1997, p. B3.

21 Guy Rocher, "Autour de la langue: crises et débats, espoirs et tremblements," in Gérard Daigle (ed.), *Le Québec en jeu: comprendre les grands défis* (Montreal: Les Presses de l'Université de Montréal, 1992), p. 442.

22 Cited in Plourde, *La politique linguistique du Québec*, p. 51. [Translation] A 1980 poll showed that among francophone respondents who had voted Yes in the referendum on sovereignty-association, support for a range of rights and services for Anglophones varied between 61 percent and 86 percent. Gagnon and Montcalm, *Quebec: Beyond the Quiet Revolution*, p. 186.

23 *Le français langue commune*, p. 15. [Translation]

24 See *Rapport de la Commission sur l'Avenir politique et constitutionnel du Québec* (Bélanger-Campeau report) (March 1991), p. 19.

25 From a letter by René Levesque addressed to Eric Maldoff, President of Alliance Québec (November 5, 1982), cited in Plourde, *La politique linguistique du Québec*, p. 61. [Translation]

26 This point is made by Plourde, *La politique linguistique du Québec*, p. 25.

27 See Rocher, "Autour de la langue," p. 441.

28 Gagnon and Montcalm, *Quebec: Beyond the Quiet Revolution*, p. 185.

29 Rhéal Séguin, "Poll Backs Current Language Law," *The Globe and Mail*, March 23, 1996, p. A4.

30 Levine, *The Reconquest of Montreal*, p. 107.

31 "Abandoning restraint," *The Gazette*, July 23, 1974.

32 Gary Caldwell, "Le Québec anglais: prélude à la disparition ou au renouveau," in Gérard Daigle (ed.), *Le Québec en jeu: comprendre les grands défis* (Montreal: Les Presses de

l'Université de Montréal, 1992), p. 486. See also Ronald Rudin, "English-Speaking Québec: The Emergence of a Disillusioned Minority," in Gagnon (ed.), *Québec: State and Society*, p. 345. Rudin notes that Anglo-Quebecers had a long history of out-migration to the rest of Canada, which facilitated the departure response.

33 Gagnon and Montcalm, *Quebec: Beyond the Quiet Revolution*, p. 181.

34 Rudin, "English-Speaking Québec," p. 347.

35 See the *Report of the Commission of Inquiry on the Position of the French Language and on Language Rights in Québec: Book I* (Chairman: Jean-Denis Gendron) (Quebec: Government of Quebec, 1972), p. 215, and Sorecom Inc., "Les mass média, l'attachement à sa langue et les modèles linguistiques au Québec en 1971," Étude E17 conducted for the Gendron Commission (Quebec: Éditeur officiel du Québec, 1973), p. 195.

36 Uli Locher, *Les anglophones de Montréal: émigration et évolution des attitudes 1978-1983* (Quebec: Conseil de la langue française, 1988), p. 77.

37 Gary Caldwell has noted, however, that Allophones (Italians and Portuguese, for example) remained loyal to the Quebec Liberal Party in the 1989 election. See Caldwell, "Le Québec anglais," p. 498.

38 Rudin, "English-Speaking Québec,"

39 See the "Politique gouvernementale relative à l'emploi et à la qualité de la langue française dans l'Administration," adopted by the Quebec Cabinet on November 12, 1996.

40 Denis Lessard, "Les Québécois partagés en deux blocs sur tous changements à la Loi 101," *La Presse*, March 2, 1996, p. A8.

41 *Le français langue commune*, p. 220.

42 *Le français langue commune*, p. 137.

43 *Le français langue commune*, pp. 68-69.

The Bilingual Air Traffic Control Crisis (1976)

1   In 1963, only nine air traffic controllers (out of 110), 15 radio operators (out of 135) and 12 aviation electronic technicians (out of 150) were Francophones. Toward the mid-1970s, the situation was completely reversed: out of over 200 radio operators and 275 air traffic controllers in Quebec, "...only a handful of the former and about sixty of the latter were unilingual anglophones." Sandford F. Borins, *The Language of the Skies: The Bilingual Air Traffic Control in Canada* (Montreal: McGill-Queen's University Press, 1983), pp. 23-24.

2   As early as July 1970, the Lisson report had recommended that bilingualism be authorized in bilingual districts. See Office of the Commissioner of Official Languages, *Our Two Official Languages Over Time* (Ottawa: Office of the Commissioner of Official Languages, 1990), p. 18; Michael Benedict, "Air-Language Row: A Step-by-Step History," *Toronto Star*, June 28, 1976, p. C3; Borins, *The Language of the Skies*, pp. 25-27, 45.

3   For a discussion of the main arguments against bilingualism, see Borins, *The Language of the Skies*, pp. 31-36.

4   Robert Bourassa recalls that the Gens de l'air "invoked Bill 22 when they decided to take action: 'we want to speak French in Quebec now that French is the official language of Quebec'." Robert Bourassa, *Gouverner le Québec* (Montreal: Fides, 1995), pp. 111-12. [Translation]

5   "Pilots and controllers distorting real issue, Trudeau says," *The Toronto Star*, June 24, 1976, p. A14.

6   "The air strike's over," *Toronto Star*, June 28, 1976, p. A1.

7   John F. Conway, *Debts to Pay: English Canada and Quebec from the Conquest to the Referendum* (Toronto: James Lorimer, 1992), p. 95.

8 Quoted in Robert Bothwell, Ian Drummond and John English, *Canada Since 1945: Power, Politics and Provincialism* (Toronto: University of Toronto Press, 1981), p. 356. See also "Because of Ottawa's haste," *The Globe and Mail* June 21, 1976, p. 6.

9 Borins, *The Language of the Skies*, pp. 157-59. See also William Johnson, "Pilots won't budge in bilingual battle," *The Globe and Mail*, June 26, 1976, p. 1.

10 See "How to Fire a Fan," *The Globe and Mail*, June 26, 1976, p. 6. "Trudeau Clears the Air," *The Toronto Star*, June 24, 1976, p. B4; and "Pilots Arrogant to Defy the Law," *The Toronto Star*, June 26, 1976, p. B2.

11 Borins, *The Language of the Skies*, p. 154.

12 Borins, *The Language of the Skies*, p. 174.

13 Kenneth McRoberts, *Quebec: Social Change and Political Crisis*, 3rd ed. (Toronto: McClelland and Stewart, 1988), pp. 236-27.

14 Bothwell, Drummond and English, *Canada Since 1945*.

15 Milton J. Esman, "The Politics of Official Bilingualism in Canada," *Political Science Quarterly*, Vol. 97, no. 2 (Summer 1982), p. 250.

16 Borins, *The Language of the Skies*.

17 Borins, *The Language of the Skies*, pp. 153-55.

18 Conway, *Debts to Pay*.

19 Bothwell, Drummond and English, *Canada Since 1945*, p. 396.

The Election of the Parti Québécois and the Referendum on Sovereignty-Association (1976-1980)

1 From 1973 on, René Lévesque and Claude Morin gradually altered the Parti Québécois policy of declaring sovereignty as soon as it came to power, in favour of an "étapiste" or step-by-step approach to sovereignty. The adoption of this strategy caused tension within the party. On this subject, see Robert Barberis and Pierre Drouilly, *Les illusions du pouvoir: les erreurs stratégiques du gouverne-ment Lévesque* (Montreal: Éditions Sélect, 1980); Vera Murray, *Le Parti québécois, de la fondation à la prise du pouvoir* (Montreal: Hurtubise HMH, 1976), pp. 191-95.

2 For example, Claude Ryan, then editor-in-chief of *Le Devoir*, supported the PQ:
> As it had campaigned on the theme of good government, and since the Liberal government was running out of steam, I had taken a position in favour of the Parti Québécois...all the while dissociating myself from its sovereignist option.

Claude Ryan, *Regards sur le fédéralisme canadien* (Montreal: Boréal, 1995), p. 118. [Translation]

3 Bill 22 made French the official language of Quebec. In protest, many Anglophones withdrew their support for the Quebec Liberal Party in favour of the Union Nationale. André Bernard, *Québec : élections 1976* (Montreal: Hurtubise HMH, 1976), pp. 135-38. See also in this book, the essay on "Quebec's Language Laws."

4 In 1970, the Parti Québécois obtained 23 percent of the popular vote and seven seats in the National Assembly, in 1973, 30 percent of the popular vote and six seats. None of the PQ's top candidates was elected in those two elections. Murray, *Le Parti québécois*, p. 181.

5 Kenneth McRoberts, *Misconceiving Canada: The Struggle for National Unity* (Don Mills, ON: Oxford University Press, 1997), p. 148.

6 For an analysis of the various proposals put forward during this period, see Peter H. Russell, *Constitutional Odyssey: Can the Canadians Become a Sovereign People?* (Toronto: University of Toronto Press, 1992), pp. 92-106; McRoberts, *Misconceiving Canada*, pp. 148-55; Guy Laforest, *Trudeau and the End of a Canadian Dream* (Montreal: McGill-Queen's University Press, 1995).

7 In *L'option* (Montreal: Les Éditions de l'homme, 1978), pp. 331-46; Jean-Pierre Charbonneau and Gilbert Paquette explain why sovereignists found the 1978 White Paper proposals insufficient.

8   Edward McWhinney, *Canada and the Constitution 1979-1982: Patriation and the Charter of Rights* (Toronto: University of Toronto Press, 1982), p. 4. See also Russell, *Constitutional Odyssey*, pp. 95-99.

9   Patrick J. Monahan, *Constitutional Law* (Concord, ON: Irwin Law, 1997), pp. 144-45.

10   Before 1980, the sovereignty-association option never had more than 35 percent of popular support. Édouard Cloutier, "La stratégie référendaire," in Yves Bélanger and Michel Lévesque (eds.), *René Lévesque: L'homme, la nation et la démocratie* (Montreal: Les Presses de l'Université du Québec, 1991), pp. 167-68.

11   Among the PQ's initiatives around this time: Bill 101, measures to protect agricultural property, creation of the Société de l'assurance-automobile du Québec, anti-scab legislation, legal aid, legislation on the financing of political parties, the establishment of Lazure abortion clinics, and socioeconomic summits. It was, in brief, a period of state interventionism.

12   The referendum question reflected the evolution of the Parti Québécois's constitutional position. It expressed the desire to reach, with the rest of Canada, a new agreement based on the principle of the equality of nations — while maintaining an economic association with Canada. Moreover, it committed the government to holding a second referendum before effecting any change in Quebec's political status. In other words, the Parti Québécois asked only for a mandate to negotiate.

13   Quoted by Graham Fraser, *PQ: René Lévesque and the Parti Québécois in Power* (Toronto: Macmillan, 1984), p. 227.

14   "And Now to Be Honest," *The Globe and Mail*, November 16, 1976, p. 6. Prime Minister Trudeau and the leaders of the two opposition parties made the same observation. John King, "PQ Has Mandate to Rule, Not Separate, PM Says," *The Globe and Mail*, November 16, 1976, p. 1.

15   "What Mr. Levesque Wants," *The Globe and Mail*, November 17, 1976, p. 6. See also Frederick J. Fletcher, "Public Attitudes and Alternative Futures," in Richard Simeon (ed.), *Must Canada Fail?* (Montreal: McGill-Queen's University Press, 1977), p. 28.

16   Richard Simeon, "Introduction," in Simeon (ed.), *Must Canada Fail?*, p. 4.

17   See for example "A Declaration of Quebec's Right to Self-Determination," published in *Canadian Forum* (February 1980), p. 6, which was signed by 20 public figures from English Canada. On the English-Canadian left and the Quebec national question, see Serge Denis, *Le long malentendu: le Québec vu par les intellectuels progressistes au Canada anglais, 1970-1991* (Montreal: Boréal, 1992).

18   See Simeon (ed.), *Must Canada Fail?*

19   Kenneth McRoberts, "English Canada and the Quebec Nation," *Canadian Forum* (February 1980), p. 12.

20   Donald Creighton, "No more Concessions: If Quebec Does Go, Let It Not Be With Impunity," *MacLean's*, Vol. 90, no. 13, June 27, 1977, pp. 25-26. See also Reginald Whitaker, "Competition for Power: Hobbes and the Quebec Question," *Canadian Forum* (January-February 1979), p. 10.

21   Prime Minister Trudeau had taken this position immediately after the Parti Québécois's election. See Pierre Elliott Trudeau, *House of Commons Debates*, 30th Parliament, 2nd Session, Vol. I (1976), p. 1036.

22   Michael D. Ornstein, H. Michael Stevenson and A. Paul Williams, "The State of Mind: Public Perceptions of the Future of Canada," in Roddick B. Byers and Robert W. Reford, *Canada Challenged: The Viability of Confederation* (Toronto: Canadian Institute of International Affairs, 1979), p. 80. The authors of this study conclude: "The politician who does ask his or her constituents about Quebec is likely to encounter both a lack of unanimity and an ignorance of the issues." (p. 107)

23 Charbonneau and Paquette, *L'option*,
    pp. 554-58.

24 Pierre Vadeboncoeur, "Les qui-perd-gagne,"
    in *Gouverner ou disparaître* (Montreal: Édi-
    tions Typo, 1993), pp. 187-88;
    [Translation] first written in February 1979.

25 Pierre Vadeboncoeur, "Le pire serait égal?",
    in *Gouverner ou disparaître*, pp. 161-62,
    [Translation] first written in July 1976.

26 Claude-V. Marsolais, Le référendum con-
    fisqué (Montreal: VLB Éditeur, 1992), p. 132.
    [Translation] See also Marcel Rioux, *Pour
    prendre publiquement congé de quelques salauds*
    (Montreal: L'Hexagone, 1980), p. 19.

27 Over 130,000 Anglo-Quebecers left the
    province between 1976 and 1981, up from
    94,000 over the 1971-1976 period. Josée
    Legault, *L'invention d'une minorité: les Anglo-
    Québécois* (Montreal: Boréal, 1992), p. 106.

28 Participation Quebec was formed on
    November 18, 1976, the Positive Action
    Committee on December 23, 1976. Legault,
    L'invention d'une minorité, pp. 41-45.

29 Quoted by Fraser, *PQ: René Lévesque and the
    Parti Québécois in Power*, p. 239.

30 For example, Kenneth McRoberts, *Quebec:
    Social Change and Political Crisis*, 3rd ed.
    (Toronto: McClelland and Stewart, 1988).

31 Jean Herman Guay, "L'évolution de l'opi-
    nion pendant la campagne référendaire," in
    Denis Monière and Jean H. Guay (eds.), *La
    bataille du Québec, troisième épisode: 30 jours
    qui ébranlèrent le Canada* (Saint-Laurent,
    QC: Fides, 1996), pp. 184-85.

32 See Nicole Laurin-Frenette and Jean-
    François Léonard (eds.), *L'impasse: enjeux et
    perspectives de l'après-référendum* (Montreal:
    Nouvelle optique, 1980); Jean-Pierre
    Bonhomme *et al.*, *Le syndrome post-
    référendaire* (Montreal: Les Éditions interna-
    tionales Alain Stanké, 1988); Marc Henry
    Soulet, *Le silence des intellectuels* (Montreal:
    Les Éditions coopératives Albert Saint-
    Martin, 1987).

The Patriation of the Constitution (1982)

1   We know today that neither Quebec nor
    any other province had the right of veto. At
    the time, before the Supreme Court of
    Canada ruled on this question, the view
    that Quebec had a right of veto was based
    on the historical precedents emerging from
    the 1964-65 (Fulton-Favreau formula) and
    1968-1971 (Victoria Charter) constitutional
    negotiations. In each case, Quebec's rejec-
    tion of the proposed constitutional amend-
    ment put an end to that round of
    constitutional reform. See Peter W. Hogg,
    Constitutional Law of Canada, 4th ed.
    (Scarborough, ON: Carswell, 1996),
    pp. 59-65; and James Ross Hurley, *La modi-
    fication de la Constitution du Canada:
    Historique, processus, problèmes et perspec-
    tives d'avenir* (Ottawa: Ministre des Appro-
    visionnements et Services Canada, 1996),
    pp. 69-71, in which the correspondence
    between René Lévesque and Pierre Elliott
    Trudeau on that matter is reproduced.

2   Patrick J. Monahan, *Constitutional Law*
    (Concord, ON: Irwin Law, 1997), p. 155.

3   However, unanimity is required for
    amendments affecting the composition of
    the Supreme Court, bilingualism in fed-
    eral institutions and the amending
    formula itself.

4   The resolution, as it was adopted by
    Parliament on December 8, 1981, con-
    tained some concessions to Quebec as well
    as to Aboriginal groups and women.
    Provisions for compensation were included
    for education and culture and an exception
    to mobility rights (section 6 of the Charter)
    was authorized in the provinces where the
    employment rate was below the national
    average. A clause protecting existing
    Aboriginal rights (section 35) was also
    added and the clause guaranteeing sexual
    equality (section 28) was excluded from
    the application of the notwithstanding

clause. Peter H. Russell, *Constitutional Odyssey: Can the Canadians Become a Sovereign People?* (Toronto: University of Toronto Press, 1992), p. 122.

5 "The Federation Stands," *The Globe and Mail*, November 6, 1981, p. 6.

6 Only 11 percent believed the opposite. "75 p. 100 des Canadiens appuient la nouvelle Constitution," *La Presse*, June 19, 1982, p. A11.

7 "The Federation Stands."

8 A November 1981 poll found that 72 percent of Canadians supported a charter of rights, "Poll Shows 72 per cent Questioned Favor Rights Charter in Constitution," *The Globe and Mail*, November 10, 1981, p. 10.

9 Alan C. Cairns, "The Charter, Interest Groups, Executive Federalism and Constitutional Reform," in David E. Smith *et al.* (eds.), *After Meech Lake: Lessons for the Future* (Saskatoon: Fifth House, 1991), pp. 13-31; Reginald Whitaker, "Democracy and the Canadian Constitution," in Keith Banting and Richard Simeon (eds.), *And No One Cheered: Federalism, Democracy and the Constitution Act* (Toronto: Methuen, 1983), p. 254.

10 "On April 17, 1982 ...," *The Globe and Mail*, April 17, 1982, p. 6.

11 Pierre Elliott Trudeau, *Memoirs* (Toronto: McClelland and Stewart, 1993), p. 327.

12 Trudeau, *Memoirs*, pp. 326-27. Jean Chrétien, who acted as Ottawa's principal representative during this round of negotiations, concurred: "There was never any night of the long knives. A compromise was reached by those who had come in good faith to a conference that was called to find compromise." See "Bring the Constitution Home," in Thomas S. Axworthy and Pierre Elliott Trudeau (eds.), *Towards a Just Society* (Markham, ON: Penguin Books, 1990), p. 304.

13 Trudeau, *Memoirs*, p. 327. See also "L'accord constitutionnel de 1982 n'a pas été un marché de dupes pour le Québec," *La Presse*, March 10, 1989, p. B3.

14 For more on this viewpoint, see Roy Romanow, John Whyte and Howard Leeson, *Canada...Notwithstanding: The Making of the Constitution* (Toronto: Carswell/Methuen, 1984), pp. 264-68.

15 Keith Banting and Richard Simeon, "Federalism, Democracy and the Future," in Banting and Simeon (eds.), *And No One Cheered*, p. 348. See also Romanow, Whyte and Leeson, *Canada...Notwithstanding*; and Robert Stanfield, "What to Do About Quebec's Isolation," *Policy Options*, Vol. 3, no. 4 (July-August 1982), pp. 6-10.

16 For Pierre Elliott Trudeau, the entrenchment of the Charter "...was meant to create a body of values and beliefs that not only united all Canadians in feeling that they were one nation, but also set them above the governments of the provinces and the federal government itself." Pierre Elliott Trudeau, *With a Bang, Not a Whimper: Pierre Trudeau Speaks Out* (Toronto: Stoddart, 1988), p. 46. On the Charter as a nation-building instrument, see also Rainer Knopff and F. L. Morton, "Nation-building and the Canadian Charter of Rights and Freedoms," in Alan C. Cairns and Cynthia Williams (eds.), *Constitutionalism, Citizenship and Society in Canada* (Ottawa: Supply and Services Canada, 1985), pp. 133-82.

17 Russell, *Constitutional Odyssey*, p. 125. See also Donald Smiley, "A Dangerous Deed," in Banting and Simeon (eds.), *And No One Cheered*, pp. 80-81.

18 Banting and Simeon, "Federalism, Democracy and the Constitution," in Banting and Simeon, *And No One Cheered*, p. 22.

19 See Roger Gibbins, "Constitutional Politics and the West," in Banting and Simeon (eds.), *And No One Cheered*, pp. 119-32; and George Woodcock, *Confederation*

Betrayed (Madeira Park, BC: Harbour Publishing, 1981).

20 For example, see the conclusions of Robert Sheppard and Michael Valpy, *The National Deal: The Fight for a Canadian Constitution* (Toronto: Macmillan, 1982), pp. 315-21; Russell, *Constitutional Odyssey*, pp. 125-26; and Edward McWhinney, *Canada and the Constitution, 1979-1982: Patriation and the Charter of Rights* (Toronto: University of Toronto Press, 1982), pp. 115-24.

21 René Lévesque, "Intervention lors de la séance de clôture de la Conférence fédérale-provinciale des Premiers ministres sur la constitution," November 5, 1981, reproduced in Gil Rémillard, *Le fédéralisme canadien: Tome II* (Montreal: Québec/Amérique, 1985), p. 661. [Translation]

22 A poll conducted from November 13 to 28, 1981, showed that 38.1 percent of Quebecers (43.4 percent of Francophones) supported the government's decision not to ratify the November accord and that 39.6 percent (33.6 percent of Francophones) did not. Guy Trudel, "Trois sondages sur le Québec d'après-novembre," *Le Devoir*, January 20, 1982, p. 13.

23 Claude Ryan, "La dualité canadienne," *Policy Options*, Vol. 3, no. 4 (July-August 1982), p. 19. [Translation] In March 1990, Justice Minister Gil Rémillard echoed this interpretation: "No Quebec government, regardless of its political allegiance, could have accepted this patriation." [Translation] Reproduced in Roch Denis (ed.), *Québec: dix ans de crise constitutionnelle* (Montreal: VLB Éditeur, 1990), p. 223.

24 Guy Laforest, *Trudeau and the End of a Canadian Dream* (Montreal: McGill-Queen's University Press, 1995), chap. 1.

25 Pierre Elliott Trudeau, "Faire progresser l'histoire," *Le Devoir*, May 22, 1980, p. 10.

26 Guy Laforest, "L'esprit de 1982," in Louis Balthazar *et al.*, *Le Québec et la restructuration du Canada, 1980-1992* (Sillery, QC: Septentrion, 1991), pp. 153-54. See also

Smiley, "A dangerous deed," in Banting and Simeon (eds.), *And No One Cheered*, p. 78.

27 Marcel Adam, "Rien n'est changé au statut du Québec," *La Presse*, March 6, 1989, p. B3. [Translation] In the summer of 1982, Marcel Rioux anticipated future developments and wrote: "It is very clear that Quebecers were had, were victims of a dirty trick...Several persons who voted *No* now understand that *No* means *No* and not *Yes*." Marcel Rioux, *Pour prendre publiquement congé de quelques salauds* (Montreal: L'Hexagone, 1980), p. 30. [Translation]

28 Claude Morin, *Les lendemains piégés* (Montreal: Boréal, 1988), p. 308. [Translation]

29 Morin, *Les lendemains piégés*, p. 372. Guy Laforest develops a similar position in *Trudeau and the End of a Canadian Dream*, pp. 47-55.

30 Jean-Louis Roy, "Le Québec est exclu et isolé," *Le Devoir*, November 6, 1981, p. 8. [Translation] See also Ryan, "La dualité canadienne," p. 18.

31 Ryan, "La dualité canadienne," p. 21. [Translation] In March 1990, justice minister Gil Rémillard agreed:

> The argument that there was nothing to do because the Quebec government was sovereignist does not hold water. René Lévesque was the head of a legitimate government that had been given a clear mandate to oppose any unilateral patriation by Ottawa.

Reproduced in Denis, *Québec: dix ans de crise constitutionnelle*, p. 224. [Translation]

32 Roy, "Le Québec est exclu et isolé," p. 6. [Translation] See also Laforest, "L'esprit de 1982," p. 149; and André Burelle, *Le mal canadien: essai de diagnostic et esquisse d'une thérapie* (Montreal: Fides, 1995).

33 See James Tully, "The Crisis of Identification: The Case of Canada," *Political Studies*, Vol. 42, Special issue (1994), p. 85.

34 Laforest, "L'esprit de 1982," p. 154.

35 Quebec, *Le Journal des débats*, Vol. 26, no. 9 (1981), p. 462.

36   Quebec, *Le Journal des débats*, Vol. 26, no.12 (1981), p. 605.

37   On December 6, 1982, eight months after the proclamation of the Constitution Act of 1982, the Supreme Court of Canada rejected Quebec's claim.

38   Richard Gwyn, "Masters in Our Own House," *Toronto Sun*, April 17, 1982, p. A1.

Chapter 5 : The Economic Debates

The Churchill Falls Contract (1969)

1   For a detailed account of the origins and development of the project, see Philip Smith, *Brinco: The Story of Churchill Falls* (Toronto: McClelland and Stewart, 1975).

2   This option would have involved getting the electricity from Churchill Falls to the United States by crossing the Strait of Belle-Isle by tunnel, going along the west coast of Newfoundland and then crossing the Cabot Strait by underwater cable to Nova Scotia. Frederick W. Rowe, *A History of Newfoundland and Labrador* (Toronto: McGraw-Hill Ryerson, 1980), pp. 488-89.

3   Rowe, *A History of Newfoundland and Labrador*, p. 489.

4   Maurice Jannard, "La Cour suprême donne raison à Québec contre Terre-Neuve," *La Presse*, May 4, 1984, p. A1.

5   The plaintiffs in this case included the CFLCo, Hydro-Québec, the Quebec government and two CFLCo creditors, Royal Trust and General Trust of Canada. The opposing party was represented by the Attorney General of Newfoundland.

6   Fearing an unfavourable verdict, the Quebec government tried to reach an agreement whereby an improvement of the 1969 contract would have been linked to the development of new water resources in Newfoundland. In March 1984, Premier Lévesque offered the Newfoundland premier a compromise valued by Hydro-Québec at more than $1 billion. Quebec's offer would have entitled Newfoundland to 500 additional megawatts (instead of the 800 megawatts it demanded) and doubled its hydraulic fees. "Our proposal was rejected outright in less than 72 hours, without a single counter-offer being made," Quebec's minister of energy and resources, Yves Duhaime, reported at the time. "Le jugement sur les chutes Churchill: Québec fera payer à Terre-Neuve le prix de son entêtement," *La Presse*, May 4, 1984, p. C1. [Translation]

7   Lisa Binsse, "Churchill Falls: qui dit vrai?", *La Presse*, September 26, 1996, p. E1.

8   Jeffrey Simpson, "Quebec Faces a New Challenge to Its Hydro Deal With Newfoundland," *The Globe and Mail*, September 24, 1996, p. A22.

9   Jannard, "La Cour suprême donne raison à Québec contre Terre-Neuve."

10   Jannard, "La Cour suprême donne raison à Québec contre Terre-Neuve."

11   "Newfoundland Loses its Bid to Cancel Hydro Agreement," *The Globe and Mail*, May 4, 1984, p. 1.

12   "Arbitrary Measures From our Lawmakers," *The Globe and Mail*, September 24, 1996, p. A22.

13   Cabot Martin, "The Truth Behind the Churchill Falls Deal," *The Globe and Mail*, November 23, 1996, p. D2.

14   Several months earlier, as part of its by-election campaign in Labrador, the party had asked the House of Commons to denounce the Churchill Falls contract. Chantal Hébert, "Tobin sur les traces de Clyde Wells," *La Presse*, September 28, 1996, p. B3.

15   "Mr. Chrétien and Newfoundland," *The Globe and Mail*, September 25, 1996, p. A22.

16   Roger J. Bédard, "Churchill Falls: signer d'abord, discuter ensuite," *Le Devoir*, April 1, 1969, p. 5. [Translation]

17 Gilles Lesage, "Québec est prêt à négocier, mais sur la base du jugement," *Le Devoir*, May 4, 1984, p. A1. [Translation]

18 Alain Dubuc, "Le plan B, Churchill Falls et Captain ROC," *La Presse*, September 25, 1996, p. B2. [Translation] See also Gilles Lesage, "Capitaine Canada: à l'abordage!", *Le Devoir*, September 28-29, 1996, p. A10.

19 Eric Kierans, "Tobin Hasn't Told the Full Story on Churchill Falls," *The Gazette*, November 1, 1996, p. B3.

20 Quoted in Konrad Yakabuski, "Churchill Falls Peace Advocated," *The Globe and Mail*, November 28, 1996, p. B4.

21 Mario Cloutier, "Bouchard et Tobin se disent également comblés," *Le Devoir*, March 10, 1998, p. A6; Rhéal Séguin and Sean McCarthy, "Churchill Pact to Bury Hatchet," *The Globe and Mail*, March 9, 1998, p. A1.

22 Ryan Cleary, "Business as Usual for Tobin," *The Telegram*, February 11, 1999.

23 Mario Cloutier, "Les autochtones exigent leur part," *Le Devoir*, March 10, 1998, p. A1; Mario Cloutier, "Les Innus devant l'ONU à Genève," *Le Devoir*, July 29, 1998, p. A4.

Bill S-31 and Quebec Deposit and Investment Fund (1982)

1 Yves Bélanger and Pierre Fournier, *L'entreprise québécoise: développement historique et dynamique contemporaine* (Montreal: Éditions Hurtubise, 1987), p. 174.

2 Quoted by Susan Goldenberg, *Canadian Pacific: A Portrait of Power* (Toronto: Methuen, 1983), p. 34.

3 The Trudeau government's interventions in regional economic development included the National Energy Program and certain constitutional proposals. See David Milne, *Tug of War: Ottawa and the Provinces Under Trudeau and Mulroney* (Toronto: James Lorimer, 1986), pp. 128-37.

4 Allan Tupper, *Bill S-31 and the Federalism of State Capitalism* (Kingston: Institute of Intergovernmental Relations, Queen's University, 1983), pp. 14-16.

5 Tupper, *Bill S-31 and the Federalism of State Capitalism*, p. 18; Hubert Bauch, "CP Sought PM's Help to Ward Off Caisse," *The Gazette*, December 3, 1982, p. A1; "Issue Behind Ottawa Bill is Control of Investment," *The Globe and Mail*, December 9, 1982, p. 8.

6 Tupper, *Bill S-31 and the Federalism of State Capitalism*, p. 25.

7 "Issue Behind Ottawa Bill is Control of Investment."

8 "Issue Behind Ottawa Bill is Control of Investment."

9 Tupper, *Bill S-31 and the Federalism of State Capitalism*, pp. 1-2.

10 Tupper, *Bill S-31 and the Federalism of State Capitalism*, pp. 22-23.

11 Alain Dubuc, "Caisse de dépôt: la chasse aux péquistes," *La Presse*, November 20, 1982, p. A12. [Translation]

12 Michel Vastel, "La loi S-31 ne gêne pas tellement la Caisse de dépôt à moins qu'elle veuille prendre le contrôle de CP," *Le Devoir*, November 30, 1982, p. 2.

13 "Qui a peur de la Caisse?", *Le Devoir*, December 9, 1982, p. 11. [Translation]

14 Tupper, *Bill S-31 and the Federalism of State Capitalism*, p. 21.

15 "Not Finished Yet," *The Globe and Mail*, November 26, 1982, p. 6.

16 Michel Nadeau, "Le projet S-31: un coup de jarnac à Power," *Le Devoir*, November 12, 1982, p. 11.

17 Cited in Pelletier, *La machine à milliards: histoire de la caisse de dépôt et placement du Québec* (Montreal: Québec/Amérique, 1989), p. 202. [Translation]

18 Graham Fraser, "Quebec Closes Ranks Over Investment Bill," *The Gazette*, December 7, 1982, p. B3.

19 Michel Roy, "L'opération ratée du cabinet fédéral," *La Presse*, December 9, 1982, p. A6.

20   "Rhetoric Outstrips Reality," *The Gazette*, November 27, 1982, p. B2.
21   Pelletier, *La machine à milliards*, p. 206.
22   Vastel, "La loi S-31 ne gêne pas tellement la Caisse de dépôt à moins qu'elle veuille prendre le contrôle de CP." [Translation]
23   Bélanger and Fournier, *L'entreprise québécoise*, p. 175. [Translation]

The CF-18 Maintenance Contract (1986)

1   The relevant players were: Canadair Group: Canadair Ltd. (Montreal), CAE Electronics (Montreal), Northwest Industries (Edmonton); Bristol Group: Bristol Aerospace (Winnipeg), Litton Systems of Canada (Toronto), Bendix Avelex Inc. (Montreal), Garrett Manufacturing Ltd. (Toronto), Leigh Instruments Ltd. (Ottawa); and IMP Group: IMP Aerospace (Dartmouth), Canadian Marconi Co. (Montreal), Canadian Astronautics Ltd. (Ottawa), Spar Aerospace Ltd. (Toronto), Fleet Industries (Fort Erie).
2   In January 1988, *The Globe and Mail* revealed that according to documents made public through the Access to Information Act, Bristol's price was not $3.5 million less but $65 million less. See Robert M. Campbell and Leslie A. Pal, "The CF-18 Affair," in *The Real World of Canadian Politics: Cases in Process and Policy* (Peterborough: Broadview Press, 1989), p. 20.
3   "West Outraged at CF-18 Decision," *The Gazette*, November 1, 1986, p. A1.
4   Campbell and Pal, "The CF-18 Affair," p. 35.
5   Don Braid, "CF-18 Contract May Help Doom Tories," *The Gazette*, November 1, 1986, p. B3.
6   "Pawley Has Doubts About Federalism After Contract Loss," *The Gazette*, November 6, 1986, p. A9.
7   Campbell and Pal, "The CF-18 Affair," p. 31.

8   "West Outraged at CF-18 Decision"; Geoffrey York, "CF-18 Affair Flying High as an Issue in Manitoba," *The Globe and Mail*, October 4, 1988, p. A5.
9   "West Outraged at CF-18 Decision."
10   "West Outraged at CF-18 Decision."
11   Maurice Girard, "Les libéraux du Québec optent pour Canadair," *Le Devoir*, September 4, 1986, p. 3.
12   Campbell and Pal, "The CF-18 Affair," p. 41.
13   Cited in Campbell and Pal, "The CF-18 Affair," p. 26. See also p. 19.
14   Michel Van De Walle, "CF-18: la décision fédérale consacre Montréal à titre de capitale aéronautique," *Le Devoir*, November 1, 1986, p. B1.
15   Cited in Campbell and Pal, "The CF-18 Affair," p. 22.
16   Campbell and Pal, "The CF-18 Affair," p. 39.
17   Jeffrey Simpson, *Spoils of Power: The Politics of Patronage* (Toronto: Collins, 1988), p. 375.
18   York, "CF-18 Affair Flying High as an Issue in Manitoba," p. A5.
19   Alain-G. Gagnon and A. Brian Tanguay, "Minor Parties in the Canadian Political System: Origins, Functions, Impact," in Alain-G. Gagnon and A. Brian Tanguay (eds.), *Canadian Parties in Transition*, 2nd ed. (Toronto: Nelson, 1996), p. 114.
20   Sheldon Alberts, "Ottawa Renews CF-18 Contract Despite Howls from Reformers," *The Gazette*, November 21, 1996, p. A10. In Manitoba, the CF-18 maintenance award helped set the agenda of the 1988 federal election campaign. It was one of the main issues for the Liberals and New Democrats, rivalling the free trade issue that was much debated in the country at the time. York, "CF-18 Affair Flying High as an Issue in Manitoba."
21   Quoted in Miro Cernetig, "How Western Canada remembers Robert Bourassa," *The Globe and Mail*, October 4, 1996, p. A23.
22   Alberts, "Ottawa Renews CF-18 Contract Despite Howls from Reformers."

Bill C-22 on Drug Patents (1987)

1   Robert M. Campbell and Leslie A. Pal, "Drug Deals: Globalization and the Politics of Patents," in *The Real World of Canadian Politics: Cases in Process and Policy*, 3rd ed. (Peterborough: Broadview Press, 1994), pp. 32-33; Guy Taillefer, "Quarante organismes de la santé present le Sénat de mettre fin à son obstruction," *La Presse*, September 22, 1987, p. 1.

2   Robert M. Campbell and Leslie A. Pal, "The Long and Winding Road: Bill C-22 and the Politics of Drug Patents," in *The Real Worlds of Canadian Politics,* p. 68.

3   Michael M. Atkinson and William D. Coleman, *The State, Business and Industrial Change in Canada* (Toronto: University of Toronto Press, 1989), p. 134.

4   Campbell and Pal, "The Long and Winding Road," p. 91.

5   "Les changements à la loi pourraient se buter à l'opinion publique," *La Presse*, September 2, 1986, p. B1.

6   Janice Turner, "Drug Patent Law Under Opposition Fire," *Toronto Star*, November 16, 1988, p. A26.

7   Jean-Benoît Nadeau, "La guerre des pilules: un enjeu crucial," *L'actualité*, Vol. 22, no. 5, April 1, 1997, p. 16.

8   Atkinson and Coleman, *The State, Business and Industrial Change in Canada*, p. 138.

9   Campbell and Pal, "The Long and Winding Road," p. 96.

10 Campbell and Pal, "The Long and Winding Road," pp. 96-97.

11 Paul Durivage, "Les scientifiques craignent une mollesse du gouvernement devant les pressions," *Le Devoir*, December 16, 1986, p. 9; [Translation] Jean Benoît Nadeau, "Encore une guerre des pilules?", *L'actualité*, Vol. 17, no. 17, November 1, 1992, p. 44.

12 Campbell and Pal, "The Long and Winding Road," pp. 79, 82.

13 Campbell and Pal, "The Long and Winding Road," p. 87.

14 Nadeau, "La guerre des pilules," p. 16.

15 For a comparative study of both bills on patented drugs, see Campbell and Pal, "Drug Deals," pp. 46-62.

16 Nadeau, "Encore une guerre des pilules?", p. 15.

17 Nadeau, "La guerre des pilules," p. 15.

The Canada-US Free Trade Agreement (1988)

1   G. Bruce Doern et Brian W. Tomlin, *The Free Trade Story: Faith & Fear* (Toronto: Stoddart, 1991), p. 58; See also Robert M. Campbell and Leslie A. Pal, "A Big Deal? Forging the Canada-US Free Trade Agreement," *The Real Worlds of Canadian Politics: Cases in Process and Policy* (Peterborough: Broadview Press, 1989), p. 360.

2   Campbell and Pal, "A Big Deal," pp. 316, 376; Stephen T. Easton, "Free Trade, Nationalism, and the Common Man: The Free Trade Agreement Between Canada and the United-States," *Contemporary Policy Issues*, Vol. VII (July 1989), p. 61.

3   Campbell and Pal, "A Big Deal," p. 342.

4   Mel Hurtig, *The Betrayal of Canada* (Toronto: Stoddard, 1991), pp. xiii, 265.

5   David Crane, "Free Trade Fears Rising, Poll Shows," *Toronto Star*, March 4, 1986, p. A1.

6   Doern and Tomlin, *The Free Trade Story*, p. 224.

7   John M. Strate and James R. Sellars, "Elite Opinion on Canada-US Trade Liberalization," *American Review of Canadian Studies* (Winter 1993), pp. 587, 596.

8   Marc Clark, "The Free Trade Fight," *Maclean's*, May 12, 1986, p. 20.

9   Crane, "Free Trade Fears Rising, Poll Shows,"

10 Darrel R. Reid, "The Election of 1988 and Canadian Federalism," in Ronald L. Watts and Douglas M. Brown (eds.), *Canada: The State of the Federation 1989* (Kingston: Institute of Intergovernmental Relations, Queen's University, 1989), pp. 37-42;

Richard Johnston *et al., Letting the People Decide: Dynamics of a Canadian Election* (Montreal: McGill-Queen's University Press, 1992), p. 143.

11 "Alberta Warns It 'Will Never Forget' If Opponents Scuttle Free Trade Deal," *Toronto Star*, October 28, 1987, p. A2.

12 Doern and Tomlin, *The Free Trade Story*, p. 140; Alain-G. Gagnon and Mary Beth Montcalm, *Quebec: Beyond the Quiet Revolution* (Scarborough, ON: Nelson, 1990), p. 32.

13 Jean Blouin, "Les Don Quichotte du commerce," *L'actualité* (November 1986), p. 33.

14 Coalition québécoise d'opposition au libre-échange CEQ-CSN-FTQ-UPA, *Danger, Libre-échange* (1987), p. iii. [Translation]

15 Coalition québécoise d'opposition au libre-échange CEQ-CSN-FTQ-UPA, *Danger, Libre-échange*, pp. 13, 22, 38.

16 Quoted in David Johnson, "Free Trade Scares 'Les Anglais': Bouchard," *The Gazette*, November 16, 1988, p. A11.

17 Jacques Portes, *Le Canada et le Québec au xxe siècle* (Paris: Armand Colin, 1994), p. 165. [Translation]

18 However, the Conservatives' share of the popular vote, though not as remarkable as in 1984 when they captured 211 seats with 50 percent of votes cast, was comparable to — indeed, higher than — the popular vote won by the Liberal governments of the 1960s and 1970s. Moreover, they managed to win back-to-back majorities, a feat that Trudeau never accomplished. The regional breakdown of the Conservative vote was as follows: in the Maritimes, 12 seats against 20 for the Liberals; in Ontario, 47 seats and 38 percent of the vote, against 43 seats and 39 percent of vote for the Liberals and 10 seats with 20 percent of the vote for the NDP; in the West, 48 seats against 32 seats for the NDP and only six seats for the Liberals. In Quebec, the Conservatives took 53 percent of the popular vote and 63 of the 75 seats.

Reid, "The Election of 1988 and Canadian Federalism," pp. 38-39.

19 *Letters to a Québécois Friend* (Montreal: McGill-Queen's University Press, 1990), pp. 48-59.

20 In the same vein, the Canada-Israel Free Trade Agreement, CIFTA, signed on July 13, 1996, came into force on January 1, 1997. Prime Minister Jean Chrétien and Chilean President Eduardo Frei also signed a bilateral free trade agreement on November 17, 1996, which came into effect on June 2, 1997.

Chapter 6 : Failed Reconciliation

John Meisel's introduction

1 Reginald Whitaker, *The Government Party* (Toronto: University of Toronto Press, 1977).

2 See Neil Nevitte, *The Decline of Deference* (Peterborough: Broadview Press, 1996).

3 See Arend Lijphart, *Democracy in Plural Societies* (New Haven, CT: Yale University Press, 1977); and Kenneth McRae (ed.), *Consociational Democracy* (Toronto: McClelland and Stewart, 1974), particularly part IV.

Guy Rocher's introduction

1 "The Night of the Long Knives" refers to the kitchen negotiation that took place over the night of November 4/5, 1981, in the absence of the Quebec delegation.

2 The *Cité libre* philosophy drew inspiration from the French leftist Christian magazine *Esprit*. The editor of Esprit in the postwar period was the philosopher Emmanuel Mounier, the author of a book on personalism (Le Personnalisme). He had a strong and persistent influence on the Quebec *Cité libre* team. While being pro-union, the team advocated the universalist ideology of

the person, based on the global perspective of the Jesuit Teilhard de Chardin and which, in their view, was incompatible with a nationalism that withdraws into itself to focus on a particular collectivity and its past.

The Meech Lake Accord (1987)

1   This speech was written by none other than Lucien Bouchard, who would become leader of the Bloc Québécois (1990) and the Parti Québécois (1996).

2   These five conditions were already set out in the Quebec Liberal Party program. In order to return to the negotiating table, the Liberals demanded: explicit recognition of Quebec as a distinct society; increased powers in matters of administration and integration of new immigrants; appointment of three Supreme Court judges trained in civil law; restriction of federal spending power; and right of veto on any constitutional amendment. The text of the address by Gil Rémillard is reproduced in Peter M. Leslie, *Rebuilding the Relationship: Quebec and Its Confederation Partners* (Kingston: Institute of Intergovernmental Relations, Queen's University, 1987), pp. 47-55.

3   Ratification, by large majorities, followed in: Saskatchewan (September 1987); the House of Commons (October 1987 and again in June 1988); Alberta (December 1987); Prince Edward Island (May 1988); Nova Scotia (May 1988); Ontario (June 1988); British Columbia (June 1988); and New Brunswick (June 1990).

4   The new section 2 would also have recognized Canada's fundamental dualism. It stipulated that

> the existence of French-speaking Canadians centred in Quebec but present elsewhere in Canada and English-speaking Canadians concentrated outside of Quebec but also present in Quebec, consti-

tutes a fundamental characteristic of Canada.

One role of Parliament and the provincial legislatures was to preserve this fundamental characteristic. See Peter W. Hogg, *The Meech Lake Constitutional Accord* (Toronto: Carswell, 1988), p. 11.

5   Unanimous agreement would be required for all amendments affecting the powers and composition of the Senate as well as the selection of senators, the creation of new provinces, the Supreme Court and the principle of proportional representation in the House of Commons.

6   New Brunswick, Select Committee on the 1987 Constitutional Accord, *Final Report on the Constitution Amendment 1987* (Fredericton: The Committee, 1989).

7   Ramsay Cook, "Alice in Meechland Or the Concept of Quebec as a 'Distinct Society'," in Michael D. Behiels (ed.), *The Meech Lake Primer* (Ottawa: University of Ottawa, 1989), pp. 285-94; and Michael D. Behiels, "Women's Rights: Does Meech Lake Undermine the Gains of 1982?", in Behiels (ed.), *The Meech Lake Primer*, pp. 285-94.

8   "The Welcome Pact," *The Globe and Mail*, June 4, 1987, p. 6. The day after June 3, the *Calgary Herald*, the *Vancouver Sun* and the *Chronicle Herald* supported the Accord; however, the *Winnipeg Free Press* and the *Toronto Star* expressed very strong reservations. These editorials are reproduced in *Le Québec et le lac Meech: un dossier du Devoir* (Montreal: Guérin, 1987), pp. 290-98.

9   André Blais and Jean Crête, "Pourquoi l'opinion publique au Canada anglais a-t-elle rejeté l'Accord du lac Meech?", in Raymond Hudon and Réjean Pelletier (eds.), *L'engagement intellectuel: mélanges en l'honneur de Léon Dion* (Sainte-Foy, QC: Les Presses de l'Université Laval, 1991), p. 390. According to a poll taken in early June 1987, support for the Accord varied from 46 percent in Ontario to 57 percent in the Maritimes. Reported by Kenneth McRoberts, *Misconceiving Canada: The Struggle for*

National Unity (Toronto: Oxford University Press, 1997), p. 197.

10 "This Deal Carries Too High a Price," *The Toronto Star*, May 2, 1987, and "No One Spoke for Canada," June 4, 1987. These editorials are reproduced in *Le Québec et le lac Meech*, pp. 278-79, 290-92.

11 For example, the Quebec government's 1988 adoption of Bill 178 is often considered a turning point insofar as it was used by Manitoba's premier to justify his legislature's withdrawal of the resolution on the Meech Lake Accord. Philip Resnick also suggests that Quebec's support for free trade greatly affected many English Canadians. See *Letters to a Québécois Friend* (Montreal: McGill-Queen's University Press, 1990), pp. 48-59.

12 Blais and Crête, "Pourquoi l'opinion publique au Canada anglais a-t-elle rejeté l'Accord du lac Meech?," table 1, p. 386. These figures represent responses from people whose mother tongue is English.

13 Gordon Robertson, *The Five Myths of Meech Lake* (Toronto: Methuen, 1990); Richard Simeon, "Meech Lake and Visions of Canada," in K.E. Swinton and C.J. Rogerson (eds.), *Competing Constitutional Visions: The Meech Lake Accord* (Toronto: Carswell, 1988), pp. 295-306; Peter M. Leslie, "Submission to the Special Joint Committee of the Senate and the House of Commons on the 1987 Constitutional Accord," in Clive Thompson (ed.), *Navigating Meech Lake* (Kingston: Institute of Intergovernmental Relations, Queen's University, 1988), pp. 8-28. In January 1990, a group called Friends of Meech Lake was founded in an attempt to reverse the claim that the Agreement was merely the result of Quebec's blackmail against the other provinces. Prominent Canadians such as Robert Stanfield, Stephen Lewis, Lucie Pepin, Serge Joyal, Jeremy Weber and Flora MacDonald were members of this group.

14 Public hearings were held in Manitoba, New Brunswick, Ontario, Prince Edward Island and Quebec. In August 1987, the federal government conducted its own hearings through a joint committee of the Senate and the House of Commons, and the Senate held separate hearings in March 1988.

15 Among the most well-known Liberal figures were Pierre Elliott Trudeau, Sharon Carstairs (Manitoba), Clyde Wells (Newfoundland), Frank McKenna (New Brunswick) and, more discreetly, Jean Chrétien (who would become leader of the party in 1990). In spite of reservations and rifts in the federal Liberal caucus, John Turner, then leader, ended up supporting the Accord during the two votes taken on this issue in the House of Commons. Similarly, during the federal party leadership race, candidate Paul Martin gave his support to the Accord. See Pierre O'Neil, "Paul Martin appuie inconditionnellement l'accord du lac Meech," *Le Devoir*, January 18, 1990, p. 1.

16 See Alan C. Cairns, "The Charter, Interest Groups, Executive Federalism and Constitutional Reform," in David E. Smith, Peter MacKinnon and John C. Courtney (eds.), *After Meech Lake: Lessons for the Future* (Saskatoon: Fifth House, 1991), pp. 13-31.

17 Blais and Crête, "Pourquoi l'opinion publique au Canada anglais a-t-elle rejeté l'Accord du lac Meech?," p. 390.

18 Clyde Wells, "One Canada Means No Special Privileges," in Earle Gray (ed.), *Visions of Canada: Disparate Views of What Canada Is, What It Ought to Be, and What It Might Become* (Woodville, ON: Canadian Speeches, 1990), pp. 38-45.

19 For a more detailed account of opposition from Canadian feminist groups, see Barbara Roberts, *Beau fixe ou nuage à l'horizon? L'Accord du lac Meech jugé par les groupes féministes du Québec et du Canada* (Ottawa: Canadian Institute for Research on Women, 1989), pp. 10-16, 28-46. Clarifying the Accord's impact on women's rights was one

of the conditions laid down by Premier McKenna for his approval of the Accord.

20 Quoted by Tony Hall, "What Are We? Chopped Liver? Aboriginal Affairs in the Constitutional Politics of Canada in the 1980s," in Behiels (ed.), *The Meech Lake Primer*, p. 457. For an account of the First Nations' overall objections to the Meech Lake Accord, see also Tony Penikett, "Constitutionalizing Northern Canada's Colonial Status," in Behiels (ed.), *The Meech Lake Primer*, p. 457-64; and Royal Commission on Aboriginal Peoples, *Looking Forward, Looking Back*, Vol. 1 (Ottawa: Supply and Services Canada, 1996), pp. 224-28.

21 According to Georges Arès, of the Association canadienne-française de l'Alberta,
> The most serious flaw in the ACFA's view is the lack of any obligation, at least for the federal government, to promote the duality of Canada. Parliament and the provincial legislatures have only an obligation to preserve Canada's fundamental characteristics, whereas Quebec has the responsibility to preserve and promote its distinct society.

Georges Arès, "The Accord Abandons Canada's Battered and Defenceless Minorities," in Behiels (ed.), *The Meech Lake Primer*, p. 220.

22 David Bercuson, "Meech Lake: The Peace of the Graveyard," in Roger Gibbins (ed.), *Meech Lake and Canada: Perspectives From the West* (Edmonton: Academic Printing and Publishing, 1988), pp. 17-21.

23 Wells, "One Canada Means No Special Privileges," p. 43.

24 Pierre Elliott Trudeau, "The School of Blackmail," in Donald Johnston (ed.), *With a Bang, Not a Whimper: Pierre Trudeau Speaks Out* (Toronto: Stoddart, 1988), p. 15.

25 Blais and Crête, "Pourquoi l'opinion publique au Canada anglais a-t-elle rejeté l'Accord du lac Meech?," p. 386.

26 Michel Roy, "Le Québec au Canada," *La Presse*, June 4, 1987, p. B2. [Translation]

27 Benoit Lauzière, "Un pas en avant," *Le Devoir*, May 26 and 27, 1987, reproduced in *Le Québec et le lac Meech*, p. 264. [Translation]

28 "A Hard-Won Victory," *The Gazette*, May 2, 1987, reproduced in *Le Québec et le lac Meech*, p. 269.

29 Quoted in Gilles Lesage, "Pierre-Marc Johnson mobilisera la population contre l'Accord du lac Meech," *Le Devoir*, May 2, 1987, reproduced in Roch Denis (ed.), *Québec: dix ans de crise constitutionnelle* (Montreal: VLB Éditeur, 1990), pp. 167-68. [Translation]

30 "The progress achieved exceeds my expectations," wrote Dion. However, since the concept of distinct society was not defined, the political expert from Laval University ended up refusing to support the Agreement. "Une entente dans les limites du possible," *Le Devoir*, May 7, 1987, p. 11. [Translation]

31 Daniel Latouche, "L'art de négocier: la version du lac Meech," *Le Devoir*, May 12, 1987, p. 11. [Translation] However, he too said modifications, particularly concerning the definition of distinct society, would be needed for him to support the Accord.

32 Pierre O'Neill, "Le Lac Meach [sic] a rallié les péquistes de toutes les tendances," *Le Devoir*, May 4, 1987, p. A1.

33 See "Appel au peuple du Québec," reproduced in Denis (ed.), *Québec: dix ans de crise constitutionnelle*, pp. 163-64. The positions of several organizations and nationalist parties are reproduced in *Le Québec et le lac Meech*, chap. 4.

34 Declaration of the Parti indépendantiste reproduced in *Le Québec et le lac Meech*, p. 197. [Translation]

35 Pierre Fournier, *A Meech Lake Post-Mortem: Is Quebec Sovereignty Inevitable?* (Montreal: McGill-Queen's University Press, 1991), p. 22.

36 Denis Robert, "La signification de l'Accord du lac Meech au Canada anglais et au Québec francophone," in Peter M. Leslie and Ronald L. Watts (eds.), *Canada: The State of*

the Federation 1987-88 (Kingston: Institute for Intergovernmental Relations, Queen's University, 1988), p. 154. [Translation]

37 Guy Laforest, *Trudeau and the End of a Canadian Dream* (Montreal: McGill-Queen's University Press, 1995), p. 46

38 For example, on March 28, 1990, the Liberals approved a PQ motion stipulating that the Quebec government officially reject any proposal which would constitute an amendment or modification that might change the content or the spirit of the Meech Lake Accord.

39 Daniel Bonin, "Le Québec de l'après Meech," in Douglas M. Brown (ed.), *Canada: The State of the Federation 1991* (Kingston: Institute of Intergovernmental Relations, Queen's University, 1991), p. 20.

40 Lucien Bouchard, "Le vrai pays," *Le Devoir*, June 26, 1990, p. 13. [Translation]

41 Denis Monière, *L'indépendance* (Montreal: Québec/Amérique, 1992), p. 103. [Translation]

42 Jean Herman Guay, "L'évolution de l'opinion pendant la campagne référendaire," in Denis Monière and Jean H. Guay, *La bataille du Québec: Troisième épisode: 30 jours qui ébran-lèrent le Canada* (Montreal: Fides, 1996), p. 186. In fact, the sovereignist upsurge pre-ceded the death of Meech Lake by a few months. See Mario Fontaine, "La poussée nationaliste selon cinq sondages," in Denis (ed.), *Québec: dix ans de crise constitutionnelle*, pp. 220-22; and Maurice Pinard, Robert Bernier and Vincent Lemieux, *Un combat inachevé* (Sainte-Foy, QC: Les Presses de l'Université du Québec, 1997), pp. 76-83.

43 Quoted in François Rocher, "Québec et la constitution: une valse à mille temps," in François Rocher (ed.), *Bilan québécois du fédéralisme canadien* (Montreal: VLB Éditeur, 1992), p. 34. [Translation]

The Oka Crisis (1990)

1 Robert M. Campbell and Leslie A. Pal, *The Real Worlds of Canadian Politics: Cases in Process and Policy*, 2nd ed. (Peterborough: Broadview Press, 1991), p. 326. According to Geoffrey York and Loreen Pindera, "...Oka sparked the most heated display of Indian unity in recent Canadian history." *People of the Pines: The Warriors and the Legacy of Oka* (Toronto: Little, Brown, 1991), p. 273.

2 Campbell and Pal, *The Real Worlds of Canadian Politics*, pp. 268-69.

3 "Les négociaitons avec les Mohawks sont au point mort," *Le Devoir*, July 30, 1990, p. 1.

4 The petition was published in *The Globe and Mail*, September 6, 1990, p. A7, under the heading "A Solution at the End of a Rifle Is No Solution at All."

5 Robin Philpot, *Oka: dernier alibi du Canada anglais* (Montreal: VLB éditeur, 1991), p. 149. Fifty-six percent believed that First Nations should be recognized as a distinct society. See "Canadians Willing to Give Natives One-Fifth of the Country, Poll Says," *The Gazette*, November 11, 1990, p. A7.

6 Paul Ogresko, "Reflections on Oka," *Canadian Dimension* (January-February 1991), p. 10.

7 Édouard Cloutier, "L'opinion politique québécoise en 1990-1991," in Denis Monière (ed.), *L'année politique au Québec 1991* (Montreal: Québec/Amérique, 1992), p. 241.

8 Cloutier, "L'opinion politique québécoise en 1990-1991," p. 241. Only 11 percent declared they were more favourable.

9 Campbell and Pal, *The Real Worlds of Canadian Politics*, p. 331. See also York and Pindera, *People of the Pines*, p. 231.

10 The Warriors are a nationalist group of mil-itant Mohawks inspired by the writings of Louis Hall, which call for active and armed resistance to protect the Mohawks' culture and territory. On this subject, see Gail Valaskakis, "Rights and Warriors: First

Nations, Media and Identity," *A Review of International English Litterature* (January 1994), pp. 60-74; York and Pindera, *People of the Pines*, pp. 167-90; and Peter McFarlane, "Stolen Land," *Canadian Forum* (November 1990), pp. 18-21.

11   Ogresko, "Reflections on Oka," p. 10.
12   York and Pindera, *People of the Pines*, p. 414. For an analysis of the news coverage by the English-language media from a Quebec perspective, see Philpot, *Oka*, pp. 136-48. For a better understanding of the Aboriginal point of view on the Oka crisis, see the Royal Commission on Aboriginal Peoples, *Gathering Strength*, Vol. 3 (Ottawa: Supply and Services Canada, 1996), pp. 707-09.
13   Philpot, *Oka*, p. 106. [Translation]
14   Robert Bourassa, *Gouverner le Québec* (Montreal: Fides, 1995), pp. 230-31. Among those who protested were Archbishop Desmond Tutu, Jesse Jackson, the European Parliament and the UN Human Rights Commission.
15   Kenneth McRoberts, *Misconceiving Canada: The Struggle for National Unity* (Toronto: Oxford University Press, 1997), p. 208.

The Gagnon-Tremblay-McDougall Agreement on Immigration (1991)

1   Julien Bauer, *Les minorités au Québec* (Montreal: Boréal, 1994), p. 31. It should be noted that pursuant to section 95 of the 1867 Constitution Act, immigration is a shared jurisdiction, with the federal government having paramount legislative authority.
2   Bauer, *Les minorités au Québec*; Joseph H. Carens, "Immigration, Political Community, and the Transformation of Identity: Quebec's Immigration Policies in Critical Perspective," in Joseph H. Carens (ed.), *Is Quebec Nationalism Just? Perspectives from Anglophone Canada* (Montreal/Kingston: McGill-Queen's University Press, 1995), p. 21.

3   Government of Quebec, *Canada-Quebec Accord Relating to Immigration and Temporary Admission of Aliens*, Ministère des Comm-unautés culturelles et de l'Immigration, p. 2.
4   Government of Quebec, *Canada-Quebec Accord Relating to Immigration and Temporary Admission of Aliens*, p. 3.
5   The federal government maintains sole responsibility for determining national standards and objectives relating to immigration.
6   Government of Quebec, *Canada-Quebec Accord Relating to Immigration and Temporary Admission of Aliens*, pp. B2-B3.
7   Carens, "Immigration, Political Community, and the Transformation of Identity," p. 31.
8   Since 1992, Quebec's share of Canadian immigration has been 15.1 percent (176,498 persons), compared to 19 percent (180,986 persons) for the 1987-1991 period. Government of Quebec, *Québec: prévoir et planifier: caractéristiques de l'immigration récente au Québec* (Québec: Direction de la planification stratégique du ministère des Relations avec les citoyens et de l'Immigration, 1997), p. 23.
9   Edward Greenspon and Scott Feschuk, "Ottawa Offers Immigration Deal," *The Globe and Mail*, February 27, 1997, p. A1.
10   Jeffrey Simpson, "Quebec's Immigration Deal May Be Flexible, But It's Also Profitable," *The Globe and Mail*, November 10, 1995, p. A20.
11   Bauer, *Les minorités au Québec*, p. 31. [Translation]
12   Kenneth McRoberts, *Misconceiving Canada: The Struggle for National Unity* (Toronto: Oxford University Press, 1997), p. 152.
13   Monique Gagnon-Tremblay, "Ottawa doit signer: la nouvelle entente en matière d'immigration est essentielle pour le Québec," *Le Devoir*, November 27, 1990, p. B8. [Translation]
14   Lise Bissonnette, "La première politique d'immigration," *Le Devoir*, December 5, 1990, p. A8. [Translation]

15 Reported in Paul Cauchon, "Ottawa rejette la stratégie des petits pas de Rémillard," *Le Devoir*, February 6, 1991, p. A1. [Translation] See also Monique Gagnon-Tremblay, "L'entente sur l'immigration, un modèle à suivre," *Le Devoir*, September 1, 1992, p. A13.

16 René Marleau, "Le Québec ne contrôle pas son immigration," *Le Devoir*, August 21, 1992, p. A13. [Translation]

17 See for example Daniel Turp and Alain-G. Gagnon, "Le Rapport du consensus de 1992 sur la Constitution ou l'extinction de l'Entente du lac Meech," in *Les objections de 20 spécialistes aux offres fédérales* (Montreal: Éditions Saint-Martin, 1992), p. 38. However, it should be noted that the Agreement is quasi-permanent in that both Canada and Quebec undertook not to re-open the deal unless there was agreement on how to close it again. This provision explains why Quebec is not financially penalized although it is not fulfilling its commitment on immigrant numbers.

18 Allan Thompson, "Provinces Stalling Deal on Immigrants: Ottawa," *The Toronto Star*, February 28, 1997, p. A13; and Greenspon and Feschuck, "Ottawa Offers Immigration Deal."

The Charlottetown Accord (1992)

1 Parti libéral du Québec, *Un Québec libre de ses choix*, Rapport du Comité constitutionnel du Parti libéral du Québec, January 28, 1991.

2 Commission sur l'avenir politique et constitutionnel du Québec, *Rapport* (Quebec: Secrétariat de la Commission, 1991).

3 Moreover, in the winter of 1991, the prime minister entrusted 10 teams of deputy ministers and senior civil servants with the task of reviewing the entire field of shared jurisdictions. In April he set up the Special Cabinet Committee on Canadian Unity and Constitutional Negotiations, chaired by Joe Clark.

4 Government of Canada, *Shaping Canada's Future Together* (Ottawa: Minister of Supply and Services, 1991).

5 Richard Johnston, André Blais, Elisabeth Gidengil and Neil Nevitte, "The People and the Charlottetown Accord," in Ronald L. Watts and Douglas M. Brown (eds.), *Canada: The State of the Federation 1993* (Kingston: Institute of Intergovernmental Relations, Queen's University, 1993), p. 21.

6 Cited by Alain Noël, "Deliberating a Constitution: The Meaning of the Canadian Referendum of 1992," in Curtis Cook (ed.), *Constitutional Predicament: Canada after the Referendum of 1992* (Montreal: McGill-Queen's University Press, 1994), p. 72.

7 "And Miles to Go Before We Sleep," *The Globe and Mail*, August 24, 1992, p. 26.

8 Reported by Susan Delacourt, "PM Gears Up to Fight for Accord," *The Globe and Mail*, August 24, 1992, p. A1.

9 Johnston *et al.*, "The People and the Charlottetown Accord," p. 30; and Kenneth McRoberts, *Misconceiving Canada: The Struggle for National Unity* (Don Mills, ON: Oxford University Press, 1997), p. 218.

10 Leslie A. Pal and F. Leslie Seidle, "Constitutional Politics 1990-1992: The Paradox of Participation," in Susan D. Phillips (ed.), *How Ottawa Spends 1993-1994* (Ottawa: Carleton University Press, 1993), p. 164.

11 Reluctant signatories included Clyde Wells, premier of Newfoundland, who expressed reservations about the Accord, and Michael Harcourt, premier of British Columbia, who was absent during the campaign. Moreover, support from the Liberal Party of Canada and the New Democratic Party was tepid and, on October 18, Aboriginal leaders refused to endorse the Accord, negotiated by Ovide Mercredi, Grand Chief of the Assembly of First Nations.

12 Jeremy Webber, *Reimagining Canada: Language, Culture, Community and the Canadian Constitution* (Montreal: McGill-Queen's University Press, 1994), p. 174.

13 David Elton, an early advocate of the Triple-E Senate, and Roger Gibbins, an ardent promoter of that option, were both

opposed to the Charlottetown reform. The Reform Party was also against it. Opinion polls show that more people favour abolition of the Senate than support the proposed reform. McRoberts, *Misconceiving Canada*, p. 217. Similarly, recognition of the inherent right of self-government of the First Peoples was not enough to convince Aboriginals to support the Accord in spite of the support of Ovide Mercredi. Pal and Seidle, "Constitutional Politics 1990-92," p. 167.

14   According to Johnston *et al.*, 55 percent of Canadians opposed the distinct society clause, whereas 40 percent supported it; for the 25 percent floor, 78 percent were opposed and only 16 percent supportive. See "The People and the Charlottetown Accord," pp. 24-25.

15   Quoted in Pal and Seidle, "Constitutional Politics 1990-92," p. 167.

16   Pal and Seidle, "Constitutional Politics 1990-92," p. 167.

17   Pierre Elliott Trudeau, "Quebec's Blackmail," in *Against the Current* (Toronto: McClelland and Stewart, 1996), p. 274, first published in *Maclean's*, September 28, 1992. His October 1 speech was published under the title, *Trudeau: ce gâchis mérite un gros NON!* (Outremont, QC: L'Étincelle Éditeur, 1992).

18   See "Accord Puts Handicapped in Jeopardy, Coalition Says," *Globe and Mail*, September 4, 1992, p. A4.

19   Quoted in McRoberts, *Misconceiving Canada*, p. 218.

20   Pal and Seidle, "Constitutional Politics 1990-92," p. 170.

21   Quoted in Jean Dion, "Même les autochtones ont obtenu plus que le Québec, dit Parizeau," *Le Devoir*, August 24, 1992, p. 1. [Translation]

22   François Rocher, "La consécration du fédéralisme centralisateur," in *Référendum, 26 octobre 1992: Les objections de 20 spécialistes aux offres fédérales* (Montreal: Les Éditions Saint-Martin, 1992), pp. 87-98.

23   Lise Bissonnette, "Le mur," *Le Devoir*, August 24, 1992, p. A1. [Translation] See also her editorial of July 9, following the announcement of the July 7 agreement, which consists of a single word, "NON."

24   Jean Allaire, "Le droit de savoir," in *Référendum, 26 octobre 1992*, p. 157. [Translation]

25   Johnston *et al.*, "The People and the Charlottetown Accord," p. 36.

26   The legal text of the Charlottetown Accord was released earlier in Quebec, on October 10 rather than October 13, in order to quell these suspicions.

27   See *Le Devoir*, October 1, 1992, p. A4.

28   See *Référendum, 26 octobre 1992*, pp. 45-62.

29   Allaire, "Le droit de savoir," p. 157. [Translation]

30   Reported by Curtis Cook, "Introduction: Canada's predicament," in Curtis Cook (ed.), *Constitutional Predicament: Canada After the Referendum of 1992* (Montreal: McGill-Queen's University Press, 1994), p. 7. The Aboriginal figure should be treated with caution since the margin of error may be as much as 17 percent.

31   "On to the economy," *Globe and Mail*, October 27, 1992, p. A26; and Claude Masson, "Et maintenant," *La Presse*, October 27, 1992, p. B2.

32   Alain Dubuc, "Anatomie d'un échec," *La Presse*, October 27, 1992, p. B2. [Translation]

33   For instance, responsibility for job training was transferred to the provinces. And on March 12, 1993, a resolution to amend the Constitution, to entrench the equality of the English and French linguistic communities in New Brunswick, was adopted by the House of Commons and the Senate.

The Referendum on Sovereignty-partnership (1995)

1   Reg Whitaker, "The National Unity Portfolio," in Susan D. Phillips (ed.), *How Ottawa Spends*

1995-96: Mid-Life Crises (Ottawa: Carleton University Press, 1995), p. 72; and Robert A. Young, "'Maybe Yes, Maybe No': The Rest of Canada and a Quebec 'Oui'," in Douglas M. Brown and Jonathan W. Rose (eds.), Canada: The State of the Federation 1995 (Kingston: Institute of Intergovernmental Relations, Queen's University, 1995), pp. 48-50.

2   Jean Dion, "L'unifolié à nouveau dans la tempête," Le Devoir, February 16, 1995, p. A3. See also the working document, made public by Jacques Parizeau, outlining Ottawa's objectives and strategies, "La stratégie du NON," Le Devoir, July 27, 1995, p. A7.

3   For example, Bombardier's Laurent Beaudoin declared that he might move his factories out of Quebec in the event of a Yes victory. On the role of business leaders see Michel Venne, "Le déroulement de la campagne," in Denis Monière and Jean H. Guay (eds.), La bataille du Québec: troisième épisode: 30 jours qui ébranlèrent le Canada (Montreal: Fides, 1996), pp. 41-44.

4   In January 1995, the C.D. Howe Institute released a study highlighting the negative consequences of Quebec separation. At the same time, Moody's, one of the leading US debt-rating agencies, expressed doubts about the stability of Quebec's credit rating should the vote go to the sovereignists.

5   Ed Broadbent, "Post-Referendum Canada," in John E. Trent et al. (eds.), Québec-Canada: What Is the Path Ahead? Nouveaux sentiers vers l'avenir (Ottawa: University of Ottawa Press, 1996), p. 277.

6   Quoted by Venne, "Le déroulement de la campagne," p. 58. [Translation] Ontario and Nova Scotia passed a resolution recognizing Quebec's distinct identity, while Newfoundland and New Brunswick adopted resolutions calling for constitutional recognition of Quebec as a distinct society within Canada. Barry Came, "Crusade for Canada," Maclean's, November 6, 1995, p. 23.

7   Cited in Jean Dion, "La souveraineté ne fait pas partie du paysage," Le Devoir, September 14, 1994, p. A5; [Translation] Jean Dion, "Le reste du Canada met ses gants blancs," Le Devoir, September 14, 1994, p. A4; and Jean Chartier, "La presse anglophone a mis le paquet," Le Devoir, September 14, 1994, p. A6.

8   Henry Milner, "Why Quebec Must Say No to Saying No," Inroads, no. 4 (1995), p. 9; and Michel Sarra-Bournet, Le Canada anglais et la souveraineté du Québec: deux cents leaders d'opinion se prononcent, (Montreal: VLB, 1995), pp. 154-55.

9   See for example Kenneth McRoberts (ed.), Beyond Quebec: Taking Stock of Canada (Montreal: McGill-Queen's University Press, 1995); Philip Resnick, Thinking English Canada (Toronto: Stoddard, 1994); Robert A. Young, The Secession of Quebec and the Future of Canada (Montreal: McGill-Queen's University Press, 1995); Douglas M. Brown, "Thinking the Unthinkable," in Patrick C. Fafard and Douglas M. Brown (eds.), Canada: the State of the Federation 1996 (Kingston: Institute of Intergovernmental Relations, Queen's University, 1996), pp. 23-43; and Sarra-Bournet, Le Canada anglais et la souveraineté du Québec.

10 On this account, see Charles Gordon, "Canada's Imminent Breakup Version 4," Maclean's, September 26, 1994, p. 13.

11 Anthony Wilson-Smith, "A Strong No from the Nine," Maclean's, July 1, 1995, p. 13; and Mary Nemeth, "All or Nothing," Maclean's, October 30, 1995, pp. 32-33.

12 Barry Came, "Is Separatism Dead?", Maclean's, April 24, 1995, pp. 12-16; and John F. Conway, "English Canada's Willful Blindness," Inroads, no. 4, May 4, 1995, pp. 31-32. Before the allocation of undecided respondents, support for sovereignty had reached 39 percent between January and March 1995 (14 polls). Maurice Pinard, Robert Bernier and Vincent Lemieux, Un combat inachevé (Sainte-Foy, QC: Les Presses de l'Université du Québec, 1997), table A, p. 275.

13   Brian Bergman, "A New Gambit: English Canada Is Cool to Parizeau's Unity Offer," *Maclean's*, May 8, 1995, p. 20; and Diane Francis, "The Dishonesty of the Parti Québécois," *Maclean's*, October 2, 1995, p. 17.

14   "He Said, They Said," *Maclean's*, September 4, 1995, p. 10. For a review of public sentiment, see also Nemeth, "All or Nothing"; and Pierre Martin, "L'opinion des Canadiens sur une association économique avec le Québec," *Le Devoir*, July 22-23, 1995, p. A7.

15   Nemeth, "All or Nothing."

16   Cited by Barry Came, "Crusade for Canada," p. 22.

17   "Taking the Pulse," *Maclean's*, December 25, 1995/January 1, 1996, p. 33. Eighteen percent of those surveyed believed that the demonstration had convinced a significant number of undecideds and "soft" nationalists to vote No; 43 percent that it had convinced a few.

18   Michel Venne, "Vivement le référendum," *Le Devoir*, September 14, 1994, p. A5.

19   Jean H. Guay, "L'évolution de l'opinion pendant la campagne référendaire," in Monière and Guay (eds.), *La bataille du Québec*, pp. 188-90.

20   François Rocher, "Les aléas de la stratégie pré-référendaire, chronique d'une mort annoncée," in Brown and Rose (eds.), *Canada: The State of the Federation 1995*, p. 25. See also Conway, "English Canada's Willful Blindness," pp. 31-32.

21   Jacques Parizeau, "Le contraire du repli sur soi," press conference held on September 14, 1994. Reproduced in Jacques Parizeau, *Pour un Québec souverain* (Montreal: VLB, 1997), p. 97. [Translation]

22   Jean Dion, "A pieds joints dans le bain de l'unité nationale," *Le Devoir*, September 14, 1994, p. A6.

23   Guay, "L'évolution de l'opinion pendant la campagne référendaire," p. 194.

24   Rocher, "Les aléas de la stratégie pré-référendaire, chronique d'une mort annoncée,"

p. 33. It should nonetheless be noted that 55,000 Quebecers chose to participate in the public hearings held by the 16 regional commissions and the two special-interest commissions reserved for young people and the elderly. See Commission nationale sur l'avenir du Québec, *Rapport* (Quebec: Ministère du Conseil exécutif, 1995), p. 10.

25   Commission nationale sur l'avenir du Québec, *Rapport*, p. 25.

26   Quoted in Venne, "Le déroulement de la campagne," p. 47. [Translation] On the state of federal finances and its impact on the referendum strategy, see Whitaker, "The national unity portfolio."

27   Barry Came, "Quebec Inc. Stirs," *Maclean's*, October 2, 1995, p. 22. [Translation]

28   Guy Lachapelle, "La souveraineté partenariat donnée essentielle du résultat référendaire et de l'avenir des relations Québec-Canada," in Trent et al. (eds.), *Québec-Canada*, pp. 45-53; Pinard, Bernier and Lemieux, *Un combat inachevé*, pp. 76-83; and Commission nationale sur l'avenir du Québec, *Rapport*, p. 34.

29   Lachapelle, "La souveraineté partenariat donnée essentielle du résultat référendaire et de l'avenir des relations Québec-Canada," p. 58.

30   On the importance of the tripartite agreement and the Bouchard effect on voting intentions, see Maurice Pinard, "L'effet Bouchard," *Policy Options*, Vol. 18, no. 8 (October 1997), pp. 33-37; and Pinard, Bernier and Lemieux, *Un combat inachevé*.

31   Jean Herman Guay and Denis Monière, "Conclusion," in Monière and Guay (eds.), *La bataille du Québec*, p. 257. [Translation] See also Claude Denis, "Sovereignty Postponed: On the Canadian Way of Losing a Referendum, and Then Another," *Constitutional Forum constitutionnel*, Vol. 7, no. 3 (Winter/Spring 1996), pp. 45-46, Daniel Drache, "Chock-a-Block Federalism Lessons for the Next Time," *Canada Watch*, Vol. 4, no. 2 (November/December 1995), p. 20; Édouard Cloutier, "The Quebec

Referendum: From Polls to Ballots," *Canada Watch*, Vol. 4, no. 2 (November/December 1995), pp. 37, 39.

32   André Blais, "Pourquoi le oui a-t-il fait des gains pendant la campagne référendaire?", in Trent *et al.* (eds.), *Québec-Canada*, p. 74. [Translation] See also Pinard, Bernier and Lemieux, *Un combat inachevé*, pp. 85-87.

33   Guay and Monière, "Conclusion," p. 258. See also Vincent Lemieux, "Le référendum de 1995: quelques pistes d'explication," in Trent *et al.* (eds.), *Québec-Canada*, pp. 65-69; and Pinard, Bernier and Lemieux, *Un combat inachevé*, pp. 317-53.

34   Denis, "Sovereignty postponed," p. 46. See also Daniel Latouche, "You Asked for It," *Canada Watch*, Vol. 4, no. 2 (November/ December 1995), p. 31; and Louis Balthazar, "Please, Let Us Breathe," *Canada Watch*, Vol. 4, no. 2 (November/December 1995), p. 35.

35   Martin Leblanc, "Bouchard dénonce l'amour soudain pour le Québec," *Journal de Montréal*, October 27, 1995, p. 6; John Gray, "Business as Usual Amid the Tumult," *The Globe and Mail*, October 28, 1995, p. A4. According to a poll conducted in November 1996, 56.5 percent of Quebecers attributed little or no importance to this rally. The survey nevertheless revealed that the rally had drawn considerable attention. Guy Lachapelle, "Les raisons de vote massif des Québécois au référendum," *Bulletin d'histoire politique*, Vol. 4, no. 3 (Spring 1996), p. 24.

36   For a detailed presentation of the results, see Jean Herman Guay, "Les résultats du référendum du 30 october 1995," in Monière and Guay (eds.), *La bataille du Québec*, pp. 203-52.

37   Cited in Philippe Cantin, "Parizeau blâme l'argent et le vote ethnique," *La Presse*, October 31, 1995, p. A4.

38   Pierre Drouilly estimates that nearly 60 percent of Francophones voted Yes, whereas five percent of non-Francophones at most did so. "Le référendum du 30 octobre 1995, une analyse des résultats," in Robert Boily (ed.), *L'année politique au Québec*

1995-1996 (Montréal: Fides, 1996), p. 135. See also Pinard, Bernier and Lemieux, *Un combat inachevé*, pp. 307-13.

39   Groups representing these sentiments included Howard Galganov's Quebec Political Action Committee, the Special Committee for Canadian Unity and Guy Bertrand's Citizens for a Democratic Nation. While these groups are not, as Guy Bertrand's group attests, the exclusive preserve of Anglophones, they are predominantly so. See John E. Trent, "Post-Referendum Citizen Group Activity," in Fafard and Brown (eds.), *Canada: The State of the Federation 1996*, p. 58.

40   Others also spoke out against the "the post-referendum climate, which seems to us to be unhealthy" in favour of an "open and respectful discussion of democratic values." See Marc Brière (ed.), *Le goût du Québec* (Montreal: Hurtubise HMH, 1996). [Translation] The group Forum Québec and a number of English-speaking intellectuals favoured this approach. See "Un climat postréférendaire malsain," *Le Devoir*, October 26-27, 1996, p. A6.

41   Cited in Cantin, "Parizeau blâme l'argent et le vote ethnique." [Translation] See also Daniel Turp, "Post-referendum Reflections: Sovereignty Is Alive and Well, Partnership Remains the Roadmap to the Future," *Canada Watch*, Vol. 4, no. 2 (November/December 1995), p. 1.

42   Cited in Guay, "Les résultats du référendum du 30 octobre 1995," p. 220. [Translation] See also Lise Bissonnette, "Le non de 1995," *Le Devoir*, October 31, 1995, p. 14.

43   See "The Unfinished Country," *The Globe and Mail*, October 31, 1995, p. A24.

44   Gérard Boismenu, "L'obsédante question constitutionnelle," in Boily (ed.), *L'année politique au Québec 1995-1996*, pp. 15-21. See also Group of 22, *Making Canada Work Better* (Toronto: C.D. Howe Institute, May 1996); Yves Fortier, Peter Lougheed and J. Maxwell, *Today and Tomorrow: An Agenda for Action: Report of the Confederation 2000*

Conference (Ottawa, May 1996); Trent *et al.* (eds.), *Québec-Canada*; and André Burelle, *Le mal canadien* (Montreal: Fides, 1995).

45 See the text of the press release issued at the close of the First Ministers' meeting: "Des consultations publiques pour renforcer la fédération," *Le Devoir*, September 1997, p. A7.

46 Hugh Windsor and Edward Greenspon, "Hardline on Separation Popular Outside Quebec," *The Globe and Mail*, November 16, 1996, p. A1. The question read as follows: "Do you think the federal government should focus on giving Quebec some of the changes it wants, or should it emphasize the tough conditions Quebec would have to meet if it were to leave Canada?" Plan B was supported by 57 percent of those questioned in the Atlantic provinces, 58 percent in Ontario and 70 percent in the West.

47 Roger Gibbins, "Western Canada in the Wake of the Events of 1995," in Trent *et al.* (eds.), *Québec-Canada*, pp. 255-62.

48 For example, Diane Francis, *Fighting for Canada* (Toronto: Key Porter, 1996). For discussions of the post-referendum climate, see McRoberts, *Misconceiving Canada*, pp. 241-44; Michel Sarra-Bournet, "Le choc référendaire au Canada anglais," *L'action nationale*, Vol. 85, no. 9 (September 1997), pp. 111-22; and *Canada Watch* (August 1996).

49 Reference re Secession of Quebec [1998] 2 R.C.S. 217. The Supreme Court also stated: The clear repudiation by the people of Quebec of the existing constitutional order would confer legitimacy on demands for secession, and place an obligation on the other provinces and the federal government to acknowledge and respect that expression of democratic will by entering into negotiations and conducting them in accordance with the underlying constitutional principles already discussed...The continued existence and operation of the Canadian constitutional order cannot remain indifferent to the clear expression of a clear majority of Quebecers that they no longer wish to remain in Canada...The rights of other provinces and the federal government cannot deny the right of the government of Quebec to pursue secession, should a clear majority of the people of Quebec choose that goal, so long as in doing so, Quebec respects the rights of others (pp. 28-29).

Guy Rocher's Conclusion

1 Ernest Renan, *Qu'est-ce qu'une nation ?* (Paris: Pierre Bordas et fils, 1991).

2 Renan, *Qu'est-ce qu'une nation ?*, p. 41.

John Meisel is Sir Edward Peacock Professor of Political Science Emeritus and Senior Fellow in the Centre for the Study of Public Opinion at Queen's University. He has been associated with several royal commissions, task forces and inquiries, and has acted as adviser to both the Canadian and Ontario governments. He is the author *Cleavages, Parties and Values in Canada* (1974) and *Debating the Constitution* (with Jean Laponce, 1994). His most recent publications include "Multi-nationalism and the Federal idea: A Synopsis" (1995) and "Meteor? Phoenix? Chameleon? The Decline and Transformation of Party in Canada" (with Michael Mendelsohn, 1995). In 1991 he received the Northern Telecom International Canadian Studies Award of Excellence.

Guy Rocher is Professor of Sociology at University of Montreal since 1960 and has been a Researcher at the Centre de recherche en droit public of the Faculty of Law at the University of Montreal since 1979. From 1977 to 1979, he acted as Quebec's Deputy Minister for Cultural Development. In that capacity, he participated in the development of the Charter of the French Language. He is the author of numerous books, articles, and research reports, including *Introduction à la sociologie générale* (1969), *Le Québec en mutation* (1973), *Le Québec en jeu* (in collaboration, 1992), and most recently *Études de sociologie du droit et l'éthique* (1996). Recipient of numerous distinctions, he received the 1997 Molson Award.

Arthur Silver is Professor of History at the University of Toronto. He is the author of *The French-Canadian Idea of Confederation, 1864-1900* (1982; 1997) and numerous articles in Canadian history published in many specialized journals including the *Canadian Historical Review*. He is currently preparing a book on anglophone and francophone public opinion towards Louis Riel.

1534	Jacques Cartier claims New France for the King of France
1608	Founding of Quebec City
1755 - 1762	Deportation of Acadians
1759	Battle of the Plains of Abraham
1760	Capitulation of the French Governor
1763	Treaty of Paris
	Royal Proclamation
1774	Quebec Act
1775 -	Exodus of Loyalists
1791	Constitutional Act
1834	92 Resolutions
1837 - 1838	Insurrections in Lower and Upper Canada
1839	Durham Report
1840	Act of Union
1848	Responsible government in the Canadas
1854 - 1866	Reciprocity Treaty with the United States
1867	Confederation of Nova Scotia, New Brunswick, Quebec and Ontario
	John A. Macdonald (Cons.) becomes Prime Minister
1870	Manitoba becomes a Canadian province
1871	British Columbia enters Confederation
1872	Oliver Mowat (Lib.) becomes Premier of Ontario
1873	Prince Edward Island enters Confederation
1874 - 1875	Separate Schools crisis in New Brunswick
1879	First National Policy
1884	Sudan Crisis
	Creation of the Imperial Federation League

1885	Hanging of Louis Riel
	The last spike of the transcontinental railway is put in place
1886	Honoré Mercier (Parti national) becomes Premier of Quebec
1887	First interprovincial conference
1889	Formation of the Equal Rights Association
1890	Schools issue in Manitoba
1896	Wilfrid Laurier (Lib.) becomes Prime Minister
	Formation of the British Empire League
1898	Yukon becomes a Territory
1899 - 1902	Boer War
1905	Alberta and Saskatchewan become Canadian provinces
	The remainder of Rupert's Land becomes the Northwest Territories
1908	Lomer Gouin (Lib.) becomes Premier of Quebec
1911	Robert Borden (Cons.) becomes Prime Minister
1912	Regulation 17 in Ontario
1914 - 1918	World War I
	Canada joins the League of Nations
1917	Conscription crisis
1920s	Maritimes Rights Movement
1921	William Lyon Mackenzie King (Lib.) becomes Prime Minister
1927	Old Age Pensions Act
1929	Great Depression
1930	Richard B. Bennett (Cons.) becomes Prime Minister
1931	Statute of Westminster
1932	Creation of the Canadian Radio Broadcasting Commission
1933	Report of the Quebec Social Insurance Commission (Montpetit Commission)

1934	Creation of the Bank of Canada
1935	William Lyon Mackenzie King (Lib.) is returned to power
1936	Maurice Duplessis (Union nationale) becomes Premier of Quebec
	Publication of *The General Theory of Employment, Interest and Money* by John Maynard Keynes
	Creation of the Canadian Broadcasting Corporation
1939 - 1945	World War II
1939	Adélard Godbout (Lib.) becomes Premier of Quebec
1940	Report of the Royal Commission on Dominion-Provincial Relations (the Rowell-Sirois Commission)
	Introduction of Unemployment Insurance
1942	Plebiscite on conscription
1943	Report on Post-War Reconstruction (Marsh Report)
	Report of the Advisory Committee on Health-Insurance (Heagerty Report)
1944	Federal Family Allowances Act
	Tommy Douglas (CCF) becomes Premier of Saskatchewan
	Maurice Duplessis is returned to power
1945	Canada becomes a member of the United Nations Organization
1945 - 1946	Reconstruction Conferences
1946	Hospital insurance plan in Saskatchewan
	Canadian Citizenship Act
1947	First Tax Rental Agreements
1948	Louis Saint-Laurent (Lib.) becomes Prime Minister
	National health grants program
	Adoption of the Quebec flag
1949	Newfoundland enters Confederation
	The Supreme Court of Canada becomes the final court of appeal for Canada

	Leslie M. Frost (Cons.) becomes Premier of Ontario
1951	Old Age Security Act
	Old Age Assistance Act
	Blind Persons Act
	Report of the Royal Commission on National Development in the Arts, Letters and Sciences (Massey-Lévesque Commission)
	Federal grants to universities
1952	Vincent Massey becomes the first Canadian-born Governor-General
	Birth of television in Canada
1953	Creation of the National Library of Canada
1954	Disabled Persons Act
1955	Quebec establishes its own income tax
1956	Unemployment Assistance Act
	Report of the Royal Commission of Inquiry on Constitutional Problems (Tremblay Commission)
1957	Federal Hospital Insurance and Diagnostic Services Act
	John Diefenbaker (Cons.) becomes Prime Minister
	First Tax Sharing Arrangements
1958	Adoption of the National Capital Act
1959	University Finance Agreement
	Opting-out formula
1960	Adoption of the Canadian Bill of Rights
	Jean Lesage (Lib.) becomes Premier of Quebec
	Founding of Rassemblement pour l'indépendance nationale (RIN)
1961	Saskatchewan introduces a health insurance plan
	Creation of the Office de la langue française (French-Language Bureau)
	John P. Robarts (Cons.) becomes Premier of Ontario

1963	Lester B. Pearson (Lib.) becomes Prime Minister
	First FLQ bombs explode
1963 - 1970	Royal Commission on Bilingualism and Biculturalism (Laurendeau-Dunton Commission)
1964	Youth Allowance Act
	Fulton-Favreau formula
1965	Adoption of the Canadian flag
	Quebec and Canada Pension plans
	Established Programs (Interim Arrangements) Act
	Canada-US Auto Pact
1966	Daniel Johnson (Union nationale) becomes Premier of Quebec
1967	Centennial of Confederation
	Charles de Gaulle exclaims "Vive le Québec libre!"
	Creation of the Mouvement souveraineté-association
	Confederation of Tomorrow Conference
1968	Health Insurance Act
	Jean-Jacques Bertrand (Union nationale) becomes Premier of Quebec
	The Quebec Legislative Assembly becomes the National Assembly
	Pierre Elliott Trudeau (Lib.) becomes Prime Minister
	Creation of the Parti québécois
1969	Saint-Léonard Crisis
	Official Languages Act
	Act to promote the French language in Quebec (Bill 63)
	Churchill Falls Contract
1970	Robert Bourassa (Lib.) becomes Premier of Quebec
	Federal Multiculturalism Policy

Report of the Commission of Inquiry on Health and Social Welfare (Castonguay-Nepveu Commission)

October Crisis

1971   Victoria Charter

1972   Report of the Commission of Inquiry on the Position of the French Language and on Language Rights in Quebec (Gendron Commission)

1974   Quebec's Official Language Act (Bill 22)

1975   Wage and Price Controls Policy

1976   René Lévesque (PQ) becomes Premier of Quebec

"Gens de l'air" Crisis

1977   Charter of the French Language (Bill 101)

1979   Joe Clark (Cons.) becomes Prime Minister

Report of the Pepin-Robarts Committee on Canadian Unity

1980   Pierre Elliott Trudeau is returned to power

"O Canada" becomes the national anthem

National Energy Policy

Referendum on Sovereignty-Association

1981   The Supreme Court rules on the Trudeau government's plans for unilateral patriation

1982   Bill S-31

Patriation of the Constitution

The Supreme Court rules on Quebec's right of veto

1983   Act to amend the Charter of the French language (Bill 57)

1984   The Supreme Court rules on the "Quebec Clause"

Brian Mulroney (Cons.) becomes Prime Minister

Robert Bourassa (Lib.) is returned to power

1986   Act to amend the Act respecting health and social services (Bill 142)

CF-18 maintenance contract

Edmonton Declaration

1987   Bill C-22 on drug patents

Meech Lake Accord

Creation of the Reform Party of Canada

1988   The Supreme Court rules on French unilingual public signs

Act to amend the Charter of the French language (Bill 178)

1989   Canada-US Free Trade Agreement

1990   Creation of the Bloc québécois

Oka Crisis

Citizens' Forum on Canada's Future (Spicer Commission)

1991   Allaire Report

Report of the Commission on the Political and Constitutional Future of Quebec (Bélanger-Campeau Commission)

1992   Charlottetown Accord and Referendum

1993   Jean Chrétien (Lib.) becomes Prime Minister

The Bloc québécois becomes the Official Opposition in Ottawa

Act to amend the Charter of the French language (Bill 86)

1994   Jacques Parizeau (PQ) becomes Premier of Quebec

1995   Canadian Health and Social Transfer (CHST)

National Commission on the Future of Quebec

Quebec Referendum on Sovereignty-partnership

1996   Lucien Bouchard (PQ) becomes Premier of Quebec

1997   Calgary Conference

1998   The Supreme Court rules on the right of Quebec to declare independence unilaterally

1999   Social union agreement